Beauvoir and Sartre

EDITED BY
CHRISTINE DAIGLE
AND
JACOB GOLOMB

Beauvoir and Sartre

The Riddle of Influence

INDIANA UNIVERSITY PRESS

Bloomington and Indianapolis

This book is a publication of

Indiana University Press
601 North Morton Street
Bloomington, IN 47404–3797 USA

http://iupress.indiana.edu

Telephone orders   800–842–6796
Fax orders   812–855–7931
Orders by e-mail   iuporder@indiana.edu

© 2009 by Indiana University Press

The paper used in this publication meets the minimum requirements of American National Standard for Information Sciences—Permanence of Paper for Printed Library Materials, ANSI Z39.48-1984.

Manufactured in the United States of America

Library of Congress Cataloging-in-Publication Data

Beauvoir and Sartre : the riddle of influence / edited by Christine Daigle and Jacob Golomb.
    p. cm.
   Includes bibliographical references (p.) and index.
   ISBN 978-0-253-35265-1 (cloth : alk. paper) — ISBN 978-0-253-22037-0 (pbk. : alk. paper)
1. Beauvoir, Simone de, 1908–1986. 2. Sartre, Jean-Paul, 1905–1980. I. Daigle, Christine, date
II. Golomb, Jacob.
   B2430.B344B43 2009
   194—dc22

                                                                2008025666

1 2 3 4 5   14 13 12 11 10 09

And what was [their] weapon? . . . A pen.
—*Victor Hugo, "Oration on Voltaire"*

Contents

Acknowledgments

Christine Daigle would like to thank her partner, Eric Gignac. Without his understanding and good spirits, this work would not have been possible. Her heartfelt thanks also go to Jacob, who initiated this project and was such a pleasure to work with. A better project partner is not conceivable.

Jacob Golomb would like to thank Christine for her cheerful and kind-hearted spirit and for her patience to put up with him. It was really a great privilege to work with her on this rather complicated and sensitive project, and her good judgment and hard work made it all possible.

We both would like to thank Indiana University Press and, in particular, Dee Mortensen, sponsoring editor; Laura MacLeod, assistant sponsoring editor; Miki Bird, managing editor; and Marvin Keenan, project editor. Our thanks also go to Philip Puszczalowski, whose work on the preparation of the manuscript was invaluable. We also wish to acknowledge the excellent work of Elizabeth Yoder, who copyedited the manuscript. Finally, our thanks go to all of the contributors, who made this endeavor a very pleasant one.

Abbreviations

Works by Beauvoir

A	*Anne, ou quand prime le spirituel*
AFS	*Adieux: A Farewell to Sartre*
DS	*Le Deuxième sexe*
EA	*The Ethics of Ambiguity*
Ent	*Entretiens avec Jean-Paul Sartre*
FA	*La Force de l'âge*
FC	*The Force of Circumstance*
FCh	*La Force des choses*
Inv	*L'invitée*
JG	*Journal de guerre*
LS	*Letters to Sartre*
LSFr	*Lettres à Sartre*
MA	*Pour une morale de l'ambiguïté*
Man	*The Mandarins*
MDD	*Memoirs of a Dutiful Daughter*
M-P	*"Merleau-Ponty and Pseudo-Sartreanism"*
PC	*Pyrrhus et Cinéas*
PL	*The Prime of Life*
Sade	*"Faut-il brûler Sade?"*
SCS	*She Came to Stay*
SS	*The Second Sex*
W	*When Things of the Spirit Come First*
WSD	*Who Shall Die?*

Works by Sartre

Bau	*Baudelaire*
BauFr	*Baudelaire (French)*

BN	*Being and Nothingness*
CDR	*Critique of Dialectical Reason*
CG	*Les Carnets de la drôle de guerre*
CL	*"The Childhood of a Leader"*
CPM	*Cahiers pour une morale*
EC	*"L'Enfance d'un Chef"*
EH	*"Existentialism Is a Humanism"*
EN	*L'Être et le néant*
Ex	*No Exit*
IF	*L'Idiot de la famille*
LC	*Lettres au Castor*
Mots	*Les Mots*
MT	*Modern Times*
N	*Nausea*
NFr	*La Nausée*
NE	*Notebooks for an Ethics*
QMW	*Quiet Moments in a War*
TE	*Transcendence of the Ego*
TM	*Les Temps modernes*
W	*The Wall*
WD	*The War Diaries*

Beauvoir and Sartre

Introduction

Christine Daigle and Jacob Golomb

This collection of original essays explores a thorny question: the philosophical and literary relationship between Simone de Beauvoir and Jean-Paul Sartre. These two flamboyant intellectuals have marked the philosophical, literary, and political scene of twentieth-century Europe and are still influential today in various fields. However, there is a lingering problem that we aim to explore in this international collection, namely, the question of the nature of the intellectual exchange between the two. Sartre has enjoyed a broader reception of his works, whereas the reception of Beauvoir's works has been plagued by multiple problems. Her work has not been treated with the same academic seriousness as that of other philosophers, notably Sartre's.[1] Furthermore, many of her important philosophical essays have only very recently been made available to the English-speaking world.[2]

Although not every piece of writing by Sartre has been translated, it is still undeniable that the scholarly researches devoted to his philosophy, especially in the Anglo-Saxon literary world, have been much more numerous than those devoted to Beauvoir.[3] As surprising as this may be, and despite the increased amount of attention her thought is getting, Beauvoir is still, unfortunately, not considered a philosopher in her own right for reasons we will address below.

While the present collection aims to set the record straight, we do not wish to naively adopt the opposite view of Beauvoir's and Sartre's works. If the history of the reception of Beauvoir's works is the history of an occultation from the philosophical scene, the point is not for us to simply put her in the forefront and by the same token to put Sartre in the shadow. More pointedly, we wish to explore the intricacies of their intellectual relationship in order to question how each developed their own thinking in light of the other's own development, and to examine how there might have been a crisscrossing of influence between the two. It is to this task that the contributors of this volume have dedicated themselves.

Although there were many similarities between the two thinkers' positions—philosophical, literary, and political—their differences might be significant enough to say that they proposed independent, yet related, philosophical views. After all, they both accepted the label "existentialist," and insofar as they did, they shared a similar philosophical perspective on the human condition. However, we want to critically examine the prevalent view that Beauvoir was *merely* a follower of Sartre.[4] Hence the question arises: can we respond to the claim that "had there been no Sartre, there would be no Beauvoir" with an exclamation that "had there been no Beauvoir, there would be no Sartre either"? Our aim is to check whether these claims are valid and to what extent, if any, they are justifiable. We are dealing here primarily with a rehabilitation and not with a condemnation. Thus, we hope to be able, with the invaluable assistance of the contributors to this volume, to shed some new light on the main reasons—sociological, political, and, of course, also biographical and philosophical—for Beauvoir's intentional or unintentional withdrawal from the forefront of the European intellectual stage mainly before, but even after, Sartre's death.

Beauvoir–Sartre: The Personal Affair

Beauvoir and Sartre met in the late 1920s. At the time, Sartre was a student at the École Normale Supérieure and had attempted his *agrégation* in 1928 without success (he had been too original, and the jury, which was fairly conservative, did not appreciate his style). Beauvoir was attending a conventional Catholic school for women, where she too was preparing for the *agrégation*. She was introduced to Sartre, and they studied together with other friends. The *agrégation* was very competitive. When they wrote it in 1929, Sartre was ranked first, Beauvoir second (becoming, at age 24, the youngest person ever to receive the *agrégation*). The jury had hesitated for a long time. They thought that Sartre was brilliant but that she was more rigorous and technical. They agreed that, of the two, she was the philosopher![5]

Soon after they met, they became a couple, and Sartre said to Beauvoir that although their love was a necessary one, they could still enjoy contingent affairs. The arrangement was for them to be together but to be free and, mostly, to be honest with one another and to tell each other everything about their other relationships. Beauvoir agreed. The external relationships formed by the two were certainly a shock for the bourgeois French society, who preferred (at least on the surface) a more conventional model of interrelationship. But it was precisely against such a model that the young couple rebelled. Neither wanted to be trapped in such a model. As Sartre put it poignantly in his *War Diaries:* "It was also the existential and the authentic, which we vaguely sensed beyond our petty-bourgeois rationalism" (*WD*, 77).

They were lovers of freedom (*amants de la liberté*), as one commentator has put it.[6] However, they were not lovers in the usual sense for all the time that they were together, having stopped their sexual relationship rather early. Nonetheless, the bond that held them together was very strong. They needed each other throughout their lives and were always together. They would see each other every day, and if they could not be together, they would write to each other almost every day. Beauvoir was always Sartre's first reader, fierce editor, and profound critic. He would trust her judgment entirely. He was also her reader and advisor. And, yes, also her greatest admirer, as his striking confession in his *War Diaries* attests: "The Beaver . . . is more naturally authentic than me" (*WD*, 85). In Sartre's existentialist glossary and hierarchy of types, to be authentic is the highest human level that a person can ever attain or hope to attain.[7]

After Beauvoir met Sartre, she did not pursue writing. She said she was too busy being happy and in love to want to write. It was Sartre who gave her the little push she needed to focus on her writing again. However, that does not mean that he was always behind her writing and philosophical activity. In fact, the diaries of Beauvoir, which predate her meeting with Sartre, show that she had always loved philosophy and wanted to dedicate herself to it. These diaries still did not represent a sophisticated philosophical theory, but they contain many seeds of certain concepts that will later lie at the heart of her philosophy— and possibly Sartre's—such as the concept of the Other, situation, freedom, and bad faith.

Beauvoir has claimed many times that the philosopher was Sartre and that she was merely a writer. For her, one was a philosopher only if one had elaborated a system. This seems to be quite a narrow definition indeed, given that it would exclude such great thinkers as Kierkegaard and Nietzsche. In an interview with Margaret Simons, she says:

> Sartre was a philosopher, and me, I am not; and I never really wanted to be a philosopher [thereby contradicting what she had said in her diaries].[8] I like philosophy very much, but I have not constructed a philosophical work. I constructed a literary work. I was interested in novels, in memoirs, in essays such as *The Second Sex*. But this is not philosophy. On the philosophical plane, I was influenced by Sartre. Obviously, I was not able to influence him, since I did not do philosophy.[9]

Beauvoir insists that the only influence she can have had on Sartre philosophically is through the critique she could make of his work, since she was always the first reader. This and other repeated claims that she was not a philosopher may have contributed to the prolonged downplay of Beauvoir's contribution to this field. These claims are all the more interesting when one considers Sartre's similar statement at that time: "I was always a writer first, and then a philosopher; that's just how it was."[10]

In any case, it is quite misguided to try to separate these activities, the literary and the philosophical, especially for Sartre and Beauvoir. After all, the kind of philosophy they espouse commands that they explore forms of discourse other than the traditional systematic discourse of philosophy in order to delineate more truthfully the notions they want to promote. Because they are dealing with the concrete, embodied, situated individuals that are in-the-world, novels seem perfectly suited for the exploration of the lived experience of such persons, notably the exploration of their personal authenticity or its lack.[11] The same goes for the theatre (of which Sartre was apparently more fond than Beauvoir, who wrote only one play).[12]

Both Sartre and Beauvoir emphasized philosophizing as action over abstract and sterile systematic speculations. Both preferred *vita activa* rather than *vita contemplativa* and thought that existentialist philosophy had to take on a form that was conducive to action in order to become relevant to the concrete lives of persons who conceived it.

The Philosophical Affair

How did the "philosophical affair" unfold? It unfolded via the daily conversations they had about their work and via their publications. Though Sartre was the first to publish, it does not necessarily follow that he was *always* the sole originator of ideas. In the 1930s and 40s, the major texts he published were the *Transcendence of the Ego* (1937, but written at the end of his stay in Berlin in 1934); *Nausea* (1938); the essay on emotions (1939); *The Imagination* (1940); and then, in 1943, *Being and Nothingness*, after which he struggled on the *Notebooks for an Ethics* (1947–48), which he ended up abandoning. In the 1940s, the major texts Beauvoir published were *She Came to Stay* (1943), *Pyrrhus et Cinéas* (1944), *The Blood of Others* (1945), *All Men are Mortal* (1946), *The Ethics of Ambiguity* (1947), and *The Second Sex* (1949).

A close examination of the philosophical concepts dealt with in these works unveils what seems to be a crisscrossing of influence from Beauvoir to Sartre and from Sartre to Beauvoir. Many key concepts that are an integral part of both philosophies, such as freedom, the problem of the Other, situation, bad faith, authenticity, and embodiment, are dealt with in a different fashion by each of them.

The example of freedom is telling in that respect. Beauvoir has always claimed that she fully embraced the Sartrean notion of freedom. However, at the time when Sartre was working on *Being and Nothingness,* their disagreement on the nature of freedom was already marked. In *The Prime of Life,* one of her auto-biographies, Beauvoir recounts how they had a vivacious discussion about the notion of freedom at one time when Sartre was on leave from his army post in 1940. She recounts that Sartre held to a notion of *absolute* freedom, while she was more concerned with the *constraints* brought by one's situation. She was arguing that a slave or a woman in a harem could not be free in the same way as other people, whereas he would say that they were still as free as anybody else and that it was up to them to decide on the meaning of their enslavement. Beauvoir did not agree with this, however, and only gave it a token acceptance. In her autobiographical writings she affirms that she had been right all along. A scrutiny of her works in the 1940s unveils that the freedom she talks about is not a Sartrean *absolute* freedom, as delineated in *Being and Nothingness,* but rather her *own* view of freedom as situated and embodied. Beauvoir's view of being at the mercy of history and facticity was one that Sartre seemed to adopt in his later explorations of existential psychoanalysis, notably in his books about Genet and Flaubert.

There are many other examples of ideas developed by Beauvoir that have influenced Sartre, for example, her discussion of absence in her novel *L'invitée.* Her ideas about the necessity of willing the Other as free for my own freedom, as spelled out in *Pyrrhus et Cinéas* and *The Ethics of Ambiguity,* were also influential, a view that Sartre seemed to adopt in his "notorious" postwar lecture, *L'Existentialisme est un humanisme.*[13]

The necessary outcome of such a philosophical position is a view of the necessity of political and social commitment. We know that Sartre came to it too, due not only to his discovery of his own historicity while at war but also because of the influence Beauvoir's thought had on him.[14] He returned from the POW camp with the firm intention to be politically and socially committed. This startled Beauvoir at the time because she was surprised at the sudden shift in Sartre from political anarchism to commitment. If her philosophy of the 1940s can be argued to bear a necessary political extension, it is Sartre, in this case, who is taking the lead. That said, Beauvoir was ahead of Sartre many times, but she often tried to cover this. Why she did it will probably remain an unsolved riddle.

Of the "phallocentric view" (which regards Beauvoir as merely Sartre's follower and lover-assistant), Margaret Simons has said: "This view fails to recognize the originality of Beauvoir's insights and is thus unable to appreciate her considerable influence on Sartre's development of a social philosophy of existentialism."[15] This is why many recent Beauvoir scholars (including some of our contributors below) put such an emphasis on the originality and depth of her philosophical contributions, thereby opposing the view that Beauvoir herself helped to reinforce with her many statements of her own status as a non-philosopher, as a follower of Sartre, as "just a writer." The truth of the matter is probably slightly different and more moderate. It is less extreme inasmuch as it does not take Beauvoir's self-depreciating statements at face value, but it still gives them some weight.

Beauvoir and Sartre were engaged in a philosophical affair; and, as with any affair, they were both involved in it, each sometimes contributing a little less, sometimes a little more. These two great minds were not engaged in a conflictual relationship of the kind described by Sartre in *Being and Nothingness*. They were intellectually, at least, not a "hell to each other" but rather equal partners for elaborating, experimenting, and playing with common ideas.

The Riddle of Influence

Beauvoir's and Sartre's lifelong affair, which was both a love affair and a philosophical and literary affair, is problematic in a sense. Because they were so close and because they did the same kind of work, it is sometimes difficult to establish how each developed his or her own thought. Can one talk of a Sartrean philosophy completely devoid of Beauvoir's influence? And likewise, is a Beauvoirian philosophy conceivable without Sartre's influence? One may be tempted to ask whether paying attention to this question is not distracting us from more important philosophical issues and whether it really matters. After all, it is always difficult to disentangle the web of influences that are at play in a philosopher's intricate thinking. We are talking here about two existentialist philosophers who were involved in a rethinking of human experience in a postwar world that tended to become a nihilistic hell. They shared their enterprise with that of other philosophers of that movement. They can be said to have been influenced, together with other phenomenologists or existentialists, by such thinkers as Husserl, Nietzsche, and Kierkegaard. They also shared many ideas with other contemporary Continental philosophers like Heidegger, Levinas, Merleau-Ponty, and Camus.

Sartre, Beauvoir, Camus, and Merleau-Ponty were friends at the time of the rise and peak of the existentialist movement.[16] Did they influence each other? Certainly. While these friends acknowledged each other's works and welcomed each and every one's philosophical and literary output—at least most of the time—they did not merely embrace the same philosophical positions. Each had his or her own views to present, his or her own particular approaches and emphases to the problems they shared, his or her own intellectual enemies and prevalent prejudices to fight. This is also true of Sartre and Beauvoir.

Yet Beauvoir has stood in the shadow of Sartre for a considerable time. This has irritated many Beauvoir scholars, all the more since Beauvoir's own attitude may have played the major role in the way her works have been received. This is why we think the question of influence between Sartre and Beauvoir is of such importance, especially in a year that widely celebrates Beauvoir's centennial. What is at stake is to show how Beauvoir was *also* an independent and significant philosopher and to show that the Beauvoir–Sartre relationship was much more than a simple love affair but was indeed a philosophical affair, where each had something to learn from the other.

In a nutshell, the debate is as follows: some philosophers and historians of philosophy express the view that Beauvoir is *merely* a follower of Sartre. While none would express such views explicitly, their editorial choices, dismissal of Beauvoir, and constant association of Beauvoir with Sartre uncover such an attitude. Opposed to this view stand philosophers who consider Beauvoir to be an independent and original thinker. Our collection aims to contribute to the movement initiated in the past years in the field of Beauvoir studies and to portray her as an original thinker engaged in a fertile dialogue with Sartre. The collection will present a variety of views related to this issue and to the riddle of influence between Beauvoir and Sartre, for if it is true that Beauvoir should have a place in the philosophical canon as an original thinker, it remains to determine how her thought relates to that of Sartre. The aim shared by all contributions to this volume is to critically inquire about the intellectual relationship between Beauvoir and Sartre. Our wish is to present Simone de Beauvoir as a philosopher whose many phenomenological and existential insights are important and might have been influential on Sartre. Most of the contributors below agree that the influence was complex and did not always work one way.

The question of influence is not new in Beauvoirian and Sartrean scholarship. Groundbreaking work has been accomplished by several scholars, some of whom we are proud to count among our contributors. In an article published in 1981, "Beauvoir and Sartre: The Question of Influence," Margaret Simons opens up the question to the effect that Beauvoir may have contributed to the formation of Sartre's *Being and Nothingness*. In the interviews she conducted with Beauvoir, she was concerned with many things, including trying to get Beauvoir to admit to having been influential for Sartre.

Simons's work has been crucial in launching the question, and the interviews, as well as her many essays on the question, vividly fleshed out the problem.[17] Sonia Kruks and Debra Bergoffen have also tackled important aspects of the Beauvoir–Sartre philosophical relationship. In "Simone de Beauvoir: Teaching Sartre about Freedom" (as well as in her contribution to this volume), Kruks has demonstrated how Beauvoir's and Sartre's views on this key existentialist concept diverged and how it was Beauvoir's own original dealings with freedom as situated and socially interdependent that led Sartre to depart from his earlier view of freedom as absolute to one that was more workable in his works of the 1950s and, more particularly, in the *Critique of Dialectical Reason* published in 1960.[18] For her part, Bergoffen has explored *the look* and *bad faith* and how they are used very differently by Beauvoir and Sartre. In her article "The Look as Bad Faith," she discusses how Beauvoir's particular emphasis on the look allows her to devise an ethics of generosity.[19]

In 1993 Kate and Edward Fullbrook tackled the question of influence in *Simone de Beauvoir and Jean-Paul Sartre: The Remaking of a Twentieth-Century Legend*. This "revisionist biography" revisits many aspects of Beauvoir's and Sartre's lives, including that of philosophical influence. In it and other articles (including Edward Fullbrook's essay in this volume), they vigorously claim that we have to thank Beauvoir for the philosophy presented in *Being and Nothingness*.[20]

By mentioning the works of Simons, Kruks, Bergoffen, and the Fullbrooks, we do not mean to give the impression that they have been the only scholars who have dealt with these issues. However, these scholars have initiated an important movement and line of inquiry that leads us to revise conventional views of Sartre's and Beauvoir's respective philosophies and their interrelations. It is indeed the case that many others, such as William McBride, Gail Weiss, Christine Daigle, Deborah Evans, and others have significantly reflected about the question of influence as part of their independent ongoing inquiries on specific aspects of Beauvoir's and/or Sartre's philosophy.

Almost immediately after Beauvoir's death (and even before it, as the interviews with her show), the question of influence between her and Sartre stirred up heated debates, arguments, and even quarrels. The present editors feel that one hundred years after Beauvoir's birth the time has come to present a focused and sustained volume that will address this very issue. Though we do not aim at reaching a final and absolutely "true" judgment about what has become an almost insolvable question, we at least hope to be able—with the kind help of all the contributors included—to clarify this issue and the multifarious perspectives relevant here, and to point to what was really at stake: not merely a more comprehensive understanding of Beauvoir and Sartre but a more serious awareness of what we are, an understanding that both sexes are in great need of each other. Like Sartre and Beauvoir, neither sex can live without the other, and their common enterprises, intellectual and otherwise, are often reaching human greatness because they are the loving testimony that we humans, women and men, are bound to work together, to live together, and to fight our common enemies: sickness, starvation, ignorance, racial prejudices, privation, and natural disasters. We think that Simone de Beauvoir felt this deeply and passionately, as did Sartre. That may be why she really did not care about the question of influence: she was always looking at Sartre's intellectual achievements and her own as one *combined* enterprise that vividly attest to human greatness and genuine humanism.

This collection deals with the question of how Beauvoir and Sartre developed their own thinking in light of the other's own development and how there might have been a crisscrossing of influence between the two. Each of these thinkers was influenced in different stages of development by different notions that the other presented in his or her respective compositions in various times. Thus we were able to discern generally and somewhat roughly three developmental stages for each thinker:

1. The prewar phase: for Sartre this was the period of the *Transcendence of the Ego, Nausea, A Sketch for a Theory of Emotions,* and *The Imagination.* For Beauvoir it was the time when she composed *Anne, ou quand prime le spirituel* (written between 1935 and 1937, though only published in 1979). Lecarme-Tabone's and van den Hoven's essays tackle the works of that period.
2. The times of World War II and the immediate postwar period: Sartre's *Being and Nothingness* appeared in 1943, soon followed by Beauvoir's essay *Pyrrhus et Cinéas.* At the end of the war, both launch, with Merleau-Ponty, *Les Temps modernes.* They both contribute many articles and essays to the journal. Sartre works on his plays and on his *Notebooks for*

an Ethics. Beauvoir publishes *The Ethics of Ambiguity* and, in 1949, her magnum opus, *The Second Sex.* This period is, approximately, covered by the contributions of Bergoffen, Daigle, de Lacoste, Eshleman, Evans, Fullbrook, Heinämaa, Veltman, and Weiss.

3. The "political engagement" period: the period unfolding in the 1950s, with Sartre's other major work, *Critique of Dialectical Reason,* published in 1960, and Beauvoir's major novel, *Mandarins,* in 1954. This period is dealt with—again, approximately—by Kail, Kruks, and McBride.

To end this introduction on a more personal tone, due to the somewhat emotionally laden import of this collection—its dealing with such sensitive issues as feminism, machismo, sexism, and chauvinism (just to enumerate a few)—it was rather beneficial to the collection, as well as to the parties involved, that the editors represent both sexes. Here the "other sex" is the other editor, who balances the here and there one-sided presentation, counterchecks, provokes, and stimulates the whole tenor of the entire collection. Thus we can say confidently that we were very lucky to find each other for this collection. Here, as in few instances in our life, one may dare to conclude that the final result is far more than the sum of its two editors, and we naturally mean also the impressive efforts of the other contributors, whose patience, acumen, and working ethics made it all possible—not to mention the press's editors and reviewers—without whom the entire project would have deteriorated, to use Sartre's expression, into a "useless passion."

Notes

1. The story of Beauvoir's incorporation in the philosophical canon is one of a very slow appearance. She is conspicuously absent from Paul Edwards's influential *Encyclopedia of Philosophy* (1967), where Sartre benefits from his own six-page-long entry. Anthologies on Continental philosophy or existentialism rarely include her, and when they do, they often present her as a minor contributor to the existentialist movement. One recent exception to this rule is Daigle's collection, *Existentialist Thinkers and Ethics* (2006), in which a long chapter on Beauvoir (by Christine Daigle) presents her thought on par with that of other existentialist figures (see 120–41). The *Routledge Encyclopedia of Philosophy,* published in 1998, presents a good picture. Beauvoir has her own entry (as does Sartre), and she is discussed as a contributor to phenomenology, existentialism, and in particular existentialist ethics. Beauvoir has been gaining in reputation as a philosopher, but this is a rather recent phenomenon.

2. This is thanks to the new *The Beauvoir Series,* published by the University of Illinois Press under the editorship of Margaret A. Simons and Sylvie Le Bon de Beauvoir. Two books have appeared in the series so far: *Simone de Beauvoir: Philosophical Writings* (2004) and *Simone de Beauvoir: Diary of a Philosophy Student, Volume 1, 1926–27*

(2006). These volumes are the first in the series and aim (as the inside cover of the first one informs us) at "nothing less than the transformation of Simone de Beauvoir's place in the canon."

3. Thus, for example, a *Philosopher's Index* search conducted in January 2007 yielded the following results: a search for "Beauvoir" gave 149 journal entries, 121 peer-reviewed journal entries, 42 book entries, and 67 chapter/essay entries. A search for "Sartre" gave 1,475 journal entries, 845 peer-reviewed journal entries, 473 book entries, and 259 chapter/essay entries.

4. In her paper "Sexism and the Philosophical Canon" (reprinted as chapter 8 in her *Beauvoir and* The Second Sex, 101–14), Simons gives much evidence to that effect, pointing to important philosophers and historians of philosophy like Jean Wahl and Walter Kaufmann as being guilty of such a misconception and misrepresentation of Beauvoir. See especially, 103ff.

5. See Annie Cohen-Solal, *Sartre, 1905–1980,* 151.

6. Claudine Monteil, *Les amants de la liberté.*

7. See the chapter on Sartre in Jacob Golomb's *In Search of Authenticity from Kierkegaard to Camus.*

8. In her 1927 diary, Beauvoir refers to her education, to her passion for philosophy, and to her desire to develop her own philosophical ideas. See Margaret Simons, "Beauvoir's Early Philosophy," 233–43, which reproduces excerpts of the diary in the French original.

9. Simons, "Beauvoir Interview (1979)," 9. That Beauvoir should label *The Second Sex* an "essay" and add that "this is not philosophy" must be striking to anyone who has read the original French text. It is unfortunately highly probable that the flawed, not to say "fraudulent," translation by the zoologist Howard Parshley would not lead a reader to think that he was reading a philosophical treatise. For a detailed discussion, see Simons, "The Silencing of Simone de Beauvoir: Guess What's Missing from *The Second Sex*," 67, and Toril Moi, "While We Wait: Notes on the English Translation of *The Second Sex*," 37–68. Moreover, problems also plague the French reception of the work, albeit of a different type. In the French world, one could probably argue that the treatise has been less than well received. When published, it generated a wave of protests and was judged to be scandalous. Beauvoir was publicly insulted and accused of having unduly attacked the French male! This was probably not conducive to a friendly reception of her work as philosophical.

10. Our translation of "J'ai toujours été écrivain d'abord, et puis philosophe, c'est venu comme ça" (quoted in Michel Rybalka, "Les Chemins de la liberté. Notice," 1860).

11. See Golomb, *In Search of Authenticity,* chapter 2, which deals with the intimate relations between literary fiction and the moral value of authentic life in existentialism and its literature.

12. Sartre wrote a total of nine plays and adapted two more, one from Alexandre Dumas and the other from Euripides. He can thus be said to have been an accomplished playwright. Beauvoir, for her part, wrote only one play, *Les bouches inutiles.* It was finished in 1944 and first staged in 1945. She says that it was when she attended rehearsals of Sartre's *Les mouches* that the idea originated in her to try writing a play herself (see *FA*, 672).

13. We say "notorious" because it is well known that many of its claims clash in sig-

nificant ways with his previous tenets as introduced in *Being and Nothingness*. Sartre, after recognizing it, came to regret the publication of this lecture. For details, see Golomb, *In Search of Authenticity*, 156–57. However, the very fact that Sartre introduced Kantian motifs "about the necessity of willing the Other as free" in this lecture seems highly indicative of the depth of Beauvoir's influence on him in these matters.

14. Sonia Kruks has argued as much in "Simone de Beauvoir: Teaching Sartre about Freedom," 79–95.

15. Simons, *Beauvoir and* The Second Sex, 2.

16. Breaks occurred in the 1950s between Camus and Sartre and between Merleau-Ponty and Sartre. Beauvoir took up arms in the latter break, defending Sartre against Merleau-Ponty in her essay "Merleau-Ponty et le pseudo-sartrisme." The essay appeared in *Les Temps modernes*, nos. 114–15 (juin–juillet 1955): 2072–2122.

17. See Simons, *Beauvoir and* The Second Sex for a reprint of the interviews she conducted with Beauvoir in 1979, 1982, and 1985. This book also contains a reprint of her essay "Beauvoir and Sartre: The Question of Influence" from 1981. She has also published "An Appeal to Reopen the Question of Influence," 17–24, and more recently in *Les Temps modernes*, "L'indépendance de la pensée philosophique de Simone de Beauvoir," 43–52.

18. See Kruks, "Simone de Beauvoir: Teaching Sartre about Freedom." The article was reprinted with revisions in Simons, ed., *Feminist Interpretations of Simone de Beauvoir*, 79–95. A previous version in French as "Simone de Beauvoir entre Sartre et Merleau-Ponty" had been published in *Les Temps modernes* (November 1989), where Kruks was misidentified as Sonia Kraüs.

19. See Bergoffen, "The Look as Bad Faith," 221–27. Bergoffen has pursued this view of Beauvoir's ethics in *The Philosophy of Simone de Beauvoir*. Her essay "Simone de Beauvoir and Jean-Paul Sartre: Woman, Man and the Desire to be God" also tackles the philosophical relationship between the two thinkers. See also her contribution in the present collection.

20. Edward and Kate Fullbrook have also published articles on the question of the philosophical influence. See their "The Absence of Beauvoir" and "Sartre's Secret Key."

1   Getting the Beauvoir We Deserve

Debra Bergoffen

The Second Sex may be read as driven by a simple question: Why don't women rebel? Or, in Beauvoir's words, "Why is it that women do not dispute male sovereignty? . . . Whence comes this submission . . . of women" (*SS*, xxiv)?[1] Insofar as it concerns the matter of exploitation, women, like other dominated groups, are marked as the Other. When Beauvoir writes, "thus humanity is male and man defines woman not in herself but as relative to him; she is not regarded as an autonomous being. . . . She is defined and differentiated with reference to man . . . she is the incidental, the inessential as opposed to the essential" (*SS*, viii), she could easily have substituted markers of race for *man* and *woman*. The sentence could read, "thus humanity is *white* and *white people* define *native people*, or *black people*, not in themselves but as relative to them." Beauvoir herself suggests such possibilities when she compares the situation of women to that of the slave. This substitutability accounts for some of the impact of *The Second Sex*. Its category of the Other resonates beyond the confines of the text.

Beauvoir insists, however, that there is a radical difference between the otherness of women and the otherness ascribed to other oppressed groups. Other oppressed groups, remembering the moment when they were transformed from sovereign subjects into objects to be used by others, see their exploitation as a historical injustice that must and can be opposed. Appealing to their memory of life before their transformation, they call to each other in solidarity and rebel. They follow the script of the Hegelian master-slave dialectic.

No such script exists for women. There seems to be no "before," no moment when women's subjectivity was stolen from them. In this, women's otherness is more akin to that of Hindu untouchables than to that of the colonized or enslaved. It appears to be ahistorical—a matter of natural law or divine ordination. Believing in the inevitability of their otherness, women exist in a mystified condition. As mystified, they accept the "fact" of their passivity, weakness, and need for male protection. Accepting the naturalness of their condition, they accept the necessity and justness of male domination. We see the vicious circle. Women are said to be passive by nature. They are therefore by nature incapable of action—rebellion.

Were it simply a matter of women's mystification, the riddle of why women fail to rebel might be solved and resolved by combing historical archives for the moment when the transformation of women from subject to object occurred. To some extent Beauvoir takes up this quest. She soon discovers, however, that were such a moment to be discovered, it would not create the conditions of solidarity necessary for rebellious action. To understand the complexity of women's situation, we need to understand the forces at work that sustain women's otherness, that support their ongoing mystification. Furthermore, we need to understand that, given the unique situation of women as the second sex, the idea of a violent rebellion is unthinkable.

Rejecting a simple answer to her simple question, Beauvoir writes, "thus woman may fail to lay claim to the status of the subject because she lacks definite resources, because she feels the necessary bond that ties her to man regardless of reciprocity, and because she is often very well pleased with her role as the *Other*" (SS, xvii). This sentence is philosophically packed. It identifies the position of woman as the Other as both a consequence of a unique situation and as a matter of complicity. It identifies economic, sexual, and existential roots of women's continued status as the Other.

In speaking of the heterosexual bond, Beauvoir alerts us to the ways in which heterosexuality, by figuring women as the birthing body, structures them as dependent on men and in this way creates a situation where women, seeing themselves as requiring male protection for themselves and their children, elevate the value of the bond that ties them to husband and children above the value of their bonds to other women and above the value of intersubjective reciprocity. Instead of identifying with each other, women identify with the men of their culture, race, or class. Ignoring their solidarity with other women and forgoing reciprocity with men for the value of the bond, women's alignment with men is also tactical. The system of patriarchy renders them economically dependent on men.

Beauvoir's first two explanations of women's failure to rebel, that they lack definite resources and that they prefer the value of the bond to the reciprocities of equality, refer to economic-social-structural issues. Her third explanation, however, is existential. Women, for realistic, practical, and existentially unethical reasons, are content with their status as the *other*. It protects them from the anxieties and responsibilities of freedom. They are happy.

Beginning with the question: Why don't women rebel? and led by it to focus on Beauvoir's three-pronged answer alerts us to Beauvoir's unique contribution to Continental political thought. Though the answer's reference to economics alerts us to the Marxist strain of *The Second Sex*'s analysis of women's situation, the reference to the bond of the heterosexual couple and to women's satisfaction indicates that, from Beauvoir's point of view, the complexity of the oppressive structures of patriarchy cannot be captured through the single lens of economics. Taking Beauvoir's answer to the riddle of women's failure to rebel as my point of departure, I situate Beauvoir as an existential phenomenologist whose engagement with existential phenomenology is at the root of her feminist critique. Attending to the details of Beauvoir's deployment of phenomenological existential categories, I find that Beauvoir engaged Merleau-Ponty's and Sartre's phenomenological analyses of embodiment, perception, and desire to create a unique phenomenological, existential, and political position.

In previous writings I have focused on the role of the erotic in Beauvoir's thinking.[2] This chapter brings the idea of bad faith to Beauvoir's discussions of the ways in which the erotic experience of ambiguous subjectivity refutes the structures of masculine autonomous subjectivity central to patriarchal ideologies. It finds that although the erotic event has the potential to destabilize patriarchal gender codes, the long-term effects of this destabilization will depend on the extent to which bad faith loses its hold on those who embrace their patriarchal status.

In taking up the question of bad faith, I am of course calling up the figure of Sartre and treading in the mire of the Sartre–Beauvoir relationship. In taking up the concept of bad faith within the context of Beauvoir's concept of ambiguity, however, I intend to complicate this relationship so that instead of returning to the time when linking Beauvoir's name to Sartre's meant losing the name Beauvoir, we situate ourselves in a time where, instead of threatening Beauvoir's name, the name Sartre takes its place alongside another name circulating in her texts, that of Merleau-Ponty. Attending to these names, we come to a better understanding of the complexities of Beauvoir's thinking and come closer to getting the Beauvoir we deserve.

In titling this chapter "Getting the Beauvoir We Deserve," I am miming the title of Douglas Crimp's essay "Getting the Warhol We Deserve." I crib that title to signal the affinity of this piece with the project of Crimp's piece. He is concerned with Andy Warhol and the situated scholarship of cultural studies. I am interested in the current state of Beauvoir scholarship and its relationship to feminism. Pointing to Crimp is my way of signaling that we are at a unique and interesting moment in Beauvoir scholarship. We no longer have to justify Beauvoir's status as a philosopher. We can speak of her relationship with other philosophers, notably Sartre, without risking her philosophical credentials. Recalling this title also signals that the state of feminism, like the state of cultural studies, remains contested. It also speaks to my conviction that Beauvoir's work continues to operate in this contested space and that to understand its operation, itself a matter of dispute, we need to attend to the ways in which her ideas cut into the ideas of other philosophers, and the ways in which ideas that she often developed in isolation from each other form constellations of thought that remain relevant for current philosophical and feminist concerns.

The concept of ambiguity is at the center of Beauvoir's thought. It is at work in Beauvoir's depiction of intentionality and is critical to her analyses of our ethical and political relationships. It signals her debt to a phenomenological tradition that muddies the subject-object distinction. It appeals to the method of thick descriptions as it pursues the project of identifying the essential structures of the life world. Once we appreciate the ways in which the concept of ambiguity anchors and permeates Beauvoir's thought, we cannot help but turn to the thinking of Merleau-Ponty; for he, like Beauvoir, chooses the term "ambiguity" to develop the insights of the phenomenological turn.

The affinities between Beauvoir and Merleau-Ponty go beyond sharing an affinity for a particular word, however. The matter of the shared term may have drawn Beauvoir's readers to the name Merleau-Ponty, but once there, we discovered important affinities between her work and his. This strategy of reading Beauvoir and Merleau-Ponty through each other has never fallen into the traps of Beauvoir–Sartre readings. There was no extra-philosophical Beauvoir–Merleau-Ponty couple as a decoy and no directive from Beauvoir to subordinate her work to his. As these readings came on the scene in the wake of the movement to disentangle Beauvoir's voice from Sartre's, noting the affinities between Beauvoir and Merleau-Ponty became a way to erase Sartre.

If we ignore Beauvoir's affinities with Sartre, however, we risk forgetting that *The Second Sex*'s existential-phenomenological analyses of women's situations are taken up in the name of a political liberatory project. If Beauvoir's only goal was to decipher the lived experience of being a woman, showing the ways in which her phenomenological analyses are indebted to Merleau-Ponty might be sufficient. But *The Second Sex* is not an epistemological treatise. It is an ethical and political work. In showing us the how and what of the lived woman's body, Beauvoir intends for us to see that women are oppressed. Getting us to see this is the first step in enlisting us as her allies in the political and ethical project of liberating women from their subjection.

To get the Beauvoir we deserve, we need to read her as an engaged existential phenomenologist, whose central concerns were ethical and political. In *the Second Sex*, as the riddle and the answer that opened this chapter show, Beauvoir understood that the endurance of patriarchy relied on a unique intertwining of political and existential structures that implicated women and men intimately, socially, and politically. She discovered that a structural analysis that ignored what Sartre called bad faith, and/or an existential analysis that ignored what Merleau-Ponty identified as the anonymous structures of experience, would miss the mark—would have no political or existential effect. Thus, paying her debts to Sartre and Merleau-Ponty but beholden to neither, Beauvoir created a unique phenomenological political liberatory text—*The Second Sex*.

Taking advantage of this interpretive moment when we can call up the name Merleau-Ponty without erasing the name Sartre, and when we can speak of Sartre without marginalizing Beauvoir, I read *The Second Sex* as the scene of a ménage à trois, where the angles of Sartre's and Merleau-Ponty's thoughts are triangulated through the cutting edges of Beauvoir's thinking. Though neither Sartre's concepts of bad faith and the look nor Merleau-Ponty's idea of ambiguity can by themselves adequately account for women's failure to rebel, taken together, they can, when properly spliced, satisfy Beauvoir's desire to birth the independent woman.

To understand how Beauvoir's concept of ambiguity differs from Merleau-Ponty's and to understand the role Sartre's bad faith plays in this difference rely on an un-Cartesian understanding of Sartre's categories of freedom and facticity. If we read Sartre as establishing a Cartesian dualism between the domain of the fact and the domain of freedom, if we equate the domain of the fact with the *en-soi* and the domain of freedom with the *pour-soi*, we will have trouble finding a productive way of understanding the ways in which Sartre's and Beauvoir's ideas cross. Sartre, as I read him, is not a Cartesian, however. He does not understand the givens of our situation as pure materialities devoid of human intentionalities. They are facticities. That is, consciousness is not, as with Descartes, a passive meaning finder as much as it is an active meaning giver. In disclosing the meanings of the world, consciousness also constitutes them. Given that every materiality we confront is already sedimented with historical, social, political, economic, and cultural layers of intentional acts, and given that consciousness finds meaning already inhering in the materialities that confront it, it appears that materialities are meaningful in themselves. Facticities, materialities imbued with human meaning, that is, appear to be facts, material givens that seem to be immune from, and independent of, our intentionalities.

The *Being and Nothingness* category of bad faith destabilizes the apparent fact status of the facticities of our lives. Reading the vignettes of the waiter in the café, the woman on a date, the gambler, and the homosexual, we discover the ways in which the category of bad faith obfuscates the relationship between intentionality and materiality. It is true that the point of Sartre's discussions of bad faith is to reveal the powers of freedom. Freedom is not, however, privileged to the point of throwing us into the pitfalls of an idealistic constructivism. The waiter's need to earn a living is a material reality that cannot be willed or wished away; the homosexual's desires and the gambler's addictions are not mere matters of the will. The point of Sartre's bad faith is not to deny the power of these materialities, desires, and habits, but rather to refuse to treat them as facts: determining conditions immune to the meaning-giving powers of consciousness. In the process of earning a living, it is not necessary for the waiter to reduce himself to a social role. The gambler and the homosexual are responsible for the meaning they assign to their addiction and desire.

A fact is a facticity whose intentional structure is obscured by the bad faith that negates the reality of our freedom/intentionality. Reading Sartre's account of bad faith through Beauvoir, we discover that, at bottom, the category of bad faith is a political category that calls us to the task of resisting the powers that would transform facticities into facts. Comparing Beauvoir's image of the serious man in *The Ethics of Ambiguity* to Sartre's discussions of seriousness is instructive here. For both Sartre and Beauvoir, the serious man is a man who lives in a world of facts—a world where the meaning-giving powers of intentionality and the responsibilities for the meaning of the world are refused. For Sartre, seriousness is a reaction to the anguish of freedom. It is a "reassuring, materialistic, substantiation of values . . . as coming from the world rather than from my freedom" (*BN*, 78).[3] This flight from anguish is understood by Sartre as a bad faith strategy that carries ethical and psychoanalytic implications (*BN*, 797). At the end of *Being and Nothingness*, Sartre promises to devote a future work to these ethical considerations (*BN*, 798). That work never appeared during his lifetime.

Beauvoir tells us that her *Ethics of Ambiguity* fulfills Sartre's promise. This is not, however, the whole story; for though she, like Sartre, makes it clear that the serious man's refusal of freedom is a bad faith individual failure, she does not take up Sartre's directive to investigate this failure through the lens of existential psychoanalysis. For Beauvoir, this bad faith betrayal of freedom cannot be adequately dealt with at the individual level. Its political and collective effects demand our attention. The bad faith of the serious man wears a Nazi uniform. Beauvoir writes:

> The serious man is dangerous. It is natural that he makes himself a ty-
> rant. Dishonestly ignoring the subjectivity of his choice, he pretends that
> the unconditioned value of the object is being asserted through him. . . .
> The serious leads to a fanaticism . . . of the Inquisition . . . the Vigilantes of
> America. (*EA*, 49–50)

The category of bad faith, even when Beauvoir moves it from the realm of the personal to the domain of the political, is not without its problems. For many, the problem lies in the way bad faith privileges freedom over facticity when it destabilizes the fact status of the materially given. Seeing this privileging as more nuanced than many of Sartre's critics allow, I find that though Sartre recognizes the ways in which our freedom is contextualized and thereby not absolute, he does not recognize the ways in which the power of the subject to destabilize the fact status of facticities are also contextualized. Granting that the freedom of the subject is not absolute, he nevertheless holds the subject absolutely responsible. As I see it, when Sartre's analyses of bad faith locate the dynamics of bad faith within the structures of consciousness such that it is the meta-stabilities of consciousness that lie at the root of our faith in the lie we tell ourselves, he gives the social forces that produce and support that faith in the lie a pass—they remain invisible. Making these forces visible is one of the critical projects of *The Second Sex*.

Beauvoir's appeal to the concept of ambiguity predates *The Second Sex*. *The Ethics of Ambiguity*—a book Beauvoir tells us she wrote to provide the ethics invited by, but absent in, *Being and Nothingness*'s analyses of bad faith—invokes the name Sartre throughout its pages. The title of the text, however, bears Merleau-Ponty's signature. Between the name within the text and the signature on the text, we are alerted to the fact that something is going to happen to the concept of bad faith as it is transferred from Sartre's to Beauvoir's pen. Merleau-Ponty's concept of ambiguity is going to set it on edge. The full impact of crossing bad faith with ambiguity will have to wait for *The Second Sex*, for though Beauvoir uses the concept of ambiguity in *The Ethics of Ambiguity*, she does not exploit the ways in which it obliges us to look beyond individual responsibility until she interrogates the situation of women.

The concept of ambiguity, like the concept of bad faith, destabilizes the fact status of the given. With the concept of bad faith, this destabilization occurs at the site of the individual. With the concept of ambiguity, it is at work in the broader field of anonymous economic, social, cultural, and psychological forces. Once the concept of ambiguity is in play, the bad faith posed by the woman in the café can no longer be confined to a matter of this woman's negotiation of her sexual embodiment. It can no longer be confined to the question of this woman on this date. It must attend to the heterosexual codes that sexualize her body and that situate her in the position of going on a date—which is not to say that this scene does not concern this woman on the date. We need the category of bad faith to keep the individual in play and to remember that what the woman does on this date is decided, not determined; but we need to situate the category of bad faith within the horizon of the concept of ambiguity to examine the interplay between the forces that situate the woman in the café and the café behavior that can either reinforce or disrupt the power of those forces. For with the category of ambiguity in play, we are directed to interrogate the codes of heterosexual normativity that position her body as the target of his sexual "advances."

One way to get at the unique way Beauvoir triangulates the thought of Sartre and Merleau-Ponty is to examine the way she redeploys the concept of ambiguity. In Merleau-Ponty there is no idea of bad faith to complicate the dynamics of ambiguity. In Sartre, the dynamics of ambiguity as described in the look, for example, are isolated from the machinations of bad faith. With Beauvoir, ambiguity and bad faith travel together. They are intimate companions. We see the difference this intimacy makes if we examine the distinct ways in which Sartre, Merleau-Ponty, and Beauvoir depict the ambiguity of the perceiver-perceived relationship.

In traditional philosophy, the distinction between the perceiver and the perceived is established as the difference between a subject and an object. With Merleau-Ponty, this difference is ruined. One cannot be a perceiver without being perceived. One cannot be a perceiving subject without also, and necessarily, being an object of perception. This simultaneity of our subject and object status constitutes the ambiguity of the lived body. We are not one (the subject) or the other (the object) but one (the subject) *and* the other (the object). There is nothing willed about this ambiguity. It is a necessary and anonymous structure of our existence.

With Sartre, this ambiguity of the lived body becomes the stuff of the look. The anonymous dynamics of perception are aligned with Hegelian accounts of power and desire. The structure may be anonymous; the existential experience is not. I struggle against this loss of subjectively experienced freedom that comes with becoming the object of another's gaze. I resist the ambiguities of the perceptual situation. In Sartre's hands, the anonymous dynamics of perception lose their perceptual innocence. They become the ground of political and ethical struggles. It is, I think, because Sartre sees these struggles of/for freedom as grounded in the anonymous, inevitable structures of perception that he does not bring his analysis of bad faith to his concept of the look. Whereas in his discussion of bad faith, Sartre holds me responsible for evading my freedom by becoming what the social and/or individual Other makes of me, in his analysis of the look, Sartre does not hold me responsible for becoming an object for the Other or for objectifying the Other. This move is left to Beauvoir.

Whereas Sartre's analysis of the look relies on a dynamic analogous to the continuous oscillation and simultaneity of perceiving and being perceived as described by Merleau-Ponty, Beauvoir sees that the anonymous forces at work in the dynamics of perception lose their fluidity once they are taken up by the desires that structure the social and political fields. She dissects the ways in which the dynamics of the struggle for freedom, the look, can become reified such that certain people come to "legitimately" occupy the position of the subject, while others are "legitimately" objectified as the Other. The subject-object dichotomy, in other words, is not simply an innocent epistemological error. It is the ground of an oppressive politics that renders its oppression invisible by reifying the flows of anonymous perceptual structures. Calling humanly constituted reifications natural facts, this politics transforms mutable historical structures into natural realities, thereby foreclosing the possibility of demands for change.

In *The Second Sex,* Beauvoir interrogates the ways in which the anonymous forces of perception become exploitive in order to strip historical perversions of the subject-object ambiguity of their seemingly natural reality. Her discussion in the chapter on biology is especially instructive here. If ever there seemed to be a fact that justified women's second-sex, dependent status, it would seem to be the fact of the biology of their reproductive bodies. If Beauvoir can make the case that even the authority of biology is not sufficient to establish a fact of the human condition, she will have made deep inroads into the ideology of facts. The chapter on biology critiques this ideology in a most interesting way. It opens with discussions of animal life that lure us to accept the "fact" status of women's reproductive bodies. Then, after being led to believe that Beauvoir intends to convince us that biology is destiny, Beauvoir alters course. Showing us the wizard behind the curtain, she turns the fact back into a facticity. Thus, the chapter's narrative repeats the strategy of presenting a facticity as a fact in order to retrace the steps through which a facticity is transformed into a fact.

Beauvoir's discussion of women's reproductive bodies is especially provocative. She describes women from puberty to menopause as the plaything of the species, as alienated from their bodies, as the site of a conflict between the species and the individual. "Woman," Beauvoir writes, "is of all mammalian females at once the one who is most profoundly alienated . . . and the one who most violently resists this alienation" (SS, 30). Only "the crisis of menopause" delivers women from "the servitude imposed by her female nature . . . [only then] she is herself, she and her body are one" (SS, 31). Everything so far seems to belie the reality of women's facticity. Then Beauvoir's analysis takes a turn. "Certainly," Beauvoir writes, "these facts cannot be denied [but] . . . in themselves they have no significance" (SS, 34). Women's violent resistance to their alienation to the species provides the phenomenological grounds on which Beauvoir can insist that "the bondage of woman to the species is more or less rigorous according to the number of births required by society and the degree of hygienic care provided for pregnancy and childbirth" (SS, 33). Another experience of woman, her experience of maternity as a unique autonomy (SS, 35), gives Beauvoir the opening to dispute the idea that pregnancy is only an alienated experience of a service to the species. It authorizes her to write, "the facts of biology take on values that the existent bestows on them" (SS, 36). Nature, in short, is a facticity. So much for the myth that biology is destiny.

Current reproductive technologies and family planning techniques make it even clearer today than when *The Second Sex* was written that the female birthing body is no more natural than the female nonreproductive body. While it is certainly not the case that we had to wait for current technologies to challenge the idea that biology is destiny, it is the case that today's technologies make it clear that the biological possibilities of the birthing body can either be normalized as mandates or understood as ambiguities whose meanings remain to be determined. Western history, the only history that I am at all competent to address, is replete with women in earlier eras who found nonreproductive ways of living their birthing bodies. Some of these women were called spinsters and were pitied. Others were called heroines. Still others were admired for their spirituality. The difference that technology makes is that what was once seen as an aberration that was either pitied or praised has now been normalized. The female birthing body has lost its fact status. Its visibility as a facticity is secured. With this visibility comes an awareness of the politics of reproduction—a politics too tangled to explore here except to say this: reproductive and family planning technologies make it clear that the female birthing body is no more necessary than the female nonreproductive body unless we invoke the argument for the preservation of the species—an argument that seems to have little standing when the subject turns to such issues as nuclear weapons, biological warfare, or global warming.

Beauvoir's chapter on biology and current reproductive and family planning technologies confronts us with the "fact" that there are no natural facts but only anonymous normalization forces that create facts out of facticities. It shows us how the concept of ambiguity in grounding the concept of facticity is essential to the liberation project of *The Second Sex*. For it is the ambiguity of the woman's birthing body that distinguishes it from other female animal bodies. The woman's body is an embodied intentionality. It is both the materiality that births the next generation and the intentionality that resists becoming a slave to the species. It is both a natural object that embodies the anonymous forces of menstruation, pregnancy, and lactation, and a human subject who lives these forces and gives them meaning.

The chapter on biology also shows us how collective human forces obfuscate the ambiguity of the birthing body by giving it the status of a fact. Now we see the social face of bad faith. Working through this chapter, we are moved from the site of an individual woman on a date who refuses to acknowledge the ambiguous interplay of her body and self in order to escape the demands of freedom, to the collective site of a patriarchal order that refuses to recognize the ambiguity of the birthing body in order to escape the threat that "unnatural" women would pose to the ideology of masculinity, which establishes men as autonomous and women as dependent. The chapter on biology shows us how reducing the ambiguity of women's embodiment to a natural fact supports the construct of the masculine autonomous subject. It hints at an alternative model of subjectivity when it identifies women's experience of pregnancy as a unique mode of autonomy. Beauvoir does not develop this idea of pregnancy as a mode of autonomy, but if we bring this idea to her discussions of women's resistance to becoming a slave to the species, we can see that it is not pregnancy that is a threat to women's subjectivity, but pregnancy coded as subordination to the species. It is a small step from identifying women as subordinate to the species, to positioning them as subordinate to and dependent on men. In this way the ambiguity of the birthing body, that is, women's experience of pregnancy as both an alienation and a unique mode of subjectivity, and the threat it poses to patriarchal ideologies are put out of play.

We are back to the riddle of rebellion. Why don't these experiences become the ground of resistance? Why have they not become a source of political action? The answer, for Beauvoir, lies in the unique ways in which the forces of ambiguity and bad faith play off each other.

Reading *The Second Sex*, we see that though for Sartre bad faith is merely a matter of individual modes of consciousness and behavior, for Beauvoir it is more complicated; for the individual who engages in bad faith is both the product of anonymous social forces and the creator of the meaning of the world. As the product of alienating social codes, women may, like those Beauvoir cites in the introduction, accept their alienation. As creators of the meaning of the world, they may, like the women in the chapter on biology, appeal to their experience of subjectivity to resist it. The question concerns the difference between these two attitudes. Why is it that some women experience their subjectivity and find in this experience a resource for resistance to the forces that alienate them from their subjectivity? Why is it that other women either lack this experience of authentic subjectivity or do not find it grounds for resistance? Attending to these questions brings us to Beauvoir's concept of the appeal. For at least part of her answer is that it is women's isolation from each other that isolates them from their experienced subjectivity—that for these individual experiences to be felt as something other than an individual aberration, a woman must discover that her experience of subjectivity is shared by other women. This discovery is essential for political action; for if it is the case that it is as individuals that we are responsible for unmasking the structures of oppression, it is also and necessarily the case that undoing these structures requires collective action—the appeal.

In *The Ethics of Ambiguity* the descriptions of the appeal are gender neutral. There, Beauvoir writes: "thus we see that no existence can be validly fulfilled if it is limited to itself. It appeals to the existence of others" (*EA*, 67). And, she continues:

> To will oneself free and to will that there be *being* are one and the same choice. . . . [W]e can neither say that the free man wants freedom in order to desire being or that he wants the disclosure of being by freedom. These are two aspects of a single reality. And whichever be the one under consideration, they both imply the bond of each man with all others. This bond does not immediately reveal itself to everybody. . . . [T]he first movement is to hate [the Other, but] to will that there be being is also to will that there be men by and for whom the world is endowed with human signification. One can reveal the world only on a basis revealed by other men. (*EA*, 70–71)

Two things are notable here. The first is the unique meaning of freedom; the second is the truth of the bond. Freedom, understood as an ethical and political category, concerns the Other. Though it is through the dynamics of freedom that I as an individual reveal the meaning of the world, the meaning I reveal is grounded on the meanings others have bequeathed to me. Moreover, it is only by engaging the Other that I can express the desires and powers of freedom in ethically and politically legitimate ways. Though for Beauvoir, like Sartre, transcendence is the mark of human condition, for Beauvoir my being as transcendence is also and necessarily a being for and toward others. This truth of freedom, which Beauvoir identifies as the truth of our bond with others, is neither immediately evident nor immediately experienced as a bond of reciprocity. Like Sartre, Beauvoir indicates that our relationship to the Other is immediately experienced through the dynamics of the look. From her gender-neutral perspective of *The Ethics of Ambiguity*, Beauvoir does not yet see the places where the bond is affirmed, and as affirmed becomes a means of subjugation. What she does see, however, is that there is a direct relationship between the refusal to affirm the bond and the forces of oppression.

To understand what Beauvoir means by oppression, we need to focus on this idea of freedom as necessarily entailing appealing to and engaging others. Beauvoir writes:

> Only man can be an enemy for man; only he can rob him of the meaning of his acts and his life because it also belongs only to him alone to confirm it in its existence, to recognize it in actual fact as a freedom. . . . It is this interdependence which explains why oppression is possible and why it is hateful. As we have seen, my freedom, in order to fulfill itself, requires that it emerge into an open future; it is other men who open the future to me, it is they who setting up the world of tomorrow, define my future; but if, instead of allowing me to participate in this constructive movement, they oblige me to consume my transcendence in vain . . . they are changing me into a thing. (*EA*, 82)

Oppression, then, is grounded in the refusal to move beyond the immediate experience of the Other as enemy, the look. It rejects the vulnerability of our interdependence for the security of reducing the Other to a thing. Thus, oppression cannot be adequately explained in terms of material deprivation. It must be understood more fundamentally as finding myself in a world where my future is defined by the Other, where being reduced to a thing, I am "condemned to mark time hopelessly in order merely to support the collectivity" (*EA*, 83).

We need to take this definition of oppression with us to *The Second Sex* to appreciate that Beauvoir is not being hyperbolic when she describes women of all classes as oppressed and when she describes the situation of women as analogous to that of the slave. Moreover, we find *The Ethics of Ambiguity* anticipating the importance Beauvoir will ascribe to the role that the myth of woman and the role that the "facts" of biology play in women's oppression when she notes that oppressors stave off revolt by converting their historical ideologies, facticities, into facts of nature. "One cannot," Beauvoir notes, "revolt against nature" (*EA*, 83).

In *The Second Sex*, the idea of the appeal is reframed to address the particulars of women's situation. Here she argues that myths of woman and the heterosexual bond have created a situation where "women do not authentically assume a subjective attitude. . . . They have gained only what men have been willing to grant" (*SS*, xxv). More controversially, Beauvoir claims that "the whole of feminist history has been man-made. . . . Just as in America there is no Negro problem but rather a white problem . . . the woman problem has always been a man problem . . . men created values, mores, religion. . . . Feminism itself was never an autonomous movement. . . . When [women] have intervened in the course of world affairs, it has been in accord with men, in masculine perspectives" (*SS*, 128–29).

The point of this observation is to distinguish between an appeal and a supplication. An appeal is grounded in an authentic experience of subjectivity. Absent this experience, women's demands for change will be framed within the categories of patriarchy. In arguing for maternity leave, for example, they will accept the offer of extended sick leave. Allowing pregnancy to be equated with illness, they will reinforce men's position as the authority that determines the meaning of the world. No idea of the pregnant woman as autonomous will emerge so long as she is referred to as ill. No challenge to male subjectivity will be heard. Women will receive what men are willing to give and will receive what they get only on the terms prescribed by patriarchy.

In linking the possibility of the appeal to an authentic experience of subjectivity, however, Beauvoir also links it to the refusal of bad faith. For if it is true that women's experience of authentic subjectivity has been hijacked by the myth of woman, it is also true that women are responsible for exposing the mystifications of patriarchy. No one else will do it for them. A politically effective appeal can only be made by those who refuse to be defined by the Other—by those who refuse the lure of the look—a seduction that by reducing women to a thing also saves them from the responsibilities of freedom. Beauvoir argues that to avoid this seduction, women must embrace their situation as historical not natural.

Whether Beauvoir is justified in accusing the feminist movements of her times of being inauthentic is not the issue here. The issue concerns the basis for a feminist movement that asks for something other than what men are willing to give. Here *The Second Sex* provides criteria for judging Beauvoir's claim about the feminism she knew, as well as current feminist movements; for if we follow *The Second Sex*, a movement is only justified in calling itself a women's movement if it is grounded in demystified women's experiences. Teaching us how to distinguish mystified experiences from authentic ones is a central project of *The Second Sex*.

In *The Second Sex*, Beauvoir calls for the end of a sexual politics, and by extension the end of all politics, which by invoking the representation of another human being as the Other betrays the phenomenological truth of our lived ambiguity. The politics of the appeal is an alternative to the violent and violating politics of the look. For an appeal to be heard, however, there must be some common ground between the one who speaks and the one spoken to. Phenomenologically speaking, that ground must be some shared experience. The question for a feminism pursuing Beauvoir's politics of the appeal concerns the possibility of a shared experience that might serve as a common ground among women and a common ground between men and women.

When it concerns the possibility of women's forming a liberation movement, their shared embodied experience of alienated subjectivity can provide the ground that opens the space for women to appeal to each other across class, race, and culture lines. When it concerns the possibility of women's appeal being heard by men, the ground must be an experience of a shared human ambiguity.

The experience of shared ambiguity that Beauvoir discusses in some detail (though not to be mistaken for the only experience) is the heterosexual experience of the erotic. Attending to Beauvoir's discussions of the erotic returns us to the question of the look and to the challenge that Merleau-Ponty's descriptions of ambiguity present to Sartre's claim that conflict constitutes our original and enduring relationship to the Other. In bringing a gendered eye to both Sartre's and Merleau-Ponty's accounts of the structure of consciousness, Beauvoir finds that while Merleau-Ponty provides the experiential ground for a politics that speaks of a shared world, Sartre shows us how and why the givens of the shared perceptual world are negated in the social and political worlds. Reading Sartre, we can conclude that perceptual experience will not lead us to Beauvoir's politics of the appeal. Interestingly, however, in discerning the ways in which a phenomenology of our relationship with others leads to the erotic body, Sartre's descriptions of the caress direct us to the ways in which the erotic draws us to each other in uniquely ethical ways.

Sartre's analysis of the caress is brief (*BN*, 507–509; 516–17). As caressed and caressing, the lived body embraces its facticity. As caressed and caressing, I live my body as flesh, contingency, presence. I live the risks of facticity. In the caress, "my body is made flesh in order to touch the other's body with its own facticity" (*BN*, 507). Sartre finds, however, that the caress, the passivity of the flesh that forgoes the power of possession for the risks of relationship, is unsustainable. It is relegated to the position of foreplay—a means toward the end of sexual intercourse, understood by Sartre as an act of possession that ruptures "that reciprocity which was precisely the unique goal of desire" (*BN*, 517).

Sartre abandons the hope of the caress. He writes: "We shall never place ourselves concretely on a plane of equality . . . where recognition of the Other's freedom would involve the Other's recognition of our freedom" (*BN*, 528). This abandoned hope, however, is retrieved in that famous footnote that reads: "These considerations do not exclude the possibility of an ethics of deliverance and salvation. But this can be achieved only after a radical conversion which cannot be discussed here" (*BN*, 534, n. 13).

As abandoned by Sartre, this hope finds a home in Beauvoir's thought. What from Sartre's point of view is an inevitable failure—the caress that reveals my reciprocal bond with the Other will inevitably end up as an erotics of sadism or masochism—is from Beauvoir's perspective a patriarchal perversion of the dynamics of intentionality. As Beauvoir describes it, intentionality joyfully embraces the pleasures of non-possession. It forgoes the alienating pleasures of possession, submission, and domination for the joy of the unique goal of desire—reciprocity. The passion of the erotic that embodies this joy carries the hope of a political transformation. Beauvoir writes:

> As a matter of fact, man like woman, is flesh . . . she like him in the midst of carnal fever, is a consenting voluntary gift, an activity; they live out in their several fashions the strange ambiguity of existence made body. . . . In both sexes is played out the same drama of the flesh and the spirit, of finitude and transcendence; both are gnawed away by time and laid in wait for by death, they have the same essential need for one another; and they can gain from their liberty the same glory. If they were to taste it, they would no longer be tempted to dispute the fallacious privileges, and fraternity between them would then come into existence. (*SS*, 728)

Beauvoir does not ask for an ethical conversion. Instead, she looks to the reciprocity of the erotic to provide an experiential ground for the emergence of a politics of the appeal. This politics translates the experience of erotic reciprocity into the imperative of the bond. It reads this imperative as requiring us to accept the ambiguity of our condition. As politicized, this ambiguity obliges us to engage each other in constituting the meaning of the world. It obliges us to translate the erotic risks of facticity into the political risk of entering the space of contested meaning making. It rejects retreats into the securities of bad faith and refuses to revert to the violence of the look.

Beauvoir's politics of the appeal is more suggestive than developed. Its suggestions, however, as grounded in the facticity of the erotic, save us from making the mistake of understanding the appeal as a speech act limited to the rules of rational discourse or operating at some level of abstraction. Taking our cue from Beauvoir, we learn that we must understand feminist politics as a concrete politics of passion that speaks of and for the joy of our embodied intentionalities and desires.

What is fully developed in Beauvoir's thought is an existential phenomenology that transformed a phenomenological thinking that did not notice its patriarchal silences and biases into a resource for a feminist phenomenology and politics that taught us to treat facts as facticities, to expose the operations of the sedimented powers of facticities, to cut through the seductions of bad faith, and to save the ambiguously anonymous structures of perception and the reciprocal passions of the erotic from the demands of the look. I read these developed dimensions of her thought reflexively and proactively. Reflexively, they are tools for critiquing her thought and ours. Proactively, they function as an appeal to give her ideas a future by pursuing their possibilities.

Notes

1. I am using the 1974 Vintage edition of *The Second Sex.*
2. See Bergoffen, *The Philosophy of Simone de Beauvoir,* 141–84; and "Simone de Beauvoir and Jean-Paul Sartre: Woman, Man and the Desire to Be God," 409–18.
3. I am using the 1956 Washington Square Press edition.

2 Where Influence Fails: Embodiment in Beauvoir and Sartre

Christine Daigle

In an article on Sartre's sexist psychoanalysis, Margery Collins and Christine Pierce begin by stating that "Sartre's view of human nature and relationships would seem, on the face of things, to preclude such sexist bias. Moreover, one suspects that the vigilance of Simone de Beauvoir might have prevented such a disaster."[1] The authors' argument is that Sartre's view of human beings wherein "existence precedes essence" precludes a sexist view of women, since such a view would require that women have an essence, that there is such a thing as an a priori and fixed way of being a woman. However, the authors proceed to show that such sexism is present in Sartre's theory and that "in both his philosophy and his literary works he associates a fixed nature with the female"[2] despite what they refer to as "the vigilance of Simone de Beauvoir." Collins and Pierce seem to infer that Beauvoir's influence on Sartre ought to have been sufficient to steer him away from any sexism. Apparently this was not the case. While it has become evident that Beauvoir was successful in influencing Sartre regarding some specific questions and philosophical problems, as some other contributors in this volume have shown, it appears that she was not able to influence him in all matters. The one fundamental concept where she failed to influence him was that of embodiment, specifically the sexed nature of embodiment.

I will begin by examining Simone de Beauvoir's "Merleau-Ponty and Pseudo-Sartreanism" as a pathway to uncovering the similarities and dissimilarities between Sartre's and Beauvoir's philosophies as well as the influence Beauvoir might have exerted over Sartre. Beauvoir was always very careful in camouflaging the influence she might have had on Sartre's works, but an analysis of that essay shows a breach in that strategy. The break between Merleau-Ponty and Sartre was the occasion for Beauvoir to "defend" Sartre vis-à-vis Merleau-Ponty and allows the careful reader to see Beauvoir's philosophy at work.[3] A close examination of the arguments presented by Beauvoir reveals that the Sartre she defends is in fact the Sartre as "infiltrated" by her thought. However, there are certain points at which her influence fails. If it seems that she is somewhat successful in bringing Sartre to open up his stringent conception of absolute freedom to consider the more important role of situation, she is not, however, as successful in exerting influence in relation to embodiment.[4] Despite the fact that Sartre had devoted lengthy sections of *Being and Nothingness* to a discussion of the body and to analyses of sexuality, the being for-itself that emerges from the book is still a somewhat "asexual" being. Beauvoir's *The Second Sex* determines that there is no such thing as an asexual being and that one's sex largely determines one's being for-itself and being for-others. Beauvoir's analyses point to the fact that a supposedly asexual for-itself would in fact be male. Thus, if we follow her analyses, the "subject" of Sartre's phenomenological ontology is an all-powerful, absolutely free male being. Beauvoir, however, presents the subject as an ambiguous being that is a situated embodied freedom. In what follows, I will discuss how this divergent view of the for-itself and embodiment might lie at the root of their ultimately divergent views on alterity and ethics. I will propose that Beauvoir's influence on Sartre fails in relation to embodiment and that this might be the reason why he had to abandon his project of an existentialist phenomenological ethics.

"Merleau-Ponty and Pseudo-Sartreanism"

Beauvoir, Sartre, and Merleau-Ponty were friends and collaborators. The intellectual exchange among the three carried on over the course of many years up until the break in 1955 marked by Merleau-Ponty's publication of "Sartre and Ultra-Bolshevism" and Beauvoir's response in "Merleau-Ponty and Pseudo-Sartreanism."[5] I do not want to examine the details of the break and what triggered it.[6] Rather, I am considering Beauvoir's response to Merleau-Ponty with a concern for what it can tell us regarding her own philosophical relationship with Sartre. I believe that the content of the essay is very telling of her own philosophical stance and of where she thinks Sartre should also be standing philosophically.

Beauvoir's main claim in the essay is that the image of Sartreanism that Merleau-Ponty attacks is a construction that does not correspond to Sartre's philosophy. Merleau-Ponty's Sartre is a philosopher of the subject that is separated from its world, a thinker who makes no room for intersubjectivity and for whom there is only a plurality of subjects among which the only possible relationship is that of the alienating look, since "Merleau-Ponty is so convinced of the insularity of Sartrean consciousness" (M-P, 457). Furthermore, according to Beauvoir, Merleau-Ponty's Sartre negates history. He is thus guilty of falsifying both the ontology and the politics in Sartre. What concerns me here, however, is the phenomenological ontology and not the politics. "True," Beauvoir charges,

> Merleau-Ponty has never understood Sartre. As early as *Phenomenology of Perception*, he coldly denied the entire Sartrean phenomenology of engaged freedom. Even if the conciliation of Sartre's ontology with his phenomenology raises difficulties, one does not have the right to grab from his hands one "of the two ends of the chain," to use Merleau-Ponty's words. Such violence is even more scandalous today than ten years ago, because *throughout the development of his work Sartre has insisted more and more on the engaged character of freedom, the facticity of the world, the embodiment of consciousness, the continuity of lived experience, the totalitarian character of the entire life.* (M-P, 489; emphasis mine)

What Beauvoir says in the last part of this quotation is particularly notable. She points out herself that Sartre has evolved in his thinking and has come to put more emphasis on certain elements that might not have been compelling enough or even present in his early thought, that is, in the philosophy of *Being and Nothingness*. Beauvoir seems to be reproaching Merleau-Ponty for what looks like a too accurate reading of the ontological treatise and, more importantly, his disregard for Sartre's later works that do make room for situation, facticity, and, according to her, embodiment.

The tone of the essay is particularly striking for the reader who is familiar with the earlier essays written by Beauvoir in appreciation of Merleau-Ponty's work. Penelope Deutscher explains that the public exchange between the two in the early 1940s was quite amiable. Beauvoir's review of the *Phenomenology of Perception* was very favorable, and Merleau-Ponty's essay on Beauvoir's fiction was in the same vein of mutual appreciation. They praised each other's work as being the pathway to a "true morality." However, as Deutscher further explains, "the pair moved from that initial surplus of public amicability when Merleau and Beauvoir each declared in print that the other offered the best or even the only exemplars of ethics, to the appropriative delirium filtered through an evanescent Sartre."[7] Deutscher goes on to argue that the essay is the occasion for Beauvoir to present her own views on ethics while defending the Sartre she considers the most defensible. While I agree that the essay unveils Beauvoir's views on ethics and politics, I will argue below that it also unveils her own ontological thinking. In other words, the Sartre she is defending in the essay is in fact herself.

Interestingly, throughout the piece, Beauvoir puts the emphasis on what truly belongs to her in Sartre's thought. Part of an explanation for Beauvoir's strong reaction to Merleau-Ponty's critique may have to do with just that: she is upset that he points to the very problems that she saw plaguing early Sartreanism. She has been working hard since *Being and Nothingness* to steer Sartre toward a situated embodied freedom that enjoys ambiguous relationships with Others rather than conflictual ones. This took time, and Sartre is slowly beginning to accept some of it when Merleau-Ponty comes along in 1953 and criticizes Sartre for what she, Beauvoir, is working to correct! She charges Merleau-Ponty with reconstructive delirium, but she is guilty of it herself. She projects back on *Being and Nothingness* the most recent developments in Sartre's thought, developments that are, as I see it, the fruit of her own influence on Sartre via her own ethical writings: *Pyrrhus and Cinéas, The Ethics of Ambiguity,* and *The Second Sex.* We see an instance of this projecting back when she claims that, in Sartre, "nothing comes from freedom but from the situation" (M-P, 470).[8] Sartre may have made that statement in *Being and Nothingness,* but absolute freedom is so overpowering that it outweighs such a claim. The weight on situation rather than freedom is a Beauvoirian idea that he has come to embrace throughout his later years.

I agree with Deutscher, who suggests that "it is the Sartreanism she [Beauvoir] believes ought to be defended that is defended," for the early Sartre cannot be defensible for Beauvoir when her own thought diverges in significant ways from his own regarding freedom, embodiment, alterity, and ethics. What does she then resent in Merleau-Ponty's attack? Possibly the fact that he fails to see how she has finally been successful in influencing Sartre, at least with regard to freedom and the acknowledgment of facticity and situatedness. If she is closer philosophically to Merleau-Ponty, as has been convincingly argued by some scholars,[9] and if Merleau-Ponty fails to see how Sartre is moving closer to her own views and hence to his own, it has to be a bitter disappointment for her, even if she is constantly and carefully deluding herself about her own role in Sartre's philosophical development.

However, Beauvoir is not completely successful in pointing Sartre in the "right direction." And her irate tone in response to Merleau-Ponty could also have been caused by Merleau-Ponty's ability to point out those elements of Sartre's thought that she is incapable of changing. If she is successful in making Sartre abandon his stringent notion of absolute freedom, and if she is successful in making him admit the importance of facticity and situation, I think her success in relation to embodiment is much less striking if not completely absent. This failure to influence him in relation to embodiment is also a failure to influence his views on alterity and intersubjectivity. So she is only partially successful in making Sartre adopt her views. In her response to Merleau-Ponty, she pretends that Sartre espouses the ideas that she is holding in her own philosophical essays and novels. That is "reconstructive delirium" on her part, and she is in fact reading her own thought into his.

It has been shown, by Kruks and others, that Sartre's evolution toward a notion of situated freedom is the result of Beauvoir's influence on his thought. She had refused from very early on the idea that freedom was absolute and had given only a token acceptance to his idea. This is probably the point on which she is most successful in influencing him. Other authors in this volume have pointed to additional elements in Sartre's thought that could be the result of Beauvoir's influence, such as the evolution of his view on alterity.[10] While the notions of freedom and alterity and their manifestations are crucial because they lie at the root of an existential ethics, the view of the individual as an embodied consciousness is also essential to the development of such an ethics. It is in relation to embodiment that I think Beauvoir's influence fails. Despite her more refined view of embodiment that unveils the fundamental ambiguity of human beings, Sartre sticks to his views that, in the end, make him a dualist: consciousness is embodied only insofar as it uses its body in order to transcend it toward its own projects.

Embodiment and Sexuality in Sartre

The body makes its first appearance in Sartre's *Being and Nothingness* as he discusses the concept of bad faith. To illustrate how one may be in bad faith, he describes the situation of a woman at a romantic rendezvous. The man grabs her hand, and she abandons it to him: "but she *does not notice* that she is leaving it. She does not notice because it happens by chance that she is at this moment all intellect. . . . And during this time the divorce of the body from the soul is accomplished; the hand rests inert between the warm hands of her companion—neither consenting nor resisting—a thing" (*BN*, 97).[11] If Sartre was a self-proclaimed Cartesian dualist and had presented the for-itself as an amalgam of mind and body, two radically different substances, this example would not come as a surprise. It would indeed be possible for the woman to divorce herself from her own body. However, Sartre claims that the for-itself *is* its body. As a conclusion to the example, he says that there are two aspects to human reality, facticity (i.e., the body) and transcendence (i.e., consciousness), and that these aspects "ought to be capable of a valid coordination" (*BN*, 98). How is this coordination to be achieved? Sartre struggles throughout his treatise to find a solution to this problem, and I don't find his dealings with the body to be entirely satisfactory.

The body's next appearance in *Being and Nothingness* is in the chapter on the immediate structures of the for-itself. However, the analysis of embodiment remains minimal in this chapter. It is not until the encounter with the Other, which emerges out of the experience of being looked at, that the for-itself truly experiences embodiment.[12] It is at one's body that the Other is looking. Again, there seems to be a divorce between consciousness and the body as Sartre explains that there is a distance between my consciousness and that of the Other, and that distance is occupied by our bodies: "The Other is first the being for whom I am an object; that is, the being *through whom* I gain my objectness" (*BN*, 361). Through experiencing such original reactions of shame, fear, and pride, consciousness comes face to face with its own factical being: the body. One must be a body-in-the-world in order to feel shame. While felt in the depths of one's consciousness, the look of the Other is only possible onto one's embodied presence. "Thus, my being-for-others—i.e., my Me-as-object— . . . is a perfectly real being, *my* being as the condition of my selfness confronting the Other's selfness confronting me. It is my *being-outside*" (*BN*, 380).

Even if the body makes its appearance in the treatise at a rather late stage, it is necessary from the outset that consciousness be embodied. Sartre's phenomenological ontology leads him to distinguish between a being in-itself and a being for-itself. The for-itself is an embodied consciousness; that is, it is a consciousness that exists as conscious (of) the world. It can be conscious (of) insofar as it is anchored in the in-itself as an embodied being. The body allows consciousness to have experiences and thus to exist. As a result, the body is presented as being the condition of existence for consciousness. I am situated in the world, and my situation, my facticity, is my body. The body is "the contingent form which is assumed by the necessity of my contingency" (*BN*, 408). If I exist, it is necessary that I have a body and that I be in a situation. But it is contingent that I have this body and that I be in this situation.

In the chapter on the body, Sartre explains the difference between the body-for-me and the body-for-others.[13] While I can exist as my body, I cannot be said to fully exist as my body-for-others. While an examination of the Other and her body may lead us to think that the body is merely an instrument for consciousness, Sartre insists that my body is action. When I use my hand to lift a glass, the hand is part of a complex of relations between my project and the resistance of objects, that is, the glass and its heaviness. My body is action, and I live it as such. He explains that action is our being-in-the-world. We need a world in order to have a body, this particular body that is the immediate presence of the for-itself to things. The body is both the point of view and the starting point that I am and that I surpass. As a project, the for-itself is not what it is and is what it is not. I am my body insofar as I transcend it toward a project. It is an instrument in that sense. But, consciousness exists as its body, it lives as body, it is the body. Sartre illustrates this with the example of reading with pain in the eyes. If I am reading while my eyes are in pain, the pain colors my experience of reading. I do not know my pain, I live it. My body is constantly present as me. I am not conscious of it, but as conscious, I exist as my body. "To be conscious is always to be conscious of the world, and the world and body are always present to my consciousness although in different ways" (*BN*, 439–40). As I am reading with pain in my eyes, my body is always present; it forms the background of my consciousness, a painful one as my eyes hurt. I can pay attention to the pain and make it the focus of my experience, or I can focus on the reading itself. But even if I choose the latter, the pain is not expelled from my consciousness. If my body or one of its parts hurts, my consciousness is a hurtful consciousness.[14]

Sartre insists: we exist as embodied consciousness. However, presenting the body also as merely a tool, or hindrance, deflates this claim. There are good reasons why the reader leaves the treatise unconvinced by Sartre's stringent notion of embodiment. The descriptions of the chapter "Concrete Relations with Others" that immediately follow the chapter "The Body" contribute to that. In "Concrete Relations with Others," Sartre explores relations of love, language, masochism, indifference, desire, hate, and sadism. I want to examine Sartre's descriptions of sexual relations between individuals now because they can tell us of a slight shift occurring in relation to Sartre's view of embodiment. More specifically, they indicate a shift toward a purely instrumental view of the body.

Sartre's Descriptions of Sexual Relations

Sartre explains that our relations to others rest on the situated body. However, he insists that the body is not "the instrument and the cause of my relations with others. But the body constitutes their meaning and marks their limits" (*BN*, 471). Yet, in the closest relations among individuals, sexual relations, the body is used by the for-itself as an instrument. In love, the for-itself tries to seduce the Other by objectifying itself and thus attempts to capture the Other's subjectivity. The for-itself makes its own flesh into a fascinating object to captivate the Other. However, what is aimed at is not the body of the Other, but rather her or his consciousness. Yet the difficulty is that, for Sartre, there is this unbridgeable distance between consciousnesses. All one can encounter, ultimately, is the body of the Other.[15] Desire aims at the Other's consciousness, but this consciousness is incarnated. The body of the Other is desirable as an unveiling of her consciousness. "In desire I make myself flesh in the presence of the Other in order to appropriate the Other's flesh" (*BN*, 506). This encounter of flesh is the encounter of consciousnesses that are sexed bodies. What does Sartre make of the sexuality of the for-itself?

For him, the sexual attitudes of the for-itself lie at the foundation of all other attitudes. Sexuality is as fundamental as the upsurge of the for-itself. He questions: "Man, it is said, is a sexual being because he possesses a sex. And if the reverse were true? If sex were only the instrument and, so to speak, the *image* of a fundamental sexuality? If man possessed a sex only because he is originally and fundamentally a sexual being as a being who exists in the world in relation with other men" (*BN*, 499)?

Despite this attempt at presenting the for-itself as a sexual being, Sartre's suggestion falls somewhat flat. He acknowledges that human beings are sexual beings, that is, that we exist sexually for each other, but fails to acknowledge sexual difference and how it colors consciousness's embodiment and hence its own existence as embodied consciousness. In desire, I unveil "simultaneously *my* being-sexed and *his* being-sexed, *my* body as sex and *his* body" (*BN*, 500). But this unveiling of sex remains strangely asexual. Sartre does not explore the implications of sexual difference. Furthermore, the body's sexuality is relegated to the background as he emphasizes the sexuality of consciousness. The shift has thus occurred from an embodied consciousness to a consciousness that uses the body.

To recapitulate: the gender of the body that he so closely examines does not seem to be an important factor. True enough, Sartre discusses sexuality and sexual relations. But even when he does so, encounters seem to take place between asexual for-itselves. When he discusses sexual relationships as tied with the notion of love, he speaks in terms of a consciousness that seeks to seduce and capture the Other as consciousness. Even the sexual act is an attempt at acquiring the consciousness of the Other. Because, in the ontological set-up, the Other's consciousness is always inaccessible and because all I encounter is a body, my desire for the Other is a desire to captivate the Other's consciousness. I always have a somewhat easy access to the body of the Other, but this is not true of the Other's consciousness. Furthermore, whenever Sartre discusses the body as sexed, he fails to acknowledge how the sexed experience will taint the for-itself's experience of the world. He seems to simply adopt a stereotypical macho view of the female body as passive and the male body as active. Interestingly, he came very close to breaking these stereotypes while discussing coitus. On that occasion, he talks of the passivity of the penis: contra the common understanding of the male's coital activity as active, Sartre insists that even during coitus, it is the whole body that is active, that puts the sexual organ in motion. The penis is no more active than the vagina. Sexual organs, of both sexes, are passive. It is the whole body, and hence the whole consciousness, the for-itself, that sets the sexual organ in motion. This further strengthens an instrumental view of the body, one that does not cohere with the view of consciousness as fully embodied.[16]

To make matters worse, Sartre engages in a description of slime and holes that leads him to identify the female sexual organs as a lack, as an "appeal to being," an "*appel d'être*," an "appeal for flesh," an "*appel de chair*." The vagina as hole wants to be filled. It is a lack, it is lacking in flesh. This all starts with his explanation of the nature of the slimy and the affective reaction of disgust it triggers in people.[17] The slimy reveals a signification that gives the being in-itself. While in contact with the slimy, the whole world has meaning as slimy. Slime is said to be the "revenge of the In-itself" and the for-itself that risks touching it "risk[s] being dissolved in sliminess" (*BN*, 777). Consciousness is afraid of the slimy since it runs the risk of its ideas being "glued." The horror of slime is the same as the horror of stagnation. Consciousness as project and as transcending is horrified by the stickiness of the slimy.[18]

From the slimy and the child's experience of it, Sartre slips into a discussion of holes. Children are fascinated by holes. The child fills holes, sticks a thumb in his mouth, a finger in a crack, and so forth: "The hole is originally presented as a nothingness 'to be filled' with my own flesh; the child can not restrain himself from putting his finger or his whole arm into the hole. It presents itself to me as the empty image of myself" (*BN*, 781). Holes are emptinesses that require to be filled. The for-itself is the only being for whom there can be holes, and he feels an urge to fill them. Sartre explains: "Thus to plug up a hole means originally to make a sacrifice of my body in order that the plenitude of being may exist; that is, to subject the passion of the For-itself so as to shape, to perfect, and to preserve the totality of the In-itself" (*BN*, 781).

From this, Sartre's analysis "naturally" slips into a discussion of the female sex as hole. Again, Sartre unveils his macho view of sexuality and falls into the trap of stereotypes.[19] I quote at length what has infuriated a great number of feminists and what ought to have been unpleasing to Simone de Beauvoir:

The obscenity of the feminine sex is that of everything which "gapes open." It is *an appeal to being* as all holes are. In herself, woman appeals to a strange flesh which is to transform her into a fullness of being by penetration and dissolution. Conversely woman senses her condition as an appeal precisely because she is "in the form of a hole." This is the true origin of Adler's complex. Beyond any doubt her sex is a mouth and a voracious mouth which devours the penis—a fact which can easily lead to the idea of castration. The amorous act is the castration of the man; but this is above all because sex is a hole. We have to do here with a *pre-sexual* contribution which will become one of the components of sexuality as an empirical, complex, human attitude but which far from deriving its origin from the sexed being has nothing in common with basic sexuality. . . . Nevertheless the experience with the hole, when the infant sees the reality, includes the ontological presentiment of sexual experience in general; it is with his flesh that the child stops up the hole and the hole, before all sexual specification, is an obscene expectation, an appeal to the flesh (*BN*, 782).

This appeal is yet another expression of the for-itself's fundamental desire to be a for-itself-in-itself. The for-itself lacks the self-completeness of being and wants to be *an* in-itself. Consciousness, using its body, fills being, makes itself a fullness of being. The body is thus seen and used as an instrument in the for-itself's attempt to be rather than to merely exist.[20] Sartre's views on the sexed nature of bodies seem to ignore how the whole experience of the for-itself, how the for-itself exists itself, is transformed by its sexed nature. The for-itself seems to be asexual and at the same time to have a body that is sexed. However, if it is true, as Sartre seems to want it sometimes, that the for-itself is embodied, then the for-itself must be sexual. He affirms as much when discussing the fundamental sexuality of the human being but fails to carry the point to its conclusion. Furthermore, the asexuality of the for-itself seems merely artificial, since the picture he draws is that of a for-itself that is active, transcending—in a word, male. The female human being that is a gaping hole secreting slimy mucus and wanting to be filled by male flesh and mucus bears no trace of transcendence and thus can hardly be imagined to be a free consciousness projecting itself. In contrast, the male human being fulfills the mission of the for-itself of making being be, by its abstract activities as well as by its sexual activity, filling the holes it encounters and sacrificing its own flesh in so doing.

I think it is fair to conclude from this analysis that Sartre does an inadequate job of grounding embodiment. His multiple statements to the effect that

"I am my body" do not carry the point. The reason for this is the multiple other occasions where the body is presented as a tool, as something one uses, as a vehicle for consciousness. As Vintges points out, "in his *Being and Nothingness,* Sartre states that human beings are always situated and that consciousness does not exist independently from their bodily position in the world. In fact, however, he strongly opposes all bodily incarnation as immanence, and thus bad faith, and advocates lucid, pure conscious existence (i.e., transcendence) as the only authentic human existence."[21] In contrast, Beauvoir takes the view that consciousness is embodied seriously and pushes it to its limits. She is closer to Merleau-Ponty's views on the body-subject and yet goes further than he does in presenting a gendered phenomenology wherein the for-itself is indeed sexual and wherein sexual difference truly matters.[22] For her, the body is a sexed body, and the sexuality of the body colors and shapes the whole experience of the world of the for-itself since it is an embodied gendered consciousness.

Beauvoir's Gendered Phenomenology

In *The Second Sex,* Beauvoir is interested in investigating what it means to be a woman. She presents a phenomenological analysis that acknowledges sexual difference and its impact on consciousness. Going much further than Sartre, she presents a more rigorous view of embodiment. As Bergoffen explains, "[Beauvoir] insisted that as concrete, embodied, and situated, we are also always and necessarily sexed and gendered."[23] It has been argued that Beauvoir began to part ways with Sartre as early as *The Ethics of Ambiguity,* where she defines human beings as essentially ambiguous.[24] While I find this convincing and think that the parting of ways occurred even earlier, it is to *The Second Sex* that I will devote my attention, for it is in this essay that one finds Beauvoir's views on embodiment in their full-blown elaboration.

In part 1, chapter 1, "The Data of Biology," Beauvoir articulates her views on embodiment. It is crucial for her to distinguish between the biological body and the social body. While it is impossible to deny that there are sexual differences among human beings, she argues, these differences take on meaning only in the social realm. Biologically, they determine the human being in that it makes the individual a sexed being, but in themselves, these sexual categories do not carry any meaning.[25] In her *Ethics of Ambiguity,* Beauvoir said as much when she claimed that "the body itself is not a brute fact. It expresses our relationship to the world, and that is why it is an object of sympathy or repulsion. And on the other hand, it *determines* no behavior" (*EA,* 41).

The human being exists in a world, and this presence in and to the world requires that one be embodied. It is as body that one is in the world: "To be present in the world implies strictly that there exists a body which is at once a material thing in the world and a point of view toward this world; but nothing requires that this body have this or that particular structure" (SS, 7).[26] Later she continues: "But it nevertheless remains true that both a mind without a body and an immortal man are strictly inconceivable" (SS, 7). There is a profound union between mind and body. Man is his body. Is woman her body? Beauvoir hesitates here because of all the meaning that sexual differentiation acquires as human beings perform their tasks for the species. The male is his body and never feels alienated from it. The female, however, sees her body taken by the male, "violated [the French violée is better translated as "raped"], the female is then alienated—she becomes, in part, another than herself. She carries the fetus inside her abdomen. . . . Tenanted by another, who battens upon her substance throughout the period of pregnancy, the female is at once herself and other than herself" (SS, 22).[27] Only the female human being experiences her body as other than herself. The male provides his semen, but his body remains intact in its individuality. The female who performs her task for the species becomes other than herself.

Interestingly, it is the very fact that she can experience the sexual act of reproduction and pregnancy as alienation that unveils the bonds between the consciousness and the body for the female. Her body is herself, and she feels alienated, taken by the male or the species, when her body is penetrated by the male or when another body grows in her own. She is then different than herself. These experiences threaten the bond between her consciousness and her body; they challenge her being conscious as this body that she is. The human female resists the intrusion of the species in her body. Beauvoir interprets the various changes in puberty as well as the physiological reactions to pregnancy, such as vomiting, as a way for woman to attempt to resist its becoming a reproductive tool for the species. The individual asserts itself against this. Beauvoir further interprets menopause as the freeing of oneself from the shackles of the species. The woman is then "delivered from the servitude imposed by her female nature . . . she is no longer the prey of overwhelming forces; she is herself, she and her body are one" (SS, 31).

For Beauvoir, sexual differences ought not to be disregarded. Since one is one's body, one is necessarily of one sex or of another. The data provided by biology thus provides us with insight into the differences between male and female consciousnesses. However, Beauvoir is adamant: as important as these biological facts are, they do not determine woman in any way. The facts are important, "for, the body being the instrument of our grasp upon the world, the world is bound to seem a very different thing when apprehended in one manner or another. This accounts for our lengthy study of the biological facts; they are one of the keys to the understanding of woman. But I deny that they establish for her a fixed and inevitable destiny" (*SS*, 32–33).

The body of the human being is not a thing, she insists, it is a situation, "it is the instrument of our grasp upon the world, a limiting factor for our projects" (*SS*, 34). Consciousness is situated. It is this body as situation. This particular body that I am makes me, as conscious being, who I am. But as a being that exists, I am not what I am and I am what I am not, to borrow one of Sartre's formulas for the for-itself. I am a project, constantly transcending myself and making myself.

Therefore, what matters is not the body as it is, but what I make of it, what I, as consciousness, make of myself. What matters for woman, given her biology, is the meaning given to her bodily situation. From thence follows the famous opening sentence of Book 2 of *The Second Sex*: "One is not born, but rather becomes, a woman" (*SS*, 267). If woman is prevented from giving her body her own meaning by a sociohistorical context of oppression, she cannot accomplish herself authentically as a human being. This is what Beauvoir goes on to demonstrate in the remainder of Book 1 as well as for the major part of Book 2. As Bergoffen puts it, "[*The Second Sex*] examines the ways patriarchy coagulates sexual differences into systems of otherness that hide the human being's fundamental ambiguity."[28]

Beauvoir had already defined the human being as ambiguous in her *Ethics of Ambiguity*. For her, there is a threefold ambiguity at the heart of the human: the human is immanent and transcendent, the human is free and yet has to make itself free, and the individual is in conflict with the Other and yet needs the Other to fulfill oneself.[29] The human being is both consciousness and body; it is an embodied consciousness, and this means that the individual is a sexed embodied consciousness. Beauvoir's discussion of sexuality shows that it is in the erotic experience that one most fully realizes this. Thus she says: "The erotic experience is one that most poignantly discloses to human beings the ambiguity of their condition; in it they are aware of themselves as flesh and as spirit, as the other and as subject" (*SS*, 402). While Beauvoir's analysis of the lived experience of woman shows that the erotic encounter is lived as conflictual, it need not be that way. She proposes that it is the history of male oppression that has created this situation but that authentic human beings could have a different, and better, erotic experience. Beauvoir describes it in terms of generosity.[30] I quote the following lengthy passage because it is crucial in marking the difference between Beauvoir's and Sartre's views of sexuality:

The dissimilarity that exists between the eroticism of the male and that of the female creates insoluble problems as long as there is a "battle of the sexes"; they can easily be solved when woman finds in the male both desire and respect; if he lusts after her flesh while recognizing her freedom, she feels herself to be the essential, her integrity remains unimpaired the while she makes herself object; she remains free in the submission to which she consents. Under such conditions the lovers can enjoy a common pleasure, in the fashion suitable for each, the partners each feeling the pleasure as being his or her own but as having its source in the other. . . . Under a concrete and carnal form there is mutual recognition of the ego and of the other in the keenest awareness of the other and of the ego. . . . The dimension, the relation of the *other* still exists; but the fact is that alterity has no longer a hostile implication, and indeed this sense of the union of really separate bodies is what gives its emotional character to the sexual act; and it is the more overwhelming as the two beings, who together in passion deny and assert their boundaries, are similar and yet unlike. . . . All the treasures of virility, of femininity, reflect each other, and thus they form an ever shifting and ecstatic unity. What is required for such harmony is . . . a mutual generosity of body and soul. (*SS*, 401–402)

So while it is true that historically women and men have not been able to enjoy such harmonious relationships, there is nothing inherent in their being that precludes such relationships. For Beauvoir, it is clear that the encounter with the Other is problematic, that one puts oneself at risk. But the outcome is not necessarily conflict. Rather, it can be an authentic achievement of ambiguity.

The erotic experience also reveals the ambiguity of one's own sexuality. True to what she has said about biological facts and how they may fail to determine the individual, Beauvoir insists that woman's sexuality is both feminine and masculine, as is that of man: "As a matter of fact, man, like woman, is flesh, therefore passive, the plaything of his hormones and of the species, the restless prey of his desires. And she, like him, in the midst of the carnal fever, is a consenting, a voluntary gift, an activity; they live out in their several fashions the strange ambiguity of existence made body" (*SS*, 728).[31] However, in order for any human being to be able to flourish as an ambiguous being, it is necessary that some social, economic, and cultural changes happen. As she states in her conclusion: "When we abolish the slavery of half of humanity, together with the whole system of hypocrisy that it implies, then the 'division' of humanity will reveal its genuine significance and the human couple will find its true form" (*SS*, 731).

Where Influence Fails

I believe that Beauvoir's influence on Sartre's philosophy has been tremendous. Among other things, she has shaped his ideas on presence/absence and his ideas on freedom from a notion of absolute freedom to that of a situated freedom.[32] These are major things. However, Sartre resists being influenced on the notion of embodiment, and this is why their respective philosophies remain different. He could have been influenced on this issue as well as on the others, since we find seeds of the view of ambiguity and of a gendered phenomenology already in *She Came to Stay*,[33] which is taken to be determinant for his views on presence/absence. The views on freedom evolve over the 1940s. It takes *Pyrrhus and Cinéas*, *The Ethics of Ambiguity*, and *The Second Sex* to make Sartre move to this view in his writings of the 1950s. However, he does not budge on embodiment. Beauvoir thus fails to "convert" him to a more rigorous (from the phenomenological point of view) view of embodiment and of the individual as sexed qua embodied. He remains trapped in a dualist, sexist, macho view, despite Beauvoir's vigilance.

Being and Nothingness's take on the body remains instrumentalist, despite the repeated claims that consciousness is its body. Consciousness uses its body, and the entrapment in the body is a permanent danger for it, as unveiled by the analysis of the slimy and the discussion on sexuality. Beauvoir presents a more complex view that champions ambiguity. The human being is consciousness, and it is truly body; it is truly an embodied, sexed consciousness. She therefore presents a gendered phenomenology wherein the experience of the human being in the world is shaped by one's sex. From the phenomenological point of view, for our own grasp on the world, it does matter what sex our body is. While Sartre had failed to acknowledge it, Beauvoir makes it the basis of her own inquiry.

Besides showing that theirs is not "one philosophy" and unveiling them as independent yet related thinkers, this important point of contention between Beauvoir and Sartre has serious consequences. This analysis may help us understand why and how Beauvoir can successfully elaborate an "ethics of ambiguity," while Sartre fails to carry the project of delineating an existentialist ethics to its end. The *Notebooks for an Ethics* shows Sartre struggling with the notion of conversion to the Other, one that he cannot fully explicate, caught as he is in the quandaries of *Being and Nothingness*. Beauvoir is in a better philosophical position, having elaborated a gendered phenomenology that sees humans as ambiguous beings capable of reciprocity and generosity despite the risk they may incur at the hand of the Other.

Influence fails in relation to embodiment in both ways. Beauvoir fails to influence Sartre, and he can be charged of sexism as he has repeatedly been. But Sartre also fails to influence Beauvoir as she sticks to her views of the embodied sexed consciousness, thus allowing her to fulfill the promise laid down by him in the conclusion of *Being and Nothingness* of devising an ethics on existential-phenomenological grounds. If she succeeds, and I think she does, it is on her own terms, thanks to her views on embodiment.[34]

Notes

1. Collins and Pierce, "Holes and Slime," 112.
2. Ibid.
3. Other contributors to this volume have also tackled the link between Beauvoir and Merleau-Ponty. See, for example, Bergoffen's and Eshleman's chapters.
4. As we will see, Sartre fails to fully take into account the body as situation. He does come to acknowledge the role of situation in relation to freedom, but this has more to do with socioeconomic constraints than with constraints related to one's embodied being.
5. See William McBride's contribution in this volume, chapter 11, "Taking a Distance: Exploring Some Points of Divergence between Beauvoir and Sartre."
6. I can only recommend the excellent collection edited by Jon Stewart, *The Debate Between Sartre and Merleau-Ponty*. This collection of essays gathers entries that tackle diverse aspects of the relationship and the break between the two thinkers as well as Beauvoir's participation in it.
7. Deutscher, "Reconstructive 'Delirium.'" See also Debra Bergoffen's take on this in her *Philosophy of Simone de Beauvoir*, 16–24.
8. Sonia Kruks has put forth a very convincing argument to the effect that it was Beauvoir who steered Sartre to a better understanding of the weight of situation. See her "Simone de Beauvoir: Teaching Sartre about Freedom."
9. See, for example, Bergoffen, *Philosophy of Simone de Beauvoir*; Langer, "Beauvoir and Merleau-Ponty on Ambiguity"; Heinämaa, *Toward a Phenomenology of Sexual Difference*. See also note 22 below.
10. See, for example, the chapters by Debra Bergoffen and Gail Weiss in this volume.
11. I am using the 1992 Washington Square Press edition.
12. It is not my goal here to analyze "the look" in Sartre. Instead, I am considering this part of Sartre's theory only insofar as it reveals something about Sartre's views on embodiment. After all, it is as body that a consciousness can be looking at an Other and be looked at.
13. The full analysis of the body appears rather late in the treatise. While it can be argued that it should have been presented earlier, I think there is a good reason for this analysis to occur where it does. For Sartre, what matters is not the body as it is, but the body for me. We can know the body as it is only very abstractly, from a scientific point of view, for example, as it is the being-for-others. The body for me is experienced as objectness (via the Other). It is thus necessary to have discussed the Other first.

14. This could have been the ground for Sartre to better acknowledge the sexed nature of bodies and to come to a gendered phenomenology similar to what Beauvoir will have to propose in *The Second Sex*. However, he shies away from this, and immediately after the chapter on the body he returns to an instrumentalist/dualist view of the body.

15. Other contributors to this volume have tackled the notion of alterity in Sartre; therefore, I will not expand on this. See the chapters by Debra Bergoffen, Guillermine de Lacoste, Michel Kail, and Gail Weiss in this volume.

16. Sartre's view here could be more inconsistent than I initially thought. On the one hand, the "whole body" is responsible for putting in motion the sex organ in the sexual act *and yet,* on the other hand, the "whole body" is *not* a whole body, since it is comprised of at least one passive part, the sex organ. Speaking of the whole body as putting the sexual organ in motion would thus consist in an instrumental view of (a part of) the body, i.e., the sexual organ. Thanks to Christopher Wood for pointing this out to me.

17. Guillermine de Lacoste and Sara Heinämaa also provide analyses of Sartre's dealings with the slimy in their contributions to this volume.

18. I think much could be deducted from this theoretical analysis of slime about Sartre's own phobia. He presents this horror of slime as a universal reaction, but I think the reader can come up with as many examples as I of their own enjoyment at playing with slimy things (as children or adult). While a common nightmare is to be sinking in moving sands, a good number of people do enjoy mud baths, a slimy experience if there is one! My own preferred contact with the slimy as a child was through the purchase of containers of slime. Shaped like a garbage can, it contained slimy green stuff that you could play with for hours, just for the fun of feeling the sliminess. Its name? Slime! No doubt Sartre would have hated such a toy. Personalia aside, I think the analysis of slime is interesting in relation to what follows it regarding the female sex organs. The vagina and vulva are not "dry" in the same way the penis and testicles are. There is a humidity of the female sex that brings it close to slime. In a sexual encounter with the vagina, mucus covers the flesh. Given what Sartre has said of slime, the sexual encounter with the female sex organ will be horrific. The same cannot exactly be said of the penis, even as the sexual act is often concluded by the ejaculation of mucus. The male sex remains dry in its erection. It is covered with mucus only as it interacts with the female sex. The ejaculation of mucus means, in fact, to sever oneself from one's own slimy substance rather than to become gluey with slime. The male sex is in danger only while in contact with the sliminess of the female sex. Not only a mouth that devours, the vagina is a hole secreting slime that is dangerous to the male sex organ.

19. For a different, yet very interesting, approach to this problem, see Michel Kail, "Le masculin et le féminin."

20. Sartre's analyses of sexuality uncover an instrumentalist view of the body. Another interesting instance where this view of the body emerges is the example of hiking. In part IV, chapter 1, "Being and Doing: Freedom," Sartre explains that what I do with my fatigued body is a result of my overall project (*BN*, 585–89). He talks of a person engaged in the activity of hiking and experiencing fatigue. In this instance, it is particularly striking how Sartre undermines the physiological import of the body's tiredness to place emphasis on the freedom of consciousness: if the hiker gives in to his fatigue, it is freely that he does so. While Sartre had previously explained how pain in one's eyes was transformative of the being for-itself of that consciousness experiencing the pain, he

fails here to acknowledge that the body's fatigue will be transformative and can actually take over the freedom of consciousness. In any case, such an analysis unveils a view of the body as an instrument of the project that consciousness is. The hiker uses her body as a tool and can freely decide to use it despite the instrument's fatigue. All is a "matter of will." Aside from showing a poor appreciation on Sartre's part of physiological demands of the body, this example also shows how Sartre puts emphasis on consciousness as being in command.

21. Vintges, "*The Second Sex* and Philosophy," 50.

22. Laura Hengehold has pointed to that in her essay "Beauvoir's Parrhesiastic Contracts." She argues that for Beauvoir the sexual being-with of human beings is understood as a situation and that, as such, biological facts take on meaning that remains indeterminate so as to leave things open for the for-itself. She notes that Beauvoir follows Merleau-Ponty in regarding the body as a situation but goes further by recognizing "the gendered nature of bodily situation in *The Second Sex* (the generic human is presumed to be male); but from the fact that 'femininity' is a specific situation we can also infer that 'masculinity' is a situation defined, empowered, and limited by reference to women" (197). Kristana Arp makes a similar argument in "Beauvoir's Concept of Bodily Alienation." She argues that Beauvoir is closer to Merleau-Ponty than to Sartre, who remains trapped in dualism (165). But, she argues, Beauvoir also goes beyond Merleau-Ponty, whose view is good for men only (166). Without entering the debate in detail, I would add that it is not clear at all that Merleau-Ponty is successful in overcoming dualism even in his later writings where some scholars find him to be successful in that relation.

23. Bergoffen, "Marriage, Autonomy, and the Feminine Protest," 103.

24. See, for example, Karen Vintges's argument in "*The Second Sex* and Philosophy." She thinks that Beauvoir's starting point may have been Sartrean, but that she moves away from it as she develops her thinking on situation and ambiguity in her ethical essays and her thought on the sociohistorical in *The Second Sex*. For my part, I think that Beauvoir never agreed with the views on the body presented by Sartre. I agree rather with Hengehold, who sees a strong connection with Merleau-Ponty rather than Sartre. I also think that Beauvoir presented these views on embodiment in *She Came to Stay*, albeit not fully conceptualized and articulated but only in its earliest forms. Notes in her early diaries also confirm this. In her student diary, she notes about Merleau-Ponty: "Those problems that he [Merleau-Ponty] lives in his mind, I live them with my arms and my legs. Has he ever known months when all the days were only tears?" (*Diary of a Philosophy Student: Volume 1, 1926–27,* 293). As early as 1927, then, Beauvoir displays a distaste for rationalism or any view that would dissociate consciousness from its body. Merleau-Ponty, it seems, from Beauvoir's diaries, leaned this way at the time. However, when he focuses on the notion of the body-subject in his *Phenomenology of Perception,* he meets with approval by Beauvoir (see the earlier part of this chapter). Could she have influenced Merleau-Ponty and steered him toward a notion of the body-subject that moves him away from such early rationalism?

25. Kristana Arp and Julie Ward present detailed analyses of this distinction between the biological and the social body in their respective articles. See Arp, "Beauvoir's Concept of Bodily Alienation," and Ward, "Beauvoir's Two Senses of 'Body.'" Ward argues that, in this chapter, Beauvoir presents a social-constructivist view of the body and

that "the body itself should, on Beauvoir's grounds, come to be seen as a cultural and historical idea, not as a natural fact" (238).

26. I am using the 1989 Vintage edition of *The Second Sex*.

27. It is passages such as these that have infuriated many gynocentrist feminists who criticize Beauvoir's take on pregnancy and maternity. What they fail to acknowledge, however, is the descriptive point of view adopted by Beauvoir here. While she observes that biology determines the female to this role, she insists later in the book, in a good existentialist fashion, that woman is not entirely determined by her biology and that she remains free to reject or accept this biological determinism. Beauvoir does not say that a woman who decides freely to become a mother is less of a woman than the one who refuses to perform her biological task as defined by the species. On the contrary, she wishes that every woman who becomes a mother does so from a free authentic decision. Only then will pregnancy and motherhood be a valid ethical choice for the woman. Constance Mui has a very interesting take on this in "Sartre and Marcel on Embodiment." In this context, she argues that Beauvoir's view of female embodiment is negative. While I disagree with that, I think her analysis of how, for Beauvoir but also for Sartre and Marcel, the body and the way one is one's body shape one's consciousness is compelling (see, specifically, 117).

28. Bergoffen, "Out from Under," 192.

29. Bergoffen points out that in *The Second Sex,* Beauvoir "proposes a new understanding of the subject: subjectivity = the ambiguity of the body" ("Out from Under," 191).

30. I defer here to Bergoffen's chapter in this volume for a detailed analysis. See also her *Philosophy of Simone de Beauvoir.*

31. In "Sexuality in Beauvoir's *Les Mandarins,*" Barbara Klaw proposes that Beauvoir "problematizes sexuality, constructing it as both feminine and masculine for both sexes, and she revalorizes the female sex" (198). She shows that the novel *Les Mandarins* is also a celebration of the body and that in it Beauvoir applies the views she had elaborated in *The Second Sex.*

32. Edward and Kate Fullbrook have provided evidence for the former (see their *Simone de Beauvoir and Jean-Paul Sartre: The Remaking of a Twentieth-Century Legend* and their essay "The Absence of Beauvoir," as well as Edward Fullbrook's "*She Came to Stay* and *Being and Nothingness*" and his chapter in this volume. Sonia Kruks has convincingly argued for the latter (see note 8 above).

33. While I have not made the case for this claim in this paper, it could easily be done. See Edward Fullbrook's chapter as well as his many publications with Kate Fullbrook.

34. See my "The Ambiguous Ethics of Beauvoir" for a detailed discussion.

3 The Question of Reciprocal Self-Abandon to the Other: Beauvoir's Influence on Sartre

Guillermine de Lacoste

The question of reciprocal self-abandon to the other might appear inconsequential when one deals with the question of the influence of Sartre on Beauvoir or vice versa. Yet, as will become evident below, it is at the very core of each's *vécu* (lived experience), and each's *pensée*—that is, the evolution of their individual oeuvres.

In a long section of Simone de Beauvoir's 1974 *Entretiens avec Jean-Paul Sartre,* Sartre discusses candidly with her his original negative reaction to self-abandon to the Other. But to our great surprise, he also ascertains that the ideal basis for reciprocity in a love relationship is the equal self-abandon of each partner to each other, and Beauvoir totally agrees. This assertion is certainly in complete opposition to Sartre's well-known stance, which stresses the activity of the project, and transcendence away from the contingency of the body, that is, passive and feminine self-abandon. As we begin to scrutinize Sartre's assertion to Beauvoir about mutual self-abandon to the other and try to determine when and how Beauvoir influenced Sartre on the subject, it is interesting to remember that, yes, it is she who introduced the question of self-abandon to the other in her "Woman in Love" chapter of *The Second Sex*—but that she was most negative about it there.

It is quite apparent that "Woman in Love" is a tacit acquiescence of the virulent androcentrism found in Friedrich Nietzsche's *Gay Science* (which Beauvoir quotes at length in that chapter): "I will never admit the claim that man and woman have equal rights in love. These do not exist," Nietzsche writes adamantly.[1] And a little further: "Woman wants to be taken, wants someone who takes, who does not give himself away."[2] And he goes on to explain that woman wants to abandon herself totally, in love, but that a man who would want to do likewise would simply not be a man. Beauvoir's reaction is well known. She agrees with Nietzsche that woman has the propensity to give herself completely, to abandon herself totally to the man she loves. Woman thus hopes to find herself, Beauvoir explains. But instead, because her lover objectifies her, she suffers a deep alienation (*une aliénation profonde* in the French text—translated as "self-abandonment" by Parshley), and loses herself. In that chapter, Beauvoir exhorts women to become like men, to fulfill themselves, not through self-abandon to the other, but through action in the world (*SS*, 642–78; *DS*, 477–507).[3]

We learn from Beauvoir's *La Force de l'âge* that in her own life, when she had first fallen in love with Sartre, twenty years before *The Second Sex*, she had abandoned herself completely to him. She had let herself be subjugated by him in the same way, she explains, that she had once been subjugated by her friend Zaza: "In both cases, I preserved my peace of mind. So fascinated was I by the other person that I forgot myself, so much indeed that no part of me remained to register the statement: I am nothing" (*FA*, 64). What of course played an essential role in both cases was the lack of reciprocal self-abandon of the other person. Zaza was so taken up by her large extended family and her many activities that she had not, in the earlier years of her friendship with Simone, abandoned herself emotionally to her in return. Sartre's case was quite different. As Beauvoir explains in *La Force de l'âge*, when she fell in love with him, she experienced a great "*trouble*" in his presence. Note that the French word *le trouble* is a "false friend" since it does not mean the English "trouble," as Hazel Barnes renders it in her translation of *L'Être et le néant*. Rather, it is a very deeply felt, irresistible impulse to abandon oneself completely to the person one loves—with the complete expectation of the reciprocal abandon of the other. When not reciprocated—which Beauvoir soon realized was the case in her relationship to Sartre—it can create havoc in the one who feels *le trouble*. In Beauvoir's case, it was especially shattering because Sartre had convinced her that they were "pure translucid consciousnesses," with nothing opaque in them, and that this was the basis of their freedom (*FA*, 20). This is why *le trouble* created "an intimate discordance between the emotions of [her] body and [her] decisions" (*FA*, 67). She became incapable of containing the violence of her desire, which submerged her defenses and mired her freedom in her flesh. (Note the negative connotation of flesh and its opposition to pure consciousness.) *Le trouble* became so brutal during that period that she came to call her non-sated desire "a poisoned tunic" and her *trouble* "a secret ailment which rotted my bones—a shameful malady" (*FA*, 68).[4] Let's note here that instead of placing the blame on Sartre's inability to abandon himself in return for her *trouble*, Beauvoir placed all the guilt on herself. What I consider to be a very healthy *trouble* became for her "the poisoned tunic," "the secret ailment," "the shameful malady" (*FA*, 68).

But to go back to the *Entretiens*, Sartre admits there that he did not abandon himself to any of the women with whom he had a relationship. He took, but did not allow himself to be taken; that is, he did not give himself to the other (*Ent*, 400). He performed the active objective part of the act and left out the passive subjective aspect, which would have involved self-abandon and *jouissance*.[5] For, he explains to Beauvoir, there existed within him *une coupure* (a cleavage), which made him resist self-abandon to the other. This led to a "cleavage between what the other could receive and give" in relation to him, and to the impossibility of reciprocity between both partners (*Ent*, 400). At one point in the *Entretiens*, Beauvoir suggests to Sartre that the overdevelopment of his active side led to self-control and coldness on his part. And, Sartre adds, "almost to a slight taste of sadism, since in the end the other person was yielded, and I was not." "I was not?" he asks himself, and he answers: "I was, but what was yielded was nothing to me, since at that very moment I was the active principal" (*Ent*, 415). The rest of this particular part of the dialogue is worth quoting not only because of its content but also because it shows so well the hermeneutics of the Beauvoir/Sartre dialogue:

> BEAUVOIR: You mean insofar as you are pure activity, and the other is pure passivity, there is something virtually sadistic about it?
> SARTRE: Yes, since activity opposed to passivity, is also that which represents sadism.
> BEAUVOIR: Because the other is reduced to the state of an object, whereas the normal would be reciprocity.
> SARTRE: Just so. (*Ent*, 415)

From this dialogue, it is obvious, then, that for both Sartre and Beauvoir (by the time of the *Entretiens* in 1974), in an authentic love relationship, each partner takes and is taken, that is, gives her/himself to the other. Each partner plays an active, objective role as well as a passive, subjective role, which involves self-abandon to the other and *jouissance*. Each partner is one within her/himself, which leads each to treat the other as subject and to the possibility of reciprocity between them (*Ent*, 399, 415).

Throughout a great deal of the dialogue, Beauvoir probes Sartre in an attempt to get him to enunciate the reasons for his own lack of self-abandon to the other. First he admits to her that his subjective relation to his body was always unpleasant, that he never enjoyed, in fact, being in his body. Beauvoir suggests to him that this is probably why he always hated to abandon himself on the grass, or on the beach, much preferring to sit on a hard, sharp stone. "And, was this not actually a moral refusal of abandon to your body?" she queries (*Ent*, 387). Sartre acquiesces that his ideal of the way one "should be" excluded self-abandon to one's body and to the other, which he linked to loss of control in the slimy, to contingency and to the subjective. Rather, what counted for him and became "the fact of being human" was to be in control of the "real objective world" and to thrust himself toward the future through activity (*Ent*, 402).[6]

He recounts to Beauvoir that during his childhood he viewed his body "as a center of action, neglecting the sensation and passivity aspect" (*Ent*, 398). He often played at Pardaillan, the then popular hero of Michel Zevaco's adventure stories, who kills the hundreds of enemies who attack him, much like today's boys, who imagine themselves as Luke Skywalker, the hero of *Star Wars*. Again pressed by Beauvoir to look further back for the source of his abhorrence of self-abandon, Sartre agrees with her that it is probably his horror of his mother's self-abandon. But neither he nor Beauvoir pinpoint in the *Entretiens* in what his mother's self-abandon consisted. From various clues, I have become convinced that, in his own sensibility, "mother" and "self-abandon" were also linked in another way—as a repressed fantasmatic desire to abandon himself to his mother—that is, to commit incest with her.[7] Thus, his Pardaillan games stressing activity and his prodigious intellectual activity throughout much of his life were both ways for him to become an autonomous subject, first by staving off, then by coming to terms with, his desire for self-abandon to his mother.

Sartre is thus the perfect example of Lacan's theory that, as Judith Butler writes, "the subject comes into being, that is, begins to posture as a self-grounding signifier within language, only on the condition of a primary repression of the pre-individuated incestuous pleasures associated with the (now repressed) maternal body."[8] Moreover, Lacan insists that the masculine subject tries to hide the repression on which his would-be autonomy is grounded. This is certainly what Sartre did—most cleverly, throughout his life—until the *Entretiens*, during which he became completely transparent. However, he left some clues that I use throughout this essay.

There are various reasons why Poulou, as young Sartre was called, was not able to work out his fear of embodiment (which was the result of his repressed desire for self-abandon to his mother) as well as most boys do. Their reaction is to run away from their fear of embodiment "by joining other boys in aggressive games of action and adventure; by turning to their father's clean and neutral physicality; and by looking for escape from immanence and for symbolic freedom in the social world outside the home."[9] For Poulou, however, the first two ways of escape were barred. He was completely excluded by his peers, never accepted by a single group of boys playing Pardaillan in the Luxembourg gardens: "Always imploring, always excluded," Sartre observes laconically fifty years later (*Mots*, 111). And of course, he never knew his father. The fact that, as he writes, his mother "was all mine" (*Mots*, 24), and that conversely he was everything to her, only complicated further his efforts to run away from his fear of embodiment.[10] What is certain is that this repressed desire played a most important role in his relationships with women and in the way he chose to focus his intellectual endeavors throughout his life.

Nausea can be read, for example, as the allegory of Sartre's own struggle against his desire for self-abandon to his mother. For Roquentin, the sudden uncontrolled giving-in of his body to passivity or self-abandon is a completely negative experience, accompanied by strong nausea. The abandon of "all things" which "gently, tenderly, were letting themselves drift into existence like those relaxed women who burst out laughing and say 'It is good to laugh,' in a wet voice" is a lure and a veneer (*N*, 172). When this veneer melts, what remains are "soft, monstrous masses, all in disorder, naked in a frightful, obscene nakedness" (*N*, 172). Self-abandon is here definitely a "*laisser-aller*," a letting-go, with its full negative connotation. Roquentin has lost the customary control or mastery that his rationalism gave him—and existence has "lost the harmless look of an abstract category" (*N*, 172). It invades him, masters him, weighing on him like a great motionless beast. Only the stiffening of his body, as for activity, makes nausea temporarily vanish for a short while (*N*, 38).

We also find Sartre's struggle against self-abandon to the other, again seen in a negative light, in *Being and Nothingness*'s section on the slimy. There we find the in-itself as the slimy, displaying itself like the overripe breast of a woman lying on her back—and there is the possibility that it will absorb the for-itself in a feminine revenge, for being appropriated by the for-itself. This surreptitious appropriation of the for-itself could mean the loss of control or mastery from which only activity can save it. "I am no longer the master in arresting the process of appropriation," Sartre writes (*BN*, 609).[11]

Except for the brief statement of Sartre's 1974 new ideal of reciprocity in a love relationship, reached through a blend of mutual self-abandon and activity—with which Beauvoir agrees completely—I have so far dealt only with Sartre and Beauvoir's negative views of "self-abandon to the other." Hers was an overt reaction dictated by androcentrism's completely negative view of woman's self-abandon to the other, exemplified by Sartre's own response to her *trouble;* his was a covert reaction, triggered by his psychological problems with his mother, generated by society's prohibition of incestuous impulses in sons and then by androcentrism's view of self-abandon as taboo for men. Behind both reactions loomed androcentrism's certitude of male superiority due to mastery and domination—through the construction of difference between self and other, and of male autonomy and subjectivity based on the objectification of the other; to androcentrism's assertion that male activity in sexuality is the norm; and to its denigration of self-abandon to the other as implying loss of mastery, of activity, and of self.[12]

But how did Beauvoir and Sartre reach the positive view of self-abandon to the other that they discuss in the *Entretiens?* Both Beauvoir's and Sartre's main texts suggesting a positive view of self-abandon to the other date from the same period, the second half of the 1940s, *The Second Sex* having been written from 1946 to 1949, and *Notebooks for an Ethics* during 1947 and 1948.[13] Hidden here and there in the main text of *The Second Sex,* about women's alienation in a patriarchal society, are a few positive strong passages about mutual self-abandon to the other and reciprocal love. Debra Bergoffen refers to these passages as portraying Beauvoir's "muted voice," which she opposes to Beauvoir's "dominant voice" in *The Second Sex.*[14] They are obviously the result of an *"expérience vécue"* by Beauvoir herself, in her relationship to Nelson Algren, who abandoned himself to her and she to him during their passionate liaison of 1947–48. That experience is recounted in *La Force des choses,* in which Beauvoir writes in one pithy sentence that she experienced with Algren, as does Anne with Lewis, in *Les Mandarins,* "the dazzlement of a deep harmony" (*FCh,* 141).[15]

In the first of *The Second Sex* passages conveying Beauvoir's "muted voice," she writes that "sex pleasure in women is a magic spell; it demands complete abandon" (*SS,* 376; *DS* II, 162). This "abandon" has been interpreted by Jo-Ann Fuchs as a "mindlessness" similar to the listlessness of the southern slaves.[16] But this is not at all what Beauvoir meant. In her view, woman's complete "abandon" corresponds, rather, to the fact that she is "profoundly beside herself because her whole being is moved by desire and excitement," and to her longing for oneness with her lover (*SS,* 396; *DS* II, 162).

If, however, a lover takes without giving, or gives pleasure without receiving, the woman feels that she has been used, objectified, and the union does not take place. Only if giving and receiving are combined, or, as Beauvoir writes a little later, "if the words to receive and to give become interchangeable does the union take place" (*SS,* 167; *DS* II, 401). This means that each lover respects each other's freedom, and in mutual recognition regards the other as a free subject.[17]

Then a reciprocity develops, and there is on both sides "the revelation of self by the gift of self" (*SS*, 505–506; *DS* II, 667). It then follows, as Debra Bergoffen explains, that woman's autonomy is not obliterated, that her self is not lost."[18] It is interesting that in her long 1955 essay "Faut-il brûler Sade?" re-marked by Bergoffen in 1997,[19] Beauvoir stresses the strong opposition that existed in Sade between lucidity and *le trouble* (which he never experienced).[20] Does not this opposition remind us of the original clash, which took place at the time of Beauvoir's early love for Sartre, between the pure translucid consciousness—which Sartre had convinced Beauvoir that they were—and the great *trouble* she experienced in his presence? And because Sartre was terribly afraid of Beauvoir's *trouble*, she had come to see it as a shameful malady. But by 1955, Beauvoir had learned the great value of *le trouble*, which impels one to abandon oneself to the other. She writes: "Through *le trouble*, existence is seized in itself and in the other as subjectivity and passivity at once: through this ambiguous unity, the two partners intermingle; each is delivered of her/his self-presence [translucid consciousness], and attains an immediate communication with the other" (Sade, 35).[21]

There at first appears to be a strong confluence between *The Second Sex* and *Notebooks for an Ethics*, although we do not know of any exchange between Beauvoir and Sartre about the *Notebooks*. Beauvoir does not discuss them in *La Force des choses* (which covers the period from 1945 to 1963), as she usually does with all of Sartre's works. She only makes a brief comment that Sartre abandoned (in 1950) his study on morality, for what appears to be obscure reasons.[22] In both texts the emphasis is on, to begin with, the lover's respect for the other's freedom. In full reversal of his *Being and Nothingness* theory, according to which love entails subjugation of the other's freedom in both masochism and sadism, Sartre now writes that there is no love "without deeper recognition and reciprocal comprehension of freedoms" (*NE*, 414). He goes on to explain (and on this point he is partially going further than Beauvoir) that reciprocal comprehension can only happen when I manage to get rid of my ego, which separates me from myself (in self-presence), and consequently from the other. And he surprises us by writing in a tone that is at once Zen- and Derrida-like: "The ego exists to lose itself. It is the gift" (*NE*, 418). He is here deconstructing himself, three decades before Jacques Derrida would begin his own deconstruction. For is not the gift about which Sartre is speaking the gift of *différance*—or dispersed identity—which runs counter to the identity of self-presence, which relies on difference between self and other?[23] The link between Sartre and Derrida is Marcel Mauss's 1923 *Essai sur le Don*, which Sartre discusses at length in *Notebooks* and to which Derrida and other postmoderns often refer.[24]

As Sartre goes on to discuss his notion of generosity, it becomes obvious that the earlier confluence between Beauvoir's thought and his has all but disappeared. But the reason is not difficult to find. I discussed earlier how Beauvoir's "muted voice" in *The Second Sex* and her notion of "erotic generosities" was a consequence of her deep reciprocal love with Nelson Algren, which she experienced while she was in the throes of writing *The Second Sex*. It is interesting to discover that Sartre's notion of generosity was also the result of a deep love affair, with Dolores Vanetti (the mysterious "M" in Beauvoir's memoirs), which he was experiencing at the time he was writing his *Notebooks*. This is not surprising, for we are dealing here with two existentialists; and the gist of existentialism is that it is about *expériences vécues,* not abstract notions. The experiences are then transformed into their theories by the authors.[25]

Actually Sartre's liaison with Vanetti began early in 1945, when he went to New York for the first time. And it was he who, inadvertently, threw Beauvoir into Algren's arms two years later. Beauvoir had been extremely distressed about Vanetti—for this was the first time that a contingent love of Sartre's was turning out to be a fully reciprocal "necessary love."[26] When she had questioned Sartre about Vanetti upon his return from his four-month stay in the United States in 1945, Sartre had replied, "Dolores means an enormous amount to me—but it is you I am with" (*FC,* 82). This enigmatic remark did not appease Beauvoir.

Sartre had already gone back to the United States to see Vanetti for two months in 1946 when, in 1947, he asked Vanetti to be with him in Paris during the four months that Beauvoir was to spend in the United States, giving conferences at various universities. But in May, at the very end of her stay, Sartre wired Beauvoir, asking her to remain in the United States another ten days to extend Vanetti's time with him. Beauvoir, who had been eagerly waiting to see Sartre again, was terribly upset. She began to yearn to be in a man's arms. It was then that she called Algren, whom she had met briefly earlier that year. It appears that he was as ready as she for a fling. According to Céline Léon, the liaison with Algren was a retaliation for Sartre's affair with Vanetti.[27] I believe that it began, rather, as a compensation, but that it immediately became a most authentic, passionate, completely reciprocal love.

In contrast to the many details Beauvoir gives us about Algren and their relationship in *La Force des choses* and in *Les Mandarins,* we have very few facts about Vanetti and the kind of relationship Sartre had with her. But since Sartre wrote his *Notebooks* at the time of his very serious liaison with her, I believe that we can deduce that it was especially that relationship Sartre had in mind when he speaks of generosity as an "unveiling/creator" in *Notebooks*. Had he not written to Beauvoir that Dolores is "a poor and charming creature"?[28] So he writes in *Notebooks*: "In pure generosity, I assume myself as losing myself, so that the fragility and finitude of the other exists absolutely as revealed within the world" (*NE*, 507). I actually make myself, he continues, the one through whom the loved one's finitude finds safety. And Sartre enumerates the different roles I as lover take to ensure this: that of guarding the loved one's finitude, that of protecting her from danger, that of savior, secretly acquiescing in her "fragility" and "secret weakness" (*NE*, 508).

Sartre evidently thought that he was here close to Heidegger's notion of solicitude and to Beauvoir's notion of generosity. But his condescendence toward the loved one (evidently the "poor fragile woman" who needs protection) is definitely Heidegger's "leaping in and dominating" rather than his "leaping forth and liberating."[29] The scathing letter that Beauvoir wrote Sartre about Vanetti, after meeting her in New York (upon her arrival there for her conferences), although obviously sparked by an understandable jealousy, was right on target: "If you're a male, and you're driven by an imperialistic passion for generosity, you couldn't find anyone more appropriate."[30] There is no doubt that the *Notebooks'* depiction of the lover as "creator" of the extremely fragile, vulnerable "finitude/object" of the loved one, who depends on the lover almost for her very being, makes the lover into a Pygmalion.[31] Although Sartre means to show here the receptivity of the lover to the loved one, the overly active, overprotective attitude of the "lover" certainly replicates Sartre's own difficulties in being receptive and giving in a love relationship.

By the time of *Notebooks* and of the Vanetti liaison, Sartre had definitely made some progress since the days of his and Beauvoir's first love—when he was terrified of her self-abandon to him and obviously did not reciprocate. He seemed by now to be better able to accept a woman's self-abandon and to partly reciprocate by giving himself, in his own way, although he did write Beauvoir from New York that "Dolores' passion . . . literally scares me, particularly since that's not my strong suit."[32] His deep love affair from 1962 to 1967 with Lena Zonina, which Rowley uncovers for the first time, certainly helped him make further progress. For she was a strong, independent woman, interpreter for the Soviet Writers Union, and she was a mother. Her whole being radiated the force of independence and the joy of motherhood.[33]

With the exception of Beauvoir's 1955 "Faut-il brûler Sade?" which I discussed briefly above, neither Beauvoir nor Sartre produced any more texts on self-abandon to the other, as such, during the period between *The Second Sex/ Notebooks* and the 1974 *Entretiens*. I view their trajectory during that period as a successful search for and return to the early idyllic mother, before she became,

The Question of Reciprocal Self-Abandon to the Other 57

for each, devouring or smothering—before, that is, her unrelenting, devouring control of her daughter, in the case of Simone, or before she smothered her son with such feminizing affection that he had to repress his feminine side and his fear of incest with her, in the case of Poulou.

Beauvoir's *Une Mort très Douce* shows a new aspect of self-abandon to another, the result of another *expérience vécue* for Beauvoir. For that text can be read as the experience of her renewed experience of self-abandon to her mother after a break of some forty years. She writes there that since her adolescence she had hidden behind thick psychological walls in order to escape her mother's control. But as her mother lay dying, she felt the irresistible urge to abandon herself to her again as she had during her early childhood. She let go of the emotional constraints she had built between them. She wrenched her mother out of "the framework, the role, the set of images in which [she] had imprisoned her."[34] She finally let go, in fact, of the abstractions, the conceptualizations by which she had separated herself from her mother.[35] And she abandoned herself to the old tenderness she had once felt for her, to the compassion that now tore her apart, to the solidarity she felt with this dying woman—her mother.

From the epilogue of *Une Mort très Douce*, we realize the great importance for Beauvoir of this renewed self-abandon to her mother. For she mentions there that her mother had always played a major role in her dreams, blending with Sartre, and the three of them being happy together, until her mother attempted renewed control and the dream turned into a nightmare.[36] The renewed self-abandon thus enabled Beauvoir to heal the wound caused by her mother's excessive control in her childhood and to have more open, truthful, uncontrolled relationships, which were outside the necessary/contingent category, such as the one she developed shortly after her mother's death with Sylvie Le Bon, a young philosophy student. Le Bon went on to have an independent career as a philosophy professor like Beauvoir herself.[37] I believe this contributed to give Beauvoir the self-assurance she shows in the 1974 *Entretiens*.

As might be expected, Sartre's search for and return to the early idyllic mother was fraught with more difficulties than Beauvoir's but was more spectacular in the end. The mother has an especially important role in two of his works during that period, *Les Mots* and *L'Idiot de la famille*. He wrote these simultaneously and intermittently for a number of years—beginning in the early 1950s—going through a number of versions of each until the publication of *Les Mots* in 1963 and of the first two volumes of *L'Idiot* in 1971 and the third in 1972. We know from an interview about *L'Idiot* that Sartre had with Michel Contat and Michel Rybalka that he insisted that Anne-Marie, the mother of the autobiography, was "not only devoted but full of tenderness."[38] But a careful deciphering of the subtext of *Les Mots* indicates that she was, in fact, the arche-typal phallic mother, who used Poulou for her own satisfaction and prevented his separation from her, emotionally and erotically—with the results that we saw. Sartre depicts Caroline, the mother of the biography, as a mother by duty, and cold as ice. According to him, Gustave, her son, reacts to his mother's cold-ness by viewing her as half-male and unabashedly desiring self-abandon to the (m)other all his life.

But what is most interesting for us here is Sartre's discovery of the body as flesh—as he opposes his paradigm of the perfect mother, in which he extols the notion of flesh, to Caroline's poor mothering. This discovery will certainly in-fluence Sartre's view of self-abandon to the other in the *Entretiens*. He writes that the mother must become flesh in order to "feed, nurture, caress the flesh of her flesh," thus instituting between her and the child a libidinal, even erotic, re-lationship (*IF*, 57).[39]

But Sartre was unable at that point to translate his notion of flesh in the mother-child relationship to that of sexual relations between adults. Flesh is still for him there, female passive submission (although Sartre allows that her flesh "blossoms"). The male is agent, who desires and takes. But his body can-not flourish unless he becomes feminine and flesh, and abandons himself passively—which is taboo for Sartre in *L'Idiot*. My guess is that Sartre wrote these sections fairly early on, anytime from the late 1950s to the mid-60s. More-over, he probably had in mind Flaubert himself, whose blatant desire for self-abandon, throughout his life, riled Sartre greatly, since he repressed that same desire in himself for a long time.

I believe that at least four factors contributed to Sartre's progressive self-transformation: (1) The 1968 student revolution was a turning point for him: he learned that what counted most was not to emit ideas or give advice, but to listen to what these young student revolutionaries had to say—an impor-tant step toward the receptiveness essential to reciprocal self-abandon. (2) His mother's death in 1969, which was a real liberation for him since for the first time he did not need to repress his desire of self-abandon to (a)(n) (m)other.[40] (3) Beginning in 1970, his new involvement with the French Maoists and their leader Pierre Victor (alias Benny Lévy). This was the first time that he was fully accepted by a group of revolutionaries. This led him to the self-acceptance nec-essary for self-abandon.[41] (4) His blindness, in 1974, forced him to give up writ-ing and to communicate with others through interviews (among which were the 1974 *Entretiens* with Beauvoir) and thus to open himself up (as opposed to his writing, which had tended to shut him up within himself).

So Sartre was ready, by 1974, to integrate Beauvoir's full notion of self-abandon to the other with his own. (Beauvoir had once told Margaret Simons, "you know, one receives influences only when one is ready for them.")[42] As Simons has well shown, this is certainly not the first time that Sartre "received an influence" from Beauvoir (notably the influence of the social and historical context on individual action and the linking of freedom with reciprocity).[43] This time, however, there is an important difference. Beauvoir is extremely self-assured in the way she questions Sartre and attempts to lead him in the direction she desires, very much in the manner of Socrates questioning Phaedrus about the meaning of love; and Sartre is obviously openly acquiescing to Beauvoir's mentorship as a way of acknowledging the integration of her idea of self-abandon to the other in reciprocity, with his.

Beauvoir's self-assurance and Sartre's acquiescence to it in the *Entretiens* has led to two types of criticisms of their tenor. According to the first type, that of those who do not want Sartre to have changed and to now hold a positive view of self-abandon to the other, Beauvoir imposed her own notion on Sartre in the same way that Benny Lévy imposed his notion of messianism on him in *Hope Now*—thus, like Lévy, taking advantage of a "feeble-minded" and "physically deteriorated old man."[44] According to the second type of criticism, it is Beauvoir who did not want Sartre to have changed. Thus, Jean-Pierre Boulé and Geneviève Idt have accused Beauvoir of "constructing," in these interviews, the image of the Sartre that she wanted to show the world (not changed, still the same), in order to deflate the Benny Lévy interviews' new image of Sartre, which she so decried.[45]

In order to evince that Sartre's ideas about the mother in *Hope Now* were inextricably linked to his complete self-transformation during the period between 1975 and 1980 (after, that is, the 1974 *Entretiens*), I offer here two samples of his interviews during these years. In an interview with Catherine Chaine, for example, he reaffirms to her, and reinforces, the notion of reciprocal giving and receiving that he discussed with Beauvoir. "Tenderness one receives, tenderness one gives, the two are linked and there only exists a general tenderness, both given and received," he tells her.[46] (And he asserts his growing awareness of his femininity to Jean Le Bitoux and Gilles Barbedette of *Le Gai Pied*. When they question him about Mathieu's and Roquentin's lack of virility, he comments: "Those correspond more or less to what I ask about myself.")[47]

During her fifty-year intellectual relationship with Sartre, Beauvoir had always been his sounding board. With *Hope Now,* she was confounded by the fact that this role had been taken by a young Jewish man, Benny Lévy, whom she saw as her rival. And so she could not fathom the full portent of Sartre's new thinking and viewed it, as Toril Moi notes, as "a lack of loyalty, during their final years, and his betrayal of what she took to be their common ideals."[48] But in her biography of Sartre, Annie Cohen-Solal gives a fairly objective account of what took place concerning the publication of the *Hope Now* interviews in the *Nouvel Observateur*. She writes that the staff of *Les Temps Modernes*, all seasoned Sartreans, tried to stop its publication because, as Horst (the only Sartrean who was faithful to Sartre at that point) told Jean Daniel, the editor of *Le Nouvel Observateur*: "They are all defending the Temple." But in fact, Sartre himself told Jean Daniel a little later: "The itinerary of my thought eludes them all, including Simone de Beauvoir."

Sartre's psychoanalytic and feminist interpretation of the mother in *Hope Now*, his replacement of Freud's "father as totem" with the "mother as totem," daringly reverses the mother's place as the one who, in the Oedipus complex, is interdicted, through the castration of the child (or the neurotic adult), to that of the one who interdicts, in a strong but gentle manner.

This new mother is neither dominated/controlled, nor dominating/controlling. She does not attempt to master everyone, yet she is strong. She is not driven by action in the world, yet she is fully present in it—exactly what Sartre would have liked a "father-mother" to be.

It is difficult to assess how far Sartre had, at that point, become conscious of the essential role that *le Castor* (as he had always called Beauvoir) played in his self-transformation, or the "triangulation"—as psychoanalysis terms it—he had achieved by the time of the *Hope Now* dialogues.[49] I view this triangulation as being at the heart of his notion of the "mother as totem." And I see *le Castor* (on the bottom left corner of the triangle), in the place of the father who interdicts. (Had she not, from the late 1930s onward, played a masculine role, that of Sartre's censor, of his "little judge"?) But she is also (on the bottom right corner of the triangle) in the place of the mother, along with Anne-Marie—who is not phallic anymore. They both give fully of themselves: Anne-Marie to her Poulou, and *le Castor* to her *"tout cher petit être"* (as she calls Sartre most often in her *Lettres à Sartre*), without possessiveness. So Sartre has been "triangulated" in a most unorthodox yet viable manner. This has enabled him to move from the patriarchy, which had bred in him a fear of self-abandon to (a)(n) (m)other, a fear of the flesh, and of the feminine. He has fulfilled his *Notebooks'* ideal of getting rid of his ego and has joined a universe without fears.[50] He is at peace with himself and exudes this peace. The *Gai Pied* journalists who interviewed him during the last months before his death spoke of his freshness and his extreme kindness.[51]

If Beauvoir could have been Sartre's sounding board once again and thus have discussed his ideas with him as they were evolving, she certainly would have been more accepting of his *Hope Now* ideas. She would have realized that they were actually the *dénouement* of her notion of reciprocal self-abandon to the other, which Sartre had integrated with his, under her mentorship, in the *Entretiens*. And she would have been quite surprised to discover the fundamental role she had played in bringing about the self-transformation/triangulation that he achieved during his last years.

Notes

1. Nietzsche, *Gay Science*, 318.
2. Ibid., 319.
3. I am using the 1953 Knopf edition for the English references and the 1949 Gallimard edition for the French page numbers.
4. Beauvoir is referring to the poisoned tunic that, according to Greek mythology, Nessus used to kill his rival Hercules.
5. I use the French term *jouissance* for lack of an appropriate term in English. It implies pleasure, yes, but much more than pleasure because it entails reciprocity. Lacan will attribute *jouissance* to women and to certain mystics, and distinguishes it from pure phallic pleasure. Lacan, *Le Séminaire de Jacques Lacan, Livre XX: Encore, 1972–1973*. Translated by Bruce Fink as *The Seminar of Jacques Lacan, Book XX: Encore, 1972–1973*. Note that Fink translated *jouissance* as "enjoyment" or "pleasure," which it is not.
6. The whole thrust of Jean-Pierre Boulé's *Sartre, Self-Formation and Masculinities* (2005) is about this attempt of Sartre to be in control of his feelings and of the world through action and the rational.
7. "Fantasmatic" is a psychoanalytic term. Its roots are "phantasm" and "fantasy." But in psychoanalytic parlance, it has to do with a partially unconscious desire, which is attempting to become conscious through various activities—such as Poulou's emulation of his hero Pardaillan, or the writing of his own stories.
8. Butler, *Gender Trouble*, 45.
9. Becker, *Denial of Death*, 39–40; and Wehr, *Jung and Feminism*, 11.
10. Lacoste, "Sartre's Itinerary from Self-Presence," 284–89.
11. In her interesting essay "Where Influence Fails: Embodiment in Beauvoir and Sartre," chapter 2 in this volume, Christine Daigle deals at length with Sartre's *Being and Nothingness* section on the slimy and analyzes fruitfully what is for him the relation between the slimy and sexuality.
12. Diprose, *Bodies of Women*, 67–75.
13. The French version of the *Notebooks* was published posthumously by Arlette Elkaïm-Sartre in 1983.
14. Bergoffen, *Philosophy of Simone de Beauvoir*, 3.
15. See also Barbara Klaw, "Sexuality in Beauvoir's *The Mandarins*," 193–221.
16. Fuchs, "Female Eroticism in *The Second Sex*," 309.
17. Toril Moi discusses at length how in *L'Invitée* Beauvoir exemplifies the difficulty of this respect of the other's freedom. "Speaking out, Françoise risks it all: her meta-

physical freedom, her self-respect as an acting subject, her sense of her own femininity, and Gerbert's friendship," Moi writes (*Simone de Beauvoir*, 140). Moi's five-page exegesis of Beauvoir's text on Françoise's predicament indicates a keen appreciation of Beauvoir's own reflection on the subject. Moi also points out that we learn from a letter of Beauvoir to Sartre that the Françoise/Gerbert episode was in fact a fictionalized version of an episode in Beauvoir's own life while on a camping trip with *le petit* Bost (*LSfr*, I, 62).

18. Bergoffen, "Out from Under," 190.

19. I dealt with that theme and how it related to Beauvoir's and Sartre's own early relationship in a paper, "Le Trouble chez Beauvoir (re)marqué par Bergoffen," presented at the Société Américaine de Philosophie de Langue Française meeting at the APA convention in Washington, D.C., in 1998, shortly after the publication of Bergoffen's book.

20. Bergoffen, *Philosophy of Simone de Beauvoir*, 34.

21. This is my own translation.

22. Citing Sartre himself, she writes that he had convinced himself that "the ethical attitude appears when the technical and the social techniques render positive conduct impossible. Morality is a set of idealistic tricks to enable one to live with what the scarcity of resources and the lack of techniques impose on one." (Unpublished Sartre notes cited by Simone de Beauvoir. My translation of *La Force des choses*, 218.)

23. Derrida, "Women in a Beehive."

24. Mauss, *Essai sur le Don*.

25. Toril Moi speaks of "Beauvoir's life-long project: to break down the distinction between philosophy and life so as to endow life with the truth and necessity of philosophy, and philosophy with the excitement and passion of life" (*Simone de Beauvoir*, 147). And Sartre himself wrote to Beauvoir, in January 1940: "I'm trying neither to protect my life after the fact with my philosophy, which would be sleazy, nor make my life conform to my philosophy, which would be pedantic, instead now philosophy and life have really become one" (*QMW*, 29).

26. Sartre's passion for Olga eight years earlier had not been reciprocated and thus had not become a *necessary love* (Lacoste, "The Transformation of the Notion of Transparency," 51).

27. Léon, "Can the Second Sex Be One?" 34.

28. Rowley, *Tête à tête*, 165.

29. Heidegger, *Sein und Zeit*, 159–160.

30. Rowley, *Tête à tête*, 174.

31. It is interesting to note that Beauvoir herself actually accused Sartre of being a Pygmalion with the women he loved (*Ent*, 390). And Hazel Barnes noted that Sartre himself recognized that fact. "He regarded each woman as raw material to be molded into a form in which he, as creator, might find his image in the work he had created" (Barnes, "Sartre's *War Diaries*: Prelude and Postscript").

32. Rowley, *Tête à tête*, 163.

33. I am referring here to the photograph of Lena Zonina in Rowley's *Tête à tête* (208–209).

34. Beauvoir, *Une Mort très douce*, and *A Very Easy Death*, 30. Passages in text translated by Guillermine de Lacoste.

35. This letting-go of abstractions and of ego is an important part of abandon, what Nel Noddings calls "letting-go of my attempts to control" the other (*Caring: A Feminine*

Approach to Ethics, 116). Beauvoir experiences it but does not theorize about it in the way Sartre does in *Notebooks.*

36. Toril Moi sees Beauvoir as beginning to exorcize this dreaded image of the excessively controlling mother as early as *L'Invitée.* But according to Moi, it is not Françoise—as we might expect—who represents the mother figure, but Xavière. Did she not surreptitiously read Françoise's private correspondence, just as Madame de Beauvoir had once read Simone's letters till she was eighteen? Moi quotes *L'Invitée* a number of times to prove her point. She shows that Françoise flees Xavière's "avid tentacles which wanted to devour her alive" and later that Françoise "was at the mercy of the voracious consciousness which was waiting in the shadows to swallow her up" (*Simone de Beauvoir,* 117).

37. Rowley discusses this relationship with great tact in four or five sections of her book (*Tête à tête,* 286–87, 309–11, etc.).

38. Sartre, "Interview à propos de *L'Idiot de la famille,*" 114.

39. Bergoffen notes that there is a difference, though, between the erotic relation of the child and mother and that between two adult lovers: "As erotic, however, these relationships express the desire of the erotic. They express the fact that we cannot, as bodied beings, substitute the abstract idea of recognition for the touch that acknowledges us in our fleshed sensuality" (*Philosophy of Simone de Beauvoir,* 209–10).

40. Self-abandon to (a)(n) (m)other means that self-abandon to a mother and to an other are inextricably related. Because he had not effected the original separation from his mother, Sartre's need to keep repressing his desire of self-abandon to her meant that he was simultaneously unable to abandon himself to an other—first of all to *le Castor.*

41. Neither the FLN (the Algerian Liberation Front) nor the communists had really accepted his commitment to them.

42. Simons, "Beauvoir and Sartre," 170.

43. Ibid., 171–79.

44. Todd, *Un Fils rebelle,* 150.

45. Boulé, *Sartre Médiatique,* 162; Idt, "Simone de Beauvoir's Adieux," 366–69.

46. Sartre, "Sartre et les femmes," 74.

47. Sartre, "Interview avec Jean Le Bitoux et Gilles Barbedette," 11–14.

48. Moi, *Simone de Beauvoir,* 117. As William McBride writes: "It is an open secret that Simone de Beauvoir, to whom, over many years, Sartre had offered his writings for pre-publication criticism and correction, as she had hers to him, was strongly opposed to publication of the Sartre-Lévy dialogue" (McBride, "Sartre's *War Diaries:* Prelude and Postscript," 2).

49. In psychoanalytic parlance, triangulation takes place when the boy becomes aware of his difference with his mother and his sameness with his father, and the girl of her sameness with her mother and her difference from her father; and this implies a concomitant awareness of the relation between the mother and the father, of which they are the products. This new awareness implies a separation from the original symbiosis with the mother for both boy and girl, and a new relation with both parents: identification with the father's masculinity for the boy, and with the mother's femininity for the girl.

50. Cixous, "Extreme Fidelity," 197–205.

51. Sartre, "Interview avec Jean Le Bitoux et Gilles Barbedette."

4 Beauvoir and Sartre on Freedom, Intersubjectivity, and Normative Justification

Matthew C. Eshleman

Our freedoms support each other like the stones in an arch, but in an arch that no pillars support. Humanity is entirely suspended in a void that it creates itself by its reflection on its plenitude. (*PC*, 140)

Recognition does not come without a fight. Over the past twenty or so years, a group of professional philosophers, primarily but not exclusively composed of women, have worked diligently to move Simone de Beauvoir out of the shadow cast by Jean-Paul Sartre and to establish her as a philosopher worthy of our attention.[1] This task has been made especially difficult in an academic environment dominated by men but also by Beauvoir's often misleading and self-deprecating remarks.[2] Two tactics have played a central role in bringing Beauvoir into prominence. The first corrects the widespread and mistaken assumption that Beauvoir's philosophical works merely presuppose and extend Sartre's work by showing, contrary to popular opinion, that the lines of influence often go the other way round.[3] The second argues that Beauvoir's account of various concepts like freedom and intersubjectivity differ from, and, according to some, improve upon Sartre.[4] Although these two lines sometimes stand in tension with one another, overall they have been successful in many ways: the number of books recently published on Beauvoir surpasses those published on Sartre; anthologies of existentialism now, unlike in the past, contain texts by Beauvoir; and most North American Sartreans recognize the importance of Beauvoir and are open to analysis of her work at their meetings.

A cruel historical irony, however, threatens to render many of the recent victories superfluous. Eclipsed by French anti-humanism during the 1960s, the heyday of French existentialism has long since passed, and Beauvoir has not always been well received by "second wave" feminism, to say nothing of the "third wave." Fortunately, the tides are beginning to turn. Recent analyses of Beauvoir increasingly aim toward showing her contribution to various contemporary ethical and political debates, indicating a new stage in the Beauvoir studies renaissance.[5] It is, after all, one thing to establish Beauvoir as a philosopher in her own right and entirely another to show her contemporary relevance. Until Beauvoir scholars decisively achieve this latter goal, Beauvoir's work will reap little more than historical interest and will likely fade away, as so many fleeting academic cottage industries do.

Wholeheartedly behind the spirit of these efforts, I am somewhat less so toward its letter. While the influence question has played an important role in calling attention to the force and originality of Beauvoir's thought, it has sometimes been overstated, as if the influence might only go one way.[6] This is understandable from a tactical point of view; however, the lack of any serious study of Sartre's influence on Beauvoir, as problematic as this may be, makes such overstatement possible. In the second place, analysis of Sartre by Beauvoir scholars has not always been perspicuous. Like the first tactical line, arguments for Beauvoir's departures from, and, according to some, superiority over Sartre, play an understandable role in the fight for recognition, but these differences have been exaggerated, often in ways that Beauvoir would have disagreed with—and, in at least some cases, correctly so.

With some hesitation, then, this essay aims, in part, to correct treatments of Sartre—with hesitation, that is, because developing further antagonisms between Beauvoir and Sartre scholars serves only to retard the more important goal of championing Beauvoir's (and Sartre's) contributions to contemporary philosophical debates. Thus, the ensuing discussion of Beauvoir and Sartre on freedom and intersubjectivity sets the stage to show more precisely where the two philosophers part ways, but also, and more importantly, to argue that Beauvoir can make an important contribution to contemporary debates concerning normative justification in a way that has largely been unappreciated.

Freedom

Sonia Kruks develops the most sustained analysis of freedom and intersubjectivity in her well-known essay, "Simone de Beauvoir: Teaching Sartre about Freedom."[7] Since a sizable consensus that Beauvoir abandoned Sartre's early notion of absolute freedom for a more nuanced account of (situated, interdependent) freedom has formed around Kruks's essay, it provides a good place to start.[8] Kruks claims that "already in 1940 Beauvoir had insisted against Sartre that 'not every situation is equal' from the point of view of freedom."[9] Kruks attributes to Sartre an absolute view of freedom and argues, "since situations are each uniquely brought into being by an individual free project . . . we [cannot] judge one situation to be more free than another."[10] After all, "'the slave in chains is as free as his master.'"[11] So understood, Sartrean freedom does not come in degrees.

Kruks diagnoses this inadequacy of Sartre's view as follows: "My freedom is an indestructible power of nihilation, the other can never finally touch it. Instead, the other must attempt to nihilate the visible exterior of my freedom . . . but although the other objectifies what we might call the external manifestations of my freedom, I always remain free."[12] Like standard (but misleading, likely false) readings of Descartes's view of the free will ensconced by a soul impenetrable by empirical forces, Sartre's "indestructible power of nihilation" cannot account for the obvious effects of social conditioning, much less oppression. Hence, Sartre's view of absolute freedom cannot be taken seriously. In contrast, as early as 1940, Beauvoir recognized the insufficiency of absolute individual freedom and therefore replaced it (or began to replace it) with a notion of interdependent freedom that more clearly illuminates the effects of social conditioning and oppression. For once we recognize that Others fundamentally influence our existence, we must abandon Sartre's inviolable freedom and follow "Beauvoir [who] argues that freedom itself undergoes modification."[13]

Problematically, Beauvoir's view that freedom undergoes modification does not occur in print until 1949. Consequently, Kruks's claim that Beauvoir rejected absolute freedom in 1940 is potentially misleading, at least if we take Beauvoir's published material during this period—*Pyrrhus and Cinéas* and *The Ethics of Ambiguity*—as our evidence. Some of Kruks's evidence comes from Beauvoir's 1960 retrospective account (in *The Prime of Life*) of her position in 1940.[14] Perhaps Beauvoir privately held a position at odds with Sartre's during the early 1940s. Publicly, the strongest evidence comes from *The Second Sex* (1949), where Beauvoir claims that oppression corrupts or degrades transcendence into the "in-itself."[15] To be sure, in 1949, Beauvoir offers a more sophisticated account of oppression and its impact on freedom than did Sartre in 1943. But this does not take us very far: if by 1949 Beauvoir had abandoned Sartre's 1943 view, so too had Sartre.[16] Whether Beauvoir abandoned Sartre's absolute notion of freedom in the early 1940s is more complicated than Kruks suggests and for at least two reasons. First, Sartre had already rejected absolute freedom in the second half of *Being and Nothingness*.[17] Second, Beauvoir's analysis of freedom in *Pyrrhus and Cinéas* looks a lot like Sartre's purportedly absolute view, and her more nuanced account in *The Ethics of Ambiguity* does not depart significantly from Sartre's more considered view.

The first claim, that Sartre abandoned an absolute view of freedom, is not easy to discern. Only five hundred plus pages into *Being and Nothingness* does Sartre argue that my being-for-Others limits my freedom, at which point he treats the objectifying gaze of Others as a "centrifugal force" that "causes everything freedom undertakes to always have one face that freedom has not chosen" (*BN*, 526; *EN*, 609). While this claim indicates that Sartre abandoned a notion of absolute freedom often attributed to him, further evidence is required, and we do well to ask whether Sartre revised his view or was inconsistent. To answer these questions, one must trace Sartre's analysis of how Others limit my freedom, which begins with the famous keyhole example, some three hundred pages earlier in the text. Caught in the act of surreptitiously spying through a keyhole, Sartre argues for the astonishing claim that the objectifying gaze of the Other "affects my being" and causes "essential modifications [to] appear in my structure" (*BN*, 260; *EN*, 318).

The claim is "astonishing" since, to this point in *Being and Nothingness*, my "being" has been considered totally unaffected by anything except my consciousness. In the preface to *Being and Nothingness*, Sartre argues that consciousness is limited only by itself (*BN*, lv; *EN*, 22; see also *TE*, 38), which entails that "only my freedom can limit my freedom." So understood, absolute freedom is the view that freedom has no limits other than those imposed upon itself—a view difficult to take seriously. Consequently, when Sartre gives a formal analysis of the objectifying gaze of Others, doing so demands rather significant revisions to his views of being-for-itself, which now finds its limitations in Others, and, hence, freedom.

With regard to being-for-itself, Sartre explains, "so long as we considered the for-itself in *isolation,* we were able to maintain that the unreflective consciousness can not be inhabited by a self. . . . But here [in relationship to Others] the self comes to haunt the unreflective consciousness" (*BN*, 260: italics mine; *EN*, 318).[18] When Sartre says "in isolation," he refers to Parts I and II, where he employed a methodological solipsism, a point that often goes unnoticed.[19] Thus, during the abstract phases of his analysis, in isolation of Others, Sartre considered being-for-itself to be pure possibility (*BN*, 95–102; *EN*, 139–47), and the ego to be solely self-constituted (and located at the level of reflective consciousness). After introducing social reality, Sartre offers a new definition of the psychological self. The self as object is "the limit between two consciousnesses as it is *produced* by the limiting consciousness [i.e., the Other] and assumed by the limited consciousness" (*BN*, 286: italics mine; *EN*, 346). By definition, this self is no longer solely (my) possibility since "we are dealing with my being as it is written in and by the Other's freedom" (*BN*, 262; *EN*, 320). As Sartre provocatively claims,

> I am a slave to the degree that my being is dependent at the very center of a freedom which is not mine and which is the very condition of my being. Insofar as I am the object of values which come to qualify me without my being able to act on this qualification or even know it, I am enslaved. (*BN*, 267; *EN*, 326)

Sartre's revised notion of self, qua partially constituted by, and hence dependent upon, Others, in turn, demands the abandonment of absolute freedom.[20] Sartre, however, waits nearly another three hundred pages to make this clear. Only in Part IV does Sartre recognize "a truth of great importance," namely, "keeping ourselves within the compass of existence-for-itself, that only my freedom can limit my freedom, we see now, when we include the Other's existence in our considerations, that my freedom on this new level finds its limits also in the existence of the Other's freedom" (*BN*, 525; *EN*, 608).[21] Rarely noted by other commentators, Sartre abandons his initially exaggerated view of absolute freedom: freedom is not limited only by itself; it is also limited by Others. While existence precedes essence, the social world precedes individual existences; thus, when Sartre considers the fact that sociality precedes and modifies existence, he argues for social limitations to freedom.

A great deal more could be said about Sartre's considered view of freedom and what precisely Sartre means by limit. However, it should now be clear that Kruks's claim that Others only objectify external manifestations of my freedom is at best misleading. Social objectifications affect my being, essentially modify my structure, and fundamentally limit my freedom. Consequently, my choices are always only half chosen, as it were. Thus, Kruks is mistaken when she quotes from *The Ethics of Ambiguity* to evidence Beauvoir's departure from Sartre. The claim that "it is this interdependence [of freedoms] which explains why oppression is possible and why it is hateful" (*EA*, 82)[22] does not depart in any significant way from Sartre's considered view.

In fact, Beauvoir affirms this in her 1955 essay "Merleau-Ponty and Pseudo-Sartreanism," which defends Sartre against Merleau-Ponty. In that essay, she argues that Sartre developed a notion of interdependence in *Being and Nothingness,* and she offers the following quote as evidence:

> The fact of the Other is incontestable and touches me to the heart. I realize him through uneasiness; through him I am perpetually in danger in a world which is this world and which nevertheless I can only glimpse. (*EN*, 319)[23]

This quote comes after the keyhole example and before the quote given above that my being is fundamentally dependent upon Others, such that, to use Sartre's admittedly overly dramatized language, I am a slave. To be sure, Beauvoir does not always offer a consistent appraisal of Sartre. In her 1945 review of Merleau-Ponty's *Phenomenology of Perception,* Beauvoir attributes to Sartre a view of the "absolute freedom of the mind." Although Beauvoir does not elaborate upon what this view entails, if by absolute she means a mind unlimited by everything except itself, she misunderstood Sartre. Might Beauvoir have misunderstood these matters in 1945 but understood them more clearly by 1955?

Some published evidence suggests this possibility. In 1944 Beauvoir seemed to accept a Cartesian (but not Descartes's) view of freedom in *Pyrrhus and Cinéas,* evidenced below; whereas by 1947, in *The Ethics of Ambiguity,* Beauvoir refined her view. Whatever the case may be, it is not obviously true, as Kruks puts it, that "in *Pyrrhus et Cinéas,* begun while *Being and Nothingness* was in press, and again in 1947, in *The Ethics of Ambiguity,* she suggested that there might be situations of oppression in which freedom, such as Sartre describes it in *Being and Nothingness,* ceases to be possible."[24] If what Kruks means by impossible freedom is absolute freedom, Sartre had already rejected this view. Once more, it is not at all clear that *Pyrrhus and Cinéas* shows any such thing. In *Pyrrhus and Cinéas* Beauvoir argues that "a man can never abdicate his freedom; his claims to renounce it are only a masquerade that he freely performs. The slave who obeys chooses to obey, and his choice must be renewed at every moment" (*PC*, 118).[25] Along this same line, in the context of discussing an executioner's victim, Beauvoir claims, "if his victim wants to be free, she will remain free even during torture, and struggling and suffering will only elevate her" (*PC*, 124).[26] So understood, the oppressive weight of another's freedom never entirely exhausts mine, and the struggle of slaves and torture victims indicates an irrepressible freedom to resist, a freedom that the torturer can never fully extinguish without bringing about death. Of course, even if it makes sense to say that slaves and torture victims remain free, this does not mean that freedom does not come in degrees, at least not in any practical sense. What does not come in degrees is the mere fact that human beings are not things, so long as they remain human.[27]

Beauvoir offers a problematic explanation for irrepressible freedom: "As freedom the other is radically separated from me; no connection can be created from me to this pure interiority upon which even God would have no hold, as Descartes has clearly shown" (PC, 125–26). This goes too far. To the extent that one wishes to maintain an irrepressible view of freedom, the more reasonable approach should not argue that freedom is entirely cut off from everything except itself. The point here, however, is that Beauvoir's view in *Pyrrhus and Cinéas* sounds like the view Kruks attributes to Sartre, the same view that Kruks claims Beauvoir rejected, a view that I claim Sartre did not hold.

As problematic as Beauvoir's notion of radical separation may be, it stands in a clear tension with her surmised desire, à la Kruks, to account for interdependence. Perhaps Kruks is correct to suggest that Beauvoir began with Sartrean suppositions; however, due to the influence of Merleau-Ponty, she developed an agenda incompatible with Sartre's. Could it be that Beauvoir did not consciously recognize this tension, so that it was "in spite of herself" that Beauvoir argued to "some most un-Sartrean conclusions?"[28] Perhaps. But what Kruks takes to be un-Sartrean is in some cases Sartrean, and in those cases where Beauvoir does go beyond Sartre, it is unclear that she does so "in spite of herself." Beauvoir may well have been fully aware of the many times where her position is often at odds with that of Sartre. Whatever the case may be, does Beauvoir's account of interdependence in *Pyrrhus and Cinéas* contradict or stand in tension with her view of freedom qua radical separation? I argue that it does not.

Intersubjectivity

According to Kruks, Beauvoir "suggests" that freedoms "are not self-sufficient but interdependent," and she provides a quote from *Pyrrhus and Cinéas* as evidence: "For '[only] the freedom of the other is able to give necessity to my being'" (PC, 95–96).[29] Kruks, however, does not analyze what giving "necessity to my being" means or why only the freedom of Others provides this necessity. Consequently, it remains unclear whether and to what extent Beauvoir's (early) account of (absolute) freedom stands in tension with or is contradicted by her account of interdependence. It also remains unclear whether Beauvoir's account of intersubjectivity differs significantly from Sartre's. Since the above passage from *Pyrrhus and Cinéas* comes rather late in Beauvoir's analysis of intersubjectivity, a discussion of her initial analysis must come before these questions can be answered.

Beauvoir's account of intersubjectivity begins with a description of devotion in the context of clarifying existential justification. At this point in her career, existential justification should be understood very broadly in the sense of giving reasons and purposes for one's life. If some Other exhibited both absolute existence and a need for me, then, insofar as I am devoted to that absolute Other, "my being is justified since I am for a being whose existence is justified" (*PC*, 117). Devotion to a needy God would, for example, grant a foundational, noncontingent reason for me to exist, if such a needy God exists. Of course, God cannot be both needy and absolute, and foundational justification turns out to be nothing but a comforting illusion. "By positing an absolute end before me, I have abdicated my freedom; questions are no longer posed; I no longer want to be anything but a response to that appeal which requires me" (*PC*, 117). This familiar existential move announces Beauvoir's commitment to anguish in the absence of absolutes, where belief in absolutes suppresses the risk and uncertainty of existence.

While no possible being can be absolute in the required sense, Beauvoir argues that one can justify one's life through devotion to finite Others, if and only if one respects the freedom of Others: "There is devotion only if I take an end defined by the other as my end. But then it is contradictory to suppose that I could define that end for him" (*PC*, 118–19). Defining the ends for Others, as opposed to letting Others define their own ends, denies freedom and transforms devotion into, at best, some form of paternalism, or worse, of oppression. As Beauvoir explains later in the essay,

> Only the other can create a need for what we give him; every appeal and every demand comes from his freedom. In order for the object that I founded to appear as a good, the other must make it into his own good, and then I would be *justified* for having created it. The other's freedom alone is capable of *necessitating my being*. My essential need is therefore to be faced with free men. (*PC*, 129; emphasis added)

My assistance to Others must be useful to Others, from the Others' point of view. If I force "help" onto Others, especially undesired "help," my assistance may not be justified. Only when the Other takes my assistance as good can the object of my assistance (and hence one of my life's purposes) be justified. Thus, when Beauvoir says that Others necessitate my existence, she means that only through Others can my projects be justified. Contra Kruks, Beauvoir's notion of interdependence does not stand in tension with or controvert her view of irrepressible freedom, because her analysis of interdependence takes place primarily in the context of existential justification.

It is worth noting here that Beauvoir's analysis of intersubjectivity, nonetheless, rather significantly departs from *Being and Nothingness*. Sartre eventually argues (in Part III) that Others are the condition for the possibility of being a flesh-and-blood human being. However, given any intersubjective context, while the existence of Others can be ascertained via the cogito, the existence of Others cannot be deduced from the structure of being-for-itself (*BN,* 363; *EN,* 430). Contra Heidegger, Others are ultimately inessential, that is, contingent. This means that one can, without contradiction, entertain in thought the existence of a single being-for-itself. Consequently, Sartre remains committed to some version of ontological individualism. Even if Beauvoir agreed with the spirit of this analysis, she would, at the very least, have found the abstract orientation mostly irrelevant and potentially misleading.

For Beauvoir, human interdependency begins in infancy and childhood, stages of life that Sartre mostly ignores. While human reality seems to be fundamentally (and not contingently) intersubjective, whether Beauvoir accepts ontological individualism in *Pyrrhus and Cinéas* cannot easily be discerned. Beauvoir, however, argues later in *The Ethics of Ambiguity,* "I concern others and they concern me. There we have an irreducible truth. The me-others relationship is as indissoluble as the subject-object relationship" (*EA,* 72; *MA,* 104).[30] So understood, Beauvoir comes to see Others as essential and not merely factually necessary. Contrary to Sartre's ontological individualism, Beauvoir argues for an intrinsic ontological interdependence.

When it comes to ascertaining how intersubjectivity bears on questions concerning justification in Sartre, different considerations arise. Although Sartre prefigures Merleau-Ponty's claim that language comprises a third genus of being, arguing that my being-for-others is language (*BN,* 372; *EN,* 440), Sartre offers no sustained analysis of how Others are necessary to justify my projects or what this fact about language entails about values in general. One has to wait until his popular lecture, where Sartre offers his first extended analysis of normative questions, though he does make a few scattered remarks in *Being and Nothingness.* Clarifying Sartre's views on normative justification helps to set out Beauvoir's departures from, and arguably advances over, Sartre.

Sartre on Normative Justification

At the outset of *Being and Nothingness* Sartre claims, "my freedom is the unique foundation of values and . . . nothing, absolutely nothing, justifies me in adopting this or that particular value, this or that particular scale of values. As a being by whom values exist, I am unjustified" (*BN,* 38; *EN,* 76). The contingent fact that humans are a peculiar kind of being (one that lacks being), through whom values populate the world, is itself inexplicable and the freedom that gives rise to value itself unjustified. Consequently, the particular values freedom constitutes are also unjustified. Notably, Sartre does not claim that all values are unjustified. He specifies only particular values. This leaves open the possibility that some general value(s) is (are) justified, though it is not immediately clear what this might mean and Sartre does not offer much by way of any clarification. It is unsurprising, then, that many have charged Sartre with an apparently hopeless relativism.[31] Not until Sartre's 1946 popular lecture does he attempt to counter the relativism charge, though caution here is warranted, since he later distanced himself from the views espoused there. The transcript of the talk (revised into an essay by Beauvoir) nonetheless provides a helpful clue with regard to the distinction between an unjustified specific value and a justified general value (which of course turns out to be freedom).

In his "Existentialism Is a Humanism" lecture, Sartre gives his now famous example of a young man caught in indecision between leaving Nazi-occupied France to fight with the free French forces (revenging the death of his brother) or staying home to comfort his mother (who now only lives for him).[32] The choice is complicated by the fact that his mother not only grieves over the death of her other son at the hands of the Nazis, but she also distresses over the fact that her husband is a suspected Nazi sympathizer. Thus, she finds her only solace in her remaining son. What should he do? Sartre quickly enumerates various possible resources the young man might employ to determine his decision: Kantianism, Utilitarianism, Christianity, and Intuitionism. While Sartre's analysis moves too quickly, his aim is nonetheless clear, namely, to show that principles are either too general or too vague to provide any determinate action guidance.[33] Hence, Sartre's advice to the young man: "Since no a priori value can determine choice" (EH, 282), "I had only one answer to give: 'you're free, choose, i.e., invent'" (EH, 276).

Problematically, Sartre's advice suggests that all value inventions are normatively equivalent, which raises a rather obvious worry. "So you're able to do anything, no matter what!" (EH, 282). Of course, one *can* do anything one can do; the real worry regards justification. Since all particular values are unjustified and no general principle seems capable of adjudicating between actions, there seems to be no sufficient reason to do any one thing rather than any other. So understood, all actions are arbitrary, unjustified preferences, and the whole history of moral philosophy turns out to be one long, grand illusion. Putting the latter point aside for the moment, Sartre responds with a series of procedural considerations. If value-decisions always entail an element of invention, the failure to recognize the inventive element amounts to a failure to recognize the subjectivity of value. By positing objective values, then, one contradicts the subjective process of value invention. Thus, Sartre argues that he can objectively judge procedural consistency and inconsistency, insofar as commitment to value objectivity is (logically) contradictory.

Sartre admits that this judgment of contradiction is logical and not moral in character. Consequently, it is unclear whether the judgment of contradiction adequately counters the relativism criticism. However, Sartre also suggests an underlying existential contradiction that, perhaps inadmissibly, imports normative force. Since everyone is tacitly aware of the subjective nature of value (a claim maintained in *Being and Nothingness* (*BN,* 475; *EN,* 554) but not clearly articulated in "Existentialism Is a Humanism"), the affirmation of objective values, together with the implicit denial of value-inventive processes, entails not just a logical contradiction but existential dishonesty, *mauvaise foi.* It is a contradiction that one comprehends but does not admit.

Since one's awareness of the inherent unjustified nature of action (and hence the absence of a determinate decision procedure) motivates anguish, Sartre calls hiding from this awareness "cowardly." Of course, Sartre's exhortation to honestly confront the fact that our actions are inherently unjustified, and hence to stand courageously in the face of anguish, may well appear to amount to little if anything more than rhetoric. Why, after all, *should* one value existential honesty over self-deception, especially since confrontation with value invention provokes anxiety? Why not lie to oneself when doing so feels better than existential honesty?

The demand for an account of why one ought to choose existential honesty over dishonesty might itself be unreasonable, since this demand requires an answer to the skeptical question, Why be moral? Sartre would likely argue that none of the traditional answers are at all satisfying: acting morally is in your (enlightened) self-interest, or the only way to remain rational (instrumentally or otherwise), or to fulfill some intrinsic teleological end or purpose. Consequently, it would be surprising if Sartre, at least at this point in his career, thought that such a question could be answered. It is, after all, up to you to decide whether you want to live an authentic life. Nothing more can be provided. Even if we find this kind of reply to the skeptic inadequate, we still do well to ask whether this thin sketch of authenticity provides anything like the grounds of an adequate ethics. Do either the logical or existential contradictions help us to evaluate situations any more clearly than when a maxim fails to be willed as a universal law, in the Kantian sense—a principle already imputed as too general?

To begin an answer to this question, notice that if every free action results in an invented value (where the inventiveness, in part, regards the navigation of an irreducibly unique situation), then every free action, qua exercise of freedom, entails that freedom itself is valuable. So understood, every free action discloses two values: the (reportedly unjustified) value of doing whatever one does (writing this paper) and the value of exercising freedom by so doing. Consequently, the value of freedom turns out to be general, insofar as all free agents, qua exercise of free action, value exercising freedom. (Incidentally, this is true regardless of whether free agents are aware of the value of freedom implicitly contained in free actions, though for Sartre, it seems that they must be so aware.) For this reason, Sartre concludes, "though the content of ethics is variable, a certain form of it is universal" (EH, 284). All free beings that act without coercion tacitly value the exercise of freedom.

Even though the form of ethics turns out to be freedom, it is unclear whether and to what extent this step takes us any closer to an adequate ethic that avoids the very problems Sartre raises against traditional views. Might not two people perform the same action (or significantly similar actions, since no two actions can, strictly speaking, be identical) both authentically and inauthentically? Or could the same person perform the same action with these two fundamentally different attitudes? How do Sartre's procedural considerations—"knowing whether the inventing . . . has been done in the name of freedom" (EH, 284)— help adjudicate between actions in any sensible way, if every action can be performed both authentically and inauthentically? Here we do well to ask whether there are any morally relevant differences between unjustified specific values that result from an authentically affirmed, inventive procedure and unjustified specific values that result from a self-contradictory, deceptive procedure? While Sartre neither raises nor addresses this kind of question, Beauvoir does. In the process, she not only offers a considerably more sophisticated analysis of the requirements for authenticity, but she also develops the consequences of inauthenticity in a way that begins a kind of answer to the Why be moral? question.

Beauvoir on Normative Justification

Many have pointed out that Beauvoir made good on Sartre's unfulfilled promise at the end of *Being and Nothingness*—literally on the last page—to provide an existential ethic.[34] While Beauvoir's *Ethics* is not without rather significant problems, not so much for what she says as for what she does not say, it deserves considerably more attention than it has, until quite recently, received. The extremely ambitious first chapter, which weighs in at approximately ten thousand words, attempts to describe the fundamental ambiguity of human reality (in both phenomenological and ontological terms); explains why nearly the whole history of moral philosophy, including a sidebar on Marxism, fails; defends Sartre against several complex criticisms; and, if that were not already enough, lays out a groundwork for an existential ethic. Each issue taken alone requires more consideration than Beauvoir offers; consequently, considerable work remains to fill in the gaps. Although a growing body of solid secondary literature addresses *The Ethics of Ambiguity*, the secondary literature also suffers not so much from what it says but from what it does not say. Very few of Beauvoir's commentators offer an extended analysis of Beauvoir's account of normative justification. This absence is problematic because, as will be argued, the central argument in the *Ethics* sets out the necessary and sufficient conditions for normative justification, and hence authenticity.

To begin with, according to Beauvoir, a normative void comprises the space outside of human reality, a space where nothing can be said to be either valueless or valuable (*EA*, 11–12; *MA*, 15–16). Values do not exist independently of what individuals do and believe, for without humans, values do not exist at all. Only after humans populate the normative void are values disclosed. For only (ontologically) free beings can make choices, and only when these choices are freely made (in an empirical sense without excessive coercion) are values disclosed. For example, if one protests a mendacious administration's illegal war, one discloses protest as a value, so long as nothing coerces the act of protest. During Soviet-style "communism," if Russians were sometimes required to publicly demonstrate against the West, such demonstrations would not necessarily disclose the value of protesting the West, insofar as the protesters had to protest. In cases of coercive force, the process of value disclosure is compromised, vitiated, or altogether negated. Thus, all actions committed by free beings in the absence of coercion disclose values, precisely because those actions are free.[35]

However, even though all uncoerced free actions disclose values, the values disclosed are unjustified. Beauvoir claims, "every man is originally free, in the sense that he spontaneously casts himself into the world. But if we consider this spontaneity in its facticity, it appears to us only as a pure contingency, an upsurge as stupid as the clinamen of the Epicurean atom" (*EA*, 25; *MA*, 35). The analogy between original human freedom and the swerve of the Epicurean atom only goes so far. It is more than a bit strained to claim that the atom's "movement was not justified by [where it ended] which had not been chosen" (*EA*, 25; *MA*, 35). Beauvoir's point, however, is that while original freedom leads to the irruption of values into the normative void, when considered in its facticity, the disclosed "values" are something like arbitrary, unjustified preferences. Thus, if all freedom never left the original (read unreflective) level, all values would, in some sense, be normatively equivalent, in which case extreme relativism would reign.

However, just as uncoerced, free actions disclose values, free conscious acts of reflection upon previously disclosed lived values (or potential future values) give rise to the possibility of valuing those values and of disclosing meta-values employed in the critical task of justification. Only because humans can "stand back" and take a reflective "distance" from what they do can they consider their actions and evaluate them. As Beauvoir explains, "it is through this end that it sets up that my spontaneity confirms itself by *reflecting* upon itself" (*EA*, 26: italics added; *MA*, 36). However, while reflection is necessary, it is not sufficient for normative justification, because not all acts can be so confirmed.

In order to justify unreflective values, one must effect a transition from original freedom to moral freedom (*EA*, 25, 32, 41; *MA*, 35, 46, 60). The reflective affirmation, or what Beauvoir often calls "the willing of freedom" (*EA*, 25; *MA*, 35), plays a central role in this transition. It is here that we find the basis for the central argument in *The Ethics of Ambiguity*. In a widely quoted passage, Beauvoir argues, "freedom is the source from which all significations and all values spring. It is the original condition of all justification of existence. The man who seeks to justify his life must want [*doit vouloir*] freedom itself absolutely and above everything else" (*EA*, 24; *MA*, 33).[36] Thomas Anderson interprets this passage to mean that the affirmation of freedom is the most consistent attitude but that normative justification is possible without willing freedom.[37] Projecting Sartre's argument from "Existentialism Is a Humanism" onto Beauvoir's *Ethics* leads Anderson into error. Beauvoir never claims that the most consistent attitude demands the reflective affirmation of freedom; rather, she claims something quite a bit stronger, namely, that justification necessitates wanting or willing freedom.[38] There are two separate but essentially related reasons for why willing freedom is necessary (but not sufficient) for normative justification: one negative, the other positive.

Beginning with the negative reason, any justification that entails the (tacit) denial of ontological freedom (by positing objective, i.e., transcendent values) immediately undercuts itself, because doing so denies the condition for the possibility of justification, namely, ontological freedom. Here an example may be helpful. Suppose Marcel believes his actions are justified because God commands them. His reference to God entails the existence of transcendent moral values that exist independently from freedom. However, because values arise solely through (the subjective movement of) freedom, appeals to God implicitly deny the very freedom that makes such (pseudo) appeals to God possible. To invoke justification that (tacitly) denies freedom "contests the meaning of the project at the very moment that one defines it" (*EA*, 25; *MA*, 36). As a consequence,

> There then blazes forth the absurdity of a life which has sought outside of itself the justification which it alone could give itself. Detached from the freedom which might have genuinely grounded them, all the ends that have been pursued appear arbitrary and useless. (*EA*, 52; *MA*, 75)

In effect, Beauvoir offers something like a hypothetical imperative.[39] In the case of Kant, the fact that a certain action is a means to some desired end gives you a reason to perform that action. If you do not perform the means, then you cannot achieve the goal. In the case of Beauvoir, the fact that freedom provides the (only) means to normatively justify action gives you a reason to value freedom. If you do not value freedom, you cannot normatively justify your goals. It might, however, seem that the two cases are not strictly homologous and that something has gone wrong. If freedom is always implicitly valued in every uncoerced action, then doesn't the free mental act of justification, even if it appeals to transcendent values, automatically justify those values? The answer is no, but this is not immediately obvious.

Thus, Marcel's appeal to God for justification only apparently values God as a source of action guidance. What he really values, albeit implicitly, is the comfort derived from the tacit denial of his freedom, where such a tacit denial is motivated by his unwillingness to bear the burden of inventing values. The tacit denial of freedom, however, undercuts the normative force of his explicit assertion, because it denies the source of normativity. As stated above, Marcel's feigned effort to value God as a guarantor of his actions defeats itself, because he simultaneously invents the value of God, where the value of God masquerades as uninvented. Marcel is like the mythomaniac: he sends himself love letters and believes that he has a secret admirer.[40]

Thus, Marcel's failure to will freedom, and hence his failure to will the means to giving justification, results in a peculiar illusion. Marcel may enumerate various reasons for his actions (God's love for life) that give the appearance of justification. However, his justification is akin to what Husserl calls countersense. His words are syntactically correct, for example, "God demanded that I kill the abortion clinic doctor," such that they give the appearance of offering justification; however, they are empty of all justificatory content. Marcel does not offer poor justification; his assertion is tacitly incoherent. Consequently, like the swerve of the Epicurean atom, his actions amount to nothing more than unjustified preferences. As Beauvoir artfully explains, in such cases, "the spontaneity of the subject is merely a vain living palpitation" (*EA*, 25; *MA*, 36).[41]

Beauvoir states the positive requirement as follows: "Freedom must project itself toward its own reality through a content whose value it establishes. An end is valid only by a return to the freedom which established it and which willed itself through this end" (*EA*, 70; *MA*, 100). Freedom can be willed only through particular actions like writing a paper or protesting a currently mendacious regime. The value of the action's end—finishing the paper or deposing the illegitimate regime—results only because one freely chooses it. However, the validity of the end, that is, the question of whether the original value can itself be justified, arises upon the grounds of freedom. Only freedom-affirming goals can be justified, since freedom is the condition for the possibility of the valuable content of action. Thus, only actions consistent with the value of freedom can be reflectively endorsed.

However, while justification requires the reflective endorsement of my freedom, this endorsement alone does not yet achieve an authentically moral attitude; that is, it does not satisfy all of the sufficient conditions for normative justification. In cynicism, one can affirm subjective freedom, like both the passionate person and the adventurer Beauvoir discusses in chapter 2, while encroaching upon the freedom of Others.[42] Marcel, in a moment of cynicism, denies God's role and admits he freely chose to attack the abortion clinic. However, while the action is now affirmed as free, it undercuts itself in the denial of the freedom of Others. Authentic normative justification requires willing the freedom of Others.[43] Beauvoir's reasons for this are as follows.

Since all actions unfold in a social context (*EA*, 60; *MA*, 86), the social context provides the conditions for the possibility of expressing values, and hence of offering justification (*EA*, 71–72; *MA*, 102–104). For example, teaching philosophy expresses the value of education. However, the expression of this value would be impossible without students, universities, other teachers, or a philosophical tradition. Just as individual human freedom fills the normative void with values, intersubjective freedom fills it with distinctly moral values.[44] Thus, the legitimacy of teaching rides on the free, intersubjective affirmation of my activities by my students, colleagues, and the administration. If students were forced to attend class and literally chained to their desks, the value of teaching would be vitiated because the students could not, in principle, freely confer value onto my teaching. By coercing Others to do something or by doing things Others would not, in principle, freely affirm, one undermines the possibility of legitimizing these actions.

So understood, the requirement to will one's own freedom must be expanded to include Others who must be able to freely affirm your actions. Actions that Others cannot, in principle, affirm because those actions compromise their freedom cannot be morally justified. Beauvoir formulates the intersubjective requirement for justification as a principle in the following way: "The precept will be to treat the other as a freedom so that his end may be freedom" (*EA*, 142; *MA*, 206). If my activities deny the possibility of Others taking freedom as their end, it treats Others not as people but as mere instruments; consequently, Others cannot freely support my project as valuable, and hence it cannot be authentically justified. "The supreme end at which man must aim is his freedom, which alone is capable of establishing the value of every end" (*EA*, 113; *MA*, 162–63).

When put like this, Beauvoir's principle sounds very much like Kant's humanity formulation of the categorical imperative: "Act in such a way that you treat humanity, whether in your own person or in the person of any other, always at the same time as an end and never simply as a means."[45] Indeed, Beauvoir awaits a capable expositor to analyze her view in a way that simultaneously develops her deep debt to Kant (and in relationship to contemporary Kantians like Christine Korsgaard), but also in a way that works out her considerable and important departures that potentially surmount some of the well-known criticisms of Kant (and contemporary Kantians). Of the many ways that Beauvoir departs from Kant, only one can be discussed here.[46] For Kant, normative analysis reduces to reasons and intentions for acting, such that straightforward analysis of actual actions, their social implications, and their consequences are, strictly speaking, morally irrelevant. For Beauvoir, since freedom can only be expressed practically in action, analysis of authenticity involves more than consideration of reasons and intentions. To reflectively endorse freedom requires that one work to establish and/or maintain an intersubjective field of open possibilities, absent coercion, in which you and Others can express freedom (*EA*, 30, 32, 60, 80; *MA*, 43, 46, 86, 116). All the good intentions in the world amount to naught unless backed up by actions.

Consequently, the authentic affirmation of freedom cannot be merely intellectual. One does not will a maxim to express action authentically. Rather, one commits to freedom-affirming actions that open and/or maintain intersubjective fields of practical possibilities. As Beauvoir repeatedly argues in *Pyrrhus and Cinéas*, "a more demanding man knows that words cannot suffice to necessitate the object that he has founded. He asks that a real place be reserved for him on earth" (*PC*, 132). We need the concrete affirmation of our projects through the actions of Others and vice versa: students must attend our classes, the curious must observe our art, and the government must actually allocate resources for higher education. This leads to a rather thorny problem: Why can I not affirm the freedom of only the members of my tribe, while denying the freedom of nonmembers? To put this in Hegelian terms, Why cannot masters affirm, recognize, and be recognized only by other masters? Why do masters need the free affirmation of slaves, which, of course, cannot happen unless slaves are freed, and, hence, no longer slaves?

To begin an inadequate reply, the affirmation of intersubjective freedom has both ideal and practical requirements. Without the practical (engagement) requirement, normative justification is empty. However, without the ideal (universality) requirement, practical affirmation is blind. Whether less than universal justification amounts to no justification at all comes down to the question as to whether universality provides a necessary condition for normative justification. Here is a fainthearted stab: the slaveholder's affirmation of aristocratic freedom (while denying the freedom of slaves) involves a self-contradiction akin to his talking about rifles but not worrying that slaves might have them and revolt, because the word *rifle* can only refer to things within his group. Since normative objectivity requires intersubjectivity, the denial of some subjects undercuts justification.

Of course, universality would be unnecessary if justification required merely practical moments. The reduction of normative analysis to the practical comes down to the provincial supposition that the ideal requirements of freedom end with our allies. To be sure, a great deal more work needs to be done to clarify the relationship between ideal and practical requirements, and a great many other difficulties lurk on the horizon—like Beauvoir's justification of violence, and whether or to what extent Beauvoir envisions a (utopian) kingdom of ends, where intersubjective communities of freedom unfurl without any conflict. These must, however, remain projects for another day.[47]

Conclusion: A Future for Existential Ethics?

Alasdair MacIntyre famously argues that the fragmented moral structures emerging from the "enlightenment" project were gripped with an incoherence that has led to our current situation composed of intractable disagreement and dangerous forms of relativism.[48] MacIntyre offers us a well-known choice: we can either return to Aristotle, minus the metaphysical biology, preferably as read through the lens of Aquinas, or we are stuck with Nietzsche in a free-for-all where (provincial) struggles for power reign. While MacIntyre fails to understand Nietzsche (and for that matter Sartre),[49] unlike "enlightenment" philosophers (and many post-Enlightenment philosophers), Sartre and Beauvoir were well aware of the failures of the Enlightenment: "In the eighteenth century, the atheism of the *philosophes* discarded the idea of God, but not so much for the notion that existence precedes essence" (EH, 270). Not fully appreciating the consequences of rejecting God, Enlightenment philosophers continued to employ various transcendent programs to ground moral philosophy: a priori principles, an inviolable soul, human nature, teleological ends, or a Platonic realm of the forms, among others. The abandonment of God, however, requires a rejection of all transcendent efforts to found morality. Thus, Sartre and Beauvoir can, in a way, agree with MacIntyre: the Enlightenment moral project does indeed involve an underlying incoherence. It mostly amounts to countersense (but so too did the pre-Enlightenment period). However, unlike MacIntyre, Beauvoir effectively shows us that the rejection of all traditional views of transcendent normative objectivity does not demand that we either return to the (mystical) past or abandon all hope for normative objectivity. Beauvoir offers an account of normative justification that is weaker than traditional transcendent views but stronger than naïve relativism. Thus, for those who find a return to the past (Aristotle and/or Aquinas) implausible, Beauvoir offers a serious alternative to Nietzsche. Perhaps we need not choose between Aristotle and Nietzsche but between Nietzsche (or some form of post-structuralism) and vintage French Existentialism.

A final note to those dwindling members of the existentialist tribe: Beauvoir concludes the first chapter of *The Ethics of Ambiguity* with an apparently audacious claim: "Therefore, not only do we assert that the existentialist doctrine permits the elaboration of an ethics, but it even appears to us as the only philosophy in which ethics has its place" (*EA*, 34; *MA*, 48). The time has come for existentialists to throw down the gauntlet and make good on Beauvoir's apparently audacious claim. Until academia widely recognizes that an existential ethic provides a viable alternative to contemporary approaches, existentialists will, at best, live on the periphery, or at worst, slip into a forgotten past.[50]

Notes

1. Integral to this movement are various essays written by Margaret Simons that begin in the late 1970s, many of which are recently brought together in a fine collection titled *Beauvoir and* The Second Sex. See also Toril Moi's *Feminist Theory*, Eva Lundgren-Gothlin's *Sex and Existence*, Debra B. Bergoffen's *The Philosophy of Simone de Beauvoir*, and Kate and Edward Fullbrook's *Simone de Beauvoir*.

2. Beauvoir consistently but misleadingly insisted that she was merely Sartre's philosophical disciple; see, for instance, Michel Sicard's interview with Beauvoir and Sartre in *Obliques*, nos. 10–19 (1979): 325–29. In other places, Beauvoir claims that she "adhered completely to *Being and Nothingness* and later to *Critique of Dialectical*

Reason." Beauvoir scholars in recent years have, I believe correctly, argued that Beauvoir's self-portrait is inaccurate. See, for instance, Moi, *Feminist Theory*, and Sonia Kruks, "Teaching Sartre About Freedom," 79–95.

3. See Kate and Edward Fullbrook, *Simone de Beauvoir*, and Moi, *Feminist Theory*. For a more recent analysis that makes use of Beauvoir's early journals, see Margaret Simons's essay "Beauvoir's Philosophical Independence," 87–103.

4. See Kruks, "Teaching Sartre about Freedom"; Lundgren-Gothlin, *Sex and Existence*, and Arp, *Bonds of Freedom*.

5. See, for instance, the recent collection of essays edited by Lori Jo Marso and Patricia Moynagh, *Simone de Beauvoir's Political Thinking*, which argues that Beauvoir makes a "unique contribution" to political contemporary thought.

6. For an overstated account of the influence question, see Kate and Edward Fullbrook, *Simone de Beauvoir*.

7. See note 4 above.

8. For Beauvoir scholars that either quote or refer to and generally accept Kruks's analysis, see Ursula Tidd's *Simone de Beauvoir, Gender and Testimony*, 28–29; Barbara Andrew's "Beauvoir's Place in Philosophical Thought," 33; Eva Lundgren-Gothlin's "Reading Simone de Beauvoir with Martin Heidegger," p. 51, n. 15; and Kristana Arp's *Bonds of Freedom*, 6–7, 141.

9. Kruks, "Teaching Sartre about Freedom," 82.

10. Ibid., 86. Others have also argued Sartre's notion of absolute freedom leads to the absurd consequence that it does not come in degrees. See, for instance, V. J. McGill's "Sartre's Doctrine of Freedom."

11. Ibid., 84. Ursula Tidd, in *Simone de Beauvoir, Gender and Testimony*, refers to Kruks and also quotes the now infamous "slave in chains" passage in greater length (in French) in the effort to make much the same point, though with a sharper rhetorical edge. Following Kruks, Tidd claims, "Sartre's overestimation of individual willpower and choice when faced with crushing oppression leads him to the unhumanitarian and naively abstract position from which he argues that those who submit to torture do so freely" (29). Needless to say, Sartre's claim about the slave in chains has attracted a great deal of unfavorable commentary. To be sure, Sartre's unfortunate penchant for hyperbolic, misleading use of language and often controversial assertions presents a series of obstacles to giving levelheaded analysis. However, as will be argued below, exaggerated remarks like those of Tidd's indicate an underlying agenda, the absence of a close reading, and hence a superficial understanding of *Being and Nothingness*. Incidentally, one should compare Sartre's slave in chains claim with Beauvoir's claim in *Pyrrhus and Cinéas* that "the slave's chains do nothing about freedom either" (*PC*, 124).

12. Kruks, "Teaching Sartre about Freedom," 83.

13. Ibid., 84.

14. Kruks quotes Beauvoir from *The Prime of Life*, where in 1960, reflecting back twenty years to 1940, Beauvoir claims the following: "I maintained that, from the point of view of freedom, as Sartre defined it—not as a stoical resignation but as an active transcendence of the given—not every situation is equal: what transcendence is possible for a woman locked up in a harem? Even such a cloistered existence could be lived in several different ways, Sartre said. I clung to my opinion for a long time and then made only a token submission. Basically [she comments in 1960] I was right. But to have been able to

defend my position, I would have had to abandon the terrain of individualist, thus idealist, morality, where we stood" (quoted in Kruks, "Teaching Sartre about Freedom," 82). Beauvoir doesn't, as far as I know, discuss women in harems in print until her *Ethics of Ambiguity*. Even there, it is unclear to what extent her position on ontological freedom significantly departs from Sartre's, when read correctly. Of course, a lot rides on "read correctly," a point that returns below.

15. So far as I can know, Beauvoir only mentions this issue of the degradation of transcendence into the in-itself in the preface; see the 1989 Vintage Books edition, xxxv. One should note further that in this passage Beauvoir puts *in-itself* in scare quotes, clearly indicating that we should not take this claim literally. This issue returns below.

16. See, for instance, Sartre's posthumously published *Notebooks for an Ethics*.

17. All citations are to both English and French editions of *Being and Nothingness*. English quotes come from the Philosophical Library (New York, 1956) edition (and not the 1966/84 editions) and are cited as *BN*, followed by the page number. With regard to the French, in a few cases, I give slightly altered translations to those of Hazel Barnes. Citations to the French, *L'Être et le Néant*, follow the English citation and refer to the Gallimard edition, NRF (1971), indicated by *EN* and a page number.

18. Sartre equivocates in his treatment of this "essential modification" between calling it a self, Ego, and Self-as-object (*BN*, 260); Me and Me-as-Object (*BN*, 285); and character (*BN*, 349–50). Sartre settles on calling it my being-for-others (*BN*, 286), which eventually becomes an unrealizable-to-be-realized (*BN*, 527–29).

19. Sartre's methodological solipsism is explained by his employment of a Cartesian method that proceeds from the abstract and simple to the concrete and complex. For this reason, Sartre formally introduces the existence of Others only in Part III. Failure to take Sartre's Cartesian method seriously makes accurate assessment of *Being and Nothingness* as a whole impossible, for the meanings of all of his basic concepts change over the course of the text.

20. Clarifying Sartre's considered view of freedom proves difficult, since Sartre's analysis spreads out over several hundred pages and suffers from various inconsistencies, some real and others only apparent. Sartre's initial analysis of limitation occurs in Part III, chapter 1, but rather suddenly disappears for some two hundred pages until Part IV, where Sartre examines interiorization—the process of internalizing social objectifications into one's projects.

21. As in the above case, with regard to Sartre's revised notion of self, Sartre here notes his initial methodological solipsism, indicated by the phrase "keeping ourselves within the compass of existence-for-itself." So understood, once Sartre moves to the concrete level of analysis, several of his abstract claims must be abandoned, a point often unnoticed in the secondary literature on Sartre.

22. See also Kruks, "Teaching Sartre about Freedom," 83.

23. Quoted from Veronique Zaytzeff's translation in *The Debate between Sartre and Merleau-Ponty*, 454. Incidentally, Kruks briefly mentions this essay and argues that Beauvoir's reading of Sartre was now "refracted" through "Merleau-Ponty's lenses" ("Teaching Sartre about Freedom," 88). This is a bit strange. While Beauvoir's stated purpose was to show that Merleau-Ponty dealt with a straw-man Sartre, Kruks argues that Beauvoir now misread Sartre, in her defense of Sartre, due to her commitments to Merleau-Ponty. Maybe. But since the view of Sartre that Beauvoir now recognizes op-

poses Kruks's view, she qualifies Beauvoir's reading as "refracted." Kruks does not consider the possibility that Beauvoir came to more clearly understand Sartre's view in the 1950s than she had in the early 40s. This possibility is developed below.

24. Kruks, "Teaching Sartre about Freedom," 82–83.

25. Citations to *Pyrrhus and Cinéas* come from *Philosophical Writings: Simone de Beauvoir,* edited by Margaret A. Simons, Marybeth Timmerman, and Mary Beth Mader.

26. Whether Beauvoir echoes Sartre's claim that "even the red hot pinchers of the torturer do not exempt us from being free" or whether Sartre played on an earlier reference by Beauvoir to torture and slavery, I do not know. Whatever the case may be, the issue of torture was real, given the situation of the resistance movements in Nazi-occupied France, even if it was real only in a theoretical sense for Sartre and Beauvoir.

27. This issue is considerably more complicated than I am here making it out to be. Both Beauvoir and Sartre seem to equate human reality with ontological (or what Beauvoir sometimes calls original) freedom. This suggests that when a previously ontologically free being is no longer ontologically free, it cannot be human. If we suppose that certain forms of extreme oppression completely extinguish ontological (and not just merely practical) freedom without ending life, then we have to give an account of what remains and whether such a freedom-extinguished being can recuperate ontological freedom. One might begin by drawing a continuum from inert thingness to vegetative states to something like animal existence to transcendence.

28. Kruks, "Teaching Sartre about Freedom," 82.

29. Ibid., 83.

30. Unless otherwise stated, quotes come from Bernard Frechtman's translation, cited *EA* followed by a page number. The English citation will be followed by citation to the French, *Pour une Morale de L'ambiguïté* (Paris: Gallimard, 1978) as *MA*, followed by a page number. Amendments to the translation will be noted.

31. For examples of the relativism charge, see Richard Bernstein's *Praxis and Action,* 142, 149, 151–55. See also Henry Veatch's *For an Ontology of Morals,* 76–77.

32. All citations of "Existentialism Is a Humanism" (1946), hereafter cited as EH, are from *Existentialism: Basic Writings,* ed. Guignon and Pereboom.

33. Sartre argues that Kant's categorical imperative is too general. He seems to follow the spirit of Hegel's criticism that the categorical imperative is so empty that it can generate contradictory results for the analysis of any maxim; hence, it cannot generate determinate decisions in concrete contexts. By too vague, Sartre refers to the calculation problem that plagues consequentialism. The future consequences of an action are too complex; hence, calculations can be nothing more than vague impressions that offer little help.

34. Fullbrooks, *Simone de Beauvoir,* 142; Lundgren-Gothlin, *Sex and Existence,* 149; Arp, *Bonds of Freedom,* 2.

35. Here it is perhaps worth clarifying a potential misconception. To say that uncoerced, free actions disclose values does not mean that individuals simply make up or invent values by fiat or out of nothing. Born into a social world permeated with values, values are not straightforwardly created; rather, they are, in a certain sense, inherited (*EA,* 35–42; *MA,* 51–61). However, while antecedent values condition human existence, antecedent values do not necessitate that or how these inherited values are assumed, interpreted, or applied. Anticipatory values can be accepted, rejected, modified, hidden

from, or remained oblivious to. However, all of these responses involve a basic level of inventiveness, given the irreducible uniqueness of any situation and given the uniqueness of each individual's point of view. What we cannot do is exempt ourselves from contributing to the process of social value constitution, whether or not we are explicitly aware of doing so. Here a qualification is necessary, insofar as not everyone contributes to the normative universe. During childhood, values are inherited in a way that they are "accepted" as if they were transcendent, that is, as if values exist independently of the subjective process of value disclosure. And Beauvoir likens certain forms of oppression to keeping adults in a childlike state. Only at a certain point in life, and in certain situations where mystification does not result from severe oppression (*EA*, 98), does one "recognize" the role that subjectivity plays in normativity, and only then is one confronted with the inescapable fact that one must contribute to sustaining normative reality (*EA*, 39–40).

36. Examples of those who discuss this passage are Thomas Anderson, *Foundation and Structure*, 46; Linda Bell, *Sartre's Ethics of Authenticity*, 56–57; Joseph Mahon, *Existentialism, Feminism, and Simone de Beauvoir*, 42; and Kristana Arp, *Bonds of Freedom*, 90. Surprisingly, the most sustained analysis of this passage comes from Sartreans: Anderson and Bell. Anderson, however, fails to appreciate that willing freedom is necessary for justification, likely because he (mistakenly) believes that Beauvoir employs the same arguments as Sartre. However, the Sartreans generally do not spend sufficient time analyzing all of the theoretical machinery necessary to understanding Beauvoir's entire argument. Perhaps even more surprisingly, none of the Beauvoir scholars just mentioned work out the details of this argument. Though Arp responds to Bell and Anderson, she does not come to grips with the issue of justification, see note 33 above. Finally, while Mahon claims to "reconstruct her argument in accordance with the practice current in analytic philosophy" (*Existentialism, Feminism, and Simone de Beauvoir*, 35), he discusses a cluster of arguments in a rather disjointed fashion, mentions the main argument (42), but offers no sustained analysis and does not even mention the issue of moral justification.

37. Anderson claims "that I must value freedom itself if any valuation it gives to my life is to be *ultimately* meaningful" (*Foundation and Structure*, 46; italics added). A page later he continues, "man can best be 'right,' he can *best* justify his life, by choosing freedom as his ultimate value. Such a choice is best because it is most consistent with the way things are and most consistent logically. So argue Sartre and de Beauvoir" (47; italics added). In each of the passages Anderson qualifies the relation between freedom, meaning, and justification, first with "ultimately," and second with "best." So understood, affirmation of freedom only enhances meaning, or allows one to "best" justify one's existence. The reason for this qualification arises in light of Anderson's claim that one can deny freedom but still lead a meaningful and justified existence (64)—a point that fundamentally misunderstands Beauvoir.

38. Arp notes that willing freedom is necessary for justification and shares the observation that Anderson gets Beauvoir wrong because he assumes she says the same thing as Sartre. Arp, however, neither explains why willing freedom is necessary for justification nor, conversely, why denying freedom undercuts justification (*Bonds of Freedom*, 90–95).

39. On this point I am indebted to Linda Bell, who, in response to Anderson, makes

a similar point in *Sartre's Ethics of Authenticity*, 55–58. Bell's helpful discussion frames analysis in terms of willing the freedom of others—"One cannot will one's own freedom without willing the freedom of others" (52)—and of valuing freedom itself as the source of all value (55). My discussion, in many ways, merely extends Bell. Incidentally, Arp misunderstands Bell on this point when she argues that Bell does not "draw on the Sartrean insight that human freedom is the source of all values" (*Bonds of Freedom*, 89). Clearly, Bell does take this insight seriously, as quoted above. Furthermore, Arp confuses logical concerns with rhetorical concerns when she asks, "does Bell intend her argument to convince people, especially those in bad faith, that they should value their concrete freedom?" (89). Bell's point is merely a logical one that valuing freedom is a necessary condition for willing others free, and this remains true regardless of whether anyone is convinced by it.

40. Another example that elaborates the negative requirement might be helpful. Imagine that you are in love and that the one you love also loves you. Ask yourself: What makes your lover's love for you meaningful and valuable? In part, the significance of love has to do with the fact that your lover chose you as opposed to someone else. It is your look, the style with which you walk, the way you communicate, and so on that are illuminated by your lover. And in turn, what is your lover's love toward you, if not the gentle running of fingers through your hair, the sweet caress, the sharing of a midnight bottle of wine—all actions that arise out of your lover's freedom. But imagine that someone surreptitiously slipped a love potion into a drink and induced your lover's love: you happened to be the first person your lover (to-be) saw. Like an automatic washer going into its spin cycle, you have been mechanically picked, not for who you are but simply for the fact of your being seen first. Upon this discovery, do we not find something lacking? Are not our lover's "actions" simply facts because they were not chosen? The sweet caress is now simply an inert hand lying upon your flesh. Thus, the effervescent meaning of love dies away.

41. Put another way, the implicit denial of the subjective movement of freedom entailed by the positing of objective, transcendent values also implicitly denies that which makes one distinctly human, namely, freedom. Thus, one confers upon oneself a contradictory thing-like status (*EA*, 45; *MA*, 66). Since quasi-things cannot offer more than quasi-justification, the process of self-ossification effectively undermines the possibility of giving genuinely legitimating justification.

42. While all of the five main attitudes discussed in chapter 2 of *The Ethics of Ambiguity*—the sub-man, the serious, the nihilist, the passionate person, and the adventurer—all fail to meet the requirement of authenticity, the last two fail for a fundamentally different reason than the first three. Whereas the first three all deny one's own freedom, the last two affirm one's own freedom but deny the freedom of Others.

43. Karen Vintges, in *Philosophy as Passion*, 67–71, mentions the requirement to will the freedom of others. While she rightly notes the Kantian influence, she does not offer an in-depth analysis of this claim or of all the philosophical machinery necessary to unpacking it. Debra Bergoffen, in *Philosophy of Simone de Beauvoir*, mentions "moral requirements" twice in passing without explaining why the requirements are required or what the consequences of not meeting them are (87, 91). While Bergoffen does not address Beauvoir's central argument concerning normative justification, she does offer an excellent discussion of Beauvoir's account of intersubjectivity and generosity.

44. For the abstract minded: a world with only one free person might include values but those values would not be moral values. Here it might also be added that while intersubjectivity gives rise to distinctly moral (Other-regarding) values, intersubjectivity also turns out to be a necessary condition for normative objectivity. Beauvoir indicates this line of analysis at several points, for instance, when she claims, "Man can find a justification of his own existence only in the existence of other men. . . . To will oneself free is also to will others free" (*EA*, 72–73; *MA*, 103–104). However, she doesn't really work out the details in a satisfying fashion, and much more work needs to be done here. Those interested in perusing this line of analysis might follow the spirit of Husserl in *Ideas II*, where he argues, I believe convincingly, that intersubjectivity is necessary for (perceptual) objectivity.

45. Kant, *Grounding for the Metaphysics of Morals*, 36.

46. Here is a brief sketch of only a few important departures. First, Beauvoir rejects Kant's metaphysical teleology that the end for all rational autonomous beings is the formation of a good will. Second, Beauvoir rejects the possibility of moral certitude implicit in Kant's moral philosophy and replaces it with various notions of ambiguity. Third, Beauvoir takes interdependence more seriously than does Kant. Fourth, Beauvoir justifies violence in a way that Kant likely would not. Fifth, Beauvoir's analysis concludes that one has a stronger positive obligation to liberate Others than Kant's does.

47. It would be appropriate to show, here in the conclusion, how Beauvoir moves well beyond Sartre's analysis of unjustified specific values, which she does. (According to Beauvoir, specific values are unjustified only in their original constitution but not after reflective endorsement. Consequently, contra the early Sartre, not all specific values are necessarily unjustified, not all original values can be justified, and, above all, not all actions can be performed authentically. Thus, the consequences of inauthenticity are greater than merely indicating a logical contradiction. The positing of transcendent values that tacitly contradict freedom undercuts the possibility of justification and renders life absurd. Those who wish to live an existentially coherent life must will intersubjective freedom.) There are, however, bigger fishes to fry . . .

48. See MacIntyre, *After Virtue: A Study in Moral Philosophy*.

49. A coherent existentialist ethics is not a species of emotivism, as MacIntyre claims.

50. I wish to thank the editors of this volume—Christine Daigle and Jacob Golomb—for their invitation and diligent work on this volume. A very special thank-you to Douglas Lewis for first introducing me, as an undergraduate, to Simone de Beauvoir's *Ethics* (which, incidentally, I read before Sartre's "Existentialism Is a Humanism") and *The Second Sex* (again, read before *Being and Nothingness*). Doug's astute insight, nearly infinite patience, and our continuing conversations over the years have made this essay possible. Also, a thank-you to Chris Gallagher for all of the helpful comments made on an earlier draft of this essay.

5 Sartre and Beauvoir on Hegel's Master-Slave Dialectic and the Question of the "Look"

Debbie Evans

The lucidity of the dialectic of the master and slave . . . is blinding . . . no-one knows anything of him*self* if he has not grasped this movement which determines and limits the successive possibilities of man.
—Georges Bataille, *Inner Experience*

As several feminist critics have commented, Hegel's Master-Slave dialectic, which he foregrounds in his magnum opus, *The Phenomenology of Spirit*, is a privileged textual motif in the work of both Sartre and Beauvoir.[1] It first appears in Beauvoir's novel *She Came to Stay*, where the Master-Slave relation is principally re-enacted between the characters of Françoise and Xavière. Sartre's discussion of the Master-Slave relation is taken up in his early philosophical essay *Being and Nothingness*, published in the same year as *She Came to Stay*. Although Sartre undoubtedly read Beauvoir's novel as a rich and complex metaphysical text, he was certainly not prepared to share unreservedly her early passion for Hegel in *Being and Nothingness*, and in particular, her insights into the Master-Slave relationship. Sartre's implicit critique of Beauvoir's novel forms the backdrop to much of his analysis of the limitations of Hegelian idealism and the Master-Slave scenario in particular. Whereas Sartre is keen to measure his distance from Hegel, Beauvoir's close analysis of the Master-Slave dialectic produces some of her finest writing. In her best-known work, *The Second Sex*, Beauvoir takes up the Master-Slave motif in order to analyze woman's oppression under patriarchal society and her emergence as the "inessential consciousness."

Since a reworking of the Master-Slave relation appears in both the fictional and the analytical text, we could say, to borrow a post-structuralist term, that this relation *transgresses* the boundary between the literary and the philosophical by introducing an aperture between these two fields of discourse. In Georges Bataille's well-known essay "Transgression," published in the seminal work *Death and Sensuality: A Study of Eroticism and the Taboo,* he contends that transgression does not deny a limit but rather transcends and completes it. In the context of this essay, we could refine Bataille's distinction to argue that the limits or boundaries of "literature" and "philosophy" are not erased under transgression. Rather, they are confirmed in the very movement or process that surpasses them. In this respect, the limit and its overcoming must be thought of both separately and together. For Michel Foucault, transgression replaces Hegel's language of dialectical contradiction since, as he puts it, "the limit and transgression owe to one another the density of their being."[2] In other words, it is in the very *possibility* of transgression that the existence of a boundary is determined. Both the limit and the transgression mutually reinforce each other.

In the context of Hegel's Master-Slave dialectic, we could say that this textual motif both displaces and subverts the traditional boundaries between literature and philosophy. Beauvoir's 1946 essay *Littérature et métaphysique* to some degree anticipates Bataille's analysis of transgression, to the extent that she attempts a type of dialectical synthesis between the literary and philosophical text. She defends the metaphysical novel as an attempt to reconcile the separate demands of literature and philosophy. A "true" novel, she argues, is concerned with exploring the opacity and ambiguity of a "flesh-and-blood" individual in a situation, whereas a philosophical system attempts to express an abstract truth of human existence as a type of universal. What the author refers to somewhat enigmatically as "pure" literature and "pure" philosophy may initially appear to be polar opposites. However, the metaphysical novel, she argues, answers to "a profound demand of the mind" that seeks to overcome the false barriers erected between these two modes of expression. The existential novel does not merely describe or express certain pre-held abstract metaphysical truths. Neither is it, in its most crude form, "disguised philosophy."[3] As Beauvoir points out, the "true" novel *is* metaphysical to the extent that it is concerned with exploring the historical and temporal dimension of lived human experience, an experience that can never be adequately conveyed through the universal abstractness of the philosophical text.

The transgression that displaces the boundaries between the philosophical and the literary text results in each one functioning as a type of excess or *supplément* to the other. As Jacques Derrida comments, the French word *supplément* means both addition and replacement.[4] The "literary" text, not even necessarily in a self-conscious way, both supplements and replaces the boundaries of the philosophical text. The effect of this transgression is to destabilize and therefore contaminate the "pure" frontier of reason contained within the analytical text. The *supplément,* by adding to the text, is also an excess of language. The literary text exceeds or, to use a phenomenological term, *transcends* the boundaries of philosophical thought through the irreducibility of its discourse to abstract reason. Beauvoir highlights this point in *Littérature et métaphysique:* the language of the literary text remains in its singularity both opaque and ambiguous. In the final analysis, it is irreducible to any attempt to "master" either its form or content. The unfettered "space of writing" exceeds the discursive language of the analytical text, which we could say within the context of this article, must remain *enslaved* to the logic of the *logos* that here is a project of knowledge, in the sense that this project implies a search for truth and meaning.[5] Derrida makes a similar point when he claims that the "institution of fiction . . . gives *in principle* the power to say everything, to break free of the rules, to displace them."[6] He later continues, "sometimes this questioning (of the philosophical by the literary) occurs more effectively via the actual practice of writing, the staging, the composition, the treatment of language, rhetoric, than via speculative arguments."[7]

It is within this play of the textual difference between the "literary" and the "philosophical" that I would like to situate the debate concerning the appropriation of Hegel's Master-Slave dialectic by both Sartre and Beauvoir. However, in comparing their differing approaches to reading Hegel, we should be wary of assuming that one author merely intends a type of mimetic representation of the other's thought. Neither do I want to argue that each author's thought, while acknowledging a common Hegelian heritage, is nevertheless simply "different" from the other's. Using Derrida's notion of *différance,* I want to argue that each author both simultaneously builds on and deconstructs the other's handling of the dialectic.

The term *différance* itself has, according to Derrida, a "profound affinity with Hegelian discourse."[8] Neither literally a word nor a concept, neither simply active nor simply passive, the play of *différance* eludes mastery and the linear discourse of reason. It attempts to name, not "differences," but rather the "being-different" of these "differences." In other words, it is a movement that produces both divisions and differences: a temporizing detour or deferral that, as such, must inevitably challenge the *telos* of the Hegelian project. It refers to a "writing within writing": the production of an intricate "interlacing of different threads and different lines of meaning."[9] Geoffrey Bennington remarks that *différance* refers to a witticism of Derrida's, since the difference between *différence* and *différance* is only marked in writing, not in speech. In this sense, the supposed traditional hierarchical superiority of speech over writing is overturned. What is particularly relevant about Derrida's notion of *différance* is that as a textual construct it points to a play of differentiality both within and between the margins of the literary and analytical text, where the philosophical dialogue between Sartre and Beauvoir is most acutely observed.

Différance and the Master-Slave Relation in *She Came to Stay* and *Being and Nothingness*

The significance of the Hegelian epigraph to *She Came to Stay*: "Each consciousness seeks the death of the Other" (unfortunately omitted in English translations of the novel) has been signaled by several critics.[10] Toril Moi comments that by choosing an epigraph from Hegel, "Beauvoir draws our attention to the implacable hostility between consciousness and the other in existentialist philosophy."[11] Karen Vintges also draws attention to the Hegelian epigraph, reading *She Came to Stay* as philosophical literature that focuses on the relationship between Self and Other.[12] Nancy Bauer further remarks on the influence of Sartre's conflictual model of human relationships analyzed in *Being and Nothingness*, commenting that *She Came to Stay* is a "book-long Sartrean-style fight to the death."[13]

The Hegelian influence on *She Came to Stay* has been difficult to gauge in the past, partly due to Beauvoir's remarks in *The Prime of Life* that the epigraph was only selected *after* she had begun to write her novel,[14] and that when she began to read Hegel's *Phenomenology of Spirit* in the National Library in July 1940, she understood virtually nothing of his text (*PL*, 549; *FA*, 523). This is not, of course, to dispute any veracity to Beauvoir's claim. It merely indicates that she displaces the centrality of the influence of the *Phenomenology* in relation to the chronological composition of her novel.

Throughout her lifetime, Beauvoir was intent on protecting the public image she had created for herself as, in her own words, "not a philosopher," and was anxious to deflect any attention away from her philosophical achievements in *She Came to Stay*.[15] Toward the end of her life, in conversation with her biographer, Deirdre Bair, Beauvoir could still resolutely maintain that if *She Came to Stay* could be interpreted as a philosophical text at all, its debt was specifically to Sartre, whose ideas had an "exhilarating, liberating" effect on her thinking.[16] However, as Margaret Simons has pointed out,[17] we should be wary of taking Beauvoir at her word.

Beauvoir's intricate reworking of the Master-Slave dialectic in *She Came to Stay* follows the general perspective of Hegel's approach in the *Phenome-*

nology, which is to use the dialectic as a methodological tool to examine the limitations to, and development of, autonomous self-consciousness. For Hegel, the Master-Slave relationship arises when human consciousness, which is initially rooted in sense-certainty and understanding, moves beyond the desire of the world as the truth of its existence. Consciousness is first experienced as a pure undifferentiated "I" that exists in unity with other independent self-consciousnesses. However, argues Hegel, self-consciousness can only exist for another self-consciousness through being recognized. For this reason, consciousness must desire another human consciousness in order that this consciousness may recognize him. The consciousness that seeks to appropriate another self-consciousness is that of the Master. The Slave exists initially only in the form of an inessential, object-consciousness. At first, he is merely viewed by the Master as a narcissistic reflection of his own self. However, Hegel asserts that the self-consciousness of the Slave is also independent and self-contained. The Slave, as Other, must be negated by the Master in order for him to become certain of himself as an essential being. Since each self-consciousness seeks to negate otherness in the Other, each consciousness seeks the death of the other.

In the *Phenomenology*, Hegel claims that it is only through the staking of life in this way that freedom is won. The individual who does not risk his life, says Hegel, may well be recognized as a person, but he will fail to recognize the truth of his existence as a pure "being-for-self." Nevertheless, it is ultimately the Slave that represents the truth of the Master, since in reality the Master needs the Slave in order to recognize him. In Hegel's account in the *Phenomenology*, therefore, the Master does not actually kill the Slave. However, in Kojève's dramatic reading of Hegel, he transforms the Master-Slave relationship by insisting, in a theatrical *coup de force*, that the true Master *murders* the Slave.[18] Beauvoir's novel, which culminates in the murder of the Slave, Xavière, by the master-figure Françoise, would appear to replicate Kojève's interpretation of the Master-Slave relation, which in true Hegelian fashion culminates in the *telos* of death.[19]

The dialectical destiny of Xavière, her impotence and inheritance of the Slave position, will mirror Beauvoir's later discussion of women's destiny and their inheritance of a heavy past in *The Second Sex*. Although the author will, of course, refuse the idea that women have, a priori, a destiny, Beauvoir nevertheless devotes the important first section of this work precisely to a discussion of the traditional forms that a woman's destiny may take in society. Seen from this feminist perspective, the orchestrated time of the dialectic that structures the novel represents the hegemony of the male phallocentric order, aptly symbolized in the pyramidal structure of the dialectic, which culminates in a pure moment of textual *jouissance:* Hegel's intuition of absolute knowledge. This dialectical structure represents the temporality of the "Master" philosopher. In *She Came to Stay,* Xavière as the "Slave" figure represents the lostness or *délaissement* of the female Other within this order. Whereas in the *Phenomenology* the struggle to the death is portrayed as a struggle between two male consciousnesses, in Beauvoir's novel the struggle is between two female consciousnesses, with Françoise playing the role of the honorary male "Master."

In this sense, Beauvoir's literary text both transgresses and supplements the linear, phallocentric structure of the *Phenomenology.* In the *Phenomenology,* the struggle between Master and Slave occupies a relatively short section on the development of self-consciousness. However, in *She Came to Stay,* the dialectic is extensively reworked, particularly in Part Two of the novel, where Beauvoir writes an extended Master-Slave relationship, which passes through the forms of Stoicism, Skepticism, and the Unhappy Consciousness.[20] Whereas Kojève views these stages of the dialectic merely as "obscuring ideologies," for Beauvoir, on the contrary, an exploration of these stages through a literary medium is crucial to her reworking of Hegel's portrait of the development of autonomous self-consciousness. This is undoubtedly a metaphysical goal of the author's reworking of Hegel within her text: to test the limits or boundaries of a self-consciousness that, like Hegel, she views as inevitably mediated through another human consciousness.

Being and Nothingness—A Very Sartrean Image of Beauvoir's *She Came to Stay?*

As Kate and Edward Fullbrook have pointed out in their controversial study, *Simone de Beauvoir and Jean-Paul Sartre: The Remaking of a Twentieth-Century Legend* (1993), commentators have traditionally considered Beauvoir's work to be an application of Sartre's philosophical ideas. Beauvoir herself was, of course, keen to promote this public image of the couple. In 1982 she claimed in conversation with Deirdre Bair that she accepted unquestioningly the system Sartre created in *Being and Nothingness* as her *raison d'être.*[21] However, her persistent defense of Sartre's intellectual superiority was not without its difficulties. Interestingly, Sartre himself never claimed that Beauvoir was his intellectual inferior. For example, in an interview conducted with her in 1975, he claimed that he had never considered himself more intelligent than Beauvoir.[22] In response to Bair's probing about the chronology of her composition of *She Came to Stay* and its likely impact on the development of Sartre's thought in *Being and Nothingness,* Beauvoir maintained that she had barely finished fifty pages of the manuscript by the time Sartre arrived in Paris for a two-week period of army leave in February 1940.[23]

However, as the Fullbrooks have pointed out, the posthumously published correspondence between Sartre and Beauvoir tells a very different story.[24] In a letter dated 17 January 1940, Beauvoir enthuses that she will have at least two hundred and fifty pages of draft manuscript to show him when he returns to Paris on leave from the army (*LS*, 258; *LSfr*, 2:49). Margaret Simons comments: "The evidence from the war diaries and correspondence suggests that Beauvoir lied about her philosophical work in general and her work in *She Came to Stay* in particular, in order to hide the evidence in Sartre's *War Diary* (published in 1983) that he drew upon her novel in formulating his philosophy in *Being and Nothingness*."[25]

However, when we try to assess the degree of influence that Sartre's reading of *She Came to Stay* had on the formulation of his philosophy in *Being and Nothingness*, we encounter certain fundamental problems. The first is that in his *War Diary*, widely acknowledged to be a major source of *Being and Nothingness*, there are only two minor references to Hegel. Neither are there any references to Hegel in his correspondence to Beauvoir for the years 1939–40, which marked the beginning of his work on *Being and Nothingness*. Nevertheless, Sartre implicitly discusses certain aspects of Beauvoir's novel in his *War Diary* without explicitly referring to it. For example, Sartre's discussion of time is clearly inspired by his reading of the draft manuscript of Beauvoir's *She Came to Stay* in February 1940. In his *War Diary* entry dated February 19, he writes:

> The future is the world. A for-itself, whatever it may be, grasps an aspect of the world only as an opportunity to annihilate in the in-itself the lack that it itself is. Whatever the object considered may be, it is a plea to the for-itself to project itself beyond it as *causa sui*. Were it an armchair that "stretches out its arms to us," to have the project of sitting down in it is to project oneself into that armchair as the existent which has determined itself to exist as seated in an armchair, and which will exist as seated with the plenitude of the in-itself. (*WD*, 214–15;[26] *CG*, 444)

Near the beginning of *She Came to Stay*, Beauvoir describes a similar scene in a deserted theatre:

> The safety-curtain was down; the walls smelled of fresh paint; the red-plush seats were lined up in their rows, motionless and expectant. A moment ago they had been aware of nothing. Now she was there and they held out their arms. (*SCS*, 12; *Inv*, 12)

Although Sartre's comments above in his *War Diary* concerning the relationship between consciousness and the world of objects were clearly inspired by his reading of Beauvoir's nighttime description of the theatre, what is particularly interesting is the way he interprets her work. Inevitably, Sartre read Beauvoir's text, as all readers do, through the prism of his own subjectivity. The result is that his reading of the novel tends to be somewhat idiosyncratic. Beauvoir's "Hegelian" starting point in *She Came to Stay* is that consciousness finds certainty of itself in its unity with an object. The world "belongs" to Françoise because she confers unity and meaning to it. In contrast, Sartre interprets the above scene purely in terms of his own evolving phenomenological framework. Profoundly influenced by Husserl, Sartre expands on his evolving thesis, fully developed in *Being and Nothingness,* which posits the relationship between consciousness and its transcendental object as one of *lack* and *negation.* Consciousness is a project of being; it seeks to negate itself as lack through a projected union with the world of objects; the *in-itself.* However, for Sartre the project of being is doomed to failure since consciousness, as freedom, must always remain transcendent to the world. On the contrary, Beauvoir, in the above scene, demonstrates through the character of Françoise, Hegel's thesis of the essential *unity* of consciousness and the world. The chairs belong to Françoise because she has conferred meaning on them; they exist uniquely for her: "She exercised this power: her presence revived things from their inanimateness" (*SCS,* 12; *Inv,* 12).

Sartre's *War Diary* is not the only place where he attempts to interpret Beauvoir's text. In his correspondence to Beauvoir, his reference to Françoise's "obsessive fear" as the basis for a theory of temporality (*QMW,* 61; *LC,* 77) is again framed in reference to his own work: it in no way reflects an appropriation of the Hegelian dialectical temporality that underpins the structure of *She Came to Stay.* In this sense, at least, although it certainly could be argued that Beauvoir's novel inspired Sartre to begin to formulate a theory of temporality, we should not accuse Sartre of some sort of blatant plagiarism. Clearly, the "theory" of temporality glimpsed by Sartre in *She Came to Stay* is reformulated in terms of his earlier work begun in *The Transcendence of the Ego* and fully developed in *Being and Nothingness* as the brusque upsurge of consciousness that continually negates the past in its flight toward the future. I have previously argued, in fact, that *She Came to Stay* offers a parody and critique of Sartre's theory of temporality as analyzed in *Being and Nothingness.*[27] In this respect, I would argue that *Being and Nothingness* represents the culmination of his early period of philosophy rather than a radically new departure that began with his reading of Beauvoir's manuscript during February 1940.

Nevertheless, it is certain that Sartre read *She Came to Stay* as a complex metaphysical text. In a letter to Beauvoir dated 8 May 1940, he comments, "your little novel is *excellent*" (*QMW,* 174; *LC,* 2:212). However, we should be wary of falling into the trap of assuming that there is simply "one" existential philosophy principally articulated in *Being and Nothingness* and that consequently its intellectual property rights must be somehow disputed between Sartre and Beauvoir, with Beauvoir in this instance being the "originator" of Sartre's philosophy. What I want to argue is that an effect of *différance,* both as differentiation and as deferral, takes place between the writing of *She Came to Stay* and *Being and Nothingness.* In this sense, the two texts must be studied both together and separately. Sartre uses Beauvoir's literary text, and in particular her handling of the Master-Slave relationship, as a *supplément* to the development of his own thought in *Being and Nothingness* in the sense discussed earlier, namely, both "adding to" and "replacing" the philosophical text.

The latter is certainly no mimetic representation of the former. Sartre's primary concern to protect his own philosophical autonomy meant that he remained anxious to differentiate his thought from that of Hegel in *Being and Nothingness.* Indeed, at various stages in his life, and with various interlocutors, Sartre always maintained that *Being and Nothingness* was not Hegelian. In an interview with Michel Contat, he commented that he only studied Hegel seriously after World War II with the publication of Jean Hyppolite's study of Hegel's *Phenomenology of Spirit.*[28] In other words, he claimed that he only began to seriously study Hegel at least three years *after* the publication of *Being and Nothingness.* In a further interview with Michel Rybalka, he remarked that although he had a certain knowledge of Hegel, he did not think that there was any dialectic at all in *Being and Nothingness,* although certain parts resembled it.[29]

Nevertheless, I think we must draw an important distinction between Sartre's references to the lack of a dialectic in *Being and Nothingness* and his further claim that the work is not Hegelian. The absence of any dialectic does not necessarily mean in itself that there is no Hegelian influence in this work, although it is likely that Sartre's rather hurried reading of Hegel during the period of composition of *Being and Nothingness* would lead him not to recognize the full extent of the Hegelian influence on this work. Clearly, in this work Sartre was influenced by his reading of Hegel, and specifically a reading of Hegel mediated in the first instance via Beauvoir.[30]

In *Being and Nothingness,* Sartre's main objection is to Hegelian idealism, specifically (as he reads Hegel) to the abstract universality of *Geist* (mind/spirit). Crucially, in this work he links the evolution of human consciousness in the *Phenomenology* with the overriding principle of self-identity ("I am I").[31] This particular approach to Hegel gives Sartre the immediate advantage of easily being able to differentiate his own thought from, as he sees it, the transcendental idealism of the *Phenomenology* that culminates in Hegel's intuition of absolute knowledge as knowledge of the divine. For the early Sartre, as he makes clear many times in *Being and Nothingness,* consciousness is never self-identical; its being is *not* to be what it is.[32]

Furthermore, in contradistinction to Hegel's description of a human consciousness, which has to fight to establish its autonomy and the truth of its existence, for Sartre the essential freedom of consciousness is already a *given.* Unlike Beauvoir's "Hegelian" model of consciousness in *She Came to Stay,* Sartrean consciousness is not dialectically mediated. It originates in the autonomy of the pre-reflective *cogito.* This is a long-held view, first analyzed in his early essay on Husserlian phenomenology, *The Transcendence of the Ego*—a view that he appears to cling to stubbornly throughout the text of *Being and Nothingness* and beyond.[33] He is certainly not prepared to abandon this position to accommodate a more recent reading of Hegel.

However, while Sartre will refuse Hegel's "brilliant intuition," as he calls it, that the Other can determine me in my being-for-others, it is certain that the section in *Being and Nothingness* entitled "Concrete Relations with Others" is closely modeled on his reading of the Master-Slave dialectic in *She Came to Stay.* Explicitly taking up a discussion of the Hegelian epigraph to Beauvoir's novel, he declares: "What I want to attain symbolically by pursuing the death of a particular Other is the general principle of the existence of others."[34] His implicit reading of Beauvoir's text includes an analysis of the failure of the love project and the transformation of this project into sadism and masochism. He concludes that to hate one Other is to hate all others; a reading that potentially distorts the place Beauvoir accords to reciprocal relationships in *She Came to Stay.*[35]

However, Sartre is also keen to distance his thought from Beauvoir's reworking of the Master-Slave relation. He certainly has no intention of being *her* disciple. In particular, he has severe reservations concerning the legitimacy of the ending of the novel (the murder of Xavière by Françoise), a criticism that will be later implicitly taken up by Jacques Lacan, and one that Beauvoir herself is only too willing to accept.[36] Hate, Sartre claims, is a failure, since even if I abolish the Other, I can never alter the fact that he has existed. Indeed, the triumph of hate is the explicit recognition that the Other has existed. Ultimately, I can never be free of the Other since he contaminates me by forming a part of my Being-for-Others. He carries the key of my alienation to his grave. His death can never enable me to transcend the circle of conflict in my relations with the Other; it merely represents the final attempt of despair from where I re-enter the circle (*BN,* 533; *EN,* 453).[37]

Nevertheless, in spite of these reservations, Sartre is clearly already at ease in *Being and Nothingness* discussing the dialectical framework of Beauvoir's novel. He claims that my being-alienated is a "real enslavement": an oblique reference to Françoise's experience of becoming a Hegelian Slave-figure through her alienation in Xavière's eyes at the end of the novel.[38] However, after analyzing the Master-Slave relationship in this work, he can still declare at the end of the volume that "the slave in chains is as free as his master" (*BN,* 703; *EN,* 594). This is why he is so dubious about the veracity of any Master-Slave relationship, since in this scenario the freedom of self-consciousness is continually put into play. I would argue that this is the essential point of separation between the early Sartre and Beauvoir. For Beauvoir, self-consciousness on the Hegelian model is mediated via the Other, whereas in *Being and Nothingness* Sartre cannot accept that the Other can determine me in my being-for-others.

On Sartre's reading of Hegel, my being-for-others is fatefully reduced to my being-as-an-object for the Other.[39] The danger with Hegel's approach, as far as Sartre is concerned, is that it leads perilously close to the solipsist position that he is so anxious to avoid. Hegel, he claims, transforms my "being-for-others" as an object into a relation of knowledge. I am as the Other knows me to be. This knowledge is the truth of self-consciousness that can only be established by my being an object for the Other.

As Sartre comments, "the Other is of interest to me only to the extent that he is another Me, a Me-object for Me, and conversely to the extent that he reflects my Me—i.e. is, in so far as I am an object for him" (*BN,* 320; *EN,* 275). Hegel would no doubt counter this objection by affirming that self-consciousness, at this stage in the *Phenomenology,* can only exist "for-itself" to the extent that it is recognized by another. This process of acknowledgment is far from being unequivocal; it embraces "many and varied meanings."[40] However, from the beginning of his analysis, Sartre is anxious to avoid any pluralistic or ambiguous reading of Hegel's text. In terms of the Master-Slave relation, it is clear that he has specifically identified himself with the "Master." The Other remains the inessential consciousness who never becomes essential: "He is the *Slave* I am the *Master*" (*BN,* 321; *EN,* 276). What Sartre appears to reject in Hegel's analysis is that I could be in any way dependent on another self-consciousness for the truth of my being. On his analysis, this is the final outcome of the Master-Slave relation. The Other determines the truth of who I am. Hegel, claims Sartre, has reduced my being to the Other's knowledge of me. But in order for the Other to know me, I must become an object for the Other and therefore an "inessential" or slave-like consciousness—a position that is unacceptable to him.

The Question of the "Look" in *Being and Nothingness*

Sartre's theory of the "Look" is not, as several critics have argued, his reformulation of the Master-Slave relation.[41] Nevertheless, as Debra Bergoffen argues, "anonymous dynamics of perception are aligned with Hegelian accounts of power and desire."[42] Jean-François Louette argues that the petrifying "Look," or gaze of the omniscient Other, is explored in Sartre's short story "The Childhood of a Leader."[43] There are, however, also traces of an embryonic theory of the "Look" in *Nausea*, where Roquentin already speaks of "the power of my gaze" (*N*, 115; *Nfr*, 114), which is linked to the rape and subsequent murder of little Lucienne. However, Roquentin's subject status is potentially threatened by the "Look" of the (non-Hegelian) other as an alienating, petrifying gaze (*N*, 97; *Nfr*, 97). In his *War Diary*, Sartre sketches out a metaphysical base for this theory that is founded on his deep-seated desire for an inhuman, merciless self-introspection.[44]

In *Being and Nothingness*, the anonymous inhumanity of the "Look" is not just its origin in "two ocular globes" (*BN*, 346; *EN*, 297). The "Look" of the Other *masks* their eyes, which are perceived as neither beautiful nor ugly. The male "Look" is a power relation to the outside world. It is pure *jouissance*, a rape of the virginal object that has not yet given up the secret of its existence.[45] Sartre's theory of the "Look" also reveals a fundamental aspect of our "being-for-others." The "Look" of the Other makes me realize a relation to myself which is that of "being-seen." I am no longer a pure consciousness that exists for-itself. I have suddenly become transformed into an object in another's perceptual field. Clearly, in this scenario the Other who looks at me has the potential to become a quasi-Master figure. He alienates the essence of the self that I am through his gaze, brusquely revealing to me the outside of myself that is my "being-for-others."

Sartre's account of the "Look" enables him to transcend the Master-Slave scenario. His description of the violent (because nonreciprocal) power struggle of the purified "Look" is his metaphysical "reply" to Hegel, reflecting his preferred philosophical terrain in *Being and Nothingness*, which is that of the polemic, not the dialectic. This struggle precludes any final dialectical term on the Hegelian model since the Sartrean subject (the looker) could never experience himself simultaneously as an object. This interpretation would appear to confirm Sartre's later comment that "there is no dialectic at all" in this work. Although the "Look" of the Other may alienate me in my being (and so potentially reduce me to a Slave-like figure), Sartre asserts, the existence of the Other is also *dependent* on my own consciousness. In this quasi-Master role, I summon the Other into existence through recourse to the *cogito*: the individual act of self-reflective consciousness. It alone, he argues, can reveal to me the existence of other people in the world.[46]

In his account of the "Look," unlike Hegel's account of the Master-Slave relationship in the *Phenomenology*, there is no resolution to the problem of other consciousnesses. To posit a resolution, argues Sartre, would be to deny the scandal of the plurality of consciousnesses, which must necessarily *fracture* the dialectic. So rather than a type of totalizing, teleological movement progressing through different "shapes" of consciousness, what the reader encounters in the Sartrean text is the image of an infernal cycle in our relationship to the individualized Other. This is his implicit answer to the problem of Hegel's idealism manifested in the harmonious reconciliation of identical consciousnesses.

For Sartre, consciousness as absolute is not determined by another self-consciousness. This does not mean, however, that this self-consciousness has infinite freedom. The absolute consciousness still has certain boundaries, since it may be limited by another self-consciousness. In this way Sartre hopes to refute the solipsistic attitude while at the same time distancing his thought from that of Hegel.

This attitude is exemplified in Sartre's analysis of the keyhole scene in *Being and Nothingness*. The unseen presence of the Other who looks at me peering through the keyhole may brusquely reveal my "being-for-others" to me in the form of shame as I am caught "in the act." In this instance, argues Sartre (in a deliberate attempt to distance his thought from that of Hegel), my relationship with the Other as subject is not one of *knowledge*, but rather one of being (*BN*, 349–50; *EN*, 300). The Other makes me *live* the situation of my "being-for-others." However, s/he does not have the power to fix me as an object who lives permanently in the mode of my "being-for-others." I can regain my "being-for-itself" when I transcend the objective presence of others (through an act of internal negation) and realize that I am responsible for their existence. In this (ideal) scenario they remain on the outside of my consciousness, as intentional objects of perception, since ultimately, my "being-for-others" is entirely derivative of my "being-for-itself."

It is here that we come to one of the main areas of interaction between Sartrean and Hegelian thought. It concerns Sartre's objection, as he sees it, to Hegelian idealism. He considers the Master-Slave relation to be unsatisfactory to the extent that the self-consciousness of the Master is ultimately dependent on the "inessential" and "fearful" consciousness of the Slave. Yet for Hegel, the Master gains the truth of self-certainty only through the recognition of *himself* in the consciousness of the Slave. In this respect, the dialectic as a metaphor for intersubjective relationships is not simply a relation between self and Other; it is also a relation of self to self. The Master and the Slave are part of the *same* consciousness. The Other does not determine me in my being or "know" me as much as s/he permits me to "know" myself.

It is this aspect of Hegel's thought that Beauvoir had explored in depth in *She Came to Stay*. In *The Second Sex*, Beauvoir will challenge Sartre's implicit adoption of the "Master" position in *Being and Nothingness* and his critique of her portrayal of the Master-Slave relationship. Once more she will turn to the Hegelian dialectic, which, as in her first novel, she will use as a methodological tool in order to help her investigate the historic oppression of women.

Reworking the Master-Slave Dialectic: From *She Came to Stay* to *The Second Sex*

In conversation with her biographer Deirdre Bair in 1982, Beauvoir commented that by the autumn of 1946 when she began thinking seriously about the issue of gender that was to form the basis of her thinking in *The Second Sex*, "I had not yet settled on the idea of woman as the other—that was to come later . . . none of this was clear to me. It was somewhere in my head. Oh, I hate to use that word 'unconscious,' because if you write it feminist women will pounce on me, but I can't think of another, better word, so it will have to do."[47] However, Beauvoir's idea of woman as Hegelian Other, symbolized in the character of Xavière, was already firmly established in her mind from 1940 onward, when she first started to read the *Phenomenology*—at least five years *before* she started writing *The Second Sex*. This view unfortunately leads to the inescapable conclusion that Beauvoir lied to her biographer in order to conceal the truth of the Hegelian influence on *She Came to Stay*.

The common thread that links *She Came to Stay* with *The Second Sex* is the way in which Beauvoir reworks Hegel's account of the Master-Slave relation in the *Phenomenology* to take account of women's degradation as the "inessential consciousness." Although the progress of the Hegelian dialectic through its various stages, including Stoicism, Skepticism, and the Unhappy Consciousness, is largely concealed in *She Came to Stay* and only briefly scrutinized in *The Ethics of Ambiguity*,[48] Beauvoir makes explicit reference to it throughout *The Second Sex*, where she builds on the insights gained from her earlier understanding of Hegel. In the introduction to *The Second Sex*, Beauvoir states that the category of otherness "is as primordial as consciousness itself" and has been an integral part of human thought from the dawn of civilization. Furthermore, claims the author, the category of alterity, or otherness existed prior to any division of the sexes.[49] This is a crucial part of her argument concerning the situation of women in society. Women are not a priori the Other or the Slave figure; they have been historically constituted as Other. Implicitly following Hegel, she argues that to be Other or female is to be the "inessential consciousness" in contrast to the man who has set himself up as the "essential" or sovereign consciousness.

Nancy Bauer, in her book *Simone de Beauvoir, Philosophy and Feminism*, rightly challenges the simplistic view that Beauvoir merely appropriates "Sartre's" Hegel. She argues that "Beauvoir's appropriation in *The Second Sex* of the so-called master-slave dialectic in Hegel's *Phenomenology of Spirit* . . . takes place in the light of her dissatisfactions with Sartre's taking up of the dialectic in *Being and Nothingness*."[50] Bauer's approach marks an important step forward in critically evaluating the philosophical relationship between Sartre and Beauvoir. However, the main problem with an approach that interprets Beauvoir's philosophy as essentially reactive to Sartre's is the fact that it fails to take into account that it was Beauvoir, rather than Sartre, who first appropriated Hegel's Master-Slave dialectic in her novel *She Came to Stay*. In this respect, as we have already seen, it is Sartre's handling of the dialectic in *Being and Nothingness* that is reactive to his implicit reading of Beauvoir's novel.

Beauvoir's initial approach to transposing the Master-Slave relation to the problematic area of gender relations is her view that the dual structure "male-female" contains within it the seeds of conflict and oppression, since she claims that wherever there is a duality (Self-Other) there must inevitably be conflict. Human consciousness, she argues, contains within itself a fundamental hostility toward every other consciousness: "The subject can be posed only in being opposed—he sets himself up as the essential, as opposed to the other, the inessential, the object. But the other consciousness, the other ego, sets up a reciprocal claim" (*SS*, xvii; *DS* I, 17).

In *The Second Sex* as much as in *She Came to Stay*, Beauvoir is primarily interested in the dialectic as a process rather than as merely a product. The dialectical journey is important because it has enabled her to understand herself as much as it has enabled her to know the Other. The author explains this process at the beginning of the section entitled "Myths" in volume one. "Once the subject begins to affirm himself," she contends, "the Other, who limits and denies him, is none the less a necessity to him: he attains himself only through that reality which he is not, which is something other than himself" (*SS*, 139; *DS* I, 237).

Whereas Sartre, in *Being and Nothingness*, will deny that the Other is necessary to me as determining my being-for-itself, Beauvoir affirms that this is one of the most fundamental truths of the Master-Slave relationship. Her description of female oppression is the absolute antithesis of Sartre's description of the imperialistic male consciousness that can reduce the Other to a mere image or negate him through an act of pure indifference.

However, in the transposition of the Master-Slave relation to the field of gender relations, Beauvoir encounters several difficulties. As Bauer points out, she resists the simplistic solution that would make the man the Master figure in relation to the woman as Slave. Nevertheless, Beauvoir contends that patriarchal society confirms masculine sovereignty. Furthermore, throughout her essay she refers to certain women as "vassals," and at the end of her essay, Beauvoir contends that women have inherited a "long tradition of enslavement."

In order to explain this anomaly, I would argue that what we see in *The Second Sex* is a thoroughgoing transformative approach to Beauvoir's reading of Hegel. She certainly has no intention of placing him in the Master position above herself as mere disciple. What I am going to argue lies at the heart of her relationship to Hegel in this text is the way she reworks the dialectic in the field of gender relations, viewing it as essentially an ambiguous metaphysical construct. Throughout the text we see her playing with these ambiguities and dissociating certain terms, such as the "inessential consciousness" from the Hegelian framework, letting them work and stand in isolation from it.

Whereas in her novel *She Came To Stay*, the figures of Slave and female Other are merged into one character, Xavière, in *The Second Sex* they are differentiated. This approach to Beauvoir's understanding of the Master-Slave conflict marks a critical stage in the evolution of her relationship to Hegel. To be Other is no longer to be an oppressed Slave. This is, however, not to argue that Beauvoir has ceased to be influenced by Hegel, as her full-frontal denouncement of his "rationalist delirium" might indicate. In Part One of the first volume of *The Second Sex*, for example, in the section entitled "Destiny," Beauvoir deplores Hegel's bias toward ready-made values and dialectical structures. In this respect her position appears to echo Sartre's objections in *Being and Nothingness* to Hegel's "ontological idealism" and its pyramidal structure of absolute knowledge. However, unlike Sartre, Beauvoir's main objection to Hegel is not that he equates being with knowledge, but rather that he assumes the primacy of reason or logic as a basis for his philosophical system.

A significant difference between Beauvoir's approach to Hegel in *The Second*

Sex and Sartre's approach in *Being and Nothingness* is that Beauvoir, unlike Sartre, views Hegel's description of consciousness, not as an abstract theoretical model (the I=I of self-consciousness), but as embodying a truth of lived experience. Beauvoir, however, is also anxious to avoid the potential pitfall of a naïve and simplistic analogy that would transform the male into a "Master" and the woman into a "Slave" within a dialectic of oppression. The task is a difficult one. In *The Second Sex*, as the title of this work implies, Beauvoir remains within the Hegelian framework that conceptualizes a metaphysical difference between self and Other, subject and object.

Women *are* the "second sex" to the extent that a woman's identity can only be established in terms of her "otherness" or essential difference from the male. In other words, historically, women have been defined as essentially relative to men.

In order to solve the problem of the male "Master"/female "Slave" analogy, what I want to argue is that Beauvoir undertakes an implicit full-scale deconstructive approach to the dialectic in which we can trace the infinite movement of *différance* between Hegel's text and her own. What is significant in Beauvoir's reworking of Hegel is that throughout *The Second Sex*, Beauvoir, unlike Hegel, differentiates between the "inessential" or dependent consciousness and the position of the Slave. To be an "inessential" consciousness does not mean, in fact, that one is a priori a Slave. This "splitting up" of phenomenological terms is a major departure from Hegel's dialectical framework. It forms an important part of the solution to Beauvoir's earlier criticism of Hegel that he was too intent on formulating "ready-made" dialectical structures. For Beauvoir, the male-female relationship is based on a fractured dialectic, or as Sartre might term it, a dialectic with holes in it, because it resists Hegel's universalizing framework.

Her metaphysics of gender *difference* challenges the closure of the Hegelian system of the *Phenomenology* with its finite sequence of dialectically mediated stages of spirit. Her discourse remains centered at a fundamental Hegelian level in terms of the potential for conflict between the sexes. But her analysis does not stop here. The fracturing of the dialectic facilitates Beauvoir's task in *The Second Sex*, which is to attempt to reconcile the fact of women's oppression throughout history (which would assimilate her a priori with the "Slave" position), while at the same time effectively denying that women *are* Slaves in relation to men as Masters. In order to achieve this goal, she brackets, à la Husserl, the inexorable progress of the dialectic. A part of her genius in the reworking of the Master-Slave relationship in terms of gender relations has been to isolate the terms "Master" and "Slave" and make them absolute and non-relational. The man as Master or "essential consciousness" stands in radical, non-reciprocal opposition to the woman as the "inessential consciousness."

This "Sartrean" step is necessary because Beauvoir argues that women have been enclosed within a sphere of immanence and complicity with men, which has effectively precluded their participation in any struggle for recognition, let alone any "fight to the death!" In this sense, their historic situation is not comparable to the position of Hegel's Slave. In fact, although Beauvoir does not explicitly make this point, a woman may be potentially *more* disadvantaged and oppressed than Hegel's Slave, since she has never had the opportunity to transcend her situation and become the "essential consciousness" who, on the Sartrean model, lives "for-herself" (*pour soi*).

However, the major problem with Beauvoir's adaptation of Hegel's Master-Slave relationship is that she seems, almost imperceptibly at times, to assimilate a theoretical discussion of the dialectic with the situation of actual masters and slaves.[51] This is a potentially dangerous approach that is fraught with theoretical complexities. Certainly, at the time of the writing of the *Phenomenology,* actual slavery was still widespread. Yet Hegel does not relate the life experience of masters and slaves (a relationship based on material oppression) with his discussion of the Master-Slave relation. The latter is analyzed as a privileged textual/literary motif that illustrates a stage in the development of autonomous self-consciousness. A slave is in essence a person who is neither autonomous nor free, nor who has any potential to be free. The danger of assimilating a theoretical with a lived model is that the analogy may appear naïve, which is why Beauvoir is so keen in places to differentiate the situation of women from that of actual slaves.

Yet to base this distinction on the concept of alterity is a high-risk strategy. In Hegel's discussion of the Master-Slave relation, for example, he claims that the Slave finds freedom through work; an actual slave does not. Beauvoir's analysis at times tacitly conflates one position with the other. The result is often hesitation on her part as to the extent to which women may or may not be compared to actual slaves. In volume one of *The Second Sex,* Beauvoir claims that women are, if not man's "slave," then at least his "vassal."[52] Yet in volume two, the author links both prostitution and marriage (as a form of prostitution) to women's "slave" status.[53] This hesitation, which might be taken for a certain ambivalence with regard to women's position in society, has tended to confuse critics, who either see Beauvoir as forming an analogy between women and slaves or see Beauvoir as differentiating women from the position of Hegel's Slave. In fact, in her consideration of gender relationships, she is both forming the basis of a metaphysical analogy with Hegel's dialectic of oppression and, at the same time, trying to maintain some critical distance from his (as she sees it) abstract model of universal thought. For example, in his description of the Master-Slave relation in the *Phenomenology*, Hegel never asks how other self-consciousnesses are encountered, and he considers conflict as an inevitable part of the formation of an individuated, autonomous self-consciousness. Beauvoir both questions and expands on his analysis in *The Second Sex*.

In order to achieve this goal, she will attempt to intercalate Heidegger's idea of the human *Mitsein* (Being-with) with Hegel's notion of the *"reciprocal self-surrender"* of consciousnesses[54] in dialectic of reciprocity as the highest ethical form of intersubjective relationship. For Beauvoir, the *Mitsein* may exist between individuals and social groups, and she states explicitly in her introduction to *The Second Sex* that it is a relationship based on solidarity and friendship.[55]

Reciprocity and the "Look" in *The Second Sex*

Sartre, in *Being and Nothingness*, will reject Heidegger's concept of the *Mitsein* and claim that conflict is the basis of our relation to the Other.[56] A significant aspect of Beauvoir's "reply" to him in *The Second Sex* concerns her need to establish an ethical basis for gender relationships that is capable of transcending this model. In Part One of *The Second Sex*, the author outlines her response to Sartre's position: a dialectic founded on the mutual recognition of self-consciousnesses in friendship and generosity.[57]

> It is possible to rise above this conflict if each individual freely recognizes the other, each regarding himself and the other simultaneously as object and as subject in a reciprocal manner. But friendship and generosity, which alone permit in actuality this recognition of free beings, are not facile virtues; they are assuredly man's highest achievement, and through that achievement he is to be found in his true nature. But this true nature is that of a struggle unceasingly begun, unceasingly abolished; it requires man to outdo himself at every moment. (*SS*, 140; *DS* I, 238)

As in *She Came to Stay*, Beauvoir will use the Husserlian *épochè* to bracket or suspend the movement of the dialectic.[58] Her objective is the maintenance of a type of dialectical tension that she sees as the foundation of an authentic intersubjective relationship. This relationship is never given a priori; it has to be continually striven for. For Hegel, reciprocal self-surrender is one fleeting moment in the dialectical process. For Beauvoir, on the contrary, the maintenance of this position is the unsurpassable goal of our "being-for-others."

Developing her argument begun in *The Ethics of Ambiguity,* Beauvoir claims that each human freedom is sustained and completed in the Other. This claim is directly at odds with Sartre's description of the inhuman male "Look," with its negation of otherness and its implicit Master status. To this description, Beauvoir juxtaposes the necessity of a frank and unbiased interchange between the sexes, which bypasses the need for any judgmental "Look." As far as the author is concerned, a woman's "Look," in comparison to that of a man, has no "abstract severity."[59] In fact, in relation to the male, she is often required to fulfill the role of a narcissistic mirror, to reflect his own image. In this respect, her "Look" is crucial to the male project of self-affirmation, and it is here that Beauvoir implicitly contests Sartre's depiction of the perpetual self-alienation in the gaze of the Other. The female "Look" is not inhuman: it is confirmed in the presence of "two living eyes" (*SS,* 185; *DS* I, 302).

Beauvoir's transformative approach to Sartre's theory of the "Look" draws much inspiration from her reading of literature. She finds the ideal of reciprocal recognition in the work of both Stendhal and Malraux. Malraux's depiction in *Man's Estate* (*La Condition humaine*) of the reciprocal relationship between Kyo Gisors and May, in many ways, is reminiscent of the reciprocal relationship existing between Françoise and Gerbert and also between Françoise and Pierre in *She Came to Stay.* In Malraux's implicit dialogue with Sartre's conflictual model of the "Look" in this passage, Gisors comments,

> In the eyes of others, I am what I have done. . . . But to May alone he was not what he had done; and to him alone she was something quite other than her biography. . . . Men are not my fellows, they are persons who look upon me and judge me; my fellows are those who love me and do not look upon me, who love me regardless of everything . . . me and not what I have done or shall do. (*SS,* 185; *DS* I, 302)

"What makes the attitude of Kyo human and moving," claims Beauvoir, "is that it implies reciprocity and that he asks May to love him as he is, not to send back a fawning reflection" (*SS,* 185; *DS* I, 302). For Beauvoir, Malraux's account gives us an all-too-rare glimpse of the possibility of an authentic reciprocal relationship between a man and woman—one based on mutual understanding, trust, and respect.

Some Concluding Remarks

A study of Sartre's and Beauvoir's approach to reading Hegel throws into relief both the philosophical similarities and the differences between them.

Sartre, although keen to measure his distance from Hegel in *Being and Nothingness*, nevertheless adopts an implicit Master position with regard to the absolute, negating power of the "for-itself" in this work. Beauvoir in *The Second Sex*, on the contrary, analyses the Master-Slave relation from the perspective of the female who has historically incarnated certain characteristics of Hegel's Slave.

However, in the third volume of her autobiography, *The Force of Circumstance*, Beauvoir reflects that the Hegelian framework of *The Second Sex* based on the a priori categories of male-subject and female-Other was too idealistic, and that with hindsight she would have introduced a more materialistic framework. She refers to the Sartrean concepts of need and scarcity that he introduces in the *Critique of Dialectical Reason*.[60] Beauvoir maintains that this modification would not have affected the development of volume two of *The Second Sex*. Yet I have argued that the Hegelian distinction between self and Other permeates the entirety of the work. It posits what Derrida, after Bataille, would term the "restricted economy" of the *Phenomenology*, which retains the metaphysical horizon of already-anticipated meanings. Specifically, in relation to our reading of *The Second Sex*, this concerns the notion of female alterity as an already-given category of human existence. By supplementing Heidegger's *Mitsein* with the Hegelian idea of conflict and alterity, Beauvoir reinforces the binary oppositions self/Other, Master/Slave that she attacks.

In 1948, as Beauvoir was completing *The Second Sex*, Sartre published his well-known essay, *What Is Literature?* What is particularly striking in this work is the evolution of his thought concerning a privileged intersubjective relationship: that existing between a writer and his reader. The latter could well have been depicted in terms of his theory of the "Look," but he is not. The subject-object duality that had characterized the alienation of human relationships in *Being and Nothingness* is now replaced by a dialectic of reciprocity. In many ways Sartre's account of the relationship between writer and reader, who together realize a type of metaphysical absolute, reflects Beauvoir's depiction in *The Second Sex* of "the happy couple": the lovers who freely give themselves to the other, and in whom each freedom is mutually sustained and confirmed.

It is certain that both the Hegelian construction of Beauvoir's first novel, *She Came To Stay*, and her analysis of women's oppression in *The Second Sex* had a major impact on the development of Sartre's thought. His re-engagement with Hegel is clearly in evidence in his posthumously published *Notebooks for an Ethics* and in the later texts *Saint Genet* and the *Critique of Dialectical Reason*. This is, of course, not to argue that Sartre merely "stole" her ideas, or that she "adopted" his, but rather that each author as subject was engaged in a complex interchange, a reworking and questioning of ideas which as a process of *différance* would preclude any final dialectical term or synthesis of view. The questioning, like the conversations of Sartre's play *No Exit,* would remain open-ended.

Notes

1. Toril Moi, *Simone de Beauvoir;* Lundgren-Gothlin, *Sex and Existence;* Bauer, *Simone de Beauvoir, Philosophy and Feminism.*

2. Foucault, *Préface à la Transgression,* 195–96.

3. See Tidd, *Simone de Beauvoir, Gender and Testimony,* 16, for an interesting discussion of a metaphysical approach to the fictional text.

4. "The supplement supplements. It adds only to replace. It intervenes or insinuates itself *in-the-place-of*" (Derrida, *Acts of Literature,* 83).

5. See Derrida, "From Restricted to General Economy," in "Writing and Difference" (London: Routledge, 1978), 251–77. In this essay, Derrida makes the point that Hegel's dialectic corresponds to a "restricted economy" in that it is concerned with an analysis of "already anticipated" meanings that remain tied, or locked into, the logic of the logos, which he associates with a chain of linked concepts: reason, meaning, lordship, and presence. In comparison, the "space of writing" exceeds the logos of the philosophical text since it does not remain fixed to any interpretative framework.

6. Derrida, *Acts of Literature,* 37.

7. Ibid., 50.

8. See Derrida's discussion of *différance* and the Hegelian dialectic in his *Marges de la philosophie,* 3–29. See also Howells, *Derrida,* 50–52, for a useful discussion of *différance,* and Bennington, *Jacques Derrida,* 70–84, for a detailed discussion of this term.

9. Derrida, *Margins of Philosophy,* trans. Alan Bass (Hemel Hempstead: Harvester Wheatsheaf, 1982), 3; *Marges,* 4.

10. "Chaque conscience poursuit la mort de l'autre" (*Inv*).

11. Moi, *Simone de Beauvoir,* 106.

12. Vintges, *Philosophy as Passion,* 137.

13. Bauer, *Simone de Beauvoir, Philosophy and Feminism,* 267.

14. In *The Prime of Life* this sentence is translated as: "I did not . . . know Hegel's phrase about all awareness seeking the death of the Other; I did not read it till 1940" (*PL,* 381; *FA,* 361). Unfortunately, Green mistranslates the French word *conscience* as 'awareness' instead of 'consciousness,' with the result that the metaphysical basis of Beauvoir's novel tends to become somewhat obscured in this passage.

15. See, for example, Beauvoir's comments in her third volume of autobiography, *La Force des choses:* "I have already said that I had no philosophical ambition. Sartre, in *Being and Nothingness,* had sketched a total description of existence whose value depended on his own situation. . . . We always discussed his attitudes together, and sometimes I influenced him. But it was through him that these problems, in all their urgency and all their subtlety, presented themselves to me. In this realm, I must talk about him in order to talk about us" (*FC,* 4; *FCh,* 15).

16. Bair, *Simone de Beauvoir* (London edition), 232.

17. Comments made at the annual conference of Society for Existential and Phenomenological Theory and Culture (EPTC) held in Toronto, Canada, May 2006.

18. "Each person seeks the death of the other. But the murder of the other implies risking one's own death" (my translation of: "Chacun cherche la mort de l'autre. Mais le meurtre de l'autre implique la mise en péril de sa propre vie" (Kojève, *Introduction à la lecture de Hegel*, 52).

19. There is no evidence that Beauvoir ever attended any of Kojève's lectures on the *Phenomenology* given at the École des Hautes Études in Paris during the 1930s. In this respect, we can only draw a certain parallel between the murder of the Slave-figure Xavière by the Master-figure Françoise at the end of *She Came to Stay*, and Kojève's interpretation of Hegel's Master-Slave dialectic in his lectures.

20. For an analysis of these forms of consciousness in *She Came to Stay*, see my article "Beauvoir's *L'Invitée*," 65–76.

21. Bair, *Simone de Beauvoir*, 381.

22. Interview reproduced in *Conversations with Jean-Paul Sartre*, 69–92; originally published in *L'Arc*, No. 61.

23. "By February 1940 she (Beauvoir) had written what would later amount to less than fifty pages of the printed text (of *She Came to Stay*), nor did she fully conceptualize it until Sartre's first leave in that month (February 1940). . . . The parts of the earliest draft of *She Came to Stay* that Beauvoir wanted Sartre to read during his leave did not concern her main character, Françoise, but were rather about Elisabeth . . ." (Bair, *Simone de Beauvoir*, 228). Since Elisabeth is a secondary character, Beauvoir appears to indicate in this interview with Bair that by the time Sartre began his army leave, she had barely had time to conceptualize any main ideas for her novel at all.

24. See Fullbrook and Fullbrook, *Simone de Beauvoir and Jean-Paul Sartre*, 125–31, for an interesting account of Beauvoir's alleged attempts to cover up the "philosophical system" in *She Came to Stay* and her further attempts to convince her biographer that she had barely begun her novel by the time of Sartre's February 1940 leave.

25. Comments made by Simons at the EPTC conference in Toronto, Canada, May 2006.

26. I am using the 1985 Pantheon Books edition.

27. See my article "Beauvoir's *L'Invitée*," 72–75.

28. Hyppolite, *Genèse et structure*.

29. Rybalka quoted in Schlipp, *Philosophy of Jean-Paul Sartre*, 9.

30. In a letter dated 13 July 1940, Beauvoir writes: "Then I read Hegel from 2 to 5 at the Nationale. I'm beginning to understand—it's at once interesting and irritating. I'm now on the *Phenomenology of Mind*, after which I'll move on to the *Logic*. Reflecting on him and Husserl, I've realized I'd forgotten a great deal of Husserl—so you can explain him to me again, while I'll expound Hegel to you" (*LS*, 325, *LSfr*, 2:169).

31. See *EN*, 278; *BN* 322–23. I am using the 1992 Washington Square Press edition. The particular difficulty associated with Sartre's reading of Hegel in *Being and Nothingness* is that nowhere in the *Phenomenology of Spirit* does Hegel present self-consciousness as a full plenitude of being, or self-identity (I=I). In Section B of the *Phenomenology*, Hegel writes of the development of consciousness: "As self-consciousness, it is movement; but since what it distinguishes from itself is *only itself as* itself, the difference, as an other-

ness, is *immediately superseded* for it; the difference *is not,* and *it* (self-consciousness) is only the motionless tautology of, 'I am I'; but since for it the difference does not have the form of *being,* it is *not* self-consciousness" (105).

32. See, for example, Sartre, *Being and Nothingness,* especially Part Two, Being-for-itself: "The being of consciousness does not coincide with itself" (*BN,* 120; *EN,* 110). Sartrean consciousness "is what it is not, and is not what it is," making any form of a priori self-identity impossible.

33. "(Sartre) was reading Husserl and writing his essay, 'The Transcendence of the Ego,' which appeared in 1936, in *Recherches philosophiques.* Here he outlined—in a Husserlian perspective, but contrary to some of Husserl's most recent theories—the relationship between the self and the conscious mind, and also established a distinction, which he was to maintain permanently, between the conscious mind and the psyche.... My ego . . . like the ego of any other person is by its nature a recognisable phenomenon. Herein lay the foundation of one of Sartre's earliest and most stubbornly held beliefs: the autonomy of the irrational mind [the pre-reflective consciousness]" (*PL,* 217–18; *FA,* 210). In this passage, Beauvoir appears to take her distance from Sartre's early distinction between the duality of consciousness and the ego, which he assimilates with the world of objects.

34. "[H]ate is the hate of all Others in one Other" (*BN,* 533; *EN,* 452).

35. Exemplified in the Françoise-Pierre and Françoise-Gerbert relationships.

36. Lacan, *Écrits, A Selection,* 8. Beauvoir discusses the perceived weakness of the ending of her novel at the end of *The Prime of Life:* "I was not satisfied with the ending of *She Came to Stay:* murder is not the solution to the difficulties engendered by co-existence" (*PL,* 733; *FA,* 694).

37. Sartre's play *Huis Clos* (*No Exit*) is an implicit reply to Beauvoir's novel *She Came to Stay.* Originally entitled The Others, it challenges the teleological construct of Beauvoir's novel by pointing to the futility of the murder of the Other. Sartre's play is structured around a triangular relationship similar to the one in *She Came to Stay,* since it involves two women and one man: Estelle, Inès, and Garcin. In *She Came to Stay,* Françoise, jealous of the attention given to Xavière by Pierre, succeeds in murdering her. However, in *No Exit,* Estelle is deprived of this solution to the problem of the Other. Since Inès is already dead, she cannot be killed:

> INÈS [struggling and laughing]: But, you crazy creature, what do you think you're doing? You know quite well I'm dead.
> ESTELLE: Dead?
> [She drops the knife. A pause, Inès picks up the knife and jabs herself with it regretfully.]
> INÈS: Dead! Dead! Knives, poison, ropes—all useless. It has happened already, do you understand? Once and for all. So here we are, forever. [Laughs.]
> ESTELLE [with a peal of laughter]: Forever. My God, how funny! Forever.
> (*Ex,* 47)

Whereas Françoise's murder of Xavière gives *She Came to Stay* a definitive ending, in *No Exit* there is no ending because there can be no death. Since all three characters are already dead they cannot die twice. All three are doomed to spend eternity together.

38. See *She Came to Stay:* "With horror Françoise saw the woman Xavière was confronting with blazing eyes, this woman who was herself" (*SCS,* 401; *Inv,* 499).

39. Sartre comments on Hegel's dialectic that the object of the Master-Slave relationship is for each consciousness to transform the certainty of his existence into truth: "We know that this truth can be attained only in so far as my consciousness becomes an *object* for the Other at the same time as the Other becomes an *object* for my consciousness. . . . Hegel does not even conceive of the possibility of a being-for-others which is not finally reducible to a 'being-as-object'" (*BN,* 322; *EN,* 277).

40. Hegel, *Phenomenology of Spirit,* 111.

41. See, for example, George Stack, *Sartre's Philosophy of Social Existence,* 36–38: "Sartre, *malgré lui* seems fascinated by Hegel's model of the Master-Slave relationship and seems to have been unable to transcend this dramatic model of the encounter of self with the other self."

42. Unpublished conference paper entitled "Bad Faith and *The Second Sex,*" given at the annual conference of the United Kingdom Society for Sartrean Studies (UKSSS), London, October 2006.

43. Louette, "La dialectique dans 'l'enfance d'un chef,'" 127.

44. "I strip out the man in me in order to place myself on the absolute ground of the impartial spectator; the arbiter. This spectator is the disincarnate, transcendental consciousness who looks at 'his man.' Whenever I judge myself, it's with the same severity with which I would judge others, but already I am escaping myself" (*CG,* 126; my translation).

45. "To see is to *deflower*" (*BN,* 738; *EN,* 624); Sartre's emphasis.

46. The "Look" as way out of the Master-Slave dialectic is developed in Sartre's later biographical study, *Baudelaire:* "The least thing, a change of mind, a mere look into the eyes of these idols would have been enough to make his chains fall at once to the ground" (*Bau,* 49; *BauFr,* 47). I am using the 1950 New Directions edition.

47. Bair, *Simone de Beauvoir,* 382.

48. "'Each consciousness,' said Hegel, 'seeks the death of the other.' And indeed at every moment others are stealing the whole world away from me. The first movement is to hate them" (*EA,* 70; *MA,* 89). I am using the 1947 Gallimard edition.

49. "The category of the *Other* is as primordial as consciousness itself. . . . This duality was not originally attached to the division of the sexes; it was not dependent upon any empirical facts" (*SS,* xvi; *DSI,* 16). I am using the 1964 Knopf edition for the English translations of *The Second Sex.*

50. Bauer, *Simone de Beauvoir, Philosophy and Feminism,* 79.

51. According to the author, the institution of marriage mediates the most concrete application of Hegel's Master-Slave relation. See *SS,* 425; *DS II,* 327.

52. "Now, woman has always been man's dependent, if not his slave" (*SS,* xx; *DS I,* 20).

53. See, for example, "the prostitute is denied the rights of a person, she sums up all the forms of feminine slavery at once" (*SS,* 556; *DS II,* 430).

54. Hegel, *Phenomenology of Spirit,* 134.

55. See *SS,* 17: Beauvoir's idealized account of Heidegger's *Mitsein* (Being-with) as human intersubjectivity based on solidarity and friendship is problematic. Heidegger states in his *Being and Time* (1927) that death, as Dasein's ownmost potentiality for be-

ing, individuates Dasein. In other words, Dasein exists authentically as non-relational; side by side with other Dasein (308, H.263). The "being-with" of Dasein does not automatically refer to any given act of solidarity and friendship; "being-with" may include the modes of indifference and antipathy.

56. "The essence of the relations between consciousnesses is not the *Mitsein*; it is conflict" (*BN*, 555; *EN*, 470).

57. A dialectic of reciprocity between Françoise and Pierre is first outlined by the author in her novel *She Came to Stay:*

> ". . . between us there's reciprocation." [Pierre]
> "How do you mean?"
> "The moment you acknowledge my conscience, you know that I acknowledge one in you, too." (*SCS*, 301, *Inv*, 376)

58. See the ending of *She Came to Stay* for Beauvoir's suspension of the temporal movement of the dialectic: "Time had stopped" (*SCS*, 401; *Inv*, 501).

59. "[H]er measuring gaze does not have the aloof severity of a masculine gaze, it is susceptible to charm" (*SS*, 184–185; *DS* I, 301).

60. "As for the content, I should take a more materialist position today in the first volume. I should base the notion of woman as other and the Manichaean argument it entails not on an idealistic and a priori struggle of consciences, but on the facts of supply and demand" (*FC*, 192; *FCh*, 2:267).

6   Beauvoir, Sartre, and Patriarchy's History of Ideas

Edward Fullbrook

In an interview with Alice Schwarzer in 1972, Simone de Beauvoir described the situation of the female intellectual when she was young:

> In my days there were fewer women who studied than nowadays. And, as the holder of a higher degree in philosophy, I was in a privileged position among women. In short, I made men recognize me: they were prepared to acknowledge in a friendly way a woman who had done as well as they had, because it was so exceptional.[1]

In 1973, in another interview with Schwarzer, Beauvoir observed the ugly transformations in men's attitudes as women slowly shed some elements of their oppression:

> Men have obviously changed. I think that the emancipation of women has actually made them more hostile towards women than they were; they have become more aggressive, more pushy, more sarcastic and more offensive, than they were in my time.[2]

Beauvoir spoke from bitter personal experience. Few women have suffered more than Beauvoir from the consequences of this shift in the tactics of sexism. Before the publication of *The Second Sex* in 1949, Beauvoir was recognized, celebrated, and read as an innovative philosopher on both sides of the Atlantic. But by the time of her death in 1986, Beauvoir was widely and aggressively characterized as a woman whose consciousness had never been violated by an original idea.

Beauvoir's Reputation before the Backlash

We need, therefore, to remind ourselves of Simone de Beauvoir's intellectual standing in the late 1940s, on the eve of the publication of *The Second Sex*.

At that time, appreciation of her powers of original and independent thought was especially strong in France, where after the Liberation in 1944, Beauvoir's philosophical essay *Pyrrhus et Cinéas* had been rushed into print. She wrote this book in direct opposition to Jean-Paul Sartre's notion of freedom. Her book was received with great enthusiasm and became, no less than Sartre's *Being and Nothingness,* a primary vehicle for the introduction of existentialist thought to French intellectual life.

Beauvoir followed this success with numerous philosophical essays in *Les Temps modernes.* In 1947 she traveled to the United States, where her reputation as an important new French philosopher had preceded her. Indeed, American universities eagerly opened their doors to her. In a period of three months, Beauvoir lectured on philosophy at twenty-three of America's leading institutions, including Harvard, Vassar, Yale, Princeton, and Berkeley. That same year she published *The Ethics of Ambiguity.* This book was immediately translated into English and ran through several printing runs. By contrast, Sartre's *Being and Nothingness* was not available to English readers until eight years later.

After the Backlash

But as Beauvoir grew older, recognition of her philosophical achievements was progressively withdrawn. After the publication of *The Second Sex,* and especially after it inspired and informed the next wave of the international feminist movement in the 1970s, Beauvoir became a significant target for antifeminist and anti-female sentiment.

Inevitably, her credibility as a thinker was undermined. To this end, she was portrayed repeatedly as Sartre's stooge. As Alice Schwarzer notes in one of her interviews with Beauvoir, there were even those who said it was really Sartre who wrote Beauvoir's books.[3] And, of course, Beauvoir's early philosophical works were all but forgotten. She also almost disappeared from historical accounts of the development of French existentialism. In earlier accounts Beauvoir occupies a place alongside Sartre and Merleau-Ponty. But in studies written after 1970, her contributions increasingly disappeared from the historical record. Instead of being recognized as one of the foundational philosophers of French existentialism, she was demoted to the status of "Sartre's companion." In fact, at the end of her life this was her primary public identity. This female philosopher, who worked so long and courageously for the right for women to rise above the status of relative beings, died immortalized as one.

The characterization of Beauvoir as nothing but Sartre's philosophical disciple was believable in terms of patriarchal myth. Patriarchy's history of ideas is the history of men's thought. In most cases its first premise is that only men have ideas: women do not. This has traditionally been the framework that contains (and constrains) the history of human thought. In Beauvoir's case, it meant that she could attract some acceptance as a freak original female thinker, but only so long as her direct formative influence on male philosophers was not imprinted in public consciousness.

For example, when commentators emphasized that Beauvoir and Sartre expounded the same novel set of philosophical ideas in their writing, the general cultural myth quickly turned people's perception of Beauvoir upside down. Culturally, it was both inconceivable and inadmissible that it had been the woman rather than man who had been the creative source of some of their shared ideas. No argument and no evidence was necessary to effect this fundamental change in the public and historical perception of Beauvoir. And none was given. Instead, as in so many instances, the issue of which of the couple's ideas was due to the man and which to the woman was decided on the basis of gender. And of course the answer was categorical: of the new ideas shared by Sartre and Beauvoir, all of them originated with Sartre.

The Documents

However, by the time Beauvoir died in 1986, a radical re-evaluation, led by Margaret Simons and Alice Schwarzer and others, had already begun. Furthermore, when Beauvoir died, she left behind the evidence to destroy the myth of intellectual subservience that undermined her reputation as a philosopher. She had preserved all the letters and journals that she and Sartre exchanged in the period when Sartre was preparing to write *Being and Nothingness,* the work on which most of his reputation as a philosopher still rests. Beauvoir also saved her journals from her student days before she met Sartre. In 1993, these were unearthed by Margaret Simons from an obscure corner of the basement of the Bibliothèque Nationale in Paris. The 1926–27 diaries, whose philosophical precociousness almost defies belief, have now been translated into English and published, with the others soon to follow.[4]

In total, these documents preserved by Beauvoir run to eight or nine volumes. They tell a radically different story about the origin of the philosophical ideas shared by Beauvoir and Sartre than the "official" story we all more or less believed. The student journals that Margaret Simons found show that when Beauvoir met Sartre in 1929 she was already engaged in and deeply committed to philosophical inquiry on issues central to what is now called "Sartrean existentialism."

But first, to appreciate the new story of the Beauvoir/Sartre philosophical relationship, one needs to know something about the masculinist myth that it replaces and how that myth came about.

Merleau-Ponty's Reading

It has long been known that Beauvoir's novel *She Came to Stay* sets out and develops many of the philosophical ideas made famous by Sartre's essay *Being and Nothingness*. Both of these books were published in 1943. Maurice Merleau-Ponty, who was Beauvoir's and Sartre's friend and philosophical colleague, was the first to elucidate Beauvoir's novel along these lines. In 1945 he published an essay that interprets *She Came to Stay* as a philosophical text.[5] Among the arguments that Merleau-Ponty identifies in Beauvoir's novel, and that are also central to Sartre's *Being and Nothingness,* are the theories of appearances, of temporality, and of embodiment, as well as the division of reality between immanence and transcendence. Merleau-Ponty also explains how fiction is a natural medium for a phenomenological philosopher.

But the most intriguing thing about Merleau-Ponty's essay is that it makes no mention of Sartre's *Being and Nothingness.* Nor does it suggest that the philosophical arguments identified in *She Came to Stay* owe anything to Sartre. In other words, Merleau-Ponty treats Beauvoir's novel not only as a philosophical text but as an original one. About that he could have had no doubt, not just because of his years of philosophical conversation with Beauvoir prior to her writing *She Came to Stay,* but also because he knew for certain that her book was written well before *Being and Nothingness.* Beauvoir's letter to Sartre on December 23, 1940, begins: "It's very cold this morning throughout Paris and particularly in the Dôme. Merleau-Ponty's here, a few steps away, busy reading my novel" (*LS*, 356).

Hazel Barnes's Reading

But by the 1950s, Merleau-Ponty's essay and its implications were ignored. This left the way clear for later commentators to reinterpret the Beauvoir/Sartre partnership on the basis of cultural prejudices and social stereotypes rather than on the basis of knowledge. The year 1959 was a turning point. That year Hazel Barnes, the English translator of *Being and Nothingness,* wrote a book on Sartre, Beauvoir, and Albert Camus.[6] Barnes documents the point-by-point correspondence between Sartre's theory of intersubjectivity in *Being and Nothingness* and Beauvoir's presentation of the same theory in *She Came to*

Stay. This highlighting of a close philosophical resemblance inevitably leads one to ask which of these two writers created the theory. This is an extremely important point, because the theory of intersubjectivity takes up one-third of Sartre's *Being and Nothingness* and is its most renowned, influential, and original part.

Hazel Barnes's demonstration of the philosophical similarity between the two books created a conundrum in weighing the reputations of the two philosophers. They could not both, as they each implicitly claimed, be the sole creators of this theory of intersubjectivity. Three possibilities existed for settling the question of intellectual attribution. Either both philosophers had contributed to the development of the theory and therefore credit should be divided in some proportion between them, or Beauvoir alone or Sartre alone should be seen as the sole source of these deeply influential ideas.

The traditional myth of the exclusively male origins of ideas made the ascription of credit to Beauvoir unlikely and the identification of Sartre as the sole progenitor of the theory almost inevitable. Indeed, this remains the opinion of even so notable and distinguished a commentator as Hazel Barnes. In a footnote to her essay of 1959, Barnes notes that it is not clear what parts Beauvoir and Sartre respectively played in creating the theory of intersubjectivity. Nevertheless, in the body of her text, Barnes proceeds as if *Being and Nothingness* was conceived and written first, and as if Sartre alone was responsible for the shared philosophical theories and ideas. Beauvoir's philosophical originality is therefore denied. Here, for example, is Barnes on the two works under consideration:

> Although [*She Came to Stay*] and *Being and Nothingness* were published in the same year, the similarity between them is too striking to be coincidence. As with all of de Beauvoir's early fiction, the reader of *She Came to Stay* feels that the inspiration of the book was simply de Beauvoir's decision to show how Sartre's abstract principles could be made to work out in "real life."[7]

Further on, Barnes writes: "It is only after finishing [*She Came to Stay*] that one notes with amusement its step by step correspondence with Sartre's description of the subject-object conflict."[8]

What is happening here is clear, familiar, and faintly depressing. Beauvoir is represented by Barnes as the traditional "good woman," following dutifully in her man's footsteps and merely polishing and displaying his ideas. This is a typical example of the later reception of Beauvoir's thought. Little wonder then that until recently her reputation as an original philosopher was, understandably, low.

This misrepresentation of their relative achievements must have placed some kind of strain on Beauvoir's relationship with Sartre. On the one hand, Beauvoir, who was always as protective of Sartre as if he were a little boy, never said anything to harm his reputation. Beauvoir had her own reputation for ferocity, but she was just as clearly very generous. She even invented her own peculiar definition of a "philosopher" that enabled her to exclude herself from the category occupied by Sartre. On the other hand, for forty years Beauvoir, in essays and interviews, never relented in her claim that she and she alone was the originator of the philosophical ideas and arguments in *She Came to Stay*.

Where Lies the Truth?

So where is the truth in all of this? The question, as I have already noted, is highly intriguing—and highly relevant today—because it comes up against one of the central myths of Western thought.

The letters and diaries from the period, which Beauvoir so helpfully preserved, point to an answer to this question that is based on fact rather than on prejudice or on the graciousness of generosity to friends. It is useful to divide the question into two parts. First, which book—*She Came to Stay* or *Being and Nothingness*—was written first?

Sartre's biographers are divided over whether he began to write *Being and Nothingness* in late July 1940 or in the autumn of 1941. But they all agree that he wrote at least 90 percent from the autumn of 1941 onward. So when was *She Came to Stay* written? Beauvoir's and Sartre's letters tell us exactly.

Sartre left Paris and Beauvoir for military service on September 2, 1939. During their separation they exchanged letters nearly every day until Sartre was taken prisoner on June 21, 1940. They also both kept journals. In Sartre's absence, Beauvoir threw herself into writing her novel, and naturally, in her letters to Sartre, she told him about its progress. Over thirty of her letters from this period contain such references. When Sartre left Paris, her novel's first draft appears to have been already about half written, and by early December she had another 300 pages. On December 7, 1939, Beauvoir wrote to Sartre: "Since yesterday, I've been revising the novel from the beginning. I've had enough of inventing drafts; everything's in place now and I want to write some definitive stuff. I'm enjoying it enormously, and it seems terribly—quite seductively—easy" (*LS*, 200).

Over the next two months, Beauvoir keeps Sartre posted on her progress with her final draft. On January 17, anticipating Sartre's return on leave, she writes, "I really think you'll heap me with praises when you read my 250 pages"

(*LS*, 258). Beauvoir's journal says that on February 5, the morning after Sartre arrived in Paris on leave, he occupied himself reading *She Came to Stay*. Her journal mentions seven more reading sessions that he had with her novel before he left on February 15, 1940 (*JG*, 270–74). Sartre's first letter to Beauvoir after returning to military life concludes: "You've written a beautiful novel," suggesting that he had read more than just the revised first half of her novel (*QMW*, 55).

This brings us to the second half of my question: Who originated the ideas? Given that Beauvoir's book was written first, it is implausible that ideas shared by the two books did not originate with her. But it remains theoretically possible that they were Sartre's. Unfortunately, the cultural bias against crediting female intellectuals with such foundational ideas is still so strong that even this now obviously implausible possibility must be eliminated if Beauvoir is to receive her due as a philosopher.

Beauvoir's letters and war journals were not published until 1990. But Sartre's *War Diaries* were published in 1983. Sartre scholars were thrilled with what they found. They identified these journals as the place where Sartre first developed many of the philosophical ideas that were to form the framework of *Being and Nothingness*. Agreement among Sartre scholars on this point is widespread. For example, the diaries' translator writes as follows:

> The prewar years seem in retrospect to have been but an apprenticeship. . . .
> The excitement of the notebooks . . . comes from the fact they represent
> the essential transition from that apprenticeship to the full flowering of
> Sartre's talents . . . as an original philosopher, in *Being and Nothingness*
> (1943), drafts for many of whose key passages will be found here. (*WD*, x)[9]

This "flowering" of Sartre's philosophical originality, however, does not manifest itself until after the leave he spent in Paris in February 1940 and his many sessions reading *She Came to Stay*. Sartre himself noted in a letter to Beauvoir on January 9, 1940, that he has reread his journals and found them to be devoid of the originality he so craved (*LC*, 27–28). And Sartre scholars agree. It was not, they say, until after he returned from Paris that he had what they call the "turnaround of 1940," when Sartre became "Sartrean."[10]

The explanation for Sartre's amazing and sudden change from being merely the replicator of other philosophers' ideas, into a philosopher of great and purposive originality, is simple and incontrovertible. But it also runs counter to masculinist intellectual history. The explanation is that "Sartre's companion," Beauvoir, was an original thinker whose ideas provided the philosophical base he needed. Immediately following his protracted engagement with Beauvoir's text in Paris, Sartre returned to camp and filled his notebooks with the makings of *Being and Nothingness.*

Between the 17th and the 27th of February 1940, Sartre appears to have set down in his notebooks as much of the philosophical content of *She Came to Stay* as he could remember. Many, but not all, of the ideas and arguments he records are the same as those that caught the attention of Merleau-Ponty and Barnes. Sartre began by offering a slight gesture of credit to Beauvoir but quickly became carried away by the splendors of his male "originality," as in page after page, he paraphrased his companion's novel. In various essays, Kate Fullbrook and I have documented these correspondences. [11]

Ten Ways to Erase a Woman Philosopher

Although Simone de Beauvoir remains the most special of special cases, things of a general nature can be learned from her encounters with patriarchy. In particular, the history of Beauvoir's erasure as a philosopher from the history of ideas reveals an array of methods by which a woman can be made to suffer such a fate. As noted, progress has been made since her death in 1986 in making visible her importance to twentieth-century philosophy. Advances have also been made by women in achieving position and status in academic philosophy. Nonetheless, it would be supremely naïve to think that patriarchy is dead and buried when it comes to philosophy and philosophers. Therefore, it may be helpful to catalogue the effective devices used by patriarchy against Beauvoir-the-philosopher as a means of guarding against their deployment against other women philosophers. I have identified ten. I have explained above the part that the first two played in Beauvoir's erasure.

1. When in doubt about the origin of a woman's philosophical theories and ideas, credit them to her closest male associate.
2. When no longer in doubt about a woman's contribution to philosophy, ignore the facts.
3. Cite the woman out of context.

    Beauvoir's fondness for the irony and layered meanings of literary language made her an easy target, both intended and not, for the scholar's cudgel. An example is the treatment given to her inclusion in *Memoirs of a Dutiful Daughter* of the young Sartre's remark, "from now on, I'm going to take you under my wing" (*MDD*, 339). Whereas Beauvoir humorously used her lover's remark to ridicule his pretensions and inexperience, it is commonly lifted from its satirical context and offered as evidence of the nature of their relationship.

As noted earlier, Beauvoir also declared that she was not a "philosopher." Taken out of its context, this remark seems to justify her erasure. But Beauvoir explained that for her the category "philosopher" included only those who had developed a "grand philosophical system," a pursuit for which she, presaging postmodernism, had expressed her disdain in an early essay.[12] Her definition of "philosopher" excludes not only herself but also Wittgenstein and, in most years, all the participants at American Philosophical Association conferences.

4. Stop translations of the woman's philosophical works.

Until very recently most of Beauvoir's philosophical essays remained untranslated. These include the three volumes of essays published under the titles *Pyrrhus et Cinéas, L'Existentialisme et la sagesse des nations,* and *Privilèges.* In the past, Beauvoir scholars seeking to publish English translations have been unable to obtain permission from the men controlling the copyrights.

5. Expunge the philosophical sections of the woman's most-read work.

Twenty-five years have passed since the publication of Margaret Simons's "The Silencing of Simone de Beauvoir: Guess What's Missing from *The Second Sex?*" Simons's comparisons of the original French text with the zoologist Howard Parshley's English translation—from which, curiously, translations into other languages have been made—shows that he deleted most of the book's philosophical sections as well as mistranslated key philosophical terms, creating the impression that Beauvoir was philosophically illiterate. For thirty years, Beauvoir remained incensed but powerless in the face of this censorship. In 1985, on the eve of her death, she said:

> I think that it's very bad to suppress the philosophical aspect because while I say that I'm not a philosopher in the sense that I'm not the creator of a system. . . . When I put philosophy into my books it's because that's a way for me to view the world and I can't allow them to eliminate that way of viewing the world, that dimension of my approach to women, as Mr. Parshley has done. I'm altogether against the principle of gaps, omissions, condensations which have the effect, among other things of suppressing the whole philosophical aspect of the book.[13]

To date, all attempts to persuade the holders of the English translation rights to lift the censorship have failed.[14]

6. Let the woman's key texts go out of print.

Sometimes *The Ethics of Ambiguity* is in print, sometimes not. But *America Day by Day* had been out of print so long by 1998 that some university libraries kept it in the rare books room. This 1948 book is important, not so much because it offers one of the more insightful overviews of America since de Tocqueville, but because it stands in relation to *The Second Sex*, rather like Darwin's *The Voyage of the Beagle* does to *The Origin of the Species*. Beauvoir's four-month journey around America in 1947 confronted her with American racism and with the ideas of her good friend, the African American novelist Richard Wright. He imparted to her his view of race as mainly a construct of racism, that is, as socially constituted. It was this corroboration between Beauvoir and Wright, documented in *America Day by Day*, that resulted in the full-blown concept of the social other found in *The Second Sex*, and whose later use proved such a career-booster to so many white male writers—especially Sartre.

7. Never shelve the woman's books or books about her philosophy in bookshop philosophy sections.

Bookshops tend to render Beauvoir-the-philosopher invisible. My experience with major bookshops in London, New York, Boston, Cambridge (Massachusetts), Cambridge (England), and Oxford is that they shelve her books in half a dozen sections, but never in philosophy. I have found one exception. A book, now out of print, tracing Beauvoir's development of various philosophical theories in the 1930s and of the uses Sartre subsequently found for them, used to be shelved by Dillons in London in philosophy under S.

8. Read the woman's male partner's fiction as philosophical texts, and then refuse similar readings of her fiction.

For forty years, books on Sartrean philosophy have featured readings of his novel *Nausea* as a philosophical text. This practice is no odder than reading Plato's dialogues as philosophical texts, because philosophy is primarily about ideas and arguments rather than about one or more of the literary forms through which they are expressed. However, just as the Socratic method lends itself more naturally to the dialogue than to the essay, so existentialist philosophy finds in the novel an especially congenial medium of expression. Mary Warnock has explained this fact as follows:

> This insistence on the particularity and concreteness of descriptions,
> from which ontological and metaphysical and general statements may
> be drawn, is what most clearly characterizes existentialist writing—and

what, incidentally, makes it perfectly plausible for Sartre to use novels and plays . . . to convey philosophical doctrines.[15]

But Sartre partisans today, now doubtful that the facts surrounding Beauvoir's *She Came to Stay* can be ignored forever, seek to disallow philosophical readings of the woman's novel.

9. Ignore the woman philosopher's gendered situation.

Even in France today, the tradition of the "master philosopher" still rules. Yet the old Sartre/Beauvoir legend premises itself on the notion that the same public opportunities open to Sartre as an intellectual were open to Beauvoir. When seventy-five years ago Beauvoir was first considering how to bring her philosophical ideas to the forefront of world attention, her one and only viable option was to make the public identify them with well-connected men. Even today, the willingness of society, both East and West, to accept intellectual leadership from women remains in doubt.

10. Treat the woman's autobiographies as biographies of her male partner.

If one read only Sartre scholarship, one might think Beauvoir's sole accomplishments were her "biographies" of the great man. Of course, Sartre scholars are entitled to glean material about their subject from Beauvoir's autobiographies. But they have done so in a highly selective fashion: one that filters out all of Beauvoir's accounts of her and Sartre's joint development of theories—for example, bad faith—as well as her accounts of "Sartrean" innovations she made on her own—for example, the concept of freedom in situation.

Notes

1. Schwarzer, *Simone de Beauvoir Today*, 36–37.
2. Ibid., 62.
3. Ibid., 72.
4. Beauvoir, *Diary of a Philosophy Student: Volume 1*.
5. Merleau-Ponty, "Metaphysics and the Novel."
6. Barnes, *Literature of Possibility*.
7. Ibid., 121–22.
8. Ibid., 385.
9. I am using the 1984 Verso edition.
10. Fretz, "Individuality in Sartre's Philosophy," 77–80.
11. Edward Fullbrook and Kate Fullbrook, *Simone de Beauvoir and Jean-Paul Sartre*; "Sartre's Secret Key"; "Whose Ethics: Sartre's or Beauvoir's?"; "Leveling the Field"; "Beauvoir's Literary-Philosophical Method"; "Simone de Beauvoir"; *Beauvoir: A Critical Introduction*; "The Absence of Beauvoir"; "Beauvoir and Plato"; "*Le deuxième sexe* à l'épreuve du genre littéraire"; *Sex and Philosophy*; Edward Fullbrook, "An Introduc-

tion"; "*She Came to Stay* and *Being and Nothingness*"; Edward Fullbrook and Margaret A. Simons, "Simone de Beauvoir and Jean-Paul Sartre."

12. Simons, *Beauvoir and* The Second Sex, 93.

13. Ibid.

14. Note from the editors: a new translation is currently in preparation and slated to be published in the fall of 2009.

15. Warnock, *Philosophy of Sartre,* 72–73.

7 Psychoanalysis of Things: Objective Meanings or Subjective Projections?

Sara Heinämaa

At the end of *Being and Nothingness,* Sartre outlines a new philosophical approach that he calls "psychoanalysis of things"; its aim is to disclose meanings inherent in things themselves (*EN*, 646; *BN*, 765).[1] Sartre is not concerned with images, memories, or fantasies of empirical individuals, but aims at capturing the modes of being that belong to things themselves as they are given in lived experience. So his inquiry is not about our subjective impressions, but about the *objective meanings* of material things (*EN*, 645–47; *BN*, 764–66). He explains his merging of traditional psychoanalysis with phenomenological ontology in the following way:

> A psychoanalysis of *things* and of their *matter* ought above all to be concerned with establishing the way in which each thing is the *objective* symbol of being and of the relation of human reality to this being. (*EN*, 649; *BN*, 768; cf. *EN*, 632, 649; *BN*, 748, 769)

Literary similes, metaphors, and parables offer clues for such analyses, and thus they function in Sartre's work in a way similar to classical psychoanalysis.[2] Sartre argues that if we study such hints, we will be able to articulate the modes of being—"the ontological meanings"—that characterize material things and processes. We can identify, for example, the mode of being that belongs to water and liquids. To this end, we would need to study the fluid element in its different states, such as melting, oozing, and solidifying. Similarly, we can investigate fire and its forms (smoldering, burning, and sparkling) in the interest of capturing the ontological meaning of the fiery element. Sartre explains his approach by outlining an investigation into the element of snow:

When for instance I wish to determine the objective meaning of snow, I see
for example that it melts at certain temperatures and that this melting of
snow is its death. . . . When I wish to determine the meaning of this melting, I must compare it to other objects located in other regions of existence
but equally objective, equally transcendent (ideas, friendship, persons)
concerning which I can also say that they melt: money *melts* in my hands;
I am swimming and I *melt* in the water; certain ideas—in the sense of socially objective meaning—"snowball" and others *melt* away; "how thin he
has become! how he *has melted away.*" Doubtless I shall thus obtain a certain relation binding certain forms of being to certain others. (*EN*, 646–47;
BN, 766)

To motivate and explicate his "psychoanalysis of things," Sartre develops an
exemplary inquiry into the element of *slime* [*visqueux*]. His idea is to expose
sliminess as a common significative basis for a variety of human emotions and
moral attitudes (*EN*, 650, 653; *BN*, 770, 776).

Sartre's account is well known for its highly negative descriptions that relate
femininity to the baseness of the slimy. Many feminist scholars have criticized
Sartre's similes and metaphors as misogynous.[3] Christine Pierce, for example,
argues that "Sartre's analysis of slime leaves him in an ambiguous position at
best, for what emerges here is a traditional concept of the feminine—a sweet,
clinging, dependent threat to male freedom."[4]

On the other hand, some of the most well-known feminist thinkers have
based their inquiries on Sartre's account of the objective meanings inherent in
things. The best-known of such studies is Julia Kristeva's interpretation of *ab-
jects* in *Powers of Horror* (*Pouvoirs de l'horreur*). Kristeva makes no direct reference to Sartre's *Being and Nothingness*, but her approach explicitly leans on
Mary Douglas's anthropological classic *Purity and Danger*, which explains the
horrifying character of slime by reference to Sartre's analyses.[5]

Both of these ways of responding to Sartre's association of sliminess and
femininity—the critical and the constructive—have their roots in Simone de
Beauvoir's classical treatise *The Second Sex* (*Le Deuxième sexe*). The received
view has long been that Beauvoir merely worked to apply Sartre's philosophical
concepts to moral and political problems. New investigations of Beauvoir's treatise have shown, however, that she had her own philosophical insight, which
was not derived from that of Sartre but was independent and original. I will
argue in this chapter that we can also find in Beauvoir's work an interesting critique of Sartre's interpretations of ontological meanings.[6]

Thus, my aim is to introduce the main elements of Sartre's psychoanalysis of things and to present his interpretation of slime for the purposes of critical discussion. For this end, I first illuminate the philosophical background of Sartre's approach by showing how it relates to Edmund Husserl's classical phenomenology of perception. Second, I argue that Beauvoir's critique of femininity in *The Second Sex* points to a fundamental problem in Sartre's approach. Beauvoir questions Sartre's association between the slimy and the feminine by arguing that their symbolic connection depends, not on ontological meanings, but on the specific interests of individual persons. Beauvoir problematizes the universality of Sartre's account and claims that what he presents as part of our common human condition is merely a projection of a male attitude. I begin with a short account of the Husserlian background of Sartre's psychoanalysis and proceed to his discussion of the slimy. The last part of the chapter is devoted to an explication of Beauvoir's critique.

Husserlian Background: Affective Experiences

In his phenomenological investigations into the constitution of nature,[7] Husserl argues that perceived objects (objects given in sense-perception) are not neutral but attract our attention and move us in many different ways. We see things with tempting and inviting qualities—colorful things, for example, that arrest and capture our attention and make us turn toward them. We also perceive unpleasant things that drive us away, make us turn and move further away: harsh voices, sharp smells, restless movements, bright light. So we are not indifferent to the things that we encounter in perception but are clearly influenced by them: they stir us, prod us, pull us, and provoke us.[8]

Husserl uses the concepts of *affective* and *receptive* to characterize this level of perception. Following him, we can say that perceived objects actively affect us, and whenever we react or reply to their "calls," we relate to them passively. Husserl argues that such active objects are necessarily part of our experience as human beings, despite the fact that all experienced realities result from the constitutive activity of transcendental consciousness. To understand this, one needs to distinguish between two levels of activity. On the one hand, the positing acts of consciousness constitute all meaning of reality and being, knowable reality as well as perceivable reality; on the other hand, most objects of sense-perception are constituted as active, such that they can move us, attract us, and repel us.[9]

Husserl's own examples are taken from everyday situations. He describes how the stale air in a room makes him rise and open a window, how a ball approaching fast from above makes his arm rise to catch it, and how his fingers reach for tempting food.[10] What is thematized in all these cases is not any causal relation between the external object and my physical body, but the motivational force that the perceived and sensed object has on my body as I experience and live it. Husserl states: "The object stimulates me in virtue of its *experienced properties* and not its physicalistic ones."[11]

On the basis of Husserl's concepts and distinctions, French phenomenologists Sartre as well as Merleau-Ponty developed an argument to the effect that the original objects of our experience are not theoretical objects but affective things that move, attract, and repulse us (e.g., *EN*, 649–51; *BN*, 769–71; *DS* II, 155; *SS*, 399).[12] We do not see a table, for example, as a structure of wood fibers, cells, or molecules. The perceived table is not a theoretical object of natural sciences. Rather, we see the table as a practical object of everyday affairs and primarily as an attractive thing that invites our bodies to move in certain ways: we slide our hand on its smooth, cool surface as if it "demanded those movements of convergence that will endow it with its 'true' aspect," as Merleau-Ponty writes.[13]

Thus understood, affectivity is not added to perceptual things retrospectively but is constituted together with their very presence, their being (*EN*, 650–52; *BN*, 770–72).[14] Valueless theoretical objects are abstractions having a constitutive basis in primary affective objects. This means that the idea of a perception that would present the material object as pure extension and form, free of all affectivity, is an intellectual construct. Affectivity is not projected onto purely material objects of perception—there are no such objects—but affectivity is constituted together with materiality itself.[15] Sartre explains:

> The apprehension of a quality does not add anything to being except the fact that *being is there as this*. In this sense a quality is not an external aspect of being, for being, since it has no "within," cannot have a "without." (*EN*, 223; *BN*, 258)

Sartre and Merleau-Ponty offer detailed descriptions and several examples of affective perceptions and their object.[16] They describe whole life-worlds with things composed of smells, sounds, flavors, colors, light, spatial patterns, and figures. Secondary and primary qualities form totalities in which all elements are given together in mutual implication, and eventually the life-world itself is a similar totality of things connected internally to other things. As Sartre explains in *Being and Nothingness*:

The yellow of the lemon . . . is not a subjective mode of apprehending the lemon; it *is the lemon*. . . . The whole lemon extends throughout its qualities and . . . each one of the qualities is spread over the others; that is what we have correctly called "this." (*EN*, 649; *BN*, 769; cf. *EN*, 222; *BN*, 257)[17]

Sartre and Merleau-Ponty follow Husserl also in thematizing two major types of affection: attraction and repulsion. Both argue that in primary perception we encounter *attractive* things to which we respond by approaching, reaching, and grasping; and on the other hand, we experience *repulsive* things that make us dissociate and turn, draw, and move farther away. This duality of attractive and repulsive objects corresponds to the duality of our own movements: we move toward things and away from them; we stay near to things and distance ourselves from them; we grasp and reject, possess and refute.[18]

Sartre, however, argues in *Being and Nothingness,* in contrast to Merleau-Ponty, that the structures of perception are not the final results of philosophical analysis. Phenomenology cannot rest satisfied with the explication of perceptual experience but must pierce through perception to its ontological foundations. These foundations are in our existential desires and choices—not in any empirical passions, but in our decisions about our ways of relating to being. This is the fundamental task that Sartre ascribes to his existential psychoanalysis. He explains:

The yellow and the red, the taste of a tomato, or the wrinkled softness of split peas are by no means irreducible givens according to our view. They translate symbolically to our perception a certain way which being has of giving itself, and we react by disgust or desire, according to how we see being spring forth in one way or another from their surface. Existential psychoanalysis must bring out the ontological meaning of qualities. (*EN*, 645; *BN*, 764)

The quality of the slimy functions as the paradigmatic example of such an analysis. The description of the slimy is intended to illuminate the existential structure that we encounter in certain material processes and certain emotional and moral attitudes.

The Slimy: An Example from Sartre's Existential Psychoanalysis

Sartre's account of slime confronts us with a type of repulsion manifest in many kinds of experiences. The intentional objects of these experiences vary from concrete items to abstract entities, from material things to spiritual states: "A handshake is slimy, a smile is slimy, a thought and a feeling can be slimy," as Sartre explains (*EN,* 650; *BN,* 770). The concept covers a whole range of repugnance and disgust directed at evasive and sticky things: "oysters and raw eggs"; snails, leeches, fungus, and molluscs; bogholes and quicksand; liars, weaklings, and deceivers—in a word, everything "base" (*EN,* 650–52; *BN,* 770–73).[19]

Sartre explains that slime is an element or "a substance between two states"; it is an intermediate mode between solid and fluid being. Thus characterized, slime is a liquid that has started to solidify, has lost its flowing character, but has not yet reached the rigidity and firmness of solid objects.[20] It is a thickening, dense, and viscous liquid: oil, pitch, gum, honey, tar—"the agony of water" (*EN,* 654; *BN,* 774). As such it is attractive and yielding but deceptive. A living being that falls into a slimy substance seems to keep its form for some time but actually starts to merge or fuse into the soft, yielding material. The transformation is slow, all changes are inconspicuous, but in the end, no trace or impression of spontaneous movement is left. The soft surface is even—"like the flattening of the full breasts of a woman who is lying on her back" (*EN,* 654; *BN,* 755). Beings do not sink into slime as they sink into water; instead, they are devoured by the slimy, dissolved, and decomposed already when falling (*EN,* 656; *BN,* 774).

On the other hand, slime is adhesive, gluey, and sugary. It sticks to hands and sucks in everything that touches it or tries to move it. First it seems as if the slimy substance would yield and succumb, but this is deceptive, for its grip is tight and firm, even if passive:

> I open my hands, I want to let go of the slime and it sticks to me, it draws me, it sucks at me. Its mode of being is neither the reassuring inertia of the solid nor a dynamism like that in water which is exhausted in fleeing from me. It is a soft, yielding action, a moist and feminine sucking, it lives obscurely under my fingers, and I sense it like a dizziness: it draws me to it as the bottom of a precipice might draw me. (*EN,* 655; *BN,* 776)[21]

Sartre's descriptions associate slime with decomposition and dying, or more generally, with all processes in which the movement of conscious spontaneous life (the free movement of consciousness) slows down and stagnates. He argues, however, that the repugnance of slime should not be confused with fear of death or with the anguish or disgust that we may feel for our own mortality. Rather, what is at issue is the horror of an ideal, non-existential possibility that consciousness could be arrested by being (in-itself) and could lose its free movement. According to Sartre, this cannot happen: consciousness is free activity by essence, and it retains its freedom even in embodiment and corporeality. However, the ideal possibility of a completely stagnant state of consciousness remains threatening even if it cannot be realized: we can *think* it, but we cannot *live* it (*EN*, 657; *BN*, 778).

In the very same analysis, Sartre also suggests that slime associates with the feminine, and that the horror of slimy substances and feminine elements has the same signification basis: "Slime is the revenge of the in-itself. A sticky-sweet, feminine revenge" (*EN*, 656; *BN*, 777). It is exactly these sections that have been the targets of feminist critiques of Sartre since the 1960s, rejected as "pornographic,"[22] "violent," and misogynous.[23]

To approach the philosophical problems involved in Sartre's psychoanalysis, it is crucial to notice that its descriptions are motivated not so much by perceptual evidence or imaginary variation as by a certain literary tradition (e.g., *EN*, 647–49; *BN*, 767–69). The very same combination of feminine and decomposing elements that Sartre presents in *Being and Nothingness* can be found, for example, in Charles Baudelaire's poem *The Carrion* from 1855. Sartre made Baudelaire and his work the subject of his existential psychoanalysis[24] four years after the appearance of *Being and Nothingness,* but his account of the slimy seems already influenced by the boldness and strength of Baudelaire's words.[25] To demonstrate this, I quote a few verses from the poem. The text begins with an image that compares the decomposing carcass to female genitals:

> Remember that object we saw, dear soul,
> In the sweetness of a summer morn:
> At the bend of the path a loathsome carrion
> On a bed with pebbles strewn,
>
> With legs raised like a lustful woman,
> Burning and sweating poisons,
> It spread open, nonchalant and scornful,
> Its belly, ripe with exhalations.[26]

A later section describes the slow dispersed movements of decomposition:

> Flies hummed upon the putrid belly,
> Whence larvae in black battalions spread
> And like a heavy liquid flowed
> Along the tatters deliquescing.[27]

Sartre's analysis suggests that the slimy and the feminine go hand in hand and that both qualities symbolize the threat of succumbing to being (in-itself). Thus, it seems that the connection between the qualities of sliminess and femininity is based on their ontological meanings (*EN*, 652, 655; *BN*, 772, 776–77). If this holds, then the association would not just be typical of some cultures or some historical epochs; it would be universally shared by all.

Even though Sartre explicitly rejects all attempts to construe a *universal symbolism* that would cover all individual ways of living the human predicament (*EN*, 618–19; *BN*, 732), he also insists that there is an ontological foundation for all variations and that this foundation is all-encompassing, the same for all individual persons. For him consciousness is a lack of being, and its basic structure and relation to being is desire—desire to be and to have or possess being. Accordingly, all qualities and materials that we encounter in experience are understood in ontological terms, and the slimy is disclosed as "a being in which the for-itself is swallowed up by the in-itself" (*EN*, 661; *BN*, 783–84). Sartre insists that this does not lead to universalism; the argument is merely that individual variation can be, and has to be, characterized in relation to the ontological foundation: different persons relate to this foundation in different ways. Sartre explains:

> We can see the importance which the elucidation of these immediate and concrete existential categories will assume for existential psychoanalysis. In this way we can apprehend the very general projects of human reality. But what chiefly interests the psychoanalyst is to determine the free project of the unique person in terms of the individual relation which unites him to these various symbols of being. I can love slimy contacts, have horror of holes, etc. That does not mean that for me the slimy, the greasy, a hole, etc. have lost their general ontological meaning, but on the contrary that *because* of this meaning, I determine myself in this or that manner in relation to them. (*EN* 660–61; *BN*, 782)

So the claim is not, for example, that all persons reject slimy things and subjects. The objective ontological meaning of the slimy is always threatening to consciousness, but this does not imply that all individuals have negative relations to it. Instead of generalizing over individual consciousness or persons—and instead of compromising the universality of his ontological account—Sartre argues that we are confronted with new kinds of questions that concern our relations to the ontological foundation of meaning. In the case of the slimy, such questions include the following:

> If the slimy is indeed the *symbol of a being* in which the for-itself is swallowed up by the in-itself, what kind of a person am I if in encountering others, I love the slimy? To what fundamental project of myself am I re-

ferred if I want to explain this love of an ambiguous, sucking in-itself?
(*EN*, 661; *BN*, 783; my italics)

Masculine and Feminine:
Beauvoir's Implicit Critique of Sartre

Simone de Beauvoir's *The Second Sex* seems to repeat this description and analysis of sliminess: the sections in which Beauvoir discusses women's sexuality present us with a modification of Sartre's description of "the feminine revenge." Beauvoir characterized the female sex organ as "mysterious," "concealed, mucous and humid," and compares feminine desire to the preying activities of the mantis, the molluscs, and carnivorous plants. She writes, for example:

> Feminine heat is the soft throbbing of a shell. . . . Woman lies in wait like the carnivorous plant; she is the bog in which insects and children are swallowed up. She is absorption, suction, humus, she is pitch and glue, an immobile appeal, insinuating and viscous. (*DS* II, 167; *SS*, 407)

These sections are well known and have often been criticized for their misogynous undertones. Beauvoir's feminist philosophy is claimed to include Sartre's universalist theory of ontological meanings or to be based on it.[28] A more careful and comprehensive reading of *The Second Sex* shows, however, that Beauvoir does not repeat Sartre's descriptions in an affirmative way, but on the contrary, she questions them and struggles to disclose their limitations. What we have is an internal critique of Sartre's philosophical analysis. To see this, we need to insert Beauvoir's descriptions into the context of her general argument about the human condition, and to this end we need to turn back to her ethical essays, *Pyrrhus and Cinéas* (*Pyrrhus et Cinéas*) and *The Ethics of Ambiguity* (*Pour une morale de l'ambiguïté*). In addition, two non-philosophical texts prove illuminating, the early novel *Blood of Others* (*Le sang des autres*) and the late interview with Sartre, published in *Adieux: A Farewell to Sartre* (*La cérémonie des adieux*).

In all her works, Beauvoir develops a Kierkegaardian notion of human existence as an essentially paradoxical condition.[29] She argues that each subject lives in constant indecision between inwardness and externality, finitude and infiniteness, temporality and eternity, solitude and bonding (*MA*, 11–15; *EA*, 7–19).[30] These paradoxes cannot be resolved, but they can be endured and executed in different ways (*MA*, 186–87; *EA*, 133–34). Like Sartre, Beauvoir describes several alternatives: the infantile, the narcissistic, the serious, and the artistic.

In *The Second Sex*, however, she distinguishes between two dominant attitudes, one typical of men and the other characteristic of women. Following Kierkegaard, she argues that women tend to identify with carnality, finitude, and temporality; whereas men identify with spirituality, infiniteness, and eternity. These typical identifications have wide-ranging implications to our emotional, moral, and intellectual lives. In the case of men, the one-sided identification leads to a heavily charged notion of one's own embodiment. Beauvoir describes the masculine self-understanding as follows:

> He [man] sees himself as a fallen god: his curse is to be fallen from the bright and ordered heaven into the chaotic shadows of his mother's womb. This fire, this pure and active inhalation in which he wishes to recognize himself, is imprisoned by woman in the mud of the earth. He [man] would want to be necessary, like a pure Idea, like the One, the All, the absolute Spirit; and he finds himself shut up in a finite body, in a place and time he never chose. . . . The contingency of flesh . . . also dooms him [man] to death. This quivering jelly which is elaborated in the womb . . . evokes too clearly the soft viscosity [*viscosité*] of carrion for him not to turn shuddering away. (*DSI*, 245–56; *SS*, 177–78; cf. *DSI*, 274; *SS*, 197–98)

Beauvoir's descriptions of the horrifying sexuality of the female body clearly stem from Sartre's psychoanalysis. But in the context of her general argument, they do not contribute to any "psychoanalysis of *things*." Rather, they belong to her diagnosis of the masculine attitude. Thus there is a crucial difference between Beauvoir's and Sartre's arguments: whereas Sartre proposes that the horror of feminine sex has an objective basis in the ontological meanings of things and material processes—in the repugnancy of the slimy—Beauvoir argues that such experiences emerge from an imaginary identification with spirituality and eternity, which is typical of men. Her claim is that "the ontological meaning" identified by Sartre is not universal or a priori, but it is dominant merely in the experiences and theories of men who struggle to identify with the one pole of human ambiguity—with eternity, spirituality, consciousness, and freedom.

Such identifications are not unavoidable or necessary for humans. Both sexes can cultivate both sides of their existence—flesh and spirit—and thus contribute to the creation of new values and meanings. Beauvoir is not utopian here. Rather, she sees the revaluation as already happening, and she works to promote and express it. This she does critically and analytically in *The Second Sex*, and creatively and constructively in her novels.

The early novel *Blood of Others* includes sections that deepen our understanding of Beauvoir's relation to Sartre's (psycho)analysis. Here again, Beauvoir uses images that are very similar to those presented by Sartre: the feminine body is identified with plants and molluscs; it goes through a series of transformations, becoming a tree, a blossom, a medusa, a spongy and moist surface with obscure magnetic powers. These metamorphoses remind us of those depicted as slimy in *Being and Nothingness*. But here the description has no threatening or lowering connotations: being given from the point of view of a woman, the description lacks the tones of disgust and repulsion. The woman experiences her body as transforming, becoming animal, and even vegetative. But the transformation is not horrifying; it is enjoyable and liberating.[31] The slimy materiality, which in *Being and Nothingness* is described in negative terms, is thus revaluated by Beauvoir as part of the feminine experience of desire and ecstasy.[32]

While interviewing Sartre in the early 1980s, just before his death, Beauvoir asks him directly if his understanding of the slimy is informed, not by his ontological insight, but rather by his personal dispositions. The topics of their interchange range from sexuality to food and eating, but the leading philosophical theme is that of materiality.

While recording Sartre's views of different types of material reality, Beauvoir suggested in passing that his notion of the slimy originates from his "refusal of all the values that can be called vital . . . the values of nature, fecundity" (*Ent*, 448; *AFS*, 316). Sartre accepts Beauvoir's suggestion and adds that all forms of animal life arouse disgust in him—molluscs and arthropods in particular. For him, their movements indicate that their life-form belongs to "another world," "another universe," separated from humans and everything that humans can cultivate (*Ent*, 448, 470; *AFS*, 316, 332).

Beauvoir then pushes the question further and asks if it is not flesh as such that disgusts Sartre.[33] Sartre's answer is again positive, but his answer does not distinguish between his personal dislike and the human disposition: "Certainly. The origin of *the* dislike for the materiality of the shellfish certainly lies there. It is a quasi-vegetative form of existence. It is the organic in coming into existence; or existence that is organic only in that rather repulsive aspect of lymphatic flesh, strange color, a gaping hole in the flesh" (*Ent*, 471–72; *AFS*, 333; translation modified, my emphasis).

Neither Sartre nor Beauvoir makes any direct reference to the analyses presented in *Being and Nothingness*, but Beauvoir's questions aim at separating the personal from what is necessary to human existence. Her assiduous questions make clear that Sartre's supposedly ontological analyses suffer from habitual prejudices and personal preferences—a philosophical error par excellence.

Conclusion

Even though Beauvoir's critique of Sartre's notion of the slimy remains implicit, it is harsh and uncompromising. She shows that Sartre's descriptions fail to reach the deep ontological level to which they aspire. The slimy is not repulsive or horrifying as such, Beauvoir argues, but is characterized by negative values only in philosophical and literary traditions dominated by the male perspective.

Beauvoir does not reject Sartre's psychoanalysis of things, its aims, or its principal ideas. She accepts the idea that being is always saturated with values, and she works to make us aware of such qualities. She insists, however, that we should not let any personal or theoretical interests overrule experience, its multitude and variance, in our investigations of subjectivity and humanity. If the philosophical explication aims at objectivity and is to be valid for all, it must take into account not only paradigmatic examples in accordance with the traditions of philosophy and literature but also marginal experiences seldom, if ever, described by the men of letters. At the end of *The Second Sex*, Beauvoir states: "there is a whole region of human experience which the male deliberately chooses to ignore because he fails to *think* about it: this experience woman *lives*" (*DS* II, 501; *SS*, 622).

Notes

1. I am referring to the French edition of *L'être et le néant* (Paris: Gallimard, [1943] 1998) and to the English 1992 Washington Square Press edition.
2. In this project, Sartre is influenced by Gaston Bachelard, who, in his *L'Eau et les rêves*, studies meanings that belong to materials, and especially to water. Bachelard also spoke of the "psychoanalysis of plants" and named another work *La Psychanalyse du feu*. Sartre praises Bachelard for criticizing phenomenology (*EN*, 364; *BN*, 428) but distances his own analysis from that of Bachelard in two respects:
   (a) Sartre's existential psychoanalysis does not put such a strong emphasis on the descriptions and the imaginations of poets as Bachelard's accounts do, for it depends on things themselves and not on human beings. Sartre points out that the first philosophical task is to determine the objective meanings of things and materials. Only when this is done can we study and see what poets assign to things—their "vital values," in Scheler's words. Thus, Sartre argues that fundamental ontology precedes existential psychoanalysis (*EN*, 647–50; *BN*, 767–70).

(b) Existential psychoanalysis does not accept any foundation that is not self-evident, and Sartre insists that such a self-evident foundation can only be found in ontology, that is, in our relations to being and in our own modes of being. Thus neither sexuality, nor libido, nor will to power can serve as the foundation in existential psychoanalysis.

3. See, for example, Warnock, *Philosophy of Sartre;* Pierce, "Philosophy"; Collins and Pierce, "Holes and Slime"; Morris, *Sartre's Concept of a Person;* Lloyd, *Man of Reason* (Methuen, 1984), 93–102; Pilardi, "Female Eroticism," 21–27; Le Dœuff, *Hipparchia's Choice* (Blackwell, 1991), 80–82; Lundgren-Gothlin, "Gender and Ethics"; Grosz, *Volatile Bodies,* 194–95. But for a different perspective, compare Barnes, "Sartre and Sexism"; Burstow, "How Sexist Is Sartre"; Zerilli, "A Process without a Subject"; Diprose, "Generosity"; Käll, "Encountering Self and Other," "Beneath Subject and Object," "The Expressive Body," "Expressive Selfhood."

4. Pierce, "Philosophy," 496.

5. See Douglas, *Purity and Danger,* 38; Grosz, *Volatile Bodies,* 192–208.

6. I have argued elsewhere (Heinämaa, *Toward a Phenomenology;* "Introduction") that Merleau-Ponty's concept of the human subject as a *sedimented bodily formation* is the basis of Beauvoir's philosophical conceptualization of sexual difference in *The Second Sex.* In my understanding, Beauvoir distanced herself from Sartre's Hegelian view in which the human subject is a "hole in being" (*TM,* 366; *MT,* 163; Merleau-Ponty, *Phénoménologie de la perception/Phenomenology of Perception,* 249/215). She followed Merleau-Ponty in rejecting the opposition of being and nothingness and in arguing that, rather than opposing a pure nothingness to the fullness of being, the human being functions as a fold or hollow in the tissue of being. For a more detailed discussion of these two approaches and the difference between the metaphors of fold and hollow, see Heinämaa, *Toward a Phenomenology,* 53–57.

In earlier works (Heinämaa, "Women—Nature, Product, Style?"; "What Is a Woman?"), I have shown that Beauvoir's concept of the human body is neither natural-biological nor social-constructivist, but it is phenomenological and is based on the distinction between the *lived body,* on the one hand, and the *physical thing,* on the other hand. Moreover, Beauvoir distances herself from Sartre's discourse in which the living body is primarily described as a *tool* and secondarily as *flesh.* For a full explication of these conceptual distinctions, see Heinämaa, *Toward a Phenomenology,* 21–44; Käll, "Expressive Selfhood."

Despite their methodological and ontological differences, both Sartre and Merleau-Ponty rejected all *naturalistic* interpretations of psychoanalysis and argued that psychoanalysis must make a transcendental turn. For Sartre such a turn was made possible by fundamental ontology; for Merleau-Ponty it was realizable only with the help of genetic phenomenology (Merleau-Ponty, *Phénoménologie de la perception/Phenomenology of Perception,* 145–47/124–27, 184–87/157–60, 199–202/171–73).

7. Husserl develops his phenomenological account of nature in the second volume of *Ideas* and in the late work *The Crisis of European Sciences and Transcendental Phenomenology.* He worked on the former during 1912–28 with his two assistants, Edith Stein and Ludwig Landgrebe, but he never published the text. *Ideas II* was published posthumously in 1952, and it was known by Husserl's contemporaries, Merleau-Ponty among others, in manuscript form.

8. This view is quite explicit in Husserl's manuscripts from the 1920s. There we find, for example, the following statement: "Everything that is touches our feelings; every existent is apperceived in a value-apperception and thereby awakens desirous attitudes" (Husserl, *Zur Phänomenologie der Intersubjektivität*, 404–405). An unpublished manuscript is even more explicit: "Mere sensation-data, and at a higher level, sensory objects, as things that are there for the subject, but there as value-free, are abstractions. There is nothing that does not affect the emotions" (Husserl, Ms. A VI 26, 42a; cited in Drummond, "Respect as a Moral Emotion").

9. Husserl's concept of *constitution* should not be mixed up with the Nietzschean concept of *construction,* which is central in the philosophy of Foucault and his feminist followers such as Judith Butler (1990, 1993). The Husserlian concept does not involve any sense of creation. See Sokolowski, *Formation of Husserl's Concept;* and Zahavi, *Husserl's Phenomenology,* 72–77. For a critique of the constructionist notion of sexual difference, see Heinämaa, "Women—Nature, Product, Style?"

10. Husserl, *Ideen zu einer reinen Phänomenologie/Ideas Pertaining to a Pure Phenomenology,* §55, 216–18/228.

11. Ibid., §55, 217/228.

12. I am using the 1987 Penguin edition of *The Second Sex.* See also Merleau-Ponty, *Phénoménologie de la perception/Phenomenology of Perception,* 235–42/203–209, 371–73/321–23.

13. Ibid., 367/318.

14. Ibid., 235–42/203–209, 369–71/321.

15. Thus, both Merleau-Ponty and Sartre argue that only reflection can distinguish the pure *thisness* of the thing from its affective, vital, or practical qualities.

16. Sartre's account of perceptual experience is close to Heidegger's in emphasizing the practical relations that the subject has to the world.

17. See Merleau-Ponty, *Phénoménologie/Phenomenology,* 10/4–5, 373/323.

18. For Beauvoir's critique of the attractive-repulsive opposition and her related analysis of feminine eroticism, see Heinämaa, "Through Desire and Love."

19. See Merleau-Ponty, *Phénoménologie/Phenomenology,* 282–83/244–45.

20. Max Deutscher characterizes slime as "semi-fluid" (*Genre and Void,* 103).

21. Sartre elaborates: "Throw water on the ground; it *runs.* Throw a slimy substance; it draws itself out, it displays itself, it flattens itself out, it is *soft* [*molle*]; touch the slimy, it does not flee, it yields" (*EN,* 655; *BN,* 775).

22. Warnock, *Philosophy of Sartre.*

23. See Christine Daigle's argument in this volume.

24. Sartre developed his existential psychoanalysis in his studies of Flaubert and Genet, among others. See his *Saint Genet: Actor and Martyr* (*Saint Genêt, Comédien et martyr*) and *The Idiot of the Family* (*L'Idiot de la famille, G. Flaubert de 1821 à 1857*).

25. See Sartre's treatise on *Baudelaire,* 77–78, 87, 104–106, 119ff. I am using the 1967 New Directions edition.

26. Baudelaire, *Flowers of Evil.*

27. Ibid.

28. Moira Gatens, for example, claims that "the particular form of existentialism employed by Beauvoir is that developed by Jean-Paul Sartre in *Being and Nothingness*" (*Feminism and Philosophy,* 48–49).

29. For this connection, see Heinämaa, *Toward a Phenomenology*, 127–30; cf. Kierkegaard, *Sickness unto Death*, 43–44, 60–62, 99.

30. I am using the 1947 Gallimard edition for the French.

31. See Kristeva, *Colette*, 194–240.

32. Here we find a forgotten philosophical starting point of Luce Irigaray's discourse of mucous membranes, developed in *This Sex Which Is Not One* (*Ce sexe qui n'en est pas un*) and *An Ethics of Sexual Difference* (*Éthique de la différence sexuelle*).

33. Lisa Käll offers a careful explication of Sartre's concept of flesh and an argument for its crucial role in his understanding of embodiment ("Encountering Self and Other," "Beneath Subject and Object," "The Expressive Body," "Expressive Selfhood").

8 Beauvoir, Sartre, and the Problem of Alterity

Michel Kail

Translated by Kevin W. Gray

Feminist scholars of Beauvoir's works have had to wage a difficult campaign in order to have her philosophical work's originality and importance recognized. As far as I am concerned, the battle has been won; I am quite content to leave all those who persist in believing otherwise to their own devices.

It is within this framework—one of equal respect for Beauvoir's philosophical originality—that I want to reevaluate the philosophical relationship between Sartre and Beauvoir. In particular, I will examine what I will argue is Beauvoir's important influence on Sartre as he was writing the *Critique of Dialectical Reason,* and I will examine the role Beauvoir played in Sartre's construction of his theory of alterity. The problem of alterity provides us, I argue, with a useful way to examine the accuracy of my hypothesis—and I propose to examine not only the way relationships of alterity are conceived but also the respective importance each philosopher attributes to the problem of alterity.

Sartre deals with the question of alterity in his early works such as *Being and Nothingness* in a wholly classical way, even if he is already taking the first steps for a radical revision of the philosophy of the subject. Beauvoir, on the other hand, challenges classical ideas of alterity, treating the revised conception of the Other as central to her philosophy. As such, Beauvoir, unlike Sartre, is not forced to devote a special chapter to it, as is often done in well-known treatments of the "philosophy of subject." In her very first philosophical essays, Beauvoir undertakes what I am tempted to label a "banalization" of the category of alterity to which most of our contemporaries should rally: this would save us all our discussions of identity and alterity that only reproduce the most unnecessary and abstract schemes.

Sartre: From *Being and Nothingness* to *Critique of Dialectical Reason*

In this first section, I want to examine the evolution of Sartre's thought and see how the idea of alterity evolved between *Being and Nothingness* and *Critique of Dialectical Reason*. In doing so, I hope to highlight the importance of Beauvoir's contribution. Of course, to suggest that Sartre and Beauvoir reciprocally influenced each other seems self-evident, given the fact that in their intellectual alliance of equals they both were in the habit of having the other read and comment on their manuscripts before publication.

Promises Not Kept

Even before *Being and Nothingness,* Sartre wrote, in *The Transcendence of the Ego,* about the subject as a being that exists in the world. He concluded the book by writing:

> Unfortunately, as long as the *I* remains a structure of absolute consciousness, one will still be able to reproach phenomenology for being an escapist doctrine, for again pulling a part of man out of the world and, in that way, turning our attention from the real problems. It seems to us that this reproach no longer has any justification if one makes the *me* an existent, strictly contemporaneous with the world, whose existence has the same essential characteristics as the world.... This absolute consciousness, when it is purified of the *I,* no longer has anything of the *subject.* It is no longer a collection of representations. It is quite simply a first condition and an absolute source of existence. And the relation of interdependence established by this absolute consciousness between the *me* and the World is sufficient for the *me* to appear as "endangered" before the World, for the *me* (indirectly and through the intermediary of states) to draw the whole of its content from the World. (*TE,* 105–106)

In this quote, we can see the beginnings of a materialist program unburdened of any determinist dimensions while being animated by the desire for freedom that has always resided at the heart of the materialist project. The Subject, existing in the World, could not possibly be determined by an exteriority acting mysteriously on its own interiority. Through its merger with conscious intentionality, the subject is dislodged from its central and important position—intentionality materializes as the *relationship* between the Subject and the Object. The Object of the consciousness is not alternately the Subject and the Object, but the relationship itself, which organizes consciousness as a whole. Consciousness is the movement that binds Subject and Object together. What consciousness aims at through the intentionality that constitutes it is the relation Subject-Object (which becomes what Sartre will call *praxis* in *Critique of Dialectical Reason*). This is how Sartre understands freedom (i.e., consciousness) or, perhaps better, makes it absolute, having understood, contrary to philosophical tradition, that the absolute must be integrated into being-for-itself.

In other words, transcendence is absorbed into consciousness in Sartre's philosophy; consciousness is always outside of itself, or perhaps better, is a being that exists outside of itself. This means that it is not lodged in the subject, but that it takes the place of the subject.[1] For this reason, I maintain that Sartre's philosophy is a philosophy of consciousness and not a philosophy of the Subject, as many commentators have asserted (either as a mistake or out of hostility to his philosophy). Freedom is therefore not an attribute of the human subject, a tool at his disposal (which he could decide to use or not use according to a voluntarist pattern); rather, it constitutes the very existence of consciousness.

After elaborating on the consequences of the nature of consciousness in the two first parts of *Being and Nothingness,* Sartre titles the third section "Being-for-Others." While reading these two first sections may have convinced the reader that he was not reading a work of traditional philosophy, the third section undoubtedly must give any attentive reader the sense that he is reading a work by Descartes, describing a Subject preoccupied with himself and his relationship to a divine transcendence, a Subject who belatedly discovers, with regret, that the Other exists.

In Sartre, the Other enters only in this third part, most likely after having been summoned for his analysis of bad faith; the Other then proceeds to take on the dull role of an extra in the fourth part of *Being and Nothingness,* "Having, Doing and Being." In its understated coming into being, the Other only truly emerges through the negative limitations he imposes on my freedom. I believe, therefore, that in Sartre's first great philosophical work, the Other is most conspicuous for his absence.

How Sartre develops the idea of bad faith is important, for its development illustrates the role played by the Other in *Being and Nothingness.* Bad faith, which is inextricably tied to the relationship to the Other, is the behavior according to which consciousness refuses to choose between being-for-itself and being-in-itself. The behavior that Sartre warns us about manifests itself in an exemplary fashion in the being of consciousness:

> If bad-faith is possible, it is because it is an immediate, permanent threat
> to every project of the human being; it is because consciousness conceals
> in its being a permanent risk of bad-faith. The origin of this risk is the fact
> that the nature of consciousness simultaneously is to be what it is not and
> not to be what it is. (*BN*, 116)[2]

Since this behavior expresses the very being of consciousness as only existing in the presence of the Other, we are led to believe that the analysis of consciousness should be inseparable from an analysis of the Other.

Nonetheless, that is not the case. As I have argued, the concept of being-for-others only emerges in the third part of the book. Furthermore, the Other, as presented by Sartre in the passages dedicated to bad faith, suffers from inconsistency; the Other functions as a foil—as an "occasion" in Malebranche's sense of the word. In Sartre's exegesis, the Other allows for the properties of the Subject acting in bad faith to emerge. The Other is discussed in absence of all his nonessential qualities—be they social roles, gender orientations, or others—a choice that is curious in light of the fact that Sartre chooses as examples the young woman going to her first sexual encounter and the homosexual being interrogated by the so-called "champion of sincerity."[3]

In these analyses, the Other is presented in a Cartesian fashion (Descartes tells the story of looking out his window and guessing that a man was there, even if he could only see a large-brimmed hat). In *Being and Nothingness,* the Other is a silhouette instead of being the constitutive element of the for-itself (as I believe it must be). Given the importance of bad faith for Sartre's definition of consciousness, and due to the relational nature of consciousness (as revealed by the disruption that Sartre inflicts upon the philosophy of the Subject), it is a surprise that the Other is barely perceptible.

I think these preliminary remarks have shown that Sartre does not yet realize the consequences of the profound intuition that lead him to substitute, in place of the classical philosophy of the consciousness, a worldly Subject. In spite of this, he nevertheless attempts to discuss, in order, the relationship of consciousness to the world, to itself, and to the Other.

I maintain, however, that Beauvoir's approach is in fact much more fecund, for she understands from the beginning that our world is populated by other freedoms who confront our own consciousness. I will examine this later in the chapter, but first I want to continue to trace the development of Sartre's thought between *Being and Nothingness* and *Critique of Dialectical Reason.* As many scholars have noticed, the binary relation (between consciousness and the Other, in the experience of the Look) with which Sartre models human relationships in *Being and Nothingness* is replaced by the model of the third in *Critique of Dialectical Reason;* the idea of triangularity becomes central to Sartre's later thought.

Alterity Tamed, at Last

As Sartre writes toward the end of *Being and Nothingness:*

> Here we have arrived at the end of this exposition. We have learned that the Other's existence was experienced with evidence in and through the fact of my objectivity. We have seen also that my reaction to my own alienation for the Other was expressed in my grasping the Other as an object. In short, the Other can exist for us in two forms: if I experience him with evidence, I fail to know him; if I know him, if I act upon him, I only reach his being-as-object and his probable existence in the midst of the world. No synthesis of these two forms is possible. (*BN*, 400)

The subjectivity and objectivity of the Other are thus disarticulated and resistant to the synthesis of Subject-Object (which is declared in principle impossible), contrary to Sartre's promise in his phenomenology—a phenomenology that, in principle, did not accept the division of the Subject and Object.

In *Critique of Dialectical Reason,* Sartre surpasses what he wrote in *Being and Nothingness,* extending the fundamental intuition about the nature of the for-itself (developed twenty years earlier in *Being and Nothingness*) to relationships with others. In this book, first published in 1960, the starting point remains intentionality, of course, but Sartre's goal is no longer to analyze, first, the for-itself (as a substantial subject), and second, the being-for-others (as if it was only an appendix of the former). Instead, Sartre examines the process through which each individual consciousness, as *praxis,* totalizes itself. Passing from seriality, through groups-in-fusion, to the formation of social institutions, Sartre shows how the individual is both surpassed and caused to be through its inclusion in practical ensembles.

> *The entire historical dialectic rests on individual* praxis *in so far as it is already dialectical,* that is to say, to the extent that action is itself the negating transcendence of contradiction, the determination of a present totalisation in the name of a future totality, and the real effective working of matter. This much is clear, and is an old lesson of both subjective and objective investigation. (*CDR*, 80)

And yet the constituent dialectic that brings to life individual praxis and the constituted dialectic that governs practical ensembles must be kept separate in Sartre's theory. If the first has its own unity, the second only takes on a unity through common action. In a famous example, the vacationer, looking through his window, causes the roadman and the gardener to be united, including them in a world that they totalize by themselves in their own way. Since the objective and the subjective are no longer conceived of as exterior from the Other in this description, the Other affects the vacationer without its being necessary for the Other to even look at the vacationer in his room. Thus, the vacationer who totalized the other two actors is, in turn, totalized by his action and united with the two others through it.

> It is a common error of many sociologists to stop at this point and treat the group as a binary relation (individual-community), whereas, in reality, it is a ternary relation. Indeed, this is something that no picture or sculpture could convey directly, in that the individual, *as a third party*, is connected, in the unity of a single *praxis* (and therefore of a single perceptual vista), with the unity of individuals as inseparable moments of a non-totalized totalisation, and with each of them as a *third party*, that is to say, through the mediation of the group. . . . *And the relation of one third party to another has nothing to do with alterity:* since the group is the practical milieu of this relation, it must be a human relation (with crucial importance for the differentiations of the group), which we shall call mediated reciprocity. And, . . . this mediation is dual, in that it is both the mediation of the group between third parties and the mediation of each third party between the group and the other third parties. (*CDR*, 374; emphasis mine)

The passage from binary relations in *Being and Nothingness* to the introduction of the third in *Critique of Dialectical Reason* corrects the concept of alterity in Sartre's philosophy—a concept that had caused the role of mediations in society to be misunderstood. At last, Sartre was able to see that social mediations are created by a third, who is in turn encompassed by them. The desubstantialization of the subject is then finally finished, and the anachronistic sovereign Subject (left over from early existential philosophy), threatened by the existence of the Other, is over and done with. Each of us becomes instead a third in our day-to-day social interactions.[4]

Beauvoir's Decisive Intervention

I have tried to trace the path Sartre took in developing his philosophy, and how he overcame the limits to his daring philosophical project in *Being and*

Nothingness that still existed. I believe Sartre's philosophical development from *Being and Nothingness* to *Critique of Dialectical Reason* to be a process of continuous evolution and progressive enrichment (rather than a rupture). Marxism is a major part of Sartre's later philosophy, insofar as it poses a challenge that Sartre believes only existentialism to be capable of satisfying. In this section, I will try to explain how Beauvoir's influence was decisive in leading Sartre to formulate the theses first expressed in *Critique of Dialectical Reason*.

A Resolute Existentialist

The philosopher Simone de Beauvoir wrote of her existentialism:

> Our perspective is that of existentialist ethics. Every subject plays his part as such specifically through exploits or projects that serve as a mode of transcendence; he achieves liberty only through a continual reaching out toward other liberties. There is no justification for present existence other than its expansion into an indefinitely open future. Every time transcendence falls back into immanence, stagnation, there is a degradation of existence into the '*en-soi*'—the brutish life of subjection to given conditions—and of liberty into constraint and contingence. This downfall represents a moral fault if the subject consents to it; if it is inflicted upon him, it spells frustration and oppression. In both cases it is an absolute evil. (*SS*, 28–29) [5]

It is revealing that Beauvoir had chosen to use the term *ethics* to describe her philosophical position. As she is at pains to stress, the originality of existentialism resides in the fact that it integrated transcendence into the Subject, which is then framed as the need to move outside itself into the world. The essential calling of such a subject, or more precisely such a consciousness, is one of "having to be."[6] In other words, the distinction of being versus having to be is canceled out; the two terms are joined together to define the human condition. Before discussing Beauvoir's impact on Sartre, I want to clarify two important issues with how she uses the term *ethics*.

First, Beauvoir objects to Kant's formulation of moral obligation—in particular, to Kant's assumption of the existence of separate determined beings *and* completely determining obligations. Kant presupposes a determined being (complete and identical to itself) who has no reason to obey any ethical having-to-be. In that context, what would it mean, she asks, for a determined being to determine itself? Only one faculty, under Kant's formulation—namely, willpower—would be capable of justifying consciousness's passage from being to having to be. Indeed, willpower would be both the condition according to which the problem of being and obligation is stated, and the way that it is resolved (through the construction of bridges between the One and the Other). That is what defines, for her, the circle of voluntarism!

When Beauvoir speaks of an existentialist ethics as part of her argument against the essentialist conception of the human being, she does so in order to fight against the fundamental tenets of voluntarism. In this respect,[7] Beauvoir elaborates on Sartre's criticism of voluntarism, first discussed in *Being and Nothingness,* arguing that it assimilates the distinct concepts of freedom and willpower:

> Here we have arrived at the end of this exposition. We have learned that the Other's existence was experienced with evidence in and through the fact of my objectivity. We have seen also that my reaction to my own alienation for the Other was expressed in my grasping the Other as an object. In short, the Other can exist for us in two forms: if I experience him with evidence, I fail to know him; if I know him, if I act upon him, I only reach his being-as-object and his probable existence in the midst of the world. No synthesis of these two forms is possible. (*BN,* 571–72)

Voluntarism therefore presupposes a Subject sure of its objectives, who only engages his free will in order to set into motion the means to obtain certain predetermined ends. Yet action could only occur when the acting subject already knows what his predefined (transcendent) objectives are. The Subject is therefore spared the angst that haunts all freedoms capable of creating their own objectives.

This is ultimately the problem, Beauvoir argues, with all forms of philosophical determinism: each imposes on the Subject external objectives to which we are expected to submit "voluntarily." (To put it briefly, determinism is a shameful defeatism.)

Thus, Beauvoir forcibly distinguishes between the will-to-be and the will-to-disclose-being. As she writes in *The Ethics of Ambiguity,* man's original essence is unclear:

> He [man] wants to be, and to the extent that he coincides with this wish, he fails. All the plans in which this will-to-be is actualized are condemned; and the ends circumscribed by these plans remain mirages. Human transcendence is vainly engulfed in those miscarried attempts. But man also wills himself to be a disclosure of being, and if he coincides with this wish, he wins, for the fact is that the world becomes present by his presence in

it. But the disclosure implies a perpetual tension to keep being at a certain distance, to tear oneself from the world, and to assert oneself as a freedom. To wish for the disclosure of the world and to assert oneself as freedom are one and the same movement. (*EA*, 23–24)

As will-to-be, human beings deny their freedom in order to make of themselves objects. Thus, this attitude is closely related to the naïve realistic attitude that says that being and truth are always pre-given; this implies that we are obliged to turn ourselves into purely objective beings. The subjectivity that inserts itself inside a scheme of pure objective truth creates a world of men-objects. To this philosophy, the will-to-be is nothing more than the will-to-be-as-one-already-is.

Does not a will that satisfies itself with taking upon itself being as it is prove its own uselessness? It certainly does not add anything to being, which already acts in a world full of richness. Rather, by causing subjectivity's adherence to this belief, it creates the conditions for subjectivity's self-negation, for its self-devalorization (here, we must be careful to emphasize that self-negation is an activity, and not the result of passivity: self-negation is always the negation of the self *by the self*). This self-negation is avidly practiced by those who subscribe to the spirit of seriousness, as illustrated in Simone de Beauvoir's writing (Beauvoir talks about its development during childhood):

> Man's unhappiness, says Descartes, is due to his having first been a child. And indeed the unfortunate choices which most men make can only be explained by the fact that they have taken place on the basis of childhood. The child's situation is characterized by his finding himself cast into a universe which he has not helped establish, which has been fashioned without him, and which appears to him as an absolute to which he can only submit. In his eyes, human inventions, words, customs, and values are given facts, as inevitable as the sky and the trees. This means that the world in which he lives is a serious world, since the characteristic of the spirit of seriousness is to consider values as ready-made things. (*EA*, 35)

To the serious spirit, everything is objective; values are things per se.

This will-to-be is the specificity of the individual (as conceived by modern individualism); it follows the precepts of rational choice, dictated by materiality (e.g., the laws of the market). This remark is made to underline again how Sartre's and Beauvoir's positions deviate from the concept of the individual taken by voluntarist thought.

Nonetheless, in *Being and Nothingness* Sartre actually outlines a description of alterity that is very similar to the individualist position (above, I showed how Sartre's discussion of alterity deviates substantially from his description of consciousness in *Being and Nothingness*). For example, in *Being and Nothingness* he describes the so-called duel of the eyes—the moment when the Other bursts into my visual field and threatens to disintegrate my world because it is itself a pole capable of organizing the world. This moment reproduces the competition that enslaves the individual, both as Subject and Object, and renders individuals unable to relate to each other, only to be united by the capitalist hyperorganism.[8]

An Existentialist Politics

The second point that I would like to stress is that I believe we must understand the expression an "existentialist ethics" to mean an "existentialist politics." In the quote that served as an introduction to these remarks, Beauvoir describes the transcendental goal (of human freedom) as a constant striving toward the freedom of others. Our relationship to the world is a relationship to other freedoms. If we believe Hannah Arendt, it is the fact that we live in a world of men (and not man) and that their actions make politics possible. As such, Arendt encourages us to break away from traditional political philosophy, which has been more intent on examining traditional forms of domination than on creating a theory of freedom.[9] In this section, I want to ask what Beauvoir means when she speaks of willing oneself "to be a disclosure of being."

In Beauvoir's formulation, the reflexive form of the verb *vouloir,* that is, *se vouloir,* suggests that subjectivity is present and active. She writes:

> My freedom must not seek to trap being but to disclose it. The disclosure
> is the transition from being to existence. The goal which my freedom aims
> at is conquering existence across the always inadequate density of being.
> (*EA,* 30)

In short, by showing that he has no essence, man unveils the world. By showing that he lacks an essence, which might take on the form, among others, of desire, anxiety, or nausea, he shows the fullness of the being that makes up the will-to-be. Coming to grips with the fullness of being does not necessarily mean piercing the surface of phenomena to reach their hidden hearts. Being is itself no mystery; it purely coincides with itself. To sink into being would unveil nothing but being's strict identity.

However, the moment of unveiling of being forces us to keep our distance, to free ourselves from pure being (as objectivity) and to become involved in the world. Being *is,* while the world *exists* as *"being upon which a layer of meaning has been shed"* by the action of the freedom of the for-itself.

To use one of Sartre's examples, the mountain is pure being-in-itself, rigidly set in its identity; it obtains meaning only through its relationship to beings-for-themselves. To the hiker who wants to reach shelter in the next valley, it is an obstacle; to the geographer, it is part of the earth's development; for the artist, it is an opportunity for aesthetic contemplation. When Beauvoir writes that unveiling is the passage from being to existence, we must be cautious. Indeed, Beauvoir is not trying to describe a passage going from one point to another, or from one level of being to another, as when in the course of philosophical investigation we ignore the immediacy of the phenomenon to concentrate on its essence.

Indeed, existence could not possibly add being to a being defined by its fullness; being could obviously not accept any addition to itself. The unveiling of being that Beauvoir describes is the realization that being's only essence is its existence; freedom experiences itself through the denial of its own essence. To project oneself into the world, to define our own values, to deny Being, are all synonyms. The denial of Being is not an inaugural, original event. It is the renewed event of human existence that is "a striving toward," "an intentionality." By locking up being in its fullness, Beauvoir, like Sartre, subscribes to a strain of philosophy that a Neoplatonist reading of the history of Western philosophy would try to suppress, one that separates being and rationality. To claim that being is not invested with any rationality is not at all the same as preaching irrationalism; rather, it is to put all the weight of rationality on human subjectivity. Whether the world is rational depends entirely on human subjectivity and its responsibility: according to the classic expression, "We are condemned to be free."

Our Situation Is Defined by Others

Every situation exists in the world; it is not of the same order as being. It is, in fact, essentially constituted out of Others; its objectivity is conditioned by the meaning that other subjectivities cast on being.

In order to better understand Beauvoir's analysis of the concept of the situation, I want to draw an analogy between the situation and two different theories of evolution: those of Lamarck and of Darwin, each of whom thinks of the role played by the environment in very different ways.

For Lamarck, the environment is made up of a set of physical conditions to which living beings adapt in order to ensure the continued survival of their species. Lamarckism does not give an account of evolution as such, since the constant evolution of life-forms toward ever greater modes of complexity (the vitalist principle) takes care of the need to explain evolution, but he must explain the evolution of peculiarities in nature. Darwin conceives of the role played by the environment in a different way. For him, there is no question of goal-driven evolution. In defining the environment, Darwin takes into account the role played by other members of the same species: each succeeding member of the species is faced with the problem that there are too many offspring for each to survive, and thus those carrying favorable variations—according to a haphazard distribution—are more likely to survive.

I want to argue that Beauvoir's idea of the situation is Darwinian in two important ways. Just as, from a Darwinian point of view, Lamarckism has no validity, so too, from a Beauvoirian point of view, the idea of progress must be rejected. This idea of progress presupposes that being is essentially rational, and raises the status of progress to a law of being. In practical terms, it means that progress becomes a necessary, invariant, natural part of human nature. This is expressed, for example, through the commonly held belief that the improvement of productive forces is forever producing beneficial effects. Questioning progress does not, of course, mean that we can no longer speak of progress; rather, it forces us to question the value of progress and to treat it as something to which we must give meaning, not something that is imbued with value once and for all. On the contrary, progressivism limits freedom, or human transcendence, to the "willing-to-be." Beauvoir herself describes the link between progressivism and "willing-to-be" by attacking the idea of usefulness, which as far as she is concerned, poses the same problems for being as does progress:

> Such a position would be solid and satisfactory if the word *useful* had an absolute meaning in itself; as we have seen, the characteristic of the spirit of seriousness is precisely to confer a meaning upon it by raising the Thing or the Cause to the dignity of an unconditioned end. The only problem then raised is a technical problem; the means will be chosen according to their effectiveness, their speed, and their economy; it is simply a question of measuring the relationships of the factors of time, cost, and probability of success. . . . The word *useful* requires a complement, and there can be only one: man himself. (*EA*, 111–12)

From a philosophical point of view, progressivism emerged in the philosophy of history in the nineteenth century. When confronted with the idea, Beauvoir responded by criticizing it for being unable to differentiate progress from a history of being; willpower can only wish for what already is (remaining the immediate prisoner of being) and disguise itself as the will-to-be.

The fact that both Hegel's and Marx's dialectics insisted on the role of the negative might have given us the hope that both would give wide latitude to human freedom. However, we must be disappointed by the fact that this negation can only make sense in relation to overcoming a past contradiction as part of the continued forward march of progress.

As Simone de Beauvoir remarks it, correctly in my opinion,

> In Marxism, if it is true that the goal and the meaning of action are defined by human wills, these wills do not appear as free. They are the reflection of objective conditions by which the situation of the class or the people under consideration is defined. In the present moment of the development of capitalism, the proletariat cannot help wanting its elimination as a class. Subjectivity is re-absorbed into the objectivity of the given world. Revolt, need, hope, rejection, and desire are only the resultants of external forces. The psychology of behavior endeavors to explain this alchemy. (*EA*, 19–20)

Beauvoir emphasizes how existentialist ontology is opposed to dialectical materialism: a situation's meaning cannot be discovered by a contemplative subject. It can only emerge through the actions of a free consciousness who acts to affirm its own project.

As I have shown, in existentialist ontology, negation and transcendence are interiorized by the Subject. At this point, I want to show how this decision to insert transcendence and negation into subjectivity (to make of them its constitutive elements) forces Beauvoir to rethink the relation between the freedom and the situation. Indeed, this decision entails two philosophical theses: the desubstantialization of the Subject (the Subject is not, he has-to-be), and the denaturalization of being (being is *in-itself*, it is not *for* a rationality).

Put in methodological terms, these two theses lead Beauvoir to denounce the then dominant presuppositions of the social sciences and to change how we view the relationship between freedom and situation. Rather than introducing the Subject *after* having established the objectivity of the situation, Beauvoir wants instead to establish freedom and situation contemporaneously. Neither of these two terms should claim any form of anteriority. Additionally, it is not a question of accommodating two separate terms. Rather, neither has any reality without the other: freedom is nothing but the "unveiling of existence," while the situation is only that which must be unveiled. The situation cannot be reduced to a set of exterior conditions (as determinism, with its tendency to simplify and to naturalize concepts, would have it). Beauvoir argues that as soon as the conditions that define the situation are exteriorized and separated from subjectivity, they are *inevitably* naturalized. The situation is rich with both our freedom and the freedom of all others. "The situation *is* the others," dare we say.

As such, the situation is both exterior and interior:

> Thus, every man has to do with other men. The world in which he engages himself is a human world in which each object is penetrated with human meanings. It is a speaking world from which solicitations and appeals rise up. This means that, through this world, each individual can give his freedom a concrete content. He must disclose the world with the purpose of further disclosure and by the same movement try to free men, by means of whom the world takes on meaning. (*EA*, 74)

This characterization of the situation as constituted by the others justifies, I hope, the parallel I have drawn with Darwin's conception of the environment.

Regimes of Alterity

The richness of Beauvoir's analysis of the situation, as compared to Sartre's analyses in *Being and Nothingness*, is important. Juliette Simont, in her invaluable monograph on freedom in Sartre's philosophy, writes:

> In *Being and Nothingness*, the situation was merely a backdrop, the condition from which our freedom would try to free itself, or would use to reveal itself (it is this dimension of Sartrean thought that is rendered by the provocative and brisk formula: "We were never as free as under the German occupation").[10]

The situation, thought of as merely the backdrop against which freedom exerts its essence as signifier, is a legacy of the strain of thought that conceives of the necessarily confrontational relationship between the Subject and Object. As I have already mentioned, this tends to favor the analysis of the binary term subject-object, and make the analysis of the Other more difficult. The Other becomes an essentialized being.

With Beauvoir's approach, the Other becomes not only a component of the situation, but its constituent part. For Beauvoir, the situation is more than simply a confrontation between a subject and an object ruled by an interplay of representations. Consequently, Beauvoir makes it a rule to surpass the Problem of the Other that is pronounced on at such length in philosophical manuals and to study instead the various possible varieties of alterity.

In *The Second Sex,* Beauvoir is able to describe with clarity the situation that men reserve for women by subsuming them under the category of the Other. Locked up in a situation of absolute alterity, without the possibility to develop any form of reciprocal relationships, women are dominated terribly. The attention paid to this specific regime of alterity shows that rulers control the meaning of the situation by setting the very conditions that make relationships possible. They push the oppressed away from their true being and deny them both it and the world. Their mastery of the situation allows them to define the situation such that the oppressed settle naturally into a situation that has already been objectively defined:

> As we have already seen, every man transcends himself. But it happens that this transcendence is condemned to fall uselessly back upon itself because it is cut off from its goals. That is what defines a situation of oppression. Such a situation is never natural: man is never oppressed by things . . . he does not rebel against things, but only against other men. The resistance of the thing sustains the action of man as air sustains the flight of the dove; and by projecting himself through it man accepts its being as an obstacle; he assumes the risk of a setback in which he does not see a denial of his freedom. . . . Only man can be an enemy for man; only he can rob him of the meaning of his acts and his life because it also belongs only to him alone to confirm it in its existence, to recognize it in actual fact as a freedom. (*EA,* 81–82)

In Sartre's terminology from the *Critique of Dialectical Reason,* these regimes of alterity have to be understood as modes of circulation of the third. This is, I believe, proof that Sartre must have heard the Beauvoirian lesson; identity is no longer conceivable without alterity. Henceforth, Sartre conceives of identity and alterity as strict contemporaries.

As such, I believe that the attention paid to the regimes of alterity makes existentialist philosophy take a direction that forces us to speak, in all honesty, of Beauvoirian-Sartrean philosophy. Moreover, the publication of *The Second Sex* weighed on the regimes of alterity and engendered new modalities of the circulation of the third. Sylvie Chaperon writes:

> Many women, anonymous or renowned, have expressed how reading *The Second Sex* was upsetting for them. They say emotionally that it was like

meeting themselves, that the text gives words and arguments to their "ill-being." Françoise d'Eaubonne recounts: "I read *The Second Sex*. I was overwhelmed by enthusiasm: finally a woman has understood! . . . We are all avenged." Throughout her life, Simone de Beauvoir received moving letters (kept today at the Bibliothèque Nationale) that form an invaluable archive. *The Second Sex* became an important object for discussion as part of a woman's movement that was in the process of transforming itself. This second collection is oddly unknown, particularly to researchers abroad. [11]

The Second Sex is not only a political work; it is a political fact. It is, in Michèle Le Doeuff's spirited and cheerful phrase, "the movement before the movement." [12]

In *Force of Circumstance,* Beauvoir wrote that a "book is a collective object. Readers contribute as much as the author to its creation" (*FC,* 38; *FCh,* 60). This is all the more true of her masterpiece. It is true because in *The Second Sex* Beauvoir unveils the inner workings of political activity. As it becomes more established and better accepted that humanity can only be conceived within intersubjectivity, we must label this idea as intra-alterity in order to give it its full weight of meaning.

The twin themes of intersubjectivity and intra-alterity were most often developed independently of each other. Beauvoir's analyses encouraged us to put forward the hypothesis that in order to understand intersubjectivity and intra-alterity we must examine them together. Beauvoir shows us that by experiencing itself as intrinsically Other, the Subject develops and discovers his own singularity. On the basis of the experience of his own alterity, the Subject can (in the sense that it becomes possible) actually discover Others, both other than himself and other than themselves. Such is the plurality, the plurality of a double alterity, that opens up the political sphere to exploration. This is the sphere in which humanity experiences itself as (once again, in an existential sense) that which must construct itself.

This understanding of alterity modifies many of our common concepts of social order. It shows that social order should come neither from the collective will of individuals who decide, quite reasonably—after the unhappy experience of the hypothetical state of nature (wherein exists a war of "every one against every one")—to give up their sovereign power to a state authority, nor from some natural and divine transcendental principle of organization. More to the point, it might be true that our social order is, in some sense, the result of individual wills or the divine will, but it is also true that this social order can be analyzed in these words only insofar as it is abstracted from the primary political order that gives it its meaning. This abstraction deceives us, casts a spell over us, and ultimately prevents us from seeing that no order of any kind (social, economic, or cultural) precedes the political order. The mistake of all prior political philosophy is to think the political only after having supposed an ontology, which, thanks to the development of the human sciences, is based in anthropology, sociology, or economics. On the contrary, against political philosophy we must affirm that the existence of humanity is a political act, an *existence* buried beneath a social *being*.

Notes

1. Here I am summing up what I described in greater detail in my essay "La conscience n'est pas sujet."

2. I am using the 1992 Washington Square Press edition.

3. On this point, see Michèle Le Doeuff's analysis in *Hipparchia's Choice*, 55–133.

4. This is the reason why it is not possible to place Sartre in the individualist current in philosophy (be it of the ontological variety that posits individuals as independent from another or of the methodological variety that uses the assumption of each individual's independence from all others as a hypothesis to analyze social phenomena): it would commit him to the atomistic idea of the individual that he rejects. Sartre never adhered to such a point of view, even if he was never able in *Being and Nothingness* to shake himself clear of some of individualism's beliefs. Sartre's analyses should be compared with Norbert Elias's *Die Gesellschaft der Individuen*.

5. I am using the 1971 Knopf edition of *The Second Sex*.

6. It should be noted that by interiorizing transcendence, existentialism puts an end to the traditional definitions of transcendence: transcendence from above, in the spiritualist tradition (the transcendent order of values and truths); and transcendence from below, in the manner of deterministic materialism (e.g., the view that our psychological processes are strictly determined either by our socioeconomic standing or by biologism in psychology).

7. My argument here follows the more developed argument in my *Simone de Beauvoir philosophe*, 41–57.

8. "But we should be quite clear about this: the group is not a reality which exists in itself *in spite of* the 'transcendence-immanence' tension which characterizes the third party in relation to it. On the contrary, the 'transcendence-immanence' of its members creates the possibility of the group as common action. Pure immanence, indeed, would eliminate the practical organism in favor of a hyper-organism" (*CDR*, 409).

9. See Arendt, "Philosophy and Politics," 73–103.

10. Simont, *Jean-Paul Sartre, un demi-siècle de liberté*, 145–46; my translation.

11. Chaperon, "1949–1999: Cinquante ans de lecture," 359.

12. Le Doeuff, *Hipparchia's Choice* (Columbia University Press, 2007), 57.

9 Moving beyond Sartre: Constraint and Judgment in Beauvoir's "Moral Essays" and *The Mandarins*

Sonia Kruks

> When I was born, I was on rails ... the little girl of three lived on, grown calmer, in the child of ten, that of the child in the young woman of twenty, and so on. Of course, circumstances led me to develop in many ways. But through all the changes I still see myself. ... My life has been at once the fulfillment of an original project and the product and expression of the world in which it unfolded. This is why, in recounting it, I have been able to speak of many things besides myself.
> —Simone de Beauvoir, *All Said and Done*

Among her novels, Simone de Beauvoir thought most highly of *The Mandarins,* while among her nonfiction works (which she usually referred to as "essays") she most approved of *The Second Sex.* When comparing her early novel *The Blood of Others* (completed in 1943) with *The Mandarins* (completed in 1953), Beauvoir later remarks that the former was not as successful because in it she reduced her characters to "mere ethical viewpoints," presenting "simple, unambiguous, and morally edifying" conclusions through them (*PL,* 465).[1] Likewise, Beauvoir observes that in *She Came to Stay* (completed in 1941), she had used her characters above all as vehicles to make metaphysical points. Beauvoir later criticized what she called the "thesis-novel" (*roman à thèse*) as an unsatisfactory literary form, because it contradicts the proper intent of a novel: "A novel is about bringing existence to light in its ambiguities, in its contradictions."[2] Such a disclosure of ambiguity is what *The Mandarins* undertakes, and this is why she approves of it:

> Thesis-novels always impose a certain truth that eclipses all others and calls a halt to the perpetual dance of conflicting points of view; whereas [in

The Mandarins] I described certain ways of living after the war, without offering any solution to the problems that were troubling my main characters. . . . I showed some people at grips with doubts and hopes, groping in the dark; I cannot think I proved anything. (*FC*, 270–71)

Among her nonfiction works, Beauvoir was most critical of the ethico-political essays from what she later disparagingly referred to as her "moral period" (*PL*, 433). This period begins with the publication of *Pyrrhus et Cinéas*, which was written in 1943 shortly after Sartre's *Being and Nothingness* appeared and with the intent of developing some of the ethical implications of that work, which Sartre had promised but not provided. It includes a group of essays published in 1945 and 1946,[3] and culminates with *The Ethics of Ambiguity* (published in 1947). *The Blood of Others* and the "moral period" essays were, of course, all written either during the war or in the turbulent immediate postwar period. It is hardly surprising, then, that they bear a resemblance to each other in that they are all marked by the same strongly moralizing tone. Beauvoir later explained this tone as her way of responding to the dramatic collapse of her hitherto happy and stable world and to her ensuing sense of "chaos": "I had as my only recourse this verbal exorcism: an abstract morality" (*PL*, 433; *FA*, 626, my translation).

However, by the time the last of the "moral period" essays, *The Ethics of Ambiguity*, was published in 1947, Beauvoir was already at work on something very different: *The Second Sex*; and by the time its second volume was published, in November 1949, she was already busy writing *The Mandarins*. Thus, the "essay" and the novel that Beauvoir regarded as her most successful works were written consecutively. Taken together, I argue, they are indicative of a new period in her thinking in which she was increasingly breaking away from certain aspects of Sartre's early philosophy, at least as he had articulated it in *Being and Nothingness*. This new period was marked by an increasingly profound acknowledgment of the weight of situations, of what she will call *la force des choses*. Now she ceased the attempt to "exorcise" those elements of life that are beyond control of the self and instead began to recognize their presence as integral to human existence, her own and others. This new recognition profoundly informed her writings from the late 1940s onward.

A continuity of preoccupations—with questions of selfhood, freedom, responsibility, judgment, and resistance to oppression—runs throughout Beauvoir's entire *oeuvre*. But within this continuity an important change of emphasis and approach takes place. What is most striking, both in *The Second Sex* and *The Mandarins*, is Beauvoir's shift toward a notion of a self that not only makes its choices "in situation" (as Sartre had argued in *Being and Nothingness*) but is so thoroughly suffused *by* its situation that it is, to a significant degree, constituted by it. For example, when Beauvoir writes in *The Second Sex* that a woman's body "is her situation" (*SS*, 34),[4] she does not of course mean that biology is a determining factor for a woman; biology does not irrevocably set down her entire life course. However, she does mean that the facticity, or accident of birth, that requires that one grow to maturity and live one's life with a biologically female body will always be integral to one's selfhood and to one's projects.[5] Even though a female body (and likewise a male, white, black, healthy, or disabled one) may be taken up and acted upon, or "assumed,"[6] in diverse fashions, it will always be integral to who one is and thus will indelibly color how one acts. Likewise, in *The Mandarins*, the main characters learn that the facticity of being French in the 1940s profoundly suffuses their possibilities for political action. "Freedom," here, is doubly constrained. Freedom becomes not only a matter of acting within the small margins and many constraints of one's immediate situation, but also of making one's decisions as who one has already "become."

Famously, "one is not born a woman but becomes one" (*SS*, 267). But Beauvoir's statement, and her ensuing account of women's "lived experience," invoke two senses of the verb "to become": in becoming a gender, an ethnicity, a nationality, and so on, one "becomes" what one has been made by one's situation, and one also "becomes" what one has made of oneself as such a situated existent. Furthermore, depending on what one has become, one will be more likely to make certain kinds of choices in the future and less likely to make other ones. For although what we have become will not *determine* our future actions, it does strongly *predispose* us to proceed along certain paths. For example, although I may in principle be "free" to overcome the inferiority complex with which I have lived for twenty years, as Sartre insists in *Being and Nothingness*, Beauvoir's view of freedom is nearer to Merleau-Ponty's when he asserts, in criticism of Sartre, that such a transformation is not "probable."[7] Probability, Merleau-Ponty points out, is not a fiction but a real phenomenon. For if I have made my inferiority "my abode" for the last twenty years, then "this past, though not a fate, has at least a specific weight and is . . . the atmosphere of my present." Thus, he continues, "our freedom does not destroy our situation, but gears itself to it."[8] Such a "gearing" of freedom to situation is implied in Beauvoir's autobiographical comment about living "on rails" in the epigraph from *All Said and Done* with which I began this chapter.[9] Similarly Henri, a central character in *The Mandarins*, discovers that he is "on rails." Having become a Resistance activist and a prominent left-wing intellectual during the war, he is now somebody who cannot cease to remain politically committed, even though he has ambitions to withdraw from politics in order to write.

Thus, in both *The Second Sex* and *The Mandarins,* Beauvoir moves beyond the "abstractness" of her early "moral period," as she puts into question her earlier and more Sartrean characterization of the self as always free to make its own choices within its given situation. Instead, she develops an account in which selves make their choices not only as affirmations of a future but also as instantiations of a present that is heavily freighted by the past.[10] Thus, accompanying Beauvoir's greater focus on the weight of situations, in both *The Second Sex* and *The Mandarins* she gives greater attention to the particularities of lived experience, and in both works she uses phenomenological methods more fully.

Accordingly, in volume two of *The Second Sex,* women are not characterized as one homogeneous group. Rather, Beauvoir offers phenomenological descriptions of femininity as it is lived at different life stages (from childhood to old age) and by different kinds of women (e.g., heterosexual or lesbian, compliant or resistant). Likewise, as Beauvoir herself remarked, her quasi-fictional characters in *The Mandarins* cease to be above all the bearers of moral or metaphysical positions. Rather, through the use of extensive internal monologue—drawing heavily from her own experiences and those of people close to her—she presents us with descriptions of the lived experience of a particular group of people: the politically engaged non-communist Left in postwar France. However, through the evocation of the experiences of this particular group, Beauvoir illuminates for us aspects of political experience more generally. As such, without being a "thesis-novel," *The Mandarins* is still a work that speaks to concerns that persist well beyond the confines of its own era. A key theme that pervades Beauvoir's early ethico-political writings, which she further addresses in *The Mandarins* and which still matters today, concerns the nature of political judgment. In what follows, this theme is used as a lens through which one may also chart the trajectory of Beauvoir's changing views on freedom.

The "Moral Essays"

Contemporary normative approaches to judgment remain predominantly neo-Kantian, usually positing an autonomous, rational agent of judgment—either one who dispassionately weighs and assesses the virtues of general principles or else one who, concerned with judging specific courses of action or events, evaluates these impartially against such general principles in order to decide what "ought" to be (or to have been) done. In her "moral period," as we shall see, Beauvoir's focus on political judgment still broadly remains within this tradition. Of course, she does already depart from a straightforward Kantianism insofar as she insists that the self must decide "in situation" and often in situations that do not admit of a straightforward moral resolution through the application of principle. But she still attributes a strong autonomy—indeed, an "infinite" freedom—to the self.[11] She argues that others' actions may impinge only on the "outside" (*les dehors*), and thus not on the ontological freedom of an individual (*PC*, 83, 86). Thus, she also argues, each of us must judge and act alone; consequently, we must also assume full moral responsibility for our individual actions. To deny this responsibility, it follows, is to attempt to flee one's freedom; it is to act in "bad faith."

In *The Mandarins*, however, Beauvoir puts into question these tenets of her earlier work. For what the novel reveals is that making political judgments is itself a form of situationally suffused *action*. "Judging," in this fuller sense, is an activity that we can very rarely undertake detached from the facticities of our own particular lives. For these facticities will strongly color (even though they do not determine) how we view the world, and they will significantly shape what we decide and do. They will suffuse our freedom and shape our judgments in ways that Beauvoir does not admit in her early essays, in ways that Sartre does not conceive of in *Being and Nothingness*, and that generally still remain unacknowledged in neo-Kantian conceptions of judgment.

In *Pyrrhus et Cinéas*, the first essay from her "moral" period, Beauvoir initially follows Sartre's early philosophy in arguing that we are each an *ontologically* free and separate existent that, alone and through its own projects, constitutes the meaning of its own life. She makes a distinction between this ontological freedom, which she calls "*liberté*" and which she still insists "remains infinite" (*PC*, 86), and what she calls "*puissance*." The latter term refers to our concrete ability to act in the world, an ability I will refer to as our *effective* freedom. This, unlike *liberté*, she says, is "finite," so others "can augment or limit it from without [*du dehors*]" (*PC*, 86).

However, an ontological freedom that cannot realize itself in choosing effective projects, a freedom that cannot engage in meaningful action in the world, is doomed to consume itself uselessly. Thus we can realize our *liberté* only insofar as we also possess *puissance*, or effective freedom—and this is not always the case.[12] For Beauvoir adds a highly significant caveat to her account of *puissance*, one that Sartre had not made in his treatment of freedom in *Being and Nothingness*. She argues that to enjoy effective freedom we must overcome our separation from others; we must both recognize and be recognized by them. Indeed, Beauvoir points out, to imagine myself alone in the world is truly horrifying. "A man alone in the world would be paralyzed by the self-evident vanity of all his goals; he undoubtedly could not bear to live" (*PC,* 65). Without reciprocal human recognition, our lives lack the means to overcome our individual finitude. For it is only when others take up and prolong our projects that the import of our actions may travel on beyond us. Thus, through reciprocal relations of "generosity," we must seek to move beyond the conflictual relations of self and other, which Sartre had described in *Being and Nothingness.*[13] We must will for all others an enlarged capacity to act meaningfully in the actual world—that is a greater degree of *effective* freedom.

Here is the claim that makes possible Beauvoir's move toward ethics and that also integrally links her ethics to radical politics—a linkage that Sartre will begin to explore only some years later in his *Notebooks for an Ethics.* In choosing my own freedom, I must also choose to extend that of others. Not only must I (as far as is possible) recognize and respect the freedom of other individuals I encounter, but I also must act so as to maximize the realm of effective freedom for everyone. Because oppression, which negates effective freedom, is rife in the world, an ethically inspired political engagement follows from Beauvoir's account of human existence. I must endeavor "to create for all men situations which will enable them to accompany and surpass my transcendence . . . [men need] health, knowledge, well-being, leisure, so that their freedom does not consume itself in fighting sickness, misery, ignorance" (*PC,* 115).

However, as Beauvoir herself later commented, her arguments in *Pyrrhus et Cinéas* still remain too "enmeshed in individualism." She observes: "An individual, I thought, only receives a human dimension by recognizing the existence of others. Yet, in [*Pyrrhus et Cinéas*], coexistence appears as a sort of accident that each individual should somehow surmount; each should begin by hammering out his project in isolation, and only then ask the collectivity to validate it." She goes on to observe: "In truth, society invests me [*m'investit*] from the day of my birth; it is in the bosom of society, and in my own intimate relationship with it, that I decide who I am to be" (*PL,* 435; *FA,* 628–29, my translation). For the later Beauvoir, then, our "coexistence" with others is no longer contingent but rather is integral to the self; and it thus follows that the self, even conceived as a *liberté,* is always profoundly suffused by its social situation.

Because *Pyrrhus et Cinéas* still lacks such an account of the self, the essay is also, as Beauvoir says more generally of her "moral period" essays, "abstract" (*PL,* 433). In *Pyrrhus et Cinéas,* Beauvoir criticizes Kant, arguing that "respect for the human person is not generally sufficient to guide us" (*PC,* 91). An executioner and his victim are both full human beings, yet we cannot support both:

we must decide whether we let the victim perish or kill the executioner (*PC*, 91). But how do we decide? Beauvoir argues, again against Kant, that we cannot decide "objectively" and that it is not possible to adequately evaluate such dilemmas from a dispassionate or "contemplative" attitude. For "if I am removed from all situations, all givens will seem equally indifferent to me" (*PC*, 92). Thus, we must make our judgments *in situation*.

But what does it mean to decide "in situation"? Beauvoir urges us to take up, or "assume" our freedom; we are told that we can and must choose, that we are responsible for our choices, and that we are in bad faith if we deny this. But in *Pyrrhus et Cinéas* she still operates at a level of abstraction that is too far removed from the actual world, from the concrete givens in which we make our specific judgments. Thus Beauvoir becomes mired in a problem analogous to the one she attributes to Kant. For maxims such as "Act so as to choose freedom for all" and "Recognize that you alone are responsible for your acts" are, in themselves, as abstract as his categorical imperative. This becomes apparent in her subsequent "moral period" essays. For example, in "Moral Idealism and Political Realism," first published in 1945, Beauvoir sets out with only limited success to chart a course between an "idealism" that urges that we follow right principles irrespective of the consequences and a cynical "realism" that is concerned only with political efficacy.

Both the idealist's claim, that one is bound to follow a preordained principle or duty, and the realist's claim, that objective necessity requires that we act in particular ways, are forms of bad faith, Beauvoir argues. For they are both ways of evading responsibility for our own freedom and the anguish it evokes. Beauvoir agrees with Kant that "treating man as a means is committing violence against him; it means contradicting the idea of his absolute value."[14] However, in a world of oppression and conflict, it may be impossible to avoid doing violence to others. Thus, against Kant, Beauvoir also insists that it is not possible to act on behalf of "man" without sometimes treating certain men merely as means. In many situations, "whatever I may choose to do, I will be unfaithful to my profound desire to respect human life; and yet I am forced to choose; *no reality external to myself indicates my choice [aucune réalité extérieure à moi-même ne m'indique mon choix]*."[15] Neither pre-given ethical imperatives (which the Kantian autonomous self claims freely to follow), nor claims about the necessary course of History (beloved by certain deterministic Marxists) may justify our decisions. Here, says Beauvoir, is the source of the anguish that so many flee in bad faith. For we are alone in our freedom and in our responsibility; we act in a world where nothing tells us what we should decide and where we cannot avoid violence.[16]

Beauvoir takes as an example a choice that may have confronted a leader in the Resistance: one may have to decide whether or not to sacrifice the life of one man in order to save the lives of many—but either choice is a "scandal." Whichever one decides, she insists, the decision is mine alone. For "it is not reality that imposes a choice on me, it is only after I have made a choice that reality takes on any value."[17] But here we see the abstractness of Beauvoir's account. For if my decision, whether or not to save the life of a particular man, cannot be made by subsuming it under an ethical principle and is not the outcome of determining forces, how then *do* I decide? Assuming I do not just toss a coin, assuming that my decision is not wholly arbitrary, then what concretely enters into my decision-making process? Are there not factors that will strongly predispose me to decide in a certain way? Is not my freedom, as Merleau-Ponty had put it, "geared" to my situation?

In the passage I quoted above, Beauvoir insists (here paralleling Sartre in *Being and Nothingness*) that "no reality external to myself indicates my choice."[18] Certainly, she is correct insofar as no exterior reality *determines* my choice, in the strict sense of operating upon me with the full causal necessity of a physical law. Yet, as Beauvoir will later acknowledge, there still are many factors, some external and some arising from how I have *already* assumed the world in which I find myself, that will strongly *predispose* me to decide in a certain way. These factors may include pressure from others, cultural norms, ethical considerations, my rational weighing up of other pros and cons, emotional responses such as anger or love, my habitual ways of responding to dilemmas, and so on. As Merleau-Ponty had argued against Sartre,[19] between determinism and the claim that my choice is not an effect of *any* "external" factors, lie alternatives and gradations.[20] Beauvoir begins to explore some of these gradations in *The Second Sex*, when she considers the different degrees of complicity women may have in their own oppression.[21] But it is in *The Mandarins* that Beauvoir explores yet more fully this in-between zone in which our judgments are so often made.

Were there only two possible ways to explain how we arrive at a judgment, either through external determination or else through a choice made by a freedom that is "infinite," then by rejecting determinism we would make of freedom a matter of choice that is so indeterminate that it becomes arbitrary. For if being free only means that we are not determined, then why, when presented with a dilemma such as Beauvoir describes, should we not just toss a coin to decide what to do? For no one outcome would matter more than another—indeed, nothing would matter, and nihilism would follow. However, Beauvoir firmly wishes to avoid such a position.[22]

It is true that in *The Ethics of Ambiguity*, Beauvoir does say of "political choice" that it is a "wager": one "bets on the chances and risks of the measures under consideration" (*EA*, 148). However, a political choice is also far more than a wager for her. But if, as Beauvoir argues, we must make our judgments in anguished awareness of our responsibility, then we will need to give a fuller account of the ways we arrive at them than she is able to offer in her early essays. Between the bad faith claims (of idealists and realists alike) that our judgments and actions are imposed on us, and Beauvoir's bald counter-affirmation, in "Moral Idealism and Political Realism" and other essays of her "moral period," that we decide "alone" and in our "infinite freedom," we need an account that is more attentive to the experience of a self as one suffused by its situation. What Beauvoir still lacks in her early essays is a phenomenology that reveals the complex "lived experience" through which we arrive at political judgments. Such a phenomenology will reveal our choices to be neither determined nor arbitrary.

Our freedom, to recall Merleau-Ponty's phrase again, "gears itself to our situation."[23] Since we are each a situated freedom, we will each discover how the social milieu in which we live, with its normative and cultural practices, informs (even though it does not determine) our judgments. We will see how our prior decisions and actions may strongly shape (though, again, they do not strictly determine) our future ones. We will learn, in short, that we do not only decide "in" situation, but we decide as selves that are already strongly suffused by their situation. Here we need to turn to *The Mandarins*. For this is where we find Beauvoir developing such a phenomenological exploration of the making of political judgments. In *The Mandarins* we are shown how freedom and situation merge and meld, how our situation suffuses our "free" choices.

Judgment in *The Mandarins*

Beauvoir insists that "contrary to what has been claimed, it is not true that *The Mandarins* is a *roman à clé*" (*FC*, 267; *FCh*, 366, my translation). Neither *roman à clé*, nor thesis-novel; neither autobiography, nor reportage, Beauvoir describes *The Mandarins* as "an evocation" (*FC*, 270). It is an evocation in which fiction is used as a tool to present complexities of life that mere reportage could not capture. I think Beauvoir must be taken at her word: *The Mandarins* is not a *roman à clé*. The fictitious characters do not align neatly with the actual *dramatis personae* of Beauvoir's circle, and although the novel treats of the impact of actual political events of the late 1940s, the chronology is not accurate. Yet as an evocation, *The Mandarins* is also grounded in lived experience, and its "fictions" are in large measure woven from the autobiographical. Beauvoir says she put important elements of herself and of her own experiences in the postwar era into two different characters: Anne Dubreuilh and Henri Perron. It is above all through the character of Henri that Beauvoir explores the lived experience of political judgment. "Most of the time they are my own emotions and thoughts that inhabit him," she writes (FC, 269). And in an interview given when she won the Prix Goncourt, she says, "it is with regard to Henri that I tried to pose the real problems [of practical politics]."[24]

Henri Perron is a successful young novelist, Resistance activist, and editor of a Leftist daily newspaper, L'Espoir [Hope], that he co-founded during the Resistance. He struggles throughout the novel to make sense of the shifting political currents and events of the postwar period and to satisfy his diverse and conflicting desires. He wants to engage effectively and responsibly in a Leftist politics that navigates between the two great power blocks of the emerging Cold War; to find the time to write a new novel; to disengage from a stifling affair with his long-standing mistress, Paula; to enjoy other liaisons; to maintain his close friendship with Robert Dubreuilh, the older and highly charismatic intellectual who in 1935 had helped Henri to get his first novel published.

By following Henri through his dilemmas and decisions, we may begin to construct from Beauvoir's novel an account, one still absent from her "moral period" essays, of the lived experience of making political judgments. In the course of the novel, Henri has to reach a series of crucial decisions, each of which is at once personal and political, and each of which involves being a freedom whose "choice" is, he discovers, profoundly suffused by its situation. These decisions include (among others): whether to join the SRL, the new "third way" Left political organization Robert Dubreuilh is founding;[25] whether (once having joined) to agree to make L'Espoir its official newspaper; whether to publish information that is emerging about forced labor camps in the Soviet Union; whether to perjure himself to protect his mistress, who had previously had an affair with a German officer during the Occupation; whether (at the end of the novel) to exile himself to Italy to write or to stay in Paris and remain politically engaged.

I shall focus here on only one of these decisions: whether or not to turn L'Espoir into the official organ of the SRL. For in this key exemplar, Beauvoir reveals judgment to be shaped by the convergence of multiple aspects of one's situated existence. She depicts structures, histories, and events that so strongly shape Henri's process of judgment as to put into question her earlier, Sartrean, notion of liberté. Initially, we might believe that Henri is going to make a free choice of the kind Beauvoir had talked about in the "moral period" essays. For his decision is not, strictly speaking, determined by exterior forces; nor is he able to decide what to do through the application of principles. It might appear that Henri must simply "wager" and, afterwards, acknowledge his sole responsibility for what he chooses. But this is not the case. For it becomes apparent that Henri's freedom is already profoundly suffused with the world in which he now finds himself situated and that his choice is not random, but rather, it is constrained by who he has already become. Far from its being the case that nothing "external" to Henri "indicates" his choice, he discovers he is caught up in a set of strongly convergent forces that will significantly contribute to his decision.

The Mandarins begins with an account of a joyous Christmas party, held in December 1944 in recently liberated Paris. Henri has devoted himself for four years to Resistance politics, above all to publishing *L'Espoir*, and is now aching to live life more fully again. He hungrily anticipates the end of the deprivations and drudgery of the Occupation years. He yearns to travel (he has an invitation that he intends to accept to give some lectures in Portugal), and above all, he desires to write fiction again: "With no time for himself he had lost his taste for life and desire to write. He had become a machine . . . now he was determined to become a man again" (*Man*, 16). But even during this joyous Christmas celebration, Robert Dubreuilh approaches Henri and urges him to become involved with the political struggles looming in the new postwar era by participating in the SRL. In the Resistance, life had been straightforward, as had been running the paper. He knows that now "politics," in the sense of endless committees, conferences, meetings, maneuverings, and compromises, will consume his time and energies, and exasperate and bore him. However, when Dubreuilh approaches him, he does not feel he has "the right to look for an out," so he agrees to lend his name to the SRL and to "put in a few appearances" (*Man*, 18).

Already, the "impasse" is revealed. The trap is sprung. Henri wants to go back to being what he was and doing what he did before the war. But as he discovers, he is no longer the "same" Henri; for now he is also the man he has become during the war. Moreover, he must act in a new national and international configuration not of his choosing and that will, to a significant degree, define who he is and what his possibilities are. A Leftist armchair intellectual in 1939, he now knows that he is obligated to be more politically active if he is to break away from the privileges of his class, if he is not to deserve the hatred of millions of oppressed people (*Man*, 17). However, if he gets sucked into politics, he will not have time to write. Another character, the emigré Scriassine, puts this dilemma into a wider context: "French intellectuals are facing an impasse . . . their art, their philosophies [*pensée*] will continue to have meaning only if a certain kind of civilization manages to endure. And if they want to save that civilization, they'll have nothing left over to give to art or philosophy. . . . What weight will the message of French writers have when the earth is ruled by either Russia or the United States? No one will understand them anymore; nobody will even speak their language anymore" (*Man*, 43–45; Fr. 54–56, my translation).[26]

The SRL stands for a "third way," for a democratic socialist France. This must be built by creating a space between the imperialism of U.S.-dominated world capitalism and the deformed, expansionist socialism of the Soviet Union. Without an autonomous France, there will no longer be a place for meaningful cultural expression by French intellectuals. Yet even to keep such a possibility alive in the emerging Cold War context will be an all-consuming struggle.[27] For Henri and others in his circle, there is yet a further impasse within the "impasse." For their assessment is that, for all its deformations, the Soviet Union still remains the greatest force for progress. Moreover, the French Communist Party (PCF), which takes its line from Moscow, is still the party that enjoys mass working-class support in France and thus de facto represents socialist potential. The SRL must not alienate the PCF, but rather must give it critical support. But if the SRL criticizes the Soviet Union and keeps its distance from the PCF, how then will it win the mass of people to its more democratic socialist agenda? It is within the context of these multiple dilemmas that Henri struggles over the decision whether or not to make *L'Espoir* the official organ of the SRL. Over time, and as various elements come to bear on him, he shifts from insisting that *L'Espoir* must remain independent to agreeing that it will become the organ of the SRL.

After this struggle is over, and when Henri has finally agreed that *L'Espoir* is formally to become the newspaper of the SRL, he has a conversation with Robert Dubreuilh's wife, Anne. Henri is resentful about the pressure Dubreuilh has put on him to give *L'Espoir* to the SRL. "But you did agree," says Anne. Yes, Henri says, he did agree. But, he adds, it is hard not to feel resentful when you are "pushed" into doing something "against your will [*à contrecoeur*]" (*Man*, 254–55). But how does one come to make a "decision" that goes against one's will? One does not do so, Beauvoir's account suggests, only or even primarily through a process of clear reasoning and dispassionate judgment. For one is carried toward one's final judgment by the confluence of many aspects of one's situation that are not the object of one's rational deliberations.

This is not to deny that Henri spends many hours trying to decide what is the most rational course of action, considering what appear to be the objective pros and cons of the matter. On the side of keeping *L'Espoir* independent of the SRL he can, most importantly, point to the need to go on maintaining full editorial independence if he is to keep trust with his readers and with his own commitments: "Now was the time to educate readers instead of cramming things down their throats. No more dictating opinions to them; rather teach them to judge for themselves" (*Man*, 28). He can also point to the financial risk of losing readers who may be displeased if *L'Espoir* ceases to be independent. But he hears conflicting arguments from different sides: the SRL will end up in bed with the Communists and so will *L'Espoir*, warns one. To the contrary, if the SRL has a newspaper of its own, it will become too strong a force for the PCF to accept and it will be destroyed, warns another. On the side of giving the paper to the SRL, the strongest argument is that Henri is already a prominent member of the SRL: if he supports this movement, then surely he should help it to grow by providing it with a daily paper. Moreover, in the postwar situation the paper itself now needs a clear program. Its "independence" threatens to become vacuous, a way of pleasing everyone by committing to nothing. The memory of the Resistance, the moment of the paper's founding, no longer provides an adequate political program. Indeed, the Resistance is fast becoming a nostalgic myth, not an orientation to action.

But as he considers all of these arguments, Henri becomes aware of several things: one is that "concrete evidence" will never be a sufficient basis on which to arrive at a wise judgment. We never know enough to be sure that our decisions will have the desired outcome. Will the readership grow or shrink if he gives the paper to the SRL? Will the SRL grow or not as a result? On so many political matters, Henri reflects, you have to act without knowing. "First, you've got to speak, because the matter is urgent; afterwards events prove you right or wrong. 'And that's precisely what's known as bluffing,' he said unhappily to himself. 'Yes, even I bluff my readers'" (*Man*, 175). But if he is bluffing, if he fails to give his readers what he has promised them, then why defend the independence of the paper? Similarly, he tells the younger man, Lambert, one can't defend the paper's independence on the grounds that one must be free to follow one's own conscience, for this too is to act from ignorance: "'It's just a question of speaking as our consciences dictate!' Lambert said. 'Did you ever stop to think what that means?' Henri asked. 'Every morning I tell a hundred thousand people how they ought to think. And what do I guide myself by? The voice of my conscience! ... It's a gigantic swindle'" (*Man*, 177).

But if rational arguments, the "concrete evidence" we believe we possess, or our moral convictions are insufficient to justify our decisions, are we not after all in the realm of mere "wager"? Might Henri not as well toss a coin to make his decision? If he did so, however, it would turn out to be heavily weighted; it would be far more likely to come down one way than the other. For many aspects of his situation enter into how he decides. They include his personal "history"; his present desires, fears, loves, and friendships; his wider network of social connections—Paris, France, the international situation, and so on. It is Henri as the point of convergence and (to use Sartre's much later term) the "totalizer" of all of this who will "make" the decision.[28]

Although he does very seriously consider all the rational arguments, from the beginning Henri has what we might call a "gut" resistance to the idea of handing over *L'Espoir*. "No, he wouldn't give him [Dubreuilh] *L'Espoir*. That was so clear that it needed no justifying. Nevertheless, he wished he could find a few good reasons for his stand" (*Man,* 153). Why this gut feeling? Henri has created the paper, and in doing so, he has made being its editor vital to his own existence. The paper is his "world." It is not only his project but also a place where he is profoundly at home. Beauvoir describes Henri entering the offices alone, late at night: "He liked the familiar smell of stale dust and fresh ink. The offices were still empty, the basement silent. But soon a whole world would rise from this silence, a world that was his creation. 'No one will ever lay his hands on *L'Espoir*,' he repeated to himself. He sat down at his desk and stretched out" (*Man,* 166; Fr. 207, my translation).

In addition, Henri's initial gut resistance to Dubreuilh's proposal is linked to his passionate desire to become again the "old" Henri, the creative and successful writer, the man with a zest for life. But putting *L'Espoir* into the hands of the SRL will mean being sucked further into the desiccating world of politics. Already he is "dry," and he will become more so. Then writing will be impossible. There is also the matter of personal relationships, above all of Dubreuilh. Henri feels obligated to him, and his continued friendship with the older man who has been his mentor is important. But he also feels resentment and anger that Dubreuilh is making him feel guilty and is using their friendship against him. There is also Samazelle, a powerful player in the SRL. Henri actively dislikes this man and distrusts his politics, and he knows that he will have to deal with him day after day if *L'Espoir* goes to the SRL.

Why then does Henri end by deciding to give *L'Espoir* to the SRL? It is not just that he chooses a rationally justifiable or morally superior course of action across the grain of his emotional preferences. Choosing against one's will here is not a matter of choosing reason over unreason, selflessness over self-interest. Rather, it has to do with a profound shift in Henri's own *experience* of self. It has to do with his realization that, for reasons both of his own making and reasons beyond his control, his very existence has changed. "'It's funny,'" he remarks to himself, "'but whenever you do the decent thing, instead of giving you certain rights it only creates more obligations.' He had founded *L'Espoir*, and now that act was driving him to throw himself body and soul into the political madhouse" (*Man*, 190; Fr. 237, my translation).

But the problem is not only one of being "forced" into politics. For what Henri begins to realize—and to experience as a profound crisis—is that there is no going back to the prewar Henri. With regard to his desire to write, he begins to discover that the problem is not only one of lack of time—for actually he has nothing left to say! When he does sit down to work at his novel, he is blocked. The "impasse" is not merely a practical one. For now what should he say? And to whom? Who now will be his audience? His whole life lacks meaning, lacks flavor. He is "living like an engineer in a mechanical world"; he has become "dry as a stone" (*Man*, 191). But that being the case, to refuse to get yet further involved in politics on the grounds that he needs time to write is a sham. Similarly, he comes to feel that his insistence on keeping control of *L'Espoir* is a sham, for he now realizes that the paper cannot make much of a difference. In fact, he suddenly feels, he has been "playing" at being an editor. He has considered *L'Espoir* his toy, "a complete set of equipment for the little junior editor—life size. A magnificent plaything!" (*Man*, 190). He really doesn't believe in what he is doing anymore: if Dubreuilh and Samazelle still have hope that they can change the world, then they should have the paper.

In the end, Henri is overwhelmed with a sense of the futility of both his own life and of life in general. For massive structural changes in world power relations, apparently distant forces that are now being brought to bear on him locally, conjoin with other more particularistic elements of his own situation and strongly predispose Henri toward his final "choice": the decision to give up *L'Espoir* and so also to "choose" politics over writing. On the night that Henri finally arrives at the decision that he will give his paper to the SRL, he has an abrupt and terrible epiphany. He suddenly recognizes, not as a mere piece of intellectual information, for of course he "knew" this before, but as a profound shattering of his sense of his own existence, that geopolitics changes the meaning of our actions.[29] It is this devastating realization that precipitates his final decision.

Two things take place that night. One directly involves Henri, and the other seems more distant. Early in the evening, Henri has been to see Tournelle, a man whom he had known as a comrade in the Resistance and who is now a government minister. At the behest of the beleaguered old Leftists he had met during his visit to Portugal early in 1945, Henri asks Tournelle for French government support of the Portuguese Left against Salazar's Fascist dictatorship. He already knows that, because of American influence on the government, the answer will be no, but he still feels morally obligated to try. "You know the situation a well as I," says Tournelle. "How can you expect France to do anything for Portugal, or for anyone else for that matter, when she can't do anything for herself!" (*Man*, 204). Tournelle is trapped, bitter. Now he is not even sure that the Resistance had been worth all the bloodshed—and suddenly the realization hits Henri: in this new world France is no longer a world power, and what its citizens say, write, or do simply makes no difference now. "Suddenly he realized he was living in the moribund capital of a very small country. . . . Henri was nothing but an insignificant citizen of a fifth-rate power, and *L'Espoir* was a local sheet on the same level as a village weekly" (*Man*, 205). So what did it matter who controlled *L'Espoir*? He may as well give it to the SRL!

But Henri still hesitates to do the deed. It is only later that night that he arrives finally at the tipping point, as this dreadful realization is reinforced from yet another direction. For this is also the night that the triumphant Soviet army is entering Berlin. Nazism is definitively defeated—but there is no cause for celebration. *L'Espoir* is irrelevant in the new configuration, in which France, Europe—indeed, the whole world—is now the plaything of two great powers. And equally irrelevant is the project of being a writer:

> The Russians were sacking Berlin, the war was ending, or another one was beginning—how could one find pleasure in telling stories that never actually happened? . . . He was nowhere, had nothing, was nothing; there was nothing he could speak about. "Then I just have to shut up," he thought. "If I really come to terms with the inevitable, maybe I'll stop tearing myself to pieces, maybe I'll be able to bear with a lighter heart the drudgeries I'm forced to do." . . . He had believed that he lived in a very special part of the world from which every word echoed across the entire planet. But now he knew all his words died at his feet. (*Man*, 212–13; Fr. 264–65, my translation)

And so Henri goes into a bar, gets drunk with an acquaintance, and "decides" he will give *L'Espoir* to the SRL. Moreover, drunk and maudlin, he declares to himself that he will abnegate his entire life to politics and simply follow orders: "Everyone had died in the war," including him. But "it's not upsetting being dead, if you give up pretending to be alive." So now, "act, act as a team, without worrying about yourself; sow, sow again, and never reap. Act, unite, serve, obey Dubreuilh, smile at Samazelle. He'd telephone them: 'The paper is yours'." (*Man,* 215; Fr. 267, my translation)

What kind of "freedom" does Henri's decision entail? Is this an act of *liberté,* the choice of an ontological freedom that is untouched from the "outside" (*les dehors*)? Is this a choice that is in no way "indicated" by "an external reality?" And does Henri alone bear the responsibility for his final decision here? From the perspective of Beauvoir's "moral period," Henri is not only free, he is also profoundly in bad faith. He tells himself that because the world has changed he is no longer free to take responsibility for himself. Because the world has changed, he can no longer act meaningfully, so instead he will commit to blind obedience. He will abstain from questioning or judging; he will just follow orders in the SRL.[30] Furthermore, he arrives at this moment of final decision drunk! He flees his anguish by diminishing his capacity to think and see clearly.

But Beauvoir does not invite her readers to sit in judgment on Henri. We are not asked to assess him in a dispassionate mode or to evaluate his decision through a set of "abstract" criteria against which we will find him wanting. Rather, Beauvoir invites us to enter Henri's world and to discover that—from the perspective of lived experience—judgment, action, responsibility, bad faith have become much more relative matters than she and Sartre once had thought. Now, they admit of gradations and must be qualified by the fact that we so often act in an in-between zone, a place of neither *liberté* nor of determination *tout court.*[31]

When, after his final decision, Henri tells Anne that he has been "pushed" and that he has "agreed" but has done so "against his will," Beauvoir is offering us a very different account of our relations with the world than she had sketched in her early "moral" essays. Henri's "will," the freedom that Beauvoir had previously called *liberté,* is not impervious to its situation. On the contrary, it is thoroughly porous. Thus, the actions of others do not touch only the "outside" (*les dehors*) of our freedom—rather, they may radically alter it.

Through the person of Henri, Beauvoir "evokes" the realizations—emotional, intellectual, political—that she and Sartre made in the postwar period: freedom is not an "infinite" *liberté,* but rather a matter of acting within multiple constraints and as who one has already become.[32] Our judgments, it follows, are not uniquely our own. Likewise, our responsibility for what we decide is not absolutely ours alone. For we come to make our choices suffused by our situation, enmeshed within and weighted by *la force des choses.* The insights Beauvoir offers here—about freedom, constraint, and political judgment—continue to illuminate the lives of all of us. For to one degree or another, we all live our lives "on rails."

Notes

References to works translated from the French are given to the English edition. In some instances I have made a significant alteration to the English translation and added the French page number in the text, using the abbreviation Fr.

1. She is even more critical of this novel in another passage: "I wanted to speak directly to the reader, and indeed I thought I was doing so; but all the time my voice had been usurped by a sort of fatuous, didactic vampire. I was dealing with a genuine experience, yet I kept trotting out commonplace platitudes" (*PL,* 432).

2. Beauvoir, "Mon expérience d'écrivain," 447.

3. Most of these were originally published in *Les Temps modernes.* They were later republished together in *L'Existentialisme et la sagesse des nations.*

4. I am using the 1989 Vintage edition of *The Second Sex.*

5. Toril Moi gives an excellent account of how Beauvoir can maintain "both that biology is extremely important to women's situation and that it is not a destiny" (*What Is a Woman?* 62). Moi convincingly argues that Beauvoir espouses neither biological determinism nor a theory of the social construction of gender, but rather develops an account of a woman as a being "in situation" for whom the body "founds my experience of myself and the world" (63). See pages 59–83. For related arguments, see also Kruks, *Situation and Human Existence* and *Retrieving Experience;* Heinämaa, "What Is a Woman?" and *Toward a Phenomenology of Sexual Difference.*

6. Beauvoir uses the French verb *assumer.* This has the sense of "taking up responsibility for something." The English verb, *to assume,* may have a similar sense when one talks of "assuming" a burden of some kind, or of "assuming" a debt.

7. For my fuller elaboration of the argument that Beauvoir's notion of situated freedom is nearer to that of Merleau-Ponty than of Sartre, see Kruks, *Situation and Human Existence.*

8. Merleau-Ponty, *Phenomenology of Perception,* 442.

9. Indeed, in this work Beauvoir emphasizes, perhaps even more strongly than Merleau-Ponty, the continuity and stability of the self: "I have noted a great stability in what is called people's character—the entirety of their reactions in analogous circumstances. . . . Generally speaking, men and women, once they are settled into adulthood, remain consistent with themselves. Sometimes, indeed, they repeat their own conduct when they think they are being different" (Beauvoir, *All Said and Done,* 36; my translation, Fr. 55–56).

10. Beauvoir's explicit pronouncements on the nature of time generally echo Sartre's in affirming that the present takes its meaning from one's future goals. However, from the late 1940s on, she develops a more dialectical notion of time, in which the weight of the past, as well as the openness of projects toward a future, shape the meaning of the present.

11. "One may throw a man in prison, release him, cut off his arm, lend him wings; but in all cases his freedom [*liberté*] remains infinite" (*PC,* 86).

12. David Detmer, in analyzing Sartre, renders this as the distinction between "on-

tological" and "practical" freedom (*Freedom as a Value*). I think my term "effective" freedom (see also Kruks, *Situation and Human Existence*, 90ff.) better expresses what Beauvoir means when she uses the term *puissance*. For *puissance* may be thought of as "power" in the sense of enablement: power is having a capacity to do something, being effective. Moreover, if *puissance* is integral to the realization of *liberté* and if, as Beauvoir here begins to suggest, the two are not in actuality separable in lived experience, then it is no longer straightforwardly the case, as Sartre had claimed, that "the slave in chains is as free as his master" (*BN*, 550; I am using the 1956 Philosophical Library edition).

13. In *Being and Nothingness*, Sartre still describes self-other relations as paradigmatically those of objectifying and being objectified. It is only later, notably in *Notebooks for an Ethics* (written in 1947 and 1948), that he also begins to consider the possibility of generosity in self-other relations. For important treatments of Beauvoir that insist on the originality of her focus here, see Bergoffen, *Philosophy of Simone de Beauvoir*; Bauer, *Simone de Beauvoir, Philosophy & Feminism*.

14. Beauvoir, "Idéalisme moral et réalisme politique," 99.

15. Ibid., 100; my emphasis.

16. Beauvoir expands further on these predicaments in *The Ethics of Ambiguity*. Even valid projects of emancipation may involve conflicts, she notes. For example, "during the course of the last war, no [European] anti-fascist could have wanted the revolts of the natives in the British empire to be successful; on the contrary, these revolts were supported by the Fascist regimes; and yet, we cannot blame those who, considering their emancipation to be more urgent, took advantage of the situation to obtain it. Thus, it is possible, and often happens, that one finds oneself obliged to oppress and kill men who are pursuing goals whose validity one acknowledges oneself" (*EA*, 98–99).

17. Beauvoir, "Idéalisme moral et réalisme politique," 99.

18. Ibid., 100.

19. Merleau-Ponty, *Phenomenology of Perception*, 442ff.

20. Beauvoir was already aware of the divergence between Sartre and Merleau-Ponty in 1945, when she called attention to it in her review of *Phenomenology of Perception*: "While Sartre, in *Being and Nothingness*, emphasizes above all the opposition of for-itself and in-itself . . . Merleau-Ponty on the contrary applies himself to describing the concrete character of a subject who is never, according to him, a pure for-itself" ("La phénoménologie de la perception," 366).

21. For some women, oppression is so extreme that their compliance does not involve bad faith. See *SS*, xxxv.

22. Such a position has sometimes been attributed to Sartre, although it obviously cuts across the grain of his arguments (in works other than *Being and Nothingness*) for political commitment. See, for a recent example, Nancy Bauer. She cites Sartre's infamous remarks from the Conclusion of *Being and Nothingness* that "all human activities are equivalent . . . it amounts to the same thing whether one gets drunk alone or is a leader of nations," observing that it "invites the claim of nihilism" (*Simone de Beauvoir, Philosophy & Feminism*, 142).

23. Merleau-Ponty, *Phenomenology of Perception*, 442.

24. Beauvoir, "Interview de Simone de Beauvoir par J.-F. Rolland," 359.

25. The model for the SRL is the *Rassemblement Démocratique et Révolutionaire* (RDR), with which Sartre and others in Beauvoir's circle were centrally involved.

Founded early in 1948 as a nonaligned socialist organization, the RDR collapsed by the end of 1949.

26. In the novel, Anne Dubreuilh contests Scriassine's interpretation of the situation, but it becomes evident that there is more than a grain of truth to it.

27. With hindsight, it is apparent that a major theme of Beauvoir's novel is the crisis of French national identity precipitated by France's loss of status as a world power and intellectual center. Gaullism (to which Beauvoir was profoundly hostile) was, of course, also a response to this crisis.

28. I use the later Sartre's term here to suggest that, in her portrayal of Henri and others, Beauvoir already implies Sartre's later notion of the individual as a "universal singular" who totalizes his or her era. Of course, Beauvoir does not consciously articulate the methods Sartre will use in such works as *The Family Idiot* or the *Critique of Dialectical Reason,* but they are anticipated in *The Mandarins.*

29. This is of course what, much earlier in the book, Scriassine had diagnosed as the "impasse" of French intellectuals.

30. In the event, Henri does not abnegate himself in this way for long, and he later chooses expulsion from the SRL rather than consent to remain silent about the use of forced labor camps in the Soviet Union. Which elements of his life predispose Henri to this latter choice is of course another interesting story, but one I don't have space to address here.

31. In her critique of my earlier work, Gail Linsenbard simply reasserts the dualism Beauvoir has successfully overcome in *The Second Sex* and *The Mandarins.* Linsenbard asserts: "According to Beauvoir, in deciding the meaning of my situation, I thereby constitute it, I am thus never wholly passive with respect to my situation" ("Beauvoir, Ontology, and Women's Human Rights," 157–58). But the point is that we are neither fully the constitutors of our situation nor wholly its passive products. Rather, the significance of Beauvoir's account of Henri's decision is that it reveals the tensions and ambiguities of a freedom in situation. Beauvoir here discloses the dialectics of interiorization and exteriorization (to use Sartre's later terminology in the *Critique of Dialectical Reason*) through which our choices and projects are born. These dialectics profoundly confound distinctions between the constitutor and constituted that Linsenbard still seeks to maintain.

32. Thus, looking back at the "itinerary" of his own ideas on freedom, Sartre said, in a 1969 interview, and surely with an implicit acknowledgment of Beauvoir's influence: "A simple formula would be to say that life taught me *la force des choses*—the power of circumstances." He goes on, in this interview, to criticize his youthful claim (made in a preface he wrote to his early plays) that "whatever the circumstances, and wherever the site, a man is always free to choose to be a traitor or not," saying, "when I read this, I said to myself: 'It's incredible, I actually believed that!'" and contrasting his early views of freedom with those he later presented through the character of Heinrich (in *Le Diable et le Bon Dieu*): a man who is "a living contradiction, who will never choose, [who] is totally conditioned by his situation" (Sartre, "Itinerary of a Thought," 4–6).

10 Simone de Beauvoir's "Marguerite" as a Possible Source of Inspiration for Jean-Paul Sartre's "The Childhood of a Leader"

Eliane Lecarme-Tabone
Translated by Kevin W. Gray

The relationship between Simone de Beauvoir and Jean-Paul Sartre continues to fascinate both scholars and casual readers.[1] Beyond the obvious questions brought up by their lovers' pact, there is also the problem of discerning how each influenced the other intellectually. The necessary reevaluation of their relationship, carried out by Anglo-Saxon intellectuals within the last couple of decades, has resulted in a greater appreciation for Simone de Beauvoir's contributions, while nonetheless suffering from polemical excess.[2]

For instance, it is not at all clear how we can know for certain who was the first person to conceive of such-and-such an idea when we ignore the precise content of their conversations (after all, their discussions were places to hash out their philosophical ideas). The inquiry is nonetheless easier when it is a question of literary texts (and not of philosophical ones): a well-conceived chronological investigation should allow us to formulate several hypotheses. In this text, I want to show how the book *When Things of the Spirit Come First* by Beauvoir could have inspired Sartre's *The Wall*—to quote the Bible, I want to "give unto Caesar"—while at the same time reflecting on the ways the couple worked together.

Sartre and Beauvoir began to write short stories at about the same time. Michel Rybalka tells us that Sartre became interested in the early 1930s in writing full-length novels as well as short stories.[3] He only began to do this later—according to Beauvoir's *The Prime of Life*, it was during a cruise to Norway during the summer of 1935 that Sartre tried his hand "with a short piece entitled *Le Soleil de minuit,* which he lost somewhere in the Causses and never began again" (*PL,* 229; *FA,* 328). He tried again in 1936 with "Erostrate," the first of five short stories that appeared together as the volume *The Wall* in February 1939.[4]

Beauvoir, on the other hand, first tried to write novels before turning to short stories herself in 1935: "I had written two long novels in which the opening chapters held up pretty well, but which then degenerated into a mere shapeless hodgepodge. This time I determined to compose some fairly brief stories, and to discipline them rigorously from beginning to end" (*PL,* 178–79; *FA,* 255). Unlike Sartre, who collected his texts into a volume after the fact,[5] Beauvoir tried to write her collection of stories such that common ideas ran throughout the book: the same characters occur, though with different levels of prominence, from one short story to another, assuring an internal unity to the work.[6]

I want to examine the last of the five stories that make up each of the volumes that I am interested in here. Besides occupying a prominent place at the end of each volume, "The Childhood of a Leader" and "Marguerite" share a number of similar characteristics. Even though Sartre's story is longer,[7] the two stories recount the lives of their protagonists in a chronological order, starting from their childhood. Sartre begins his story with the central character, Lucien Fleurier, dressed up as a tiny angel at a childhood party, and ends during his second year of study at the École Centrale. Marguerite recounts her life from the age of three until the moment that she writes a competitive national exam (which we are led to believe is the French *agrégation*[8]), and even looks ahead to the two years that would follow the exam.

The two stories are effectively *Bildungsroman*—they retrace the path of two young students from their youth through their formative experiences (often experiences of trial-and-error) to maturity. In "The Childhood of a Leader," Sartre changes the model, denouncing the outcome of the main character's life. Lucien Fleurier becomes a leader, nonetheless making reprehensible choices (he becomes a Fascist and an anti-Semite), and falls into inauthenticity by rejecting his fundamental freedom. His experiences of growth are banal or ridiculous.[9] While Beauvoir's story is not a parody of the model, "Marguerite" also does not conform to the norms of a *Bildungsroman.* After all, the young woman's experiences are entirely negative—she has to first pass through the intellectual traps of spiritualism and surrealism before achieving a sort of intellectual freedom—the motives for which, Beauvoir confessed, are unclear.[10]

At any rate, in both cases the authors borrowed from their own personal lives to construct their chief protagonists. Even though Sartre denied it,[11] many commentators suggested that "The Childhood of a Leader," was a largely biographical work—an argument strengthened by the publication of *The Words.*[12]

As for "Marguerite," Beauvoir herself wrote that she was happy to have written this "autobiographical sequence" ("*chapitre autobiographique*") (*PL*, 181; *FA*, 258).[13] It is true that, although satirizing the religious education that Marguerite received, the author paints the character in sympathetic strokes. And generally speaking, the heroine's intellectual history corresponds to that of Beauvoir, without the positive experiences of work, friendship, and love. Any differences of fact compared with Beauvoir's life are more omissions than changes. Lucien Fleurier, who shares many of Sartre's childhood experiences, is a "possible"[14] variant of (and despised version of) his author. He is the sort of person whom Sartre might have become had Sartre had a father, money, or the right lineage. Lucien lives in bad faith; he is active in the extreme right and finally becomes the captain of industry (namely, a factory boss) he was predestined to be. As Lucien ages, the author shows nothing but greater and greater contempt for the character.[15]

The way that this episode is recounted in these short stories (ironically, in Beauvoir's case; hatefully, in Sartre's) prefigures the tones of their later autobiographies. In *The Words*, Sartre distances himself from the little "Poulou"— not so violently, however, as he does from Lucien Fleurier. While *The Words*, according to the author, describes the birth of a neurotic who sought redemption through writing before curing himself through political engagement, Beauvoir's *Memoirs of a Dutiful Daughter* retraces the steps of one woman's liberation. The relationships the two authors have with their past are clearly different— nonetheless, the two short stories are similar stops on the writers' intellectual careers.

Beyond these broad structural similarities, there are other similarities in the two works: in particular, similarities in the scenes of homosexual seduction that take place between Lucien and Bergère on one hand, and Marguerite and Marie-Ange on the other hand, with the respective intermediaries Berliac and Denis. The characters that act as intermediaries resemble each other in many ways. Denis impresses Marguerite with his "extravagant elegance" (*W*, 175; *A*, 295). Berliac shocks his classmates by wearing "coats ringed in green or purple, in the latest styles" (*CL*, 102; *EC*, 180). They each impress their circle of friends with their lack of self-consciousness and their nonconformity. The two frequent bars. They claim to be poets. They appreciate avant-garde art and literature—a taste that allows each to initiate his friend into a new circle of acquaintances: Berliac practices automatic writing and teaches the techniques to Lucien; Denis loans Marguerite *Le Manifeste du Surréalisme*. They both display a similar contempt for money, while nonetheless keeping what they have for themselves (Denis sponges money from his female friends; Berliac is always borrowing money that he never pays back) (CL, 106; EC, 186). Both of them offer up world-weary speeches on the meaning of life, give themselves over to idleness, but at the same time each (especially Denis) arranges his life so that he can live in comfort. Each is involved in a secret affair with a much older, richer, and more prestigious partner (Denis with Marie-Ange Lamblin, Berliac with Achille Bergère); they become involuntarily the mediators between their protector and their friend.

In both cases, the seducer's and seductress's encounter with their new object of desire occurs fortuitously, in a bar, under the watchful eyes of a third party (who himself becomes importunate). Marguerite and Lucien soon thereafter begin to frequent their mentor's apartment—each of which resembles the other, if only by their strange decorations. With a wink to the surrealist style of art then in vogue in France, Marie-Ange's and Bergère's apartments are both decorated with statues of primitive art (W, 191; CL, 109; A, 323; EC, 191). Inside both apartments, the protagonists smoke opium or hash cigarettes.

In each case, the seducers employ the same strategies—tender looks, affectionate actions, careful attention paid to the spiritual states of their young protégés. They talk about their physical charm, for example, the tenderness of their skin and their unkempt beauty. Marie-Ange buys Marguerite a hope chest and helps her with her makeup; Bergère teaches Lucien to knot his tie and how to do his hair (W, 197–98; CL, 111; A, 332, 334; EC, 194). Faced with these cunning suitors, Lucien and Marguerite reveal their naïveté. Simultaneously fascinated, grateful, and full of shame, the two completely misunderstand their protectors' intentions, right up until the fatal moment when each find himself trapped in the same room as their older suitor. Their brutal realization of what is happening is accompanied by disgust and terror: "But it was only when I felt her thick lips on mine that these manipulations took on a clear meaning for me. 'She wants to make love to me'" (W, 205; A, 346), Marguerite believes. Lucien suddenly thinks: "He's going to sleep with me" (CL, 115; EC, 199), and further along: "A warm, soft mouth, like a piece of raw beefsteak, was thrust against his own" (CL, 117; EC, 202). Although Marguerite manages to escape the unwanted liaison, Lucien submits, and ends up passing the night with Bergère.

Each homosexual act plays an important role in the characters' development. In Sartre's story, the future "leader" is forced to prove his (hetero)sexuality—after having erred and allowed himself to become another man's sexual plaything. The adventure that Marguerite experiences, on the other hand, is treated more as an error in recognizing her seductress's intents than as a perverse act; it illustrates the blindness of the young girl when faced with the trickery of well-thought-out seduction, as well as her complete sexual naïveté—caused by the religious education she had received. In both cases, the experience is one of an error in the character's path, not of a potentially enriching life experience. There is, however, the important difference that Lucien's consent shows that he was at first tempted by the possibility, only later to feel dominated and debased. In this way, Sartre shows that our leaders only accede to their positions in life because of their weakness and passivity. Additionally, for both Sartre and Beauvoir, the homosexuality of the seducers contributes to a devaluation of the very values they were pretending to promote—surrealism on one hand, hazy pantheistic spiritualism on the other. The revelation of these carnal desires destroys their beauteous *paroles;* in each case homosexuality is a negative character trait.

And so, let us ask, who inspired whom here? The chronology gives us a very clear response: Beauvoir wrote the collection *When Things of the Spirit Come First* from 1935 to 1937. She tells of her decision to begin this collection of short stories after a series of rejuvenating hikes in the French mountains (first alone, then with Sartre) during the summer of 1935. In a passage that is important in order to understand her personality (where she explains why she prefers writing literature to philosophy) (*PL,* 178–81; *FA,* 253–58), she tells how it took her two years to write the stories. She elaborates, showing her desire to have the stories published: "Sartre, who read my work as it progressed, approved of numerous passages" (*PL,* 181; *FA,* 258). In July 1937, the same time as Sartre's short story "The Wall" (written during February and May) appeared in *La Nouvelle revue française,* Beauvoir found the time to review the pages of *When Things of the Spirit Come First,* which her sister had typed for her (*PL,* 239; *FA,* 343). By the start of classes in 1937, she had finished the manuscript and wanted to move on to other things (*PL,* 253; *FA,* 360); it was during this period that she began to write *She Came to Stay.* To her great disappointment, the manuscript of *When Things of the Spirit Come First* was rejected—first by Gallimard, then Grasset (during the first semester 1938). Simone de Beauvoir tried to remain strong when faced with this disappointment: "The approach of the holidays, with all their alluring prospects, helped me to bury *La Primauté du spirituel* in a fairly cheerful mood" (*PL,* 261; *FA,* 374).

During the Easter vacations of 1938, after returning from the Netherlands, Beauvoir writes that she and Sartre discussed, while walking through the streets of La Rochelle, "the outcome of 'L'Enfance d'un chef' (The Childhood of a Leader), which he was then writing" (*PL,* 260; *FA,* 372). The short story was finished by the beginning of July (*PL,* 261; *FA,* 375). As such, it is very clear that Beauvoir's account of the seduction episode preceded Sartre's.

More than that, however, we can speculate with good reason that the relevant passage in "The Childhood of a Leader" was inspired by Beauvoir's experiences in Marseilles with her colleague, the English teacher "Mme. Tourmelin," who lavished her with attention up until her fiery and unexpected final declaration of love. Like Tourmelin, Marie-Ange Lamblin wears a skintight chestnut brown dress covering her generously proportioned body (*PL*, 81; *FA*, 112; *W*, 189; *A*, 318); also like her, she shows off more of her body than she should. Like Tourmelin, Lamblin claims to have fallen in love with Marguerite when she first laid eyes on her, and also like her, she asks if she must throw herself at the feet of her obsession or beg on her knees, in order to be accepted. Despite being older at the time than her character, Beauvoir showed the same lack of understanding and the same shock manifested by the younger Marguerite. Finally, I should point out that Denis has many of the same character traits as Beauvoir's cousin Jacques (albeit in exaggerated form), with whom Beauvoir was in love during her youth and of whom she wrote extensively in *Memoirs of a Dutiful Daughter*.

The character of Achille Bergère could certainly have been inspired by Jean Cocteau or André Breton, as others have suggested,[16] but as far as the character's actions are concerned (especially during the act of seduction), Sartre certainly borrowed from Marie-Ange Lamblin. Sartre seems to give a little wink to Beauvoir in situating the sexual encounter in Rouen (where she was a teacher from 1932 to 1936).[17] Nonetheless, he never admitted to borrowing the character. When asked by Michel Rybalka and Michel Contat, he said: "There is no model for this character; I invented him from scratch."[18] Beauvoir never said anything to contradict what Sartre said.

Was this an omission or an act of politeness? In both cases, the action can be explained because Sartre was writing an intensely personal work. We should observe that Sartre's need to write an autobiography predated the writing of "The Childhood of a Leader," as the writings from his youth show.[19] Beauvoir's early writings did not cause him to want to write about his past—at most, they encouraged him. More importantly, each writer had blocked out a general theme for their collection of stories. *When Things of the Spirit Come First* is at heart a critique of spiritualism: "Through the medium of individual characters and their affairs I wanted to convey something that lay beyond them: the multitude of crimes, both small and great, which hid behind a veil of spiritual hocuspocus" (*PL*, 179; *FA*, 255). In *The Wall*, Sartre wanted to examine the philosophical problem of authentic existence: "Nobody wanted to look Existence in the face. The book shows five small detours—sometimes tragic, sometimes comic—around the problem of authentic existence."[20] The structure of "The Childhood of a Leader" is stronger because it is a stand-alone short story rather than part of the ensemble like "Marguerite." Jean-François Louette argues that

in the work there is even "an underlying philosophical dialectical structure"—
one of the essential components of Sartre's philosophy.[21] In "Marguerite," the
autobiographical instinct is revealed as being more important than any desire
to use the text to advance a particular theoretical position, something that is
perhaps easier to see when we read the collection as a whole. The homosexual
encounter, which I have argued Sartre borrowed from Beauvoir, is given added
layers of meaning in Sartre's story: Sartre augments the reference to Rimbaud,
already present in "Marguerite," in order to turn the episode into a parody of
La Saison en enfer (as Genevieve Idt has shown).[22] In addition to attacking surrealism, Sartre also satirizes psychoanalysis through the way it was used by
Lucien and his mentor. Finally, the character of Berliac is given many of Nizan's
traits.[23]

Beauvoir's silence is ultimately an example of her generosity. She is happy for
the success enjoyed by *Nausea* as well as the fact that two of Sartre's stories were
being published in literary journals, even at the same time as her own book
was rejected. Instead of becoming discouraged, she looks at this bright spell in
Sartre's life with hope, thinking that it bodes well for her own potential future
success (*PL*, 260; *FA*, 373). Just after discussing with Sartre "The Childhood of
a Leader," she talks about wanting to write a book about the little girl she once
was.[24] Every time "Castor" is faced with negative thoughts, she tries to turn
them into healthy competition.

Beyond a doubt, part of what we see here is an example of the sharing of intellectual property by the two partners. Each had the right to borrow from the
memory of the other. Sartre considered using the story Beauvoir would tell of
Zaza in her writings (*PL*, 41; *FA*, 55), and he borrowed Beauvoir's experiences
for his short story "Intimacy."[25] Beauvoir nonetheless did similar things: she ap-
pointed herself master of Sartre's past when she wrote their combined biographies. Sharing, it seems, goes hand in hand with autonomy.

Notes

1. See, for example, Hazel Rowley, *Tête-à-tête*.
2. I give my own personal point of view on the subject in "Le couple Beauvoir-
Sartre face à la critique féministe," *Les Temps modernes*, no. 619 (June–July 2002): 19–
42. In this piece, I criticize the overstated case made by Kate and Edward Fullbrook in
their *Simone de Beauvoir and Jean-Paul Sartre*.
3. Sartre, *Oeuvres romanesques*, 1802.
4. "The Wall," "The Room," "Erostratus," "Intimacy," and "The Childhood of a
Leader."
5. The title of the collection is also that of the first story. Retrospectively, he brings

the stories in the volume together by accentuating the recurrent theme of the wall (taken literally or symbolically) in several of the short stories.

6. First titled *Primauté du spirituel* (Simone de Beauvoir herself also speaks of *La Primauté du spirituel*)—an ironic reference to Jacques Maritain—the volume was first published in 1979 under the title *Quand prime le spirituel* (*When Things of the Spirit Come First*). It was reissued by the collection "Folio" in 2006 with a new title, *Anne, ou quand prime le spirituel*. The new book was formatted as a novel, with each short story centering on a different female character: "Marcelle," "Chantal," "Lisa," "Anne," or "Marguerite."

7. In many ways, this short story, because of its length and the way it is treated in the volume, is practically a freestanding novella.

8. The French *agrégration* is a competitive national examination done at the end of high school for teaching positions in the national education system [Trans.].

9. See Geneviève Idt, *Le Mur de Jean-Paul Sartre*. From Idt's point of view, "Lucien est un héros romantique dégradé" [Lucien is a debased romantic hero], 157.

10. "The events that brought about Marguerite's conversion to the truth were relatively unconvincing" (*PL*, 181; *FA*, 258).

11. See Michel Contat, "Introduction: une autobiographie politique?" 4.

12. See Idt, *Le Mur de Jean-Paul Sartre*, 203–205; Josette Pacaly, *Sartre au miroir*; Jacques Lecarme, "Sartre palimpseste," 243–46.

13. See also Eliane Lecarme-Tabone, *Mémoires d'une jeune fille rangée*, 26–27.

14. The idea that the author could have turned out like this is also to be found in certain characters from *When Things of the Spirit Come First*, for example, Chantal or, to a lesser extent, Marcelle.

15. When the question was put to Sartre by Michel Contat, he said: "*le personnage n'a de commun si vous voulez avec le personnage sympathique de mes oeuvres, de Mathieu, que le sentiment qu'il a de sa contingence, seulement il réagit comme un salaud, c'est-à-dire qu'il se crée immédiatement une attitude, des droits et tout ça*" [The only similarity the character shares with the sympathetic character of Mattieu is that they both share a common feeling of their own contingency. However, unlike Mattieu, he reacts like a *salaud*, i.e., he creates for himself a special attitude, rights, etc.] Cited in *Pourquoi et comment Sartre a écrit "Les Mots,"* 4.

16. See Idt, *Le Mur de Jean-Paul Sartre*.

17. Rouen brings to mind Flaubert and Madame Bovary (we are made to think of Emma's adultery with Léon, parodied in Sartre's story).

18. Sartre, *Oeuvres romanesques*, 1855 (translation by Christine Daigle).

19. See Contat, *Pourquoi et comment Sartre a écrit "Les Mots,"* 2.

20. [*Personne ne veut regarder en face l'Existence. Voici cinq petites déroutes—tragiques ou comiques—devant elle, cinq vies*] "Prière d'insérer," cited in the Pléiade edition, p. 1807. Sartre adds: "*Lucien Fleurier est le plus près de sentir qu'il existe mais il ne le veut pas, il s'évade*" [Lucien Fleurier is the closest of the characters to feeling the true weight of existence, but rather than embracing it, he tries to flee].

21. Louette, *Silences de Sartre*, 164; [une structuration dialectique sous-jacente, d'ordre philosophique]. He argues that the three central tenets of Sartrean philosophy are found in the story (the *pour-soi*, the *pour-autrui*, and the *en-soi*).

22. See Idt, *Le Mur de Jean-Paul Sartre*, 157.

23. See Pacaly, *Sartre au miroir.*

24. She wanted "to write a book that evoked the shade of this little girl" (*PL*, 260; *FA*, 372). These two episodes (separated by only a few weeks in real life) are brought even closer together (separated by a few paragraphs) in her writings.

25. See Idt, *Le Mur de Jean-Paul Sartre*, 203. The short story, she says, *"semble plutôt issue de l'expérience de Simone de Beauvoir, quand en l'absence de Sartre, elle hantait Montparnasse en compagnie d'Olga ou d'une jeune vendeuse de chez Burma"* [seems rather to stem out of Beauvoir's experience. Beauvoir, in Sartre's absence, haunted Montparnasse with Olga and a young salesgirl from the Chez Burma].

11 Taking a Distance: Exploring Some Points of Divergence between Beauvoir and Sartre

William L. McBride

"Merleau-Ponty et le pseudo-sartrisme" shows us Simone de Beauvoir at once at her best and at her worst. As she indicated in the famous and frequently cited autobiographical text in which she explained why she supposedly chose a literary rather than a philosophical career (a self-perception that I, like no doubt most of the contributors to this volume, do not accept, based on a traditional dichotomy that she herself put into question in her essay on literature and metaphysics), she acknowledged that she was gifted, and certainly superior to Sartre, as an interpreter of the philosophies of others, but to make this her life's work did not interest her (*FA*, 228–29). Nevertheless, the polemic against Merleau-Ponty is a lengthy, detailed exercise displaying precisely this talent. At the same time, it amounts, in many respects, to "overkill." It is 50 pages long, with more than 150 footnotes. And while Merleau-Ponty, in the chapter of his *Les Aventures de la dialectique* entitled "Sartre et l'ultra-bolshévisme" that triggered Beauvoir's response, was not exactly tender with Sartre—as one can already see in the title—the polemical level of Beauvoir's attack makes her friend Merleau look like gentleness incarnate.

As Merleau-Ponty, referring to Sartre's "Réponse à Claude Lefort," the essay that, along with "Les Communistes et la paix," constitutes the main focus of his attack on Sartre and Beauvoir's defense of him, says, "for there is a Sartrean violence, more tense and less lasting than Marx's. The personal tone of the polemic with Lefort was surprising."[1] The personal tone of Beauvoir's counterattack is equally surprising, beginning with the opening sentence in which she casually claims that this professor of philosophy at the Collège de France had until recently confused Marx with Kant, and continuing right through to the final paragraph, so many pages later, in which she compares Merleau-Ponty's adult regression to the regressions of children, which often have beneficial outcomes, and sweetly expresses the hope that something similar will eventually ensue in this case. In a typical tirade near the beginning, she accuses Merleau-Ponty of a "délire reconstructeur" (M-P, 2074); much later she asserts that he has mistakenly attributed to Sartre a "délire philosophique" (M-P, 2106) according to which the individual human subject is to be regarded as "un démiurge souverain." However, the seemingly straightforwardly negative force of this word "delirium" must be tempered in light of the fact that it is the very same word— "délire [concerté]"—that she uses in her autobiography, in the passage to which I have already referred, to characterize the kind of comprehensive system that according to her marks the activity of a genuine philosopher like Sartre, activity for which she opines that "la condition féminine" is not well suited. And indeed, true to her own distinction between such system-building and the work of a philosophical commentator like Eugen Fink, in "Merleau-Ponty et le pseudo-sartrisme" Beauvoir refrains, as far as I can ascertain, from making any original assertions of her own, confining herself to the painstaking task of recovering Sartre's actual thought from Merleau's many alleged misrepresentations of it. It is no wonder, then, that this essay attracted considerable criticism from those who accused Beauvoir of indulging in excessive personal attack on Sartre's behalf (or, as it might be expressed in more vernacular language, acting as a "point person" in the service of "her man").[2]

Beauvoir's response to these accusations was, in effect, that she had become exasperated by serious misrepresentations of Sartre's philosophy and had taken upon herself a task that could have been carried out by any careful Sartre student (*FCh,* 341).[3] It should also be noted that, in the very last footnote of her essay, à propos of her admission that there might be some difficulties in reconciling Sartre's phenomenology with his ontology, she asserted that Merleau-Ponty was well aware of the fact that Sartre was in the process of writing a new work that would address this issue. The object of this reference is unclear to me; we know, for example, that Sartre only began writing the *Critique of Dialectical Reason,* which in any case does not directly confront either phenomenology or ontology (although there are of course many elements of both in that book), some two years after the publication of "Merleau-Ponty et le pseudo-sartrisme."[4] And Sartre never published a methodological work of the sort to which Beauvoir appears to have been referring in that note. Be that as it may, the attack on Merleau-Ponty might well be regarded as the purest instance of Beauvoirean philosophical self-effacement in favor of a systematic Sartrean body of thought that she understands à fond and gives no obvious indication of questioning.

But to leave it at that in our appraisal of "Merleau-Ponty et le pseudo-sartrisme" is at the very least to forget the general principle, applicable to every work of exegesis, that even the most determinedly "objective" exegete is bound to put his or her slant on the interpretation proposed, if only by the choice of emphases.[5] So even if Beauvoir wished simply and solely to rectify the misunderstandings of Sartre's thought of which she considered Merleau-Ponty to be guilty, she was bound to give her readers *her* Sartre, that is, those aspects of Sartre's early philosophy that in her mind most clearly refuted his critic. And so she did, stressing above all the extent to which facticity, the existence of objective facts in the world, was central to his entire system, and concomitantly downplaying the role of subjectivity in it. Moreover, she insisted against Merleau-Ponty that Sartre's philosophy contained the essential ingredients, so to speak, to construct a theory of social structures. As she asserted, Merleau-Ponty must be the victim of "un étrange délire" to think that Sartre denied the existence of intersubjective realities, or what Merleau-Ponty called "médiations" or "régions médiatrices" (M-P, 2082).

Well, the simple fact is that readers of *Being and Nothingness*, especially if they are unfamiliar with Sartre's later writings, are constantly impressed by his numerous references to subjectivity, and the comparatively short section of that work in which he attempts to deal with *Mitsein* (Being-with) and the "we" is to my mind one of the least convincing because of his extreme reluctance there to accord any reality to social groupings other than ones of a purely psychological nature. Of course, by the time at which the Beauvoir-Merleau exchange took place, Sartre had begun acknowledging the importance of such things in various essays cited by Beauvoir (e.g., *L'Affaire Henri Martin*), and he was to make them central in the *Critique*. Nevertheless, it has always seemed to me that the *Critique* should be regarded at least to some degree as Sartre's long, painstaking answer to the challenge that Merleau-Ponty had laid down in the essay and that had evoked such polemical fervor on Beauvoir's part—a polemic that, when viewed from afar, can be seen tacitly to have admitted the superficial justifiability of Merleau-Ponty's philosophical concerns about the excessively subjectivistic and individualistic *tone* of Sartre's early philosophy (as Beauvoir herself pointed out, Merleau had not been alone in expressing these presumably misguided concerns) while insisting very strongly and with abundant textual evidence that Merleau-Ponty had ultimately been mistaken about its content.

Thus, even in the expression of extreme solidarity with Sartre that is "Merleau-Ponty and Pseudo-Sartreanism," Beauvoir takes a distance from him. Indeed, no one familiar with their respective styles could possibly imagine that it came from his pen rather than hers (whereas one can readily believe that some essays signed by Sartre, such as, notably, "La République du silence" and other articles from the time of the liberation of Paris, may well have been written in large measure by her). And this very distance may also suggest an influence, in the form of an important stimulus to Sartre to become, in effect, a social philosopher rather than just an ontologist. But in the present essay I would prefer to place the entire issue of possible influence(s) in a somewhat different perspective by picking out and reflecting upon certain fundamental ways in which our two subjects [sic], Beauvoir and Sartre, were indeed at a distance from one another despite all the instances of closeness that can be cited. I shall undertake this exercise under three headings—differences of style, differences of theme, and differences of philosophical positions—with a view to reinforcing a recognition of a few of the most salient and, nota bene, distinct contributions that each of them, "à l'axe du vingtième siècle" as I have expressed it elsewhere,[6] made to contemporary thought.

Differences of Style

If prolixity and complexity in expression are taken to be essential qualities of a true philosopher, then I suppose Beauvoir was right to insist that she was not destined to be one. I have always been impressed by the predominance of short, declarative sentences in her prose, sentences that cry out their author's wish to state the unadorned truth, to present the facts as she sees them. (A typical example: "Il est vrai que Merleau-Ponty n'a jamais compris Sartre" (M-P, 2121). Or, the quintessential Beauvoir: "On ne naît pas femme: on le devient" (DS II, 13).) When she wishes to pack several different points into a single sentence, she makes abundant use of semi-colons, overwhelming the reader with a machine-gun-like sequence. Tastes in style change and vary, of course, and there are those who simply prefer prose that is more baroque to Beauvoir's spare modernism. But whatever may be one's aesthetic preferences, it would be difficult to deny that this style leaves much less room for ambiguity of meaning than its more flowery counterparts.

Of course, this is highly paradoxical, inasmuch as Beauvoir the philosopher famously upheld ambiguity, notably in her Pour une morale de l'ambiguïté. Here, on page after page, she shows with great precision and in an unambiguous style just why dogmatism and zealotry and the "spirit of seriousness," that notion which both she and Sartre borrowed from Nietzsche and developed in interesting new directions, are intellectually unsustainable as practical stances in the world. Hence, her conclusion: an ethics of ambiguity. Ambiguity: recognition of gray areas, softening of sharp lines, emphasis on what is in between and what is ultimately unclear. These are not ideas with which, as ideas, Sartre was very comfortable or that he tended to emphasize. On the other hand, ambiguity in all these senses was always a very important *leitmotiv* in the writings of Merleau-Ponty. *Quelle coïncidence!*

In his literary and political essays, Sartre's style is not vastly different from Beauvoir's; that is why one can well believe that she may have ghostwritten for him on occasion. In his trilogy, *The Roads to Freedom,* his style at times resembles that of her own novels in its straightforwardness and comparative absence of embellishment. And in his autobiography, *Les Mots,* we know that he made a special effort to adhere to particularly high stylistic standards, in part with a view to ironizing about the obsessive reverence for writing that he attributed to his past self and that he was now making the object of his self-criticism. In his more strictly philosophical works, by contrast, and in particular in the *Critique of Dialectical Reason,* Sartre often achieves a sloppiness of style of which Beauvoir would simply have been ashamed. Here we can find sentences that meander over line after line after line, replete with highly abstract terms with which Sartre, ironically enough, seeks definitively to capture concrete human experience—sentences punctuated by occasional colons or semicolons that, far from producing the staccato effect achieved by Beauvoir, seem designed only to prevent the reader from becoming hopelessly lost. I am not claiming that these sentences are utterly devoid of sense, or that the meaning of any single one of them, however difficult to parse, is irredeemably vague, but I am charging Sartre, above all in the *Critique,* with having used a style that often obscures rather than facilitates the achievement of comprehension by his readers.

The most familiar excuse offered for this is the pressure that he was feeling, above all as a result of world events and particularly the French war against Algeria, while he was writing the *Critique.* Beauvoir herself describes his writing practices of this period as unusual for him: "He was not working in his usual way, taking breaks, making elisions, tearing out pages, beginning them over again; during hours on end without interruption, he ground out sheet after sheet without re-reading it, as if in the stranglehold of ideas with which his pen, even at breakneck speed, could not succeed in catching up."[7] Moreover, he was consuming an entire tube of the drug corydrane each day, and more whiskey than he was able to handle at night.

But I am not convinced that these circumstances account entirely for the marked differences that distinguish Sartre's philosophical writing style, even in *Being and Nothingness* and later in *The Family Idiot,* from Beauvoir's. Much is also owed, it seems to me, to his Alsatian background, with its strong German influence, of which there was none in Beauvoir's case. It should not be forgotten that Sartre's grandfather, the only significant male personality in his youth, taught German as a profession and that Sartre himself spent a formative early adult year in Berlin becoming acquainted with Husserlian phenomenology. He was, by all accounts, linguistically challenged with respect to foreign languages, hence not fluent even as a reader, much less as a speaker, in German; nevertheless, the influence of the German language, the dominant philosophical tradition of which tends toward prolixity and complexity, seems evident in his philosophical prose. By contrast, Beauvoir (as she herself wrote to me in responding positively to my question as to whether she wished to receive copies of the papers from the first meeting of the North American Sartre Society in 1985) read English with ease, a fact that strikes me as significant in appreciating her own distinctive style, and that in any case demarcates a clear distance between them.

Differences of Theme

Whereas Beauvoir, for reasons already mentioned here (e.g., the perceived unsuitableness of such an enterprise to "la condition féminine") as well as, no doubt, others that have gone unmentioned, never undertook to elaborate a systematic ontology and certainly wrote considerably less than Sartre—though far from nothing—about political matters, the most glaring hiatus in his writing by comparison with hers obviously has to do with feminist issues. While this goes without saying, I think it important to consider more profoundly some of its implications as well as some of the ways in which it is not entirely correct. Despite the familiar pejorative references, in *Being and Nothingness,* to "holes and slime" most closely associated with the female sex that have warranted so much unfavorable feminist criticism of Sartre over the years and that constitute what would today be seen as at least a bizarre and inexcusable failure of political correctness, the fact remains that on a personal level Sartre felt very much at home in the company of women (by his own account more so than in the company of men) and that on a theoretical level his introduction of gender themes into his philosophical magnum opus was a positive historical contribution of the first order. (Consider, by contrast, how little that is of theoretical value is said about gender in the writings of Kant, Husserl, or Heidegger.) But Sartre almost never ventured into the area of feminist thinking as such. Even many of the passages about "concrete relations with others" in the English version of *Being and Nothingness* that can be read as sexually charged and that are replete with the language, for reasons having to do with English grammar that translator Hazel Barnes explains in her notes, of "his—her" convey much more of a sense of gender neutrality in the French original, where the pronominal adjectives *son* and *sa* are masculine or feminine depending on the nouns that they modify rather than on the supposed gender of the persons to whom they are referring; thus, the impression that he is necessarily referring always to heterosexual relations (ones with, on the whole, clear overtones of dominance and subordination) is not conveyed with the same certainty in these same passages in the language in which Sartre himself originally wrote them.

On the whole, the question of Sartre's alleged sexism is far more complicated and multifaceted than it is often taken to be, with such additional complications as his obvious ambivalence about homosexuality (an ambivalence that was undoubtedly exacerbated by the dominant French attitudes of the time that took it to be a rather shameful business), his apparent acceptance of Beauvoir's bisexuality, and his own comparative lack of enthusiasm for the act of sexual intercourse itself being among the many factors contributing to this complexity. And as for the advocacy of a world of gender equality that is clearly implied in Beauvoir's *The Second Sex,* Sartre both endorsed it (and apparently contributed, as usual, some suggestions to her when reading the still-unpublished manuscript) and yet at the same time suggested that he himself would not feel completely comfortable, speaking personally, if constrained to live in such a world. This helps to explain why, though identified in his own mind and in the mind of the general public as a pro-feminist thinker, Sartre's contributions to the women's movement as a philosophical phenomenon and particularly as a social norm cannot be considered either outstanding (despite the great significance, already noted, of his discussions of gender themes in *Being and Nothingness*) or clear-cut. His own belief, as expressed to Pierre Bénichou, was that, while it would be in keeping with his deepest convictions, he would not personally enjoy living in a world in which genuine sexual equality prevailed.[8]

Another obvious basic difference of theme between Sartre, at least in his early years, and Beauvoir is that of the importance of childhood in shaping a philosopher's (or anyone's) thoughts. Beauvoir's *Mémoires d'une jeune fille rangée* is a brilliant piece of writing, not merely as autobiography but also because of its explanatory dimensions. Sartre's more strictly philosophical writings—and even, in large measure, his more purely literary ventures—did not include these dimensions, connected with childhood experiences, to any significant extent until the postwar years, when they gradually became extremely prominent in his thought, culminating in his study of Flaubert as "the family idiot." There is no serious question in my mind but that he owed this *approfondissement* (deepening) of his thinking to Beauvoir's example, and in particular to the prominent role played by her analyses of childhood experiences in making *The Second Sex* such a successful philosophical work.[9] I find it especially ironic, for several different reasons, that a version of Sartre's famous eulogy of Merleau-Ponty, one that he set aside in 1961 in favor of the one that was published then in *Les Temps modernes* and later in the *Situations* series, but that was retrieved years later and published in the *Revue internationale de philosophie*, begins with an extended discussion of Merleau-Ponty's generally very happy childhood memories and some ensuing Sartrean speculation on the extent to which the differences between their respective childhoods and the effects of the latter on their later differences of temperament might in fact be seen as the principal underlying explanation of the ostensibly political quarrel that eventually drove them apart.[10]

Indeed, it is not merely her extensive philosophical use of the experiences of *childhood* that distinguishes Beauvoir's dominant philosophical themes from the early Sartre's (to say nothing of her groundbreaking and still greatly underappreciated treatment of old age in her own later years, something about which Sartre almost never wrote), but more generally the concept of *lived experience* itself, taken as a whole. It must not be forgotten (a) that Beauvoir very pointedly gave the title "L'Expérience vécue," to the entire second half of *The Second Sex* (for which her English-language translator Parshley, with typical obtuseness, substituted "Woman's Life Today"), and (b) that Sartre himself, in an important interview published in English, asserted that "the conception of 'lived experience' marks my change since *L'Etre et le Néant*."[11] While I am inclined to think that this, like so many passing assertions in interviews with both Sartre and Beauvoir, is an exaggeration and oversimplification in several respects, respects that are without much importance for present purposes, what *is* important is the fact that Sartre here readily acknowledged as a lacuna in his own early thinking a theme that occupied a most central place in Beauvoir's. Once again, we find a difference in themes that is quite striking—and extremely significant.

Differences of Philosophical Positions

But to label such discrepancies as these (concerning feminism, childhood, and the fundamental importance of lived experience) as "differences in themes," as if they were *merely* that, is to begin to recognize the slipperiness of the slope that separates themes, emphases, judgments of relative importance, from philosophical positions *tout court*. In fact, much more of philosophical difference and distinction than is usually acknowledged hinges on the ways in which different philosophers choose to present their thought, highlighting certain aspects that seem to them most significant while mentioning others only in passing. But of course their readers and successors may, and often do, find some of these "other" aspects much more important.[12] So I think that we need finally to confront directly, if we are to take seriously my own theme of "distances" between Beauvoir and Sartre, the question of just what may explain why in the last analysis, and despite all the two authors' own protestations to the contrary as epitomized in the text "Merleau-Ponty et le pseudo-sartrisme," many intelligent, careful readers nevertheless *feel* that there were, or must have been, some genuinely significant philosophical divergences between them.

A few preliminary points seem to me in order here. First, to identify significant divergences is not, or at least should not be, equivalent to belittling the one (either one) by contrast with the other. Sartre and Beauvoir were both objects of enormous hatred on the part of some readers, as a study of some of the early reviews of *Being and Nothingness* and of *The Second Sex* confirms. (And I am referring to academic reviews, with which I have some familiarity; a study of segments of the popular press of the time, with which I am not very familiar, would no doubt reveal even deeper pools of hatred.) There seems to be absolutely no doubt that they themselves greatly respected each other's work on the whole, regardless of their various contingent loves and other personal issues that arose between them. Hence, to play the game, still all too common today, of "dissing" the philosophy of one in favor of the philosophy of the other is in a sense to bring back some of these ancient hatreds and at the same time to disrespect them *both* as thinkers. Moreover—to refer directly to the central theme of the present book—if one stresses excessively the existence of a strong influence of one over the other, to the point of contending that the thought of one of them is to all intents and purposes totally, or almost totally, derivative from that of the other, then my claim that there are or may be significant philosophical differences must be false, or at best just partially true due simply to the stupidity of the deriver in failing fully to grasp the thought of his or her counterpart. And of course, I find such a conclusion unacceptable. Finally, apart from divergences, or possible divergences, the fact that there are so many obvious convergences between them should not be taken as proof that the one therefore "stole" from the other, as if the enterprise of philosophy were not fully legitimate unless undertaken without cooperation, in independence and in a spirit of intense competition. That is not philosophy as I understand it.

Here, then, are a few of the differences, in addition to those that I have already identified as "differences in themes," that strike me as most salient when I compare the philosophies of Sartre, particularly the early Sartre of *Being and Nothingness,* and of Beauvoir, particularly in her principal work in ethics, *Pour une morale de l'ambiguïté,* and in *The Second Sex* (which is also, in a very important and insufficiently studied sense, a work in ethics). I present them somewhat impressionistically and randomly, which is, I think, the only proper way to do it: others' similar lists will no doubt vary from mine to a greater or lesser extent, and there is no way of demonstrating which of us is "correct."

To begin with, there is the fact that Beauvoir wrote and published a work in ethics in the first place (in addition to the earlier *Pyrrhus et Cinéas*, about which she expressed profound reservations later on), whereas Sartre only promised to do so and then failed to "deliver." It is true that in *Pour une morale de l'ambiguïté* Beauvoir explicitly suggests that her book can be regarded as in part a second-person fulfillment of Sartre's promise, thus seeming to reinforce the idea of a philosophical partnership between them. But Sartre, as we learned years later, had by that time begun work on a massive tome in ethics with which he became increasingly dissatisfied and which he decided not to publish—a tome that, by contrast with Beauvoir's emphasis on "ambiguity," contains some elements of what could almost be called a hierarchy of values (with "generosity" occupying the highest place). There was a period during which he came to regard ethics as a bourgeois "trick," as Beauvoir herself reported in *La Force des choses* (*FCh*, 218); and later still, he began to develop a sort of Marxist ethic in a long lecture at the Gramsci Institute in Rome as well as in lectures that he had prepared to give at Cornell University but then abandoned as a protest against the escalating American war against Vietnam—but this is another story, or rather several other stories. The principal point is that there is nothing in Sartre's writings, even the posthumously published writings, that parallels or recapitulates Beauvoir's work in ethics.

Next, in the domain of ontology, as can be seen especially in *The Second Sex*, Beauvoir attributes far more importance to the polarity transcendence–immanence than Sartre ever did. It is an especially useful conceptual vehicle for her to employ in explicating men's historical domination over women as well as, of course, the possibility of this situation's finally being overcome in the foreseeable future. There is simply nothing comparable in the early Sartre. To mention this underlying comparatively positive attitude of Beauvoir's concerning the future immediately suggests another interesting contrast in philosophical perspective between her and the early Sartre. On the one hand, there is a certain gloominess about her description of the past that prevents her from ever asserting the Stoic-type freedom that Sartre gaily attributed (in words that he later came to regret) even to prisoners in jail. On the other hand, she was essentially more optimistic about the future than the early Sartre usually appears to have been. Hers was a measured optimism, to be sure, with no promise of some sort of "final victory" or end to struggle, but there are numerous texts in which she clearly takes a more positive view than he about the possibilities of human love, of some genuine human community as captured in Heidegger's concept of *Mitsein* (about which Sartre was almost never positive), and, in short, about the human adventure itself. Years later, Sartre seemed to confirm that his early worldview had been of the one-sidedly pessimistic type that I am suggesting as a contrast with Beauvoir's. In a famous text near the end of *Les Mots*, he writes the following words about his old self that to me epitomize the entire passage, and in fact the book as a whole: "Cheated to the bone and mystified, I wrote joyfully about our unhappy state. A dogmatist, I doubted everything except my being the elect of doubt."[13]

There is one sentence in particular in *Pour une morale de l'ambiguïté* that stands out in my mind as a subtle but to me unmistakable expression of Beauvoir's sense of distance from the Sartre of *Being and Nothingness,* even though, quite typically, it occurs within the context of an apparent agreement. In writing about "the serious man," a stance of which, of course, she is highly critical, she says that Hegel, Kierkegaard, and Nietzsche all ridiculed this pretentious and hypocritical attitude, and she then adds: "And *Being and Nothingness* is in large measure a description of the serious man and his universe."[14] So are we then to conclude that, contrary to the *impression* that most of us thought Sartre was intending to convey about it, *Being and Nothingness* should not be taken as a universal description of certain fundamental aspects of the human world, but only, or mainly, of the latter as lived by certain not especially admirable individuals? Interestingly enough, there are at least two among his numerous allusions to *Being and Nothingness* in his posthumously published *Notebooks* that strongly suggest that Sartre himself questioned the apparent claims to universality made in the former, though not exactly in the same terms as Beauvoir used: one at the very beginning, in which he takes it for granted that the ontology of his magnum opus is a "pre-conversion ontology" ("The very fact that the ontology of *Being and Nothingness* is a pre-conversion ontology presupposes that a conversion is necessary");[15] and one near the end, in which he says that the work describes "L'Enfer des passions" (*CPM,* 515), a limited portion of human experience that can be altered, once again, by "conversion." Clearly, neither writer thought that she or he was doing essentially the exact same thing as the other in their respective works!

This last set of reflections on their differences leads me back, somewhat to my own surprise as I have developed this line of thinking, to my original allusion to Beauvoir's expressed reason, in *La Force de l'âge,* for not regarding herself as a philosopher in the sense in which for her Sartre truly was one: she considered herself incapable of the grand "delirium" of comprehensive system-building that she identified with what it means to be a philosopher in the full sense (and which she ultimately agreed, in her important 1979 interview with Margaret Simons and Jessica Benjamin, might be a more rigid and narrow definition of "philosophy" than is generally accepted in America and in the broader English-speaking world).[16] This was one aspect of their conventional classical training that those two otherwise very unconventional thinkers, Beauvoir and Sartre, never quite managed fully to overcome—as I think they should have. But if, as I have attempted to show with a couple of examples in this final section of my essay, Sartre himself later came to recognize numerous limitations in his own efforts to achieve the sought-for ideal of systematic comprehensiveness of thought but presumably continued to strive for it anyway, while Beauvoir never harbored similar aspirations for herself, this may well constitute the most fundamental underlying explanation of all for the distances between them that it seems to me fatuous to deny. At the same time it seems to me that, philosophically speaking, the aspiration in question is itself highly problematic, an *ignis fatuus* that has been shown to be such throughout the history of the discipline; and for this reason, Beauvoir had the better of the "argument" than had her companion—or rather *would* have had the better if she had ever fully faced up to the historical truth of what I have just suggested.

In conclusion, I want to stress once again that these (inevitable) failures and gaps in the thinking of both Beauvoir and Sartre should not be taken as an excuse for diminishing the stature of either one. Both were truly among the giants of twentieth-century philosophy. Sartre's early work owes much to Husserl and Heidegger, obviously, as well as to Beauvoir herself, but that does not mean that he was a mere Heideggerean *manqué* or simply an imitator or copier. No, *Being and Nothingness* is a great and in many important respects original contribution to thought, as was, in a very different area having to do with the sociohistorical dimension of humanity, his still understudied, undervalued *Critique of Dialectical Reason* later on. Much more could of course be said about him and his very interesting philosophical evolution, for which there is no doubt that the influence of Beauvoir loomed large. As for Beauvoir, while she wrote many fewer pages of philosophical analysis than he and tended to discount, or at least greatly underestimate, the value of what she did write in this domain, these contributions are truly of great historical and philosophical importance as well. In fact, because of her breakthrough insight into the phenomenon of "the second sex" and its overwhelming importance throughout history and into present times, it is not unthinkable to consider her to have been even more original than he and ultimately to have exerted even far greater influence, not so much on Sartre, even though that was no doubt significant, but on the development of contemporary human thought itself in our ever more globalized world.

Notes

1. This and all other translations from French texts are my own, in order to ensure a certain uniformity of terminology and interpretation that is not always maintained in the various "official" published translations of French philosophers. The French original reads: "Car il y a une violence sartrienne, plus nerveuse et moins durable que celle de Marx. Le ton personnel de la polémique avec Lefort a surpris" (Merleau-Ponty, *Les Aventures de la dialectique,* 214).

2. For a different approach, see Christine Daigle's contribution in this volume, "Where Influence Fails: Embodiment in Beauvoir and Sartre."

3. She goes on to say that Merleau-Ponty was not too upset with her over her essay, at least not for long: "Il pouvait comprendre les colères intellectuelles." And, she adds, despite the great friendship they had for one another, they often argued violently, she being enraged, he responding with a smile. It is important to note that the time to which she is referring here is subsequent to that, in 1953, at which the famous and quite public rupture of the friendship between Sartre and Merleau-Ponty occurred.

4. My authority for this chronological point is *Les Écrits de Sartre,* by Michel Contat and Michel Rybalka, 338: "The work was completely composed between the end of June 1957 and the beginning of 1960" ["L'ouvrage fut entièrement composé entre la fin de juin 1957 et le début de 1960"].

5. As Merleau-Ponty expressed it, in a very positive manner and à propos of his own appropriations of Husserl: "If one believes that interpretation is obliged either to distort or to reiterate literally, that is because one wishes that the meaning of a work should be completely positive, and by right capable of being catalogued in a way that separates off what is there from what is not there. But that constitutes a misunderstanding of the work and of thinking." ["Si l'on croit que l'interprétation est astreinte ou à déformer ou à reprendre littéralement, c'est qu'on veut que la signification d'une œuvre soit toute positive, et susceptible en droit d'un inventaire qui délimite ce qui y est et ce qui n'y est pas. Mais c'est là se tromper sur l'œuvre et sur le penser."] "Le philosophe et son ombre," in *Éloge de la philosophie et autres essais,* 252.

6. McBride, "Sartre e Beauvoir all'asse del ventesimo secolo," 91–101.

7. "Il ne travaillait pas comme d'habitude avec des pauses, des ratures, déchirant des pages, les recommençant; pendant des heures d'affilée, il fonçait de feuillet en feuillet sans le relire, comme happé par des idées que sa plume, même au galop, n'arrivait pas à rattraper" (*FA,* 407).

8. See "What's Jean-Paul Sartre Thinking Lately?" 286.

9. Margaret Simons showed an acute awareness of this some years ago already in her "Sartre and Beauvoir: The Question of Influence," 25–42.

10. Sartre does *mention* this hypothesis, but only in passing, in the original published version; see "Merleau-Ponty" (1964), 258. For the posthumously published version, see Sartre, "Merleau-Ponty" (1985), 3–29. I myself have speculated on the further

irony that Merleau-Ponty himself, even though an individual's personal history and even such details as facial expressions and various psychological states play such a central role in his philosophical analyses, virtually never alluded to his own childhood in any of his writings; see McBride, "Merleau-Ponty and Sartre," 63–86.

11. Sartre, "The Itinerary of a Thought," 21. The interview was originally published in *The New Left Review* in 1969.

12. Jacques Derrrida's efforts, some more successful than others, at reading new meanings into historical texts through focusing on some of their "margins" depend on this insight.

13. "Truqué jusqu'à l'os et mystifié, j'écrivais joyeusement sur notre malheureuse condition. Dogmatique je doutais de tout sauf d'être l'élu du doute" (*Mots*, 210).

14. "Et *L'Être et le Néant* est en grande partie une description de l'homme sérieux et de son univers" (*MA*, 67; Gallimard, 1947).

15. "Le fait même que l'ontologie de *L'Être et le Néant* est une ontologie d'avant la conversion suppose qu'une conversion est nécessaire" (*CPM*, 13).

16. Simons, *Beauvoir and* The Second Sex, 10–11.

12 *Anne, ou quand prime le spirituel:* Beauvoir and Sartre Interact— from Parody, Satire, and Tragedy to Manifesto of Liberation

Adrian van den Hoven

In the 1930s Simone de Beauvoir and Jean-Paul Sartre were both working on their first literary works. Beauvoir was crafting a collection of short stories based on her adolescence and career as a budding lycée teacher in the provinces; Sartre, who was teaching in a lycée in Le Havre, was working on *La Nausée* and the short story collection entitled *Le Mur*. Sartre's novel was published by Gallimard in April 1938 and *Le Mur* in February 1939. Beauvoir was not so lucky; her collection was rejected by Gallimard and then by Grasset. It was not published until 1979 as *Quand prime le spirituel;* however, the Folio paperback edition modified it to *Anne, ou quand prime le spirituel* in order to "highlight the importance of the main character,"[1] that is, to stress the central role this character played in Simone de Beauvoir's youth. There is no doubt that the death of Anne (whose story is based on that of Elisabeth Lacoin, called Zaza in Beauvoir's memoirs) was a decisive moment in Beauvoir's life, but this new title does shift the focus away from the collection as a comprehensive overview of "the lives of young French Catholic women after WWI" to that of its main victim, Anne/Zaza.

It is unfortunate that Beauvoir's collection remained unknown for such a long time because it bears striking similarities to Sartre's literary productions of the time and could have had an equally important impact. His novel *La Nausée* is not just a devastating satirical attack on conservative provincial France but also a manifesto for a new vision of the world and humanity. It throws overboard all the old certainties, pronounces itself in favor of "absurdity as the only absolute," and points to a redirection of man's role toward the abstract and imaginary realm. On the other hand, "L'Enfance d'un chef," the final story in *Le Mur,* provides a parodic overview of the various literary, psychological, and political movements of the time and illustrates, in an ironic and satirical take on Barrès's *Les Déracinés,* how an uprooted middle-class Frenchman indeed rediscovers his origins by becoming an anti-Semitic bully and "leader." Beauvoir's collection, in turn, draws deeply on her personal experiences, parodies the conservative Catholic environment she grew up in, describes in "Marguerite" an intellectual world similar to "L'Enfance d'un chef,"[2] but has its conclusion function as a manifesto for a new woman who will go out on her own and discover the world in all its freshness and complexity.

The conclusion of Beauvoir's autobiography, *Mémoires d'une jeune fille rangée,* deals in some detail with Zaza's importance in Beauvoir's life and underlines the crucial importance of her death: "Together we had struggled against a murky destiny that had it in for us and for a long time I have thought that she paid for my freedom with her death."[3] Since that time, Zaza's correspondence and notebooks have been published,[4] and they give quite a different picture of her and, crucially, of her relationship with her mother. Beauvoir's biographers have also added greatly to the understanding of Beauvoir's youth and teaching career, as does Danièle Sallenave's "Foreword." It might have been interesting to view Beauvoir's collection of short stories through these various mirrors, but it struck me as more worthwhile to focus on its literary and philosophical significance and to demonstrate how certain of its literary techniques and approaches highlight Beauvoir's intentions and illustrate the close interaction between her and Jean-Paul Sartre. The descriptive summaries and use of selective citations of these interrelated stories will function to highlight the importance of satire, parody, free indirect discourse, interior monologue, and other devices and show Beauvoir's ability to grasp a total social universe and to use them to write her own manifesto.

As Danièle Sallenave remarks so astutely in her "Foreword": "Free indirect discourse provides the most exact and revelatory image of bad faith, that lie to oneself."[5] Importantly, Deirdre Bair notes in her biography: "In the early Thirties Beauvoir frequented the bookshops of Sylvia Beach and Adrien Monnier and read . . . Dos Passos, whom she admired greatly."[6] She read him in English, unlike Sartre, who, at her instigation, read him and other American writers, such as Faulkner and Hemingway, in translation. Her enthusiasm for Dos Passos must have been contagious because in 1939 Sartre published "Dos Passos and '1919,'" in which he focuses on the latter's use of free indirect discourse and famously concludes: "I consider Dos Passos to be the greatest novelist of his time."[7] It is interesting to speculate on the theoretical discussions Beauvoir and Sartre may have had about Dos Passos and the works they themselves were composing, because what Sartre dissects theoretically they both put into practice, not just in the works mentioned but also in their future writings. Beauvoir shows such mastery of Dos Passos's technique of free indirect discourse that it must be assumed that these discussions exercised considerable influence on both their thinking and their practice. Sartre analyzes Dos Passos's technique as follows:

> [He] has invented only one thing, an art of story-telling, but that is enough to create a universe. The novel, like life, unfolds in the present. . . . In [it] the dice are not loaded, for fictional man is free. The narrator relates from the outside what the hero would have wanted him to relate. . . . But, at the same time, the utterance[s] take on a social importance. . . . For [his characters], there is no break between inside and outside, between body and consciousness, but only between an individual's thinking and the world of collective representations. What a simple process this is, and how effective! All one need do is use [his] technique in telling the story of a life, and it crystallizes into the Social and the problem of the transition to the typical is resolved.[8]

But if Sartre finds Dos Passos's universe nightmarish and his characters bereft of a future, Beauvoir uses his technique—as well as those of others—to describe colorfully, satirically, and parodically the stultifying, oppressive, and hypocritical atmosphere of the French Catholic petty bourgeoisie of the 1920s and 30s. Unstintingly, she lays bare its repressive puritanism, its fear of sexuality, and its sanctimonious mores; and in the last story, she proudly rejects this paralyzing and debilitating universe and proclaims her independence and eagerness to discover reality in all its newness and variety. As our summaries and citations will illustrate, Beauvoir's excellent memory for detail, the telling adjectives, and the deliberately cloying phraseology show that she possessed a fine understanding of her milieu and, as a social critic, knew how to unmask the inner selves and to uncover the basic raw impulses of her characters. Additionally, unlike what the new title implies, these five stories form a coherent unit; the characters belong to the same milieu, and their lives are intertwined. Yet each can be considered a "moral" tale: Marcelle allows herself to be fooled by Denis, the so-called avant-garde poet and genius. Chantal, "the teacher from Paris," considers herself intellectually and socially superior to her provincial counterparts but prudishly rejects her two young student friends and disdains them when one of them becomes pregnant and needs her help. The more sympathetic Lisa pines after Pascal but fails to impress him; instead—to her own startled bewilderment—a total stranger accuses her of being her husband's mistress, and later in the day her dentist suggests a liaison. In a dream sequence, she ends up musing about being seduced by Pascal. Anne, the chief victim in this collection, is passionately in love with the same Pascal, but he seems incapable of appreciating the depth of her feelings and remains preoccupied with his sister Marcelle, who has been abandoned by Denis. Chantal encourages Anne in her quest for love and believes she is instrumental in Anne's liberating herself from her domineering middle-class mother's Catholic stranglehold, but in reality she limits herself to a few futile gestures. Anne goes mad and falls deathly ill when she is threatened with exile to England. After the funeral, Chantal considers both Pascal and Anne's mother as being equally guilty of Anne's death. Marguerite, Marcelle's younger sister, defies her family and follows Denis into Paris's nightlife. She discovers all the latest trends, falls in love with the exploitative Denis, and is taken in by his exotic lesbian friend Marie-Ange, who tries to seduce her. When she rebuffs her, both are thrown out. Denis returns to Marcelle, and Marguerite decides to discover for herself reality in all its complexity and richness. As is the case of the stories in *Le Mur*, their lives—with the exception of Marguerite's—are failures. Hence the final story is highly significant, because although her experiences often parallel those of Lucien Fleurier, Marguerite arrives at the opposite conclusion. Her discovery of reality has a great deal in common with Roquentin's discovery of contingency and absurdity in "The Public Park" scene of *La Nausée*, while at the same time she goes beyond it and positively embraces the world.

A more detailed description of each story helps us to discover exactly how Beauvoir uses various literary devices to reveal the social ambiance as well as the inner self and deeper motivations of her characters. The use of free indirect discourse in "Marcelle" serves admirably to make the reader uncomfortably complicit with the sugary sweet and pseudo-religious ambiance of this middle-class Catholic society: "Marcelle Drouffe was a dreamy and precocious little girl . . . [who was] extraordinarily sensitive. . . . When she thought about poor kids and little orphans . . . tears would run down her cheeks and her whole body would plunge into a delicious void" (*W,* 11; *A,* 33). In church "Marcelle would see wonderful visions: her heart melted and while sobbing she offered the sacrifice of her life up . . . to a young fair-haired God" (*W,* 11; *A,* 34). Beauvoir deliberately associates religious ecstasy and erotic desire, but in this society matters of sexuality are firmly suppressed. In the Catholic lending library, Marcelle reads "expurgated Memoirs" while "Mlle Olivier surveys the room with a stern look." All the same, "some of the . . . regular visitors aroused a passionate interest in

Marcelle: middle-aged men with a pensive gaze, their faces matured and refined by thought. [T]hey certainly belonged to [the] intellectual elite and she ardently longed for one of them to notice her some day" (*W*, 12; *A*, 35). Marcelle's imagination finds an unexpected outlet in the books her aunt has reserved for children: "Bluebeard's cruelty, the trials imposed upon Grisélidis, the unfortunate Geneviève, stark naked beneath her long hair perturbed and excited Marcelle greatly. . . . Marcelle often felt guilty of some grave offence because she was fond of quivering with repentance at the feet of a sinless, handsome and terrible male" (*W*, 13; *A*, 37). Ironically, the works meant to shield her from her sexual awakening have precisely the opposite effect. She discovers "sex" all around her: "She was thirteen when in a public toilet she spots a story in the *Petit Parisien*: a man covering an alabaster breast with eager kisses; Marcelle is haunted by this vision all day; at night, in bed, she abandons herself to it without resistance, her cheeks are on fire" (*W*, 14; *A*, 38).

During the Great War, "faced with the immensity of human suffering; [s]he stopped believing in God; she felt quite sure that Providence did not exist" (*W*, 15; *A*, 40). It is a sad irony, but her newfound atheism does not allow our timid, clumsy wallflower to fare better: The young lieutenant "who seemed so heroic" decided "to marry one of her cousins" (*W*, 15; *A*, 40). Marcelle has no choice but to find a job. She becomes "a social assistant" in a "welfare centre" (*W*, 16; *A*, 40). In the metro, she comes into a physical contact with common laborers, and "she felt a wave of intense pity" for them. She would like to talk to them about "beauty, about love and about the meaning of suffering," but the "smell of human sweat" and the contact with their "coarse, rough bodies" makes her "nauseous." When she notices her "own pathetic face in the mirror," she remarks that it "deserves the love of a hero" and she whispers: "Oh, beloved!" (*W*, 17; *A*, 42). Her romantic idealism, combined with her inability to stomach reality, has already forced her to retreat into a world of fantasy.

When she receives the visit of two members of the "Social Contact," her life seems transformed. Maurice and Paul met during the war and "have decided to revive the deep, simple friendship that existed in the trenches" (*W*, 17; *A*, 43). She accepts the invitation to open the center to all sorts of uplifting activities, but, frustratingly, the young working-class visitors view it only as a convenient meeting place. The "Social Contact" was, in fact, an idealistic attempt by progressive Catholics to redirect the class struggle into a more harmonious, socially cooperative venture. The introduction of these two men allows Beauvoir to combine history, psychological insight, and satire. Marcelle befriends Paul, and soon this devout Catholic "asked her to marry him [and] she accepted" (*W*,

23; *A*, 52). But, as he explains, he wishes to repress his "violent longings" (*W*, 25; *A*, 56) until they are married. Marcelle soon notices that "his was neither a passionate nor a troubled nature" (*W*, 26; *A*, 57).

Not long thereafter she encounters Denis Charval, a young man with poetic pretensions who has been invited to speak about Rimbaud. He initiates her into postwar libertine Paris. She drops Paul because her role is now "to save this brilliant but weak" person (*W*, 30; *A*, 65). Their wedding night is described from her point of view and demonstrates Beauvoir's understanding of female sexuality. Yet "the joys of sex" do not open Marcelle's eyes to the inflated heroic role she has reserved for herself. Denis, too lazy to work, exploits her. He introduces her to "bars, jazz, and gross, cynical ideas for the fun of it" (*W*, 37; *A*, 75), but home life bores him, and he finally takes up with her younger sister, Marguerite, whom he invites to an "American bar" against Marcelle's wishes. Nevertheless, Marcelle persists in her sacrificial role-playing and declares pompously: "In rejecting commonplace pleasures, playthings, finery and social success and easy flirtation she had always saved herself for some splendid happiness. Yet it was not happiness that had been granted to her; it was suffering. But perhaps it was only suffering that could satisfy her heart at last" (*W*, 45; *A*, 88).

When Denis leaves her, he writes her an overwrought poetic farewell in which he declares, in pseudo-dramatic fashion, that "there are beings, my poor sweet Marcelle, who refuse even love. Do you know that in Thulé there was a king who threw his golden bowl into the sea so that he might watch the rings on the water and sigh?" (*W*, 44; *A*, 86). Marcelle concludes that her "life is finished. . . . It was not happiness that was granted her but suffering." She now wishes to "reach beyond happiness" and "for the second time had the wonderful revelation of her destiny: I am a woman of genius" (*W*, 45; *A*, 87–88).

The inflated language notwithstanding, Marcelle's life is a pathetic failure, but her willful ignorance allows her the crutch necessary to maintain her illusions. Her story can be seen as an ironic comment on the Sartrean notion that the unveiling of the world will open a person's eyes to the truth. Evidently Marcelle is determined to preserve the fanciful role she has chosen for herself; she may have been taken in by her egotistical, narcissistic young "poetic genius," but she knows how to adapt her role to whatever pathetic circumstances she finds herself in and will not let reality obtrude. The hybrid nature of free indirect discourse has allowed us to participate in the workings of her psyche and simultaneously to get a glimpse of postwar Paris in all its complexity: its Catholic bourgeoisie, its working class, and its night life. Clearly, Beauvoir had understood very well the usefulness of Dos Passos's literary technique and used it to illustrate the workings of the segments of French society that she knew so well.

"Chantal" is stylistically more complex. It opens with her diary entries for the first months as a teacher in the "provinces." Narrated in the first person, it shows us a conceited Parisian who feels superior to her provincial counterparts. Part II reverts to free indirect discourse but intersperses it with dialogue. It provides an insight into the teachers' petty mentality as they debate the relative merits of their students. Next Chantal receives a visit from two of her students, Andrée and Monique. The evening ends with Chantal being invited to Monique's house for dinner; this invitation brings her both anxiety and delight. She wants to impress the members of the local elite but is unsure how they will view her. Part III focuses on Andrée, who dreams of getting away from her suffocating surroundings. She admires Chantal, but to her chagrin, the latter prefers Monique and her friend Serge. Part IV is the follow-up of Chantal's diary. She finds Andrée "depressing" but views Monique's and Serge's relationship as a fairytale and sees in them "an adorable child-couple" (W, 76; A, 138). She has just spent two weeks in Paris, where she met Anne and Pascal, the couple at the center of story four. Chantal asserts vainly that thanks to her, "life and truth will win in the end" (W, 79; A, 142). Part V takes place in Andrée and Monique's classroom. Monique is told she has been left off the honor roll, and she bursts into tears. The two meet later, and Monique reveals that she is pregnant. Andrée is sure that Chantal will help, but when Andrée informs her, Chantal exclaims disdainfully: "Have you no moral sense at all? . . . Certainly [I will] not" (W, 88; A, 158). Part VI deals with the graduation: Andrée has won the Prize for Excellence, but Monique has been forced to become engaged and is already living with her future parents-in-law. Chantal has been named to a position in Chartres, and when she encounters Andrée, she averts her eyes. Chantal sneers at Andrée, musing that she "will turn into a little pedant" (W, 91; A, 162), and Andrée realizes that from "now on she would be entirely alone," but that one day, "in spite of everything, I shall certainly end up not being young anymore" (W, 93; A, 166).

Chantal, the budding teacher, suffers from delusions similar to those of Marcelle. She uses the same romantic language and inflated style and remains incapable of seeing herself as she is. Her readings of Balzac, Proust, and Alain Fournier inform her vision of the world: "These walls contain what is most touching in provincial France" (W, 52; A, 95), she proclaims of the drab provincial town she now inhabits. Of her female students she declares: "They are not all of them agreeable, but all that is necessary to make me happy is that the charming forms of a few girls in blossom (as dear Proust would say) should stand out among those of the common kind" (*W*, 52; *A*, 96–97). However, the third-person narration is quite realistic and accurate in its description of provincial life. In Andrée we encounter the sincere views and thoughts of a bright and sensitive teenager caught between an ambitious father and a conformist aunt. Chantal's disdainful moralistic rejection of Monique's pregnancy shows that she too is a "failure," even as she blindly persists in seeing herself in a vainglorious light. While saying good-bye, Chantal imagines that she is projecting a grandiose image on the students: "At the dawn of these young lives her form would stand out forever, her slim form, so well set off in a tailored suit—a somewhat enigmatic, paradoxical form whose appearance had created such a flash in the old provincial lycée" (*W*, 91; *A*, 163). And she ends by seeing "in the depth of two dark eyes . . . her own image already becoming legendary" (*W*, 91; *A*, 163). Clearly, reality and truth have not succeeded in penetrating her consciousness; she is determined to cling to her own grandiose conception of herself.

"Lisa," the shortest story, is quite different from the others; yet it is no less fascinating because it forms a bridge with the next story. Initially, the free indirect discourse allows us to view Lisa through the eyes of her "fervent Catholic" teachers, who run a prep school for impoverished girls as well as for "the daughters of the well-to-do, pious middle-class inhabitants of Auteuil" (*W*, 97; *A*, 169). The "pious" Mlle Lambert hopes Lisa will exhibit signs of a religious calling, but these hopes are quickly dashed when "she had seen the girl sink gradually into a sterile wasting skepticism" (*W*, 98; *A*, 171). Lisa is eager to frequent the Bibliothèque nationale, where her friend Marguerite is preparing for exams and is seated next to "Wanda, a young Polish girl with green eyes" (*W*, 99; *A*, 173), an oblique reference to Wanda Kosakievicz,[9] the student Beauvoir befriended. However, Lisa really wishes to know about Marguerite's brother Pascal, whose fateful relationship with Anne is at the center of the next story. Marguerite indicates: "He'll come when he leaves the Ecole des Chartes, he'll take the A1 [bus] and be here around 5:30" (*W*, 101; *A*, 176). They also discuss Anne, "who has been so delirious, they had to move her in an isolation ward. . . . [A]ll yesterday she did nothing but call out, perpetually asking for Pascal." Lisa wants to know if "there is hope," and to herself she thinks wistfully: "Oh! How I should try to ease his sorrow. . . . If he is really unhappy, he'll accept my affection" (*W*, 103; *A*, 179).

On her way to the bus stop, Lisa spends her fare on some flowers and is accosted by an older woman who accuses her of being her husband's mistress. The startled Lisa denies everything, but it is not easy to get rid of her accuser. She would not want to "run the risk of a public scene breaking out just at the moment of Pascal's arrival: if he guessed she was waiting for him, she would die of shame" (*W,* 107; *A,* 185). While desperately rushing along, she turns around: "Pascal was behind her and he was smiling at her kindly" (*W,* 107; *A,* 185). She has five minutes to catch his interest, but he begins to talk politics, a topic that does not interest her. Then he wants to know how her work is going. She shakes her head: "It's horrible to be forced to use one's brain to make a living; it's inhuman" (*W,* 108; *A,* 187). They have arrived at the library where they pick up his sister; the two offer her a ride in the taxi. When they drop her off, she notices somewhat bitterly: "He had not noticed the flowers, of course" (*W,* 108; *A,* 188).

Lisa's hilarious and fruitless encounters make her appear as a failure, but she shows glimpses of lucidity and realism. In the second half, we find Lisa at the dentist, who enlightens her about Hindu philosophy and theosophy. He is also interested in more than her teeth: "A young girl like you needs something more than philosophy." Lisa responds: "How do you expect me to make a living?" But he retorts: "Pretty young women shouldn't be allowed to study." And when he is finished, he opines: "My Saturdays will be quite sad from now on" (*W,* 111; *A,* 193). Before leaving, she borrows her bus money from him and later she murmurs defiantly: "Perhaps one day I'll become someone's mistress." And then the older woman's phrase echoes in her mind: "My husband's mistress" (*W,* 112; *A,* 194), a clear sign that Proust's pathetic hero Swann has left an impact on the author. Just as Swann cannot keep Odette's comments about her sexual adventures from obtruding in his consciousness, Lisa continues to be reminded of the fat lady's comments to her. Back at the Institute, she narrates her day to two of her fellow students, but their chitchat tires her, and "she could not see what had given the minor events of the day their importance" (*W,* 114; *A,* 197).

The conclusion takes the form of an interior monologue, inspired by Molly Bloom's monologue in Joyce's *Ulysses.* In these musings, Lisa lets herself be gently seduced by Pascal, her "archangel dressed in shining white with a fiery sword in his chaste hands." She can feel his "archangel's hands gliding down the tender victim's body" (*W,* 115; *A,* 199).

"Lisa" may only be a sketch, but it contains a variety of encounters and techniques. Through the use of free indirect discourse, we participate in her teacher's thoughts and feelings as well as her own, while the interior monologue unveils her wishful erotic thinking. It represents an ironic counterpart to the other stories. Nothing of consequence happens to Lisa. She fails to interest Pascal, she is falsely accused of being someone's mistress, she responds realistically to the dentist's amorous advances, and her fellow students barely react to her so-called adventures. Alone in bed, she can only indulge in erotic fantasies because reality has provided her with nothing.

"Anne," the fourth story, informs the new title. This long and tragic tale is divided into four parts. It opens with a prayer, an interior monologue by Anne's mother, Mme Vignon. It reveals the psyche of a strict bourgeois Catholic: it is a mix of religiosity, self-satisfaction and practical cunning. Her goal is to marry off her daughters properly, and nothing will stand in her way. She opens the letters her daughter receives from Pascal, considers that "her first mistake" was to let her study, and reveals that she "hates . . . intellectuals." She will also make sure that "Chantal, that unbeliever, that adventuress will not be allowed in her house that year" (W, 120; A, 206). She justifies herself by appealing to God; she "begs him to spare her" and induce her daughters to "do their duty as a Christian" (W, 122; A, 208). Then the narrator switches to free indirect discourse and describes an outing whose purpose it was to introduce her daughter Lucette to another marriage prospect. She is not happy with him: "This young man does not have a job," and, she adds bitterly, "It is not a brilliant match." Mother orders her to consider what it means to be a Christian; her daughter should become a baby machine like her; she did her duty and procreated "rather than thinking about [her own] pleasure" (W, 123; A, 211). During the picnic, Anne disappears; to her mother's consternation, she has gone off for a swim. She confronts her daughter with a sermon: "You are living in the most total moral anarchy. You are frivolous and filled with sickly curiosity." Then she repeats a fragment of her prayer: "Chantal won't be allowed to set foot in the house this year." When Anne reminds her that she had promised, her mother retorts: "I wanted too much to please you, now I am sorry, I won't accept a ruined girl in my house" (W, 127; A, 217). Next she brings up Pascal's letters and raises the "cardinal" question: "Does he want to marry you?" She lectures her about the true nature of men: "They talk about ideals but they are full of base desires. That beautiful talk by Chantal and her friends only serves to justify the lowest instincts." She concludes: "You will stop having any contact with that young man" (W, 128; A, 218–19). Toward evening, Mme Vignon feels better: "God had listened to her prayer; Lucette has accepted marriage and of her own accord Anne had admitted her fault which perhaps had only been a piece of foolishness. After all, she was dutiful and obedient; in a year she would be better" (W, 131; A, 223). But reality interrupts with a loud scream; Anne has cut her foot with an axe. She explains that she only wanted to help her younger sisters. Mme Vignon realizes that Anne will be immobilized for a week and won't have to accompany

her sister on her visit to her future in-laws. And speaking to herself she wonders: "But no one would cut herself with an axe on purpose" (*W*, 131; *A*, 224).
The mixture of dialogue and free indirect discourse allows the author to navi-
gate carefully between the mother's imperious demands, disguised in Christian
terms, and Anne, who vacillates between her desire for Pascal's love and her respect for her mother's authority.

In Part II we encounter Chantal's thoughts in the train on her way to a visit
with Anne. Chantal is still the vain, self-important do-gooder we met in the
first story: "She was fully aware of the gravity of her task. . . . Ever since she
had realized that life was more important than books and concrete action than
thought, Chantal had undertaken the mission of plucking Anne away from her
environment, to destroy her prejudices and of making her an emancipated,
happy woman" (*W*, 133; *A*, 226). Again, Chantal lets her imagination run away
with her. She views Anne as "the heroine in an artistic scene" (*W*, 135; *A*, 230
[transl. changed]) and the letter she plans to write Paul Baron will be filled with
quaint and platitudinous descriptions of the Vignon's home. She also knows
that Mme Vignon hates her (*W*, 135; *A*, 231), and she enjoys her new role: "She
was rootless, without traditions, a stranger . . . the enemy." Her view is that
"marriage to Pascal was necessary, at least as a first stage, to liberate Anne from
[her family's] stifling beliefs and morals" (*W*, 136; *A*, 231–32).

However, when the two meet secretly during the night, Anne reveals: "It's
over, finished. [She] has made her sacrifice" and is "at peace" (*W*, 137; *A*, 237).
She also admits: "Once I needed to be so alone that I cut my foot with an axe,
I spent ten days on a couch and during that period they left me in peace" (*W*,
140; *A*, 237–38). Chantal plays the existentialist: "Your resignation is in fact a
definite choice: you chose peace." But Anne begs her: "Don't torment me. . . . I
can't take it anymore" (*W*, 140; *A*, 238–39). When they return home, the door is
locked and Anne climbs up to the second story window. She has lots of physical
courage but little emotional or mental strength.

Chantal is pleased with herself for "having taken Anne's interest in hand."
Anne comes back to Paris to see Pascal, but Chantal neglects her in favor of Paul
Baron, to whom she wants "to become indispensable" (*W*, 143; *A*, 243). One evening Anne knocks: "A week from today, I leave for England, mama made all the
arrangements without telling me." She hopes to meet Pascal at Anne's place and
finally receives a call from his sister Marguerite: "Pascal can't come." Anne exclaims: "I flung myself on him with all my weight . . . but now it is only pity he
feels for me." Chantal too realizes that "Pascal had not been able to give Anne
security." In spite of that, she tells her: "You will be able to persuade Pascal" (*W*,

145–46; A, 247–48). Clearly, Chantal has completely misread the situation and overestimated her own role as Anne's savior while ignoring Anne's emotional fragility and Pascal's family problems and insecurity.

In Part III the focus shifts to Pascal, who has just received a message from Anne; she wants to see him in four hours. He vacillates between "love," "sincerity," and "duty" and is disconcerted by Anne's "passion" (W, 147; A, 249). He is very much concerned with his sister Marcelle, who has just been visited by Denis, who had abandoned her: "After making an appalling scene he took all mama's and Marcelle's money by force" (W, 152; A, 257). Pascal would like to find "a meaning in [humanity's] suffering," but the ever-idealistic Marcelle remains convinced that "illness and betrayal did not pass over me in vain" (W, 149; A, 252). In an oblique reference to Anne, he remarks: "Not all illnesses emanate from the body, too ardent a soul could wear out its fleshly wrappings and destroy it" (W, 149; A, 253). When they meet, Anne reiterates that "Mama is absolutely determined to send me to England for a year." Anne wants the two of them to become engaged, but Pascal brings up his family situation and adds vaguely that they "have all the future ahead of them and [they] will write to one another." Anne retorts: "Mama . . . will undoubtedly allow me to see you once or twice before I go but afterwards our break must be complete. I must obey her" (W, 152; A, 255–58). Later, Pascal visits Chantal to await Anne's arrival. "I leave on Monday," Anne says. "I have thought it over thoroughly; my happiness is not at the mercy of a separation. Nothing can destroy it, that dawned on me suddenly like a revelation." When she is leaving, Chantal remarks with some apparent misgiving: "I haven't seen Anne so full of life for a great while"; and Pascal replies, "One can always rely on Anne, she is equal to any trial" (W, 156; A, 264). Clearly, neither one seems to have grasped the depths of Anne's despair and her ability to hide her real feelings.

Part IV gives the lie to their optimism. The focus has shifted back to Pascal. Anne is at his door; his sister lets her in, and she is obviously deranged. When Pascal shows up, he immediately takes her back to her mother. Anne wants him to kiss her for the first time. Her mother puts her to bed, and when Pascal says good-bye to her, he declares pathetically: "We are engaged now; your mother gives her consent, Anne." But she replies: "It does not matter" (W, 159–60; A, 271). Evidently, it is already too late to save Anne; Pascal's kiss and his declaration can no longer reestablish her mental equilibrium. "Anne's death comes as a surprise," and while Pascal touches her dead eyelids, he thinks: "Nothing was left of her in these mortal remains, to reach Anne's essential truth he had to look into his own heart." He does not explain what may be found there but concludes: "The doctors had talked of inflammation of the brain but a sudden at-

tack like this was hardly credible; it was much more likely that Anne was suffering from a tumor for a long while; for a long while her days had been numbered,
and her recent excessive reactions were to be put down to this hidden disease."
And he adds: "A radiant soul dwelt within him forever; she poured certainty
and peace on him: wholly and utterly he accepted the world" (W, 161; A, 273).
These are hardly the feelings of a passionate lover.

Mme Vignon's reaction is entirely in keeping with her bourgeois religiosity.
Few people attend the funeral, but she is consoled by the great number of letters
extolling "Anne's rare qualities." She creates "a simple memento" and "underlines [in Anne's diary] a magnificent page where Anne places her life and salvation in God's hands." She prays to "Anne, my little saint. . . . Help me to accept
having been the instrument of your suffering and salvation, without complaint"
(W, 161–63; A, 273–76). Her behavior indicates that no event, however tragic,
can make her deviate from her belief in her own superiority and the correctness
of her role.

Finally, the focus shifts back to Chantal. Anne's death has "revealed the
world's ugliness to her, her enthusiasm had dried up and all she wished to set
against the absurdity of fate was a clear-minded bitterness." She also knows that
the image that is being created of Anne is false: "They turned her into a mys-
tic, a votary; Mme Vignon had placed a saint in her heaven and that beautiful
figure of the woman, modeled by Chantal with such love had crumbled into
dust" (W, 164; A, 277). Yet Chantal continues to see life in fictional terms. When
she and Paul arrive by train at Uzerche, she muses, "It would be a good beginning to a novel." And in romantic terms she adopts the viewpoint of the locals
and imagines how this mysterious couple would be viewed as they are walking
toward Anne's home. When they meet Mme Vignon, her hostility toward her
resurfaces: "There was something triumphant in her suffering, the misfortune
that had struck her was not a sign from heaven, it was a sign of divine election;
she had won the game. Chantal was forever disarmed—death had abruptly can-
celled all her efforts and now there was nothing left for her at all" (W, 165; A,
277–79). After the three exchange Anne's letters, Mme Vignon remarks characteristically: "The only consolation left to us . . . is the reflection that her death
has contributed to God's greater glory." Pascal raises his head in sympathy, but
Chantal thinks angrily: "A pair of accomplices, they both of them killed her."
In fact, according to Chantal: "Anne had died from want of love. . . . These blind
creatures believe that the fantastic only exists in books. But life is made up of
improbable events, Anne's very existence was already a miracle." At this point
she imagines a literary project: "It would take a whole book to show her as she
really was, a being of flesh and fire, a beautiful heroine with an ingenuous smile

and a passionate heart." Chantal concludes in a predictably dramatic vein: "A beautiful but tragic story weighed down forever on her life. . . . [S]he already felt transfigured by its heft, from now on she would love and understand better . . . and perhaps one day she would be able to transform her painful experience into a work of serene beauty" (*W*, 165–66; *A*, 280–81 [transl. changed]).

Ironically, and just like Roquentin in *La Nausée*,[10] who projected the writing of an "adventure that could not take place," Chantal never wrote the magnificent volume that she felt Anne so richly deserved. Beauvoir's *Mémoires d'une jeune fille rangée* provide some of the biographical underpinnings for Anne/Zaza's tragic death, but as Deirdre Bair points out, Beauvoir only discovered all the facts behind her story after its publication and had remained unaware of the reasons for Zaza's (Elisabeth Lacoin's) mother's objections and the true nature of Pascal (based on Maurice Merleau-Ponty's) family situation until that time:

> For years in La Rochelle, Madame Merleau-Ponty had supposedly been the mistress of a very well-known, highly respected professor who was also married. Sartre's mother, who had also lived in La Rochelle told me that everyone there knew about it, and that it was a public scandal to see this man seated at dinner parties with his wife on one side and his mistress on the other. It was he who was the father of the other two children, Maurice Merleau-Ponty and his sister, Monique. It was an extremely serious liaison which lasted for years and years, and this gentleman took care of his two children, even though for their mother's protection they took the name of her husband.[11]

The final story, "Marguerite," completes the circle. Some of its aspects—the detailed description of Paris's intellectual and literary currents and ambiance after the Great War—are strikingly similar to Sartre's "L'Enfance d'un chef." But in Sartre's story, Lucien becomes a copy of his father and "succeeds" by regressing into a right-wing and anti-Semitic "leader" and assuming all the vicious postures of his milieu, while in this story, Marguerite decides to find her own way and ends up discovering reality in all its richness and diversity.

The initial sentence of this first-person narration incorporates the original title of the collection, "Primauté du spirituel": "In my family it was always held that the things of the spirit came first" (*W*, 169; *A*, 285). Marguerite too suffers a stifling Catholic education, frequents a private "Institute" run by "old spinsters," and is a fervent believer. She feels inclined toward mysticism, whips herself with "a little gold chain," and "loves to go to confession" (*W*, 170; *A*, 287–88). She experiences her first erotic sensation at age seven, "learns" about making babies by reading Zola and Louÿs, yet knows nothing about reality:

"That's the advantage of a Catholic education, I might have let myself be raped without thinking there was any harm in it" (*W*, 172; *A*, 290). When a priest criticizes her for not telling him all her sins, she is so ashamed she never goes back to him: "In my mind I had confused God with Father Mirande . . . but this God was so ridiculous I soon began to doubt His existence" (*W*, 172; *A*, 291). She decides to ask another priest for advice, but he wants to know, "What is this sin that has kept you so long from the sacraments?" Marguerite reacts: "That was it, I was sick of these spiritual consultations . . . he certainly helped liquidate the last vestiges of religion" (*W*, 173; *A*, 292). Now she is ready for a series of adventures that she believes will open her up to reality; but in fact, they are only its sheen, its veneer; and it is these illusions and her belief in the "magical" powers of others that will propel her for a long time.

Her brother Pascal introduces her to his friends at the Sorbonne, and she participates half-heartedly in their amusements. Marcelle introduces her to modern literature and to the "Social Contract," but she is really fascinated by Marcelle's husband, Denis. Up to now, she has only known "an expurgated edition of the world; here and there fragments of the authentic text revealed themselves but the cuts distorted it" (*W*, 174; *A*, 296). One day while she is studying, Denis remarks that "nothing is worth-while," and she feels "her ultimate reason for living vanish." Denis explains that you must "even throw . . . freedom out of the window; the day you no longer value it or anything else, only then will you truly possess it." Denis is looking for "a miracle . . . a truly gratuitous act" and promises "to show [her] *The Surrealist Manifesto*." She now discovers the "thirty-six sexual positions," and, when Denis takes her to a bar in Montparnasse, she supposedly discovers "the true world." She drinks "a gin-fizz," observes other men and women "waiting for a miracle and ready to seize it." After a "second gin-fizz," she feels herself "linked to Denis in a bond of indissoluble complicity," and now drunk, she perceives: "At all street corners, miracles burst out like fireworks" (*W*, 178–81; *A*, 298–305).

Denis leaves her sister Marcelle, and amidst her dreary home life Marguerite can only imagine that "elsewhere, at that very moment, miracles were coming into existence and, somewhere, there was Denis." She steals money to go to the bar where Denis took her; and she proclaims: "I went there like I used to go to Mass with the same fervent eagerness. I had scarcely changed Gods" (*W*, 185; *A*, 307–308). She observes prostitutes and wonders how "they had acquired their magnificent freedom." She tries to impress the clients by her outrageous behavior: "Naively I believed I could amuse them by showing off, every one knows that delusion is a kind of miracle." A man unzips his fly for her; she is invited up to an apartment but refuses the man's kiss; he likes her anyway; she is "not corrupt." She acquires "an exaggerated confidence in [her]self"; after all, why prevent "the possible occurrence of a miracle." She accepts a car ride into the suburbs; like André Gide, "she wants to refuse nothing." But she rejects the driver's advances and is lucky to get away from him: "[I] regretted nothing; I was delighted with myself for having brought an entirely absurd happening into existence." The next time she is threatened, the men empty "her bag" (*W*, 186–87; *A*, 309–16).

The third phase of her so-called education begins when she encounters Marie-Ange at the Jockey and is reintroduced to Denis. She "admires his genius; he is sometimes terrible but poets are like that." According to Denis, Marie-Ange embodies "Destiny." Marguerite wants to know why he left Marcelle. He explains: "I have always felt irresistibly attracted to Disaster." She asks: "Do you still feel that?" He shrugs his shoulders: "Who knows!" (*W*, 189–90; *A*, 319–20). Later on, after Marie-Ange throws both of them out, in what will be a surprise move to Marguerite, Denis will stealthily and sheepishly return to Marcelle.

Marguerite is invited to Marie-Ange's apartment; it is filled with bric-à-brac, typical of the Parisian avant-garde. She has led an exotic existence, and Marguerite finds her disquieting. Denis recommends her as "a guide." She asks him if "he is pleased with his existence," and he replies, echoing Roquentin's remarks: "What a funny question, one doesn't choose, things happen, one submits to them, then another day other things happen." He continues in a vein inspired by Gide: "Even gratuitous acts have consequences. . . . I am so disgusted with myself . . . the only right thing would be to do away with myself." Yet, however difficult he may be, Marguerite "loves this totally despairing man" (*W*, 190–93; *A*, 322–27). Denis's true character should have revealed itself to her by now; he is obviously only interested in sustenance and enough pocket money to indulge in his favorite pastimes, but Marguerite still has a way to go before her eyes are opened.

Marie-Ange draws her closer, but she has a violent temper and is unpredictable. She "kisses her effusively" and decides to dress her. Marguerite is embarrassed to appear naked before her, but in a Proustian vein, Marie-Ange compares her to "those women that Cranach painted." She also has her maid give her a beauty treatment. Marguerite rushes over to Denis, who remarks: "Seeing you like that, one might almost start wanting to be happy." The comment suffices to persuade her "that he loved her" (*W*, 197–98; *A*, 332–34).

One night she absolutely wants to see him and goes to a bar where two women are talking about him: "'I wonder how she gets him to do it,' said the blond one with a shrill laugh.—'He has to stuff her five times a night,' said the dark-haired one." Marguerite goes outside and cries; she confronts Denis, but he dismisses everything. She is overjoyed; even so, the phrase "five times a night" (*W,* 201–203; *A,* 339) echoes in her mind like a Proustian refrain.

Denis proposes to go to Saigon and become an opium smuggler; she is eager to come along. She could find a teaching position there and be his accomplice, but he does not want her to tell Marie-Ange.

Marie-Ange invites Marguerite back to her apartment and tells her to spend the night. When Marguerite turns off the light, she "suddenly [feels Marie-Ange's] arms around her body." After half an hour of caresses, she senses "her thick lips pressing on hers" and realizes that "[s]he wants to make love with [her]." Marie-Ange declares her feelings, but Marguerite wants to go home. Finally, Marie-Ange becomes angry: "Go if you like and never come back again" (*W,* 205–206; *A,* 345–47).

The next day Denis tells her that thanks to her he too has been "flung out." Marguerite is eager to begin their new adventure in Saigon, but one day he casually remarks that he would like to write Marcelle and see if she cares about "the trouble I am in. Pascal will help me." Marguerite retorts naïvely: "But Denis, what are you thinking of? Don't you know there is no forgiving what you did to her?" Now Denis disappears completely. When she finally corners him and declares her love for him, he answers that "one can't always do what one likes" (*W,* 207; *A,* 350–51). In fact, Denis prefers security over adventure and is about to return to Marcelle. The next evening Pascal enters her bedroom: "Marcelle has seen her husband again . . . she has decided to forgive him and resume married life." Marguerite does not want to cry; instead she "utter[s] a slight hysterical laugh" and declares: "That's utterly grotesque." Unbeknownst to her, Denis returned "three weeks ago."

Now it is time for her "to look her empty future straight in the face." She takes a long walk: "A week ago . . . she would have called out to Denis from the depths of the night and offered him a . . . miraculous escape." Now she realizes:

> Something had changed in [her]. [Not only that]: The world too was
> changing. . . . Suddenly she saw around [her] a host of objects that ap-
> peared to exist for themselves. She no longer need[ed] Denis; she can per-
> sonally possess all those things that were offering themselves to [her]; they
> offered themselves suddenly delivered from the fixed meaning in which
> [she] had enclosed them; they had cracked open their allegorical wrap-
> pings, they appeared naked, living, inexhaustible. . . . [She] left slowly, the
> world glistened like a new penny, [she] did not know yet what to do with

it but everything was possible because in the centre of things, in the spot Denis had left empty, [she] had found herself. (*W*, 211–12; *A*, 355–56)

She now realizes that she had already begun to change when she "had taken sides against Pascal and Marcelle's [moral] code" but that it had taken her "two years to become aware of all the cowardliness and hypocrisy their marvelous and pathetic dreams were and to break with them" (*W*, 212; *A*, 356).

Catherine S. Brosman remarks about the conclusion: "She has a near-epiphany when things break through their 'allegorical [mantle]' . . . but, unlike Roquentin in *La Nausée,* she sees in a positive light the richness and inexhaustibility of things, at whose center she finds her consciousness." Nevertheless, this critic concludes, "Connoisseurs of modern stories will find little to praise in these [stories]."[12] It is my opinion that in the late 1930s, in terms of writing about women, Marguerite's discovery ranks with Roquentin's discovery of contingency and his ultimate decision to focus on the abstract and imaginary realm— and in fact goes beyond it in its positive affirmation of life and acceptance of reality. It is also clear that in the 1930s Beauvoir and Sartre worked so closely together that in very different ways both managed to deal with their personal quests, problems, and obstacles in a way that allowed both of them to liberate themselves from old shibboleths, traditional points of view, and confining relationships. In *La Nausée,* Roquentin's epiphany in the Public Park functions as the *core* of the novel around which the preceding and following parts are organized. It is at the *conclusion* of this collection that Marguerite has her eyes opened, while it is the preceding events that show the traps young women fall into when they do not open their eyes to reality.

It is only when she realizes that she does not need Denis that Marguerite can begin to think like Roquentin, as the strikingly similar language indicates: "I was not surprised, I knew quite well that it was the World, the completely naked World that showed itself all at once."[13] Of course, Marguerite draws a very different conclusion from her discovery: to her, the universe is not an overwhelming, superabundant mass of objects that expels the human person. On the contrary, the discovery of reality impels her to go forward alone and make more and more discoveries. It leads to her liberation from dependency on men such as the egotistical Denis, who uses her as he sees fit, or from women such as Marie-Ange, who use their wealth and experience to seduce her. She now asserts herself as an individual who no longer waits for a male or a female savior, and instead feels sure enough of herself to personally explore all the abundant riches of this world. Thus, this collection of stories does not just show Beauvoir's mastery of literary techniques; it is also a resounding manifesto for female liberation at a time when such stances were still relatively rare.

Notes

1. Simone de Beauvoir, *Anne, ou quand prime le spirituel* (Paris: Gallimard, Folio, 2006). The "Editor's Note" states: "Simone de Beauvoir had first given her book the title 'Primauté du spirituel' [The Primacy of the Spiritual] which is also the title of a work by Jacques Maritain. For the 1979 edition she chose to replace it with 'Quand prime le spirituel.' We have modified the title a second time and it now becomes: 'Anne, ou quand prime le spirituel'" (Avant-propos de Danièle de Sallenave, p. 24).

2. See also Eliane Lecarme-Tabone's chapter in this volume.

3. As quoted in Deirdre Bair, *Simone de Beauvoir: A Biography,* 152.

4. Elisabeth Lacoin, *Correspondance et Carnets d'Elisabeth Lacoin, 1914–1929.*

5. My translation of "le style indirect libre est l'image la plus juste et le révélateur le plus sûr de la mauvaise foi, ce mensonge à soi-même" (*A*, 17).

6. Bair, *Simone de Beauvoir,* 169.

7. Sartre, "Dos Passos and '1919,'" 89.

8. Ibid., 89–95.

9. See the multiple references to Wanda Kosakievicz in Bair's *Simone de Beauvoir.*

10. Sartre, *Oeuvres romanesques,* 159.

11. Ibid., 152–53.

12. Brosman, *Simone de Beauvoir Revisited,* 48.

13. Sartre, *Oeuvres romanesques,* 159. For a more detailed analysis of the importance of *La Nausée* as a manifesto, see my "*Nausea:* Plunging below the Surface," 227–39; as well as my article "Censures et autocensure," 270–80.

13 The Concept of Transcendence in Beauvoir and Sartre

Andrea Veltman

Scholars of twentieth-century French existentialism have traditionally assumed that Simone de Beauvoir borrows her concept of transcendence from the writings of Jean-Paul Sartre. In this chapter, I work to demonstrate that Beauvoir develops her concept of transcendence independently of Sartre, with the result that the two have different notions of transcendence. In her early ethical treatise *Pyrrhus and Cinéas,* Beauvoir creates a sense of transcendence as constructive activity in the world, arguing that only transcendence can provide meaning for human existence. Not only does her concept of transcendence differ significantly from Sartre's metaphysical concept of transcendence in *Being and Nothingness,* but Beauvoir also develops this concept of transcendence with reference to a host of writers in Western literature and philosophy—including Hegel, Pascal, Horace, Valéry, Gide, and Epicurus—rather than with reference to Sartre.

Pyrrhus and Cinéas, written in 1943 at the suggestion of a publisher seeking a new contribution in existentialism, was Beauvoir's first published philosophical essay. Although Beauvoir later said that she worked consciously within a Sartrean framework in writing this and other essays, she also remarked that *Pyrrhus and Cinéas* provided an opportunity to reconcile Sartrean views on freedom with her own views on the significance of situation in undermining or encouraging the realization of freedom.[1] Largely a treatise on the justification of human existence, *Pyrrhus and Cinéas* provided Beauvoir an opportunity to explore the themes of political violence and the interdependence of human freedoms, themes she addressed as well in her novel *The Blood of Others.* Although the treatise was well received after its publication in postwar France, it has since remained relatively neglected. An English translation was finally published in 2004 by Marybeth Timmerman, Margaret Simons, and Sylvie le Bon de Beauvoir.

The uniquely Beauvoirian sense of transcendence at play in *Pyrrhus and Cinéas* continues throughout the works she published in the later 1940s. Transcendence takes on an ethical dimension when incorporated in an existentialist account of oppression in *The Ethics of Ambiguity*, in which Beauvoir makes clear that transcendence is achieved, not in the relatively ephemeral labor required for the maintenance of life, but in the "constructive movements" of men and women who set up the world of tomorrow and push the progress of humanity forward (*EA*, 82–83). The concept of transcendence gains its greatest prominence in *The Second Sex*, in which Beauvoir couples transcendence with the Hegelian concept of immanence in her analyses of female oppression. Throughout these works, Beauvoir occasionally trades between a Sartrean sense of transcendence and her own sense of transcendence, but, particularly in *The Second Sex*, the predominant meaning of the concept is not Sartrean.

It should not be surprising that Beauvoir departs from a Sartrean sense of transcendence in her early ethical treatises, *Pyrrhus and Cinéas* and *The Ethics of Ambiguity*. She writes at the outset of *The Ethics of Ambiguity* that an existentialist ethics can be founded neither upon Sartre's ontological freedom nor upon the popular sense of freedom as obtaining chosen ends, but must be founded upon a "*liberté morale*," or ethical freedom (*EA*, 24–32). The concepts of freedom and transcendence are closely related in the writings of Sartre and Beauvoir, and Beauvoir's *liberté morale*—in which human beings found our freedom in deliberately willing both ourselves and others free—is realized concretely in transcendent activity. We embrace our freedom and situate ourselves around other free beings by propelling ourselves into the world in constructive or self-expressive projects. In *Pyrrhus and Cinéas* and *The Ethics of Ambiguity*, Beauvoir derives moral and political obligations to support the freedom of others from the interdependence of human transcendences. Sartrean ontology, in contrast, not only creates a fundamental separation among human beings but also makes nonsense of a moral failure to act freely or promote the freedom of others.

In the final section of this chapter, I examine the arguments Beauvoir provides for an ethical obligation to will the freedom of others. Sartre clearly announces in *L'Existentialisme est un humanisme* that an authentic moral agent wills the freedom of others, but he simply states this claim without furnishing an explanation.[2] In *Pyrrhus and Cinéas*—a treatise written two years prior to Sartre's lecture "Existentialism Is a Humanism" in 1945—Beauvoir provides at least four arguments in favor of an existentialist moral imperative to support the freedom of others.[3] In brief, willing ourselves free requires willing the freedom of others, for a necessary condition of the full realization of our freedom is the presence of other free beings.

Transcendence in *Being and Nothingness* and *Pyrrhus and Cinéas*

In developing a phenomenology of consciousness in *Being and Nothingness,* Sartre frequently uses the term "transcendence" to describe the intentional directedness of human consciousness toward various objects. "All consciousness," he writes in his introduction on the pursuit of being, "transcends itself in order to reach an object" (*BN*, li).[4] The phenomenological content present in consciousness derives from the objects of consciousness; conscious subjectivity is in itself a nothingness, with neither content nor any determining essence. It is a pure and spontaneous movement toward the world, an intentional transcending projection toward objects which it is not. Human subjectivity indeed never fails to be a free and active transcendence, for even if one is in a state of rest, consciousness itself remains neither passive nor causally predetermined. The total freedom of consciousness stems from its spontaneous transcendence of what is given toward unrealized goals, ideals, and projects. Every conscious action involves an intentional projection or reaching outward toward what is not, and what is not can be determined only by a free intentional consciousness (*BN*, 435ff.).

In addition to describing consciousness as a transcendence toward the world, Sartre also uses the term "transcendent" to designate objectivity, as in his claim that values are not "transcendent givens independent of human subjectivity." Values, for Sartre, spring only from human subjectivity and acts of choice: we choose to distinguish flowers from weeds, or justice from injustice, while apprehending the world through categories that are not antecedently given but that depend upon our desires, interests, and purposes (*BN*, 38). On the other hand, Sartre uses the term "transcended" in describing objectification, as when one subjectivity faces another in an ineluctable mutual struggle for domination and recognition. As Sartre characterizes the basic dilemma of human relations, "one must either transcend [and therefore objectify] the Other or allow oneself to be transcended [objectified] by him. The essence of the relations between consciousnesses is not the *Mitsein;* it is conflict" (*BN*, 429).

Notably, although Sartre emphasizes the absolute freedom of transcendent subjectivity in the introduction and conclusion to *Being and Nothingness,* a substantial portion of the third part of the work characterizes human reality as comprising both free subjectivity and our embodied nature. As embodied and historically situated living beings, we are conditioned and limited by an existing and given world (*BN*, 305–26). We are embedded in facticity, the factual dimensions of ourselves ranging from our birth, race, and ethnicity; to the physiological structure of our bodies; to our past, class, and character. Because we are embodied subjectivities, we experience ourselves as situated in a concrete world, rather than as pure transcendence (*BN*, 328ff.). In spite of the limitations imposed upon us by facticity, however, Sartre maintains that we remain inescapably free, for consciousness is pure transcendence, continually negating and transcending what is given toward nonexistent potentialities. As a transcending consciousness, I am free from the factual dimension of myself, and any limitations on my freedom exist only in relation to my freely chosen projects (*BN*, 520–31).

Beauvoir's early ethical treatises, particularly *Pyrrhus and Cinéas*, use the concept of transcendence in part as Sartre uses the concept throughout *Being and Nothingness* and other works in which transcendence is associated with the movement of the for-itself and contrasted with facticity. In *Pyrrhus and Cinéas*, transcendence sometimes refers to the "perpetual surpassing" of intentional consciousness and, occasionally, to the process whereby one creates oneself at every moment through some project. Transcendence is the spontaneous directedness of consciousness at something, a reaching outward beyond oneself toward some end, or a "[throwing oneself] toward the future" (*PC*, 111). In this sense of transcendence, all human beings continually transcend themselves, for every look, act, or thought of an intentional consciousness is an act of transcendence (*PC*, 98).

The clear undertones of the Sartrean for-itself in this early characterization of transcendence has led even revisionist Beauvoir scholarship to concede a Sartrean influence on *Pyrrhus and Cinéas* in particular. Eva Lundgren-Gothlin, for example, writes that while *The Second Sex* develops a Hegelian rather than Sartrean sense of transcendence, "in *Pyrrhus et Cinéas* Beauvoir mainly uses the concept of transcendence as Sartre defines it in *Being and Nothingness*: transcendence is tied to the actions of the intentional consciousness."[5] Although Lundgren-Gothlin and other Beauvoir scholars emphatically reject the view that *Pyrrhus and Cinéas* as a whole merely parrots or defends Sartrean concepts, they see a predominant Sartrean influence on the concepts of freedom and transcendence in this work in particular.[6]

I would like to suggest that in addition to the clear Sartrean sense of transcendence present throughout *Pyrrhus and Cinéas*, this work also introduces a specifically Beauvoirian sense of transcendence as constructive activity; it does not adhere throughout to Sartre's metaphysical concept of transcendence. Beauvoir's sense of transcendence as constructive or creative activity gains greater prominence in *The Second Sex,* but it emerges here in the course of Beauvoir's response to the suggestion scattered throughout Western literature that human unhappiness arises from active engagement with the world.[7] Pascal, for instance, writes in his *Pensées* that "all the unhappiness of men arises from a single fact, that they cannot stay quietly in their own chamber."[8] Beauvoir finds this idea repeated in the French essayist Gide and prefigured in the writings of Aristippus, Epicurus, and Horace:

> It is the moral of Aristippus, that of Horace's *Carpe diem,* and Gide's *Nourritures* [*Fruits of the Earth*]. Let us turn away from the world, from undertakings and conquests; let us devise no more projects; let us remain at home, at rest at the heart of our enjoyment. (*PC,* 95)

Contrasting repose and relaxation with movement and transcendence, Beauvoir suggests, against Pascal and others, that it is *disengagement* from the world through repose that cannot provide fulfillment for human beings, for human transcendence cannot be successfully realized in states of rest (*PC,* 97–100). The basic nature of transcendence is active movement, perpetual surpassing, or going beyond the given; and transcendence is thus truly achieved, not in the enjoyment of relaxation, but in some endeavor that moves an individual beyond the present status quo toward an open future. One achieves transcendence when one "studies science, writes poetry, or builds motors" (*PC,* 110), not when one sits idly by, devising no project, or relaxing in passive enjoyment.

The contrast between passivity and activity in *Pyrrhus and Cinéas,* which is taken up into the dichotomy between transcendence and immanence in *The Second Sex,* is drawn from a host of French, German, Latin, and Greek writings. Beauvoir identifies and contests the implicit endorsements of passivity in figures such as Aristippus, Horace, Epicurus, Gide, and Pascal and develops the association between transcendence and activity with reference to Hegel, Valéry, Arland, and Chardonne, rather than with reference to Sartre (*PC,* 95–98). In fact, Beauvoir mentions Sartre only twice within the text of *Pyrrhus and Cinéas.* Her sense of transcendence as constructive activity does partly incorporate a Heideggerian and Sartrean notion of project, but the distinction developed in *Pyrrhus and Cinéas* between constructive action and the passive enjoyment of life is absent in the Heideggerian notion of project and the Sartrean sense of transcendence. Sartre's ontological conception of transcendence as the movement of the for-itself, indeed, does not permit a distinction between the constructive activity of transcendence and the passivity of rest, for intentional movements of the for-itself occur even in relaxation and withdrawal from the world.

Beauvoir's association of transcendence with constructive activity, on the other hand, enables her to respond to the suggestion made by Pyrrhus that when finished with his world conquests, he will enjoy the paradise of rest. Since restful paradise—conceived as an existence without constructive endeavors—promises only eternal tedium, Pyrrhus "lacks imagination" in suggesting that he will rest when finished with his world conquests. It is written into the human condition that we are not fulfilled upon attaining a goal but constantly surpass everything given. Associating transcendence with active pursuits in the world once again, Beauvoir writes:

> Paradise is rest; it is transcendence abolished, a state of things that is given and does not have to be surpassed. But then, what shall we do [in restful paradise]? In order for the air there to be breathable, it must leave room for actions and desires. . . . The beauty of the promised land is that it promised new promises. Immobile paradises promise us nothing but eternal ennui. . . . Once returned home, [Pyrrhus] will hunt, he will legislate, he will go to war again. If he tries to stay truly at rest, he will only yawn. (PC, 98)

Pyrrhus and Cinéas thus uses "transcendence" to refer not only to the upsurge of the for-itself, nor only to the projection of the self into the world through any conscious activity, but also to an active mode of existence, filled with accomplishments and a continual surpassing of a given state of affairs. One salient difficulty with the simultaneous presence of these concepts of transcendence in this work, however, is the incommensurability of the former Sartrean senses of transcendence with the latter sense of transcendence as constructive activity. Where the latter Beauvoirian sense excludes passivity and repose from transcendence, the metaphysical sense includes any movement of intentional consciousness, even those that occur in moments of passivity. Transcendence cannot consistently refer to any subjective movement of consciousness and yet to the considerably more circumscribed set of human actions that accomplish, produce, or push back the boundaries of the present.

Some of the literature discussing Beauvoir's use of transcendence has granted that the concepts of transcendence and immanence are "contradictory and illusive,"[9] and in the respect that incongruent concepts of transcendence occur simultaneously in *Pyrrhus and Cinéas* and in other treatises, this assessment appears warranted. However, the presence of different concepts of transcendence in *Pyrrhus and Cinéas* may also reflect the very development of the concept of transcendence in this work. The eventual maturation of the concept of transcendence in *The Second Sex*, in which transcendence designates an active, creative mode of existence, indicates that Beauvoir ultimately finds a more Hegelian sense of transcendence to be more fruitful than a metaphysical sense of transcendence. *Pyrrhus and Cinéas*, at any rate, clearly breaks beyond a Sartrean sense of transcendence to develop a sense that is more illuminating for questions concerning the human need for meaningful action in the world.

Transcendence and Immanence in *The Second Sex*

Although Beauvoir's early ethical treatises incorporate a Hegelian and Sartrean concept of transcendence, associating transcendence with activity, progression, and the surpassing movement of consciousness, it is not until *The Second Sex* that Beauvoir appropriates the Hegelian concept of immanence as a counterpart to transcendence. Once paired with immanence in *The Second Sex*, transcendence refers to constructive work and, more generally, to an active mode of existence in which one attempts to surpass the present, burst out onto the future, and remain free from biological fate. Immanence, by contrast, designates the round of futile and largely uncreative chores necessary to sustain life as well as a mode of existence marked by passivity, ease, and submission to biological fate.

The concepts of transcendence and immanence in *The Second Sex* are multifaceted and simultaneously descriptive and normative, but the metaphysical meanings of transcendence largely drop out in *The Second Sex*, and transcendence and immanence become delineated primarily in terms of a typology of activities or active and passive modes of existing. The account of oppression developed in *The Ethics of Ambiguity* using the distinction between maintenance and progression is imported in full into *The Second Sex*, together with the thesis that an authentically lived existence requires that one establish reason for being for oneself through transcendent activities. Activities of transcendence include precisely those activities of progress, creation, and discovery that are opposed to the mere maintenance of life in *The Ethics of Ambiguity*, while the mechanical chores that minister to the life process are here activities of immanence.[10]

The Introduction to *The Second Sex* does contain two salient descriptions of transcendence in terms of Sartrean ontology,[11] but the majority of *The Second Sex* delineates transcendence and immanence primarily as a typology of activities.[12] Transcendence and immanence are contrasted not only in terms of their relation to time—transcendence expands present horizons into the future, whereas immanence perpetuates the present—but also in terms of what transcendence and immanence accomplish. Achieved "in work and action" (SS,[13] 183), transcendence engages the individual in the world and situates him or her among other freedoms by laying a foundation for a new future, creating an enduring artifact, enabling individual self-expression, transforming the world, or in some other fashion contributing positively to the constructive endeavors of the human race. Transcendent activities—precisely the same as those distinguished from maintenance labor in *The Ethics of Ambiguity*—enable us to surpass the present "toward the totality of the universe and the infinity of the future" (SS, 471).[14]

Immanence, on the other hand, produces nothing durable through which we move beyond ourselves but merely (1) perpetuates life or (2) maintains the status quo. Activities of immanence include not only the everyday labors that sustain and repair the body and mind, like cooking, cleaning and, presumably, television watching, but also bureaucratic paper pushing and biological functions such as giving birth. Beauvoir occasionally characterizes immanence as repetitive and uncreative (SS, 65–69; 474–78), although immanence is not defined against transcendence in terms of its repetitiveness or uncreativity, for activities of immanence can involve creativity or self-expression in like manner as activities of transcendence can involve repetition. Activities of immanence are characteristically futile—immanence consumes time and labor but accomplishes nothing—and the combination of necessity and futility involved in maintenance labor, in turn, makes some forms of immanence necessarily repetitive. The labor required to cook, clean, wash, or rake leaves, for instance, is necessary for the maintenance of life but is eventually negated and brought to nothing once taken up into the endless cycle of life itself (SS, 474–478).

Since activities of immanence merely sustain life and achieve nothing more than its continuation, they cannot themselves serve as the justifying ground for living. *The Second Sex* employs a contrast between life and existence that mirrors the point made in *The Ethics of Ambiguity* concerning the inability of maintenance activities to lend meaning to human existence. "Life," Beauvoir writes here, "does not carry within itself its reasons for being, reasons that are more important than the life itself" (SS, 68). Reason for living must be established through some activity that reaches beyond the maintenance of life itself toward the future; otherwise one labors to maintain life in the absence of an initial reason for laboring to maintain life. Putting the matter in terms of the reproduction of species-life as a whole, Beauvoir writes:

Here we have the key to the whole mystery. On the biological level a species is maintained only by creating itself anew; but this creation results only in repeating the same Life in more individuals. . . . In the animal, the freedom and variety of male activities are vain because no project is involved. . . . Whereas in serving the species, the human male also remodels the face of the earth, he creates new instruments, he invents, he shapes the future. (*SS*, 68)

Surpassing the repetition of biological life, man has historically represented transcendence, given his participation in the activities that set up the world over and against nature: he remodels the earth, creates new values, takes risks, fights, progresses, conquers—in short, he accomplishes what transcends the maintenance of life itself. Woman, on the other hand, has originally represented immanence, the repetition of life, given her bondage to the natural functions of childbirth and childrearing (*SS*, 65–69).

Notably, the reinterpretation of transcendence and immanence given above provides a partial defense of Beauvoir against contemporary feminist critics who maintain that *The Second Sex* incorporates a masculinist philosophical framework. Genevieve Lloyd and Charlene Haddock Siegfried, for instance, have assumed that Beauvoir's concepts of transcendence and immanence are imports of Sartrean metaphysics; these critics and others argue that the masculine elements of Sartrean existentialism render it inadequate for analyzing the female condition. As Siegfried summarizes her understanding of Beauvoirian transcendence:

Transcendence refers to nothing less than the central thesis of Sartrean existentialism. . . . The free subject, in ordering his life, makes of himself something. . . . While the object is always some definite thing, the subject is nothing insofar as the subject, freed from all constraints, unconditionally chooses to choose and thus continuously creates and re-creates his self.[15]

Associating transcendence with free subjectivity and immanence with facticity, Siegfried proceeds to argue that the transcendence/immanence dichotomy glorifies male transcendence as a human value while undermining an acknowledgment of specifically female values based in women's experiences. Similarly, Lloyd argues that Beauvoir's indebtedness to the concepts of "Sartrean immanence" and "Sartrean transcendence" "left its [male] mark on the very concepts of 'transcendence' and 'immanence.'"[16]

These feminist critiques of Beauvoir clearly rest on a misinterpretation of her concepts of transcendence and immanence. Beauvoirian immanence emerges in *The Second Sex* primarily with reference to Hegel and Marx. Sartre, indeed, rarely employs the term "immanence," preferring instead to speak of facticity and of the ontological given being-in-itself.[17] Furthermore, whereas Sartrean transcendence stands opposed to facticity rather than to the labor necessary to maintain life, Beauvoir associates transcendence primarily with constructive activity, using the dichotomy between transcendence and immanence to distinguish activities that lend life meaning from those that cannot. As I have shown, Beauvoir associates transcendence with Sartrean metaphysics only briefly in the Introduction to *The Second Sex*, but these initial associations betray the deeper meaning of Beauvoirian transcendence as developed throughout *The Second Sex* and other works.

Moreover, feminist critiques of *The Second Sex* as antithetical to feminine values overstate Beauvoir's denigration of maternity and do not acknowledge that Beauvoir's normative dichotomy between transcendence and immanence itself holds potential to critique continuing inequities in the institutions of motherhood and marriage. Although Beauvoir indeed does not admire feminine values, and although transcendence indeed distinguishes the human being, Beauvoir's view of motherhood is not unremittingly bleak. Her negative characterization of giving birth as an uncreative function has been distinguished in recent revisionist literature from her more positive portrayal of motherhood in the chapter on motherhood in *The Second Sex*.[18] In this discussion, Beauvoir notes that motherhood can be an enrichment for existence and can enable women to develop the value of generosity, although her larger point is that motherhood cannot alone serve as a reason for being (*SS*, 511; 522–27).

Critiquing the institution of motherhood rather than the experience of mothering, Beauvoir herself claims not that mothering per se is an activity of immanence but that the occupations consequent upon motherhood tend to mire women in immanence. Writing on the situation of women in antiquity, for instance, Beauvoir characterizes the domestic labors associated with raising children as activities of immanence, rather than motherhood itself as immanence:

> *The domestic labors* that fell to her lot because they were reconcilable with the cares of maternity *imprisoned her in repetition and immanence;* they were repeated from day to day in an identical form, which was perpetuated without change from century to century; they produced nothing new. (*SS*, 63; emphasis added)

The principal obstacle that motherhood presents to the free pursuit of transcendence is not the care of children itself (for childrearing can enable women to create relatively durable human beings) but the tendency of motherhood to relegate women to activities of immanence in the private realm.

As I have argued elsewhere, Beauvoir's distinction between transcendent activity and labors of immanence can, in fact, lend positive support to a feminist critique of gender inequities in marriage and divisions of domestic labor.[19] An ethics directed by the pursuit of transcendence has, as an advantage over other ethical theories, a means of judging qualitatively inequitable divisions of domestic work. Beauvoir not only captures the basic character of housework as unfulfilling labor but also establishes a need to participate in work that lends meaning to human existence. A Kantian ethics, by comparison, can establish a moral wrong in qualitatively inequitable divisions of domestic labor if such divisions of labor treat women merely as means, but it is a normative distinction between transcendent work and immanent labor that underpins a moral obligation to share less-fulfilling forms of domestic maintenance labor. Since the transcendence/immanence dichotomy functions as a normative framework for critiquing inequitable divisions of domestic work, this dichotomy is, in fact, an important component in arguing for the continuing relevance of *The Second Sex*.

Ethical Freedom and the Freedom of Others

In this final section, I would like to examine Beauvoirian transcendence in the context of her concept of ethical freedom. In recent years, Simone de Beauvoir scholars have been at pains to point out that by emphasizing the notion of situated freedom and by distinguishing an ethical freedom apart from Sartre's ontological freedom, Beauvoir lays a groundwork for an existentialist ethics where Sartre does not.[20] For Sartre, human beings are always free within a given situation to choose our course of conduct and impose an interpretation or an attitude upon our situation; ontologically, the slave is as free as his master and can choose an authentic response to his objectification.[21] In shifting away from radical Sartrean freedom, Beauvoir argues at the outset of *The Ethics of Ambiguity* that if freedom is identified with the pure nothingness of subjectivity and all human beings are inescapably free, it becomes senseless to speak of moral failures to act freely or to promote the freedom of others (*EA*, 26; 24–32). Noting an incompatibility between the conception of freedom needed for an ethics of ambiguity and that present in *Being and Nothingness*, Beauvoir writes:

> Now Sartre declares that every man is free, that there is no way of his not being free. When he wants to escape his destiny, he is still freely fleeing

it. Does not this presence of a so to speak natural freedom contradict the notion of an ethical freedom [*liberté morale*]? What meaning can there be in the words *to will oneself free,* since at the beginning we *are* free? It is contradictory to set freedom up as something to be conquered if at first it is something given. (*EA*, 24)

Rather than relying on the notion of freedom at play in *Being and Nothingness,* Beauvoir speaks instead of a *liberté morale,* a normative rather than ontological freedom that is deliberately willed and can be abdicated in "laziness, heedlessness, capriciousness, [or] cowardice" (*EA*, 25). To assume an ethical freedom is to found ontological freedom, to "effect the transition from [ontology] to morality by establishing a genuine freedom on the original upsurge of our existence" (*EA*, 25).[22]

To assume an ethical freedom in willing oneself free is not an empty formula: ethical freedom is realized in engagement with the public world and in constructive activities, rather than in passivity, laziness, or idle enjoyment (*EA*, 78–81). Human beings do not truly exist apart from doing something, and it is therefore human action, in which we create and change the world, open up new possibilities to one another, or at least justify and reinvent the status quo, that first defines the freedom of an existentialist ethics. The creation of science, art, architecture, philosophy, and so forth exist in this light, not simply for their own sakes, nor for the achievement of progress or enlightenment, but also for the sake of realizing human freedom:

The constructive activities of man take on a valid meaning only when they are assumed as a movement toward freedom; and, reciprocally, one sees that such a movement is concrete: discoveries, inventions, industries, culture, paintings, and books people the world concretely and open concrete possibilities to men. (*EA*, 80–81)

Whatever may be the particular content of an ethically free action, it aims to propel the individual into the world through her engagement in some project and, simultaneously, to open possibilities for the future for oneself and others.

As a willing oneself free, ethical freedom is realized in transcendent activities, or in other words, it is the ability to achieve transcendence, where transcendence is the surpassing of the present into the future through a creative endeavor that produces something durable or enables individual self-expression. "Transcendence" and "freedom" are, in fact, frequently used interchangeably by Beauvoir: both terms can designate either the surpassing movement of consciousness itself or the founding of consciousness in a creative project. However, Beauvoir does distinguish "freedom" from "transcendence": where "transcendence" is fundamentally a surpassing movement and a projecting of oneself into the world, in Beauvoir's early ethical writings "freedom" often refers to the fundamental Sartrean separateness of each human being and, occasionally, to the absence of coercion or causal determination. Writing on human interdependency in *Pyrrhus and Cinéas,* Beauvoir distinguishes human freedom from the transcendent projecting of the self: "Freedoms are neither united nor opposed, they are separate. It is in projecting himself into the world that a man situates himself in situating other men around him" (*PC,* 108). Whereas individual freedoms are initially separate, it is in the transcendent project that we situate ourselves in a human world and create an interdependency out of an initial separateness.

Ethical freedom cannot be realized in the absence of a world populated with other free human beings, and willing oneself free therefore requires willing the freedom of others. Throughout *Pyrrhus and Cinéas* and *The Ethics of Ambiguity,* Beauvoir sets out four arguments, explicated below, that appeal to the interdependency of human freedoms in demonstrating that the freedom of others is a necessary condition for the realization of our own freedom. The primary ethical and political implication of our need for the freedom of others is that we must not only avoid the inherently inconsistent objectification of others but also work to create a social order that enables others to realize their transcendent potential.

First, freedom cannot be realized in transcendent projects except against a backdrop of a human world infused with meanings and significations that are created by free beings. Without the existence of other free beings whose communications and practices create shared meanings, transcendent projects would be, if not impossible, meaningless. This point, Kristana Arp notes, is a recapitulation of Edmund Husserl's insight that consciousness is the source of human signification, although Beauvoir emphasizes that the significations necessary for transcendent projects originate in shared human practices rather than in consciousness itself.[23] The shared communications and practices of human agents create "a human world in which each object is penetrated with human meanings" (*EA,* 74). If one denies the human character of objects in the world by denying the subjectivity of those who manufacture the world, one becomes like a thing oneself, as when "the parasite [i.e., the slave owner] ignores the human character of the objects which he uses. In the tools, the machines, the houses, and the bread he eats, he does not recognize the mark of any freedom. Only the matter remains, and to the extent that he depends upon only matter, he is also matter and passivity . . . a thing among things" (*PC,* 132).

Secondly, in the absence of a world constituted of other free individuals, nearly all human action becomes disturbingly absurd. That is, there would be little reason for acting unless there are other consciousnesses in the world (or outside of it) who can observe us acting. The inherently performative dimension of action is indeed evident precisely in considering that action becomes vain at best, if not altogether futile, if performed for no audience. Because human beings have a deep need for action—we could neither stand living nor realize our freedom unless we act—we must will that there be a human world with consciousnesses who observe us acting. As Beauvoir writes, "a man alone in the world would be paralyzed by the manifest vision of the vanity of all his goals. He would undoubtedly not be able to stand living" (*PC*, 115). If an individual alone in the world were to build an artifice, draw in the sand, keep a journal, gesture, create any non-utilitarian object, attempt to communicate or accomplish anything at all, he would find himself in the position of acting only for his own recognition. Accomplishment would become ridiculous. An individual alone in the world must therefore "strive, like Ezekiel, to resuscitate humanity, or he will have nothing left to do but die" (*PC*, 135).

To be sure, in a world without other consciousness, actions that secure the sustenance of life itself or enable locomotion in the world serve these immediate utilitarian ends. But an individual alone in the world lacks a reason for constructive activity, for without humanity the projects that motivate the drive to create become futile. Without humanity, my projects can neither have meaning nor enable communication with another: "Only through . . . objects that I make exist in the world," Beauvoir writes, "can I communicate with others. If I make nothing exist, there is neither communication nor justification" (*PC*, 129). Of course, sometimes one is satisfied to act in the absence of other consciousnesses: one can take a solitary walk, kick a stone, appreciate nature, or climb mountains all in solitude. However, one would not be satisfied to act in solitude for her entire existence. Even the child who finishes painting a drawing must run to show her parents, for without an eye that looks at it, the drawing accomplishes nothing (*PC*, 116).

Furthermore, it is not sufficient that there be just any witnessing eye upon our projects; the recognition of a slave, a vassal, or a child is not enough. "My essential need is to be faced with free men," for I seek not simply to be perceived by another consciousness but to have my actions understood (*PC*, 129). We must be faced with others who are our peers or equals (*mes pairs*), or our approximate peers, so that we can make appeal to others who have the capacity to appreciate the meaning and significance of our actions. Sometimes our actions appeal to a long posterity—as in the project of the architect—and other times only to our contemporaries, but in order that our actions not become "lost in the void, there must be men ready to hear me . . . , and these men must be my peers" (*PC*, 137). If the men and women around us are unfree, our projects fall on deaf ears, and we have no one to hear us or to accompany us in our transcendence. Presumably, however, if those who witness and validate our projects have a greater amount of freedom or are more equipped for transcendence than ourselves, we still achieve self-expression and establish a reason for our actions, even if we cannot always join their projects in turn.

Thirdly, willing ourselves free requires that we be faced with other free beings for the reason that we continually act with or against others in transcendent projects, and we need other free individuals to take up our work in their own projects. The entirety of human projects do not form a progressive continuous succession, but individual freedoms intermingle and draw from one another in the collective projects of humankind, even when individuals oppose one another's projects (*PC*, 109). Pushing back the boundaries of music, achieving progress in science or medicine, or inventing and enacting a solution to a social problem require acting with—or against—other free beings, and we therefore need the existence of other freedoms in developing and positioning our own transcendent work. Even the scholar or the artist who works primarily in private requires the free transcendence of others, for their work takes its departure from what others are doing and calls out to others to serve as a basis for new work. "The writer does not want simply to be read; he wants to have influence; he wants to be imitated and pondered. The inventor asks that the tool he invented be used" (*PC*, 132). Indeed, if our projects fail to play a role in the work of others but are ultimately taken nowhere, our projects "fall back upon themselves" rather than serving as a mode of transcendence and become like inert and useless objects (e.g., *PC*, 135).

Finally, Beauvoir claims in her fourth argument that the particular plans and projects in which human freedoms intertwine fundamentally aim to project ourselves into the future, and we need other free beings to carry our work forward:

> I myself cannot go backwards, because the movement of my transcendence is carrying me ceaselessly forward, and I cannot walk toward the future alone. (*PC*, 137)

The idea that transcendence propels us in the direction of the future, indeed, runs throughout most of Beauvoir's works and is a predominant theme in her play *Who Shall Die?* In this work, a group of townspeople face a low store of food while fighting a war for political independence and toil away at building a bell tower to ring out their eventual victory. They labor under the presumption that they will justify their present toiling and struggling by thrusting themselves toward the future: one character comments, "without this impulse which throws us forwards, we would be no more than a layer of mildew on the face of the earth" (WSD, 39).

In later works, Beauvoir continues to argue that the future secures a justification for present living and that, since action unfolds toward the future, the future is "the meaning and substance of all action" (EA, 127). Our work will not find an ultimate positive meaning in future work unless other free individuals link their work with our own and carry our work forward. Of course, forming and carrying out transcendent work also requires looking into the past and building on the past work of others, but since transcendence cannot alter the past and aims instead at the future, we need there to be other free beings in the present or future who can take up our work within their own and move it forward. Therefore, in securing a future for our projects, we must work to ensure that others can realize the full dimension of their transcendence.

These four arguments provide a foundation for working toward equitable social and economic structures by demonstrating that the social and material condition lived by others affects our freedom. I need others to attain my level of freedom so that I can carry out and give meaning to my projects, and I should therefore support social situations that secure the conditions of transcendence for other women and men. As Beauvoir summarizes, "I must . . . endeavor to create for all men situations which will enable them to accompany and surpass my transcendence. I need their freedom to be available to make use of me, to preserve me in surpassing me. I require for men health, knowledge, well being, leisure, so that their freedom does not consume itself in fighting sickness, ignorance, misery" (PC, 137).

Even in *Pyrrhus and Cinéas,* Beauvoir thus breaks beyond Sartrean conceptions of freedom and transcendence to sketch an existentialist moral imperative to support the freedom of others. Sartre, by contrast, did not offer arguments for valuing the freedom of others, and he emphasized the absolute freedom of transcendent subjectivity, in spite of recognizing with Beauvoir that human beings are embodied subjectivities, historically situated in a concrete world. Unlike Sartre, Beauvoir emphasizes not just the facticity of existence but also the interdependence of human transcendences, arguing that the pursuit of transcendence situates us in a human world and creates a need for the recognition of other free beings. An authentic ethical freedom for Beauvoir thus cannot be assumed without simultaneously willing the freedom of others.

Notes

1. In *The Prime of Life*, Beauvoir notes that *Pyrrhus and Cinéas* enabled her to reconcile Sartre's views on freedom with ideas she "upheld against him in various conversations" concerning the significance of situation (*PL*, 434–35). Beauvoir describes *Pyrrhus and Cinéas* as written within a Sartrean framework in an interview with Michel Sicard entitled "Interférences," 325–29.

2. Some Sartre scholars, including Thomas Anderson, Robert Stone, and Linda Bell, have attempted to reconstruct Sartrean arguments for willing the freedom of others; however, they acknowledge that their reconstructive efforts are speculative, based primarily on implications of Sartre's claims and suggestions he makes throughout his writings (Anderson, *Sartre's Two Ethics*; Stone, "Freedom as a Universal Notion," 137–48; Bell, review of Anderson's *Foundation and Structure of Sartrean Ethics*, 223–34).

3. As noted above, *Pyrrhus and Cinéas* was published in 1944 but written in 1943. According to biographer Deirdre Bair, Beauvoir informed Bair that she sketched ideas for *Pyrrhus and Cinéas* in the fall of 1942 (Bair, *Simone de Beauvoir: A Biography*, 639, n. 28).

4. In *Transcendence of the Ego*, Sartre similarly characterizes consciousness as a transcendence of what is given and as a sphere of free and uncaused activity (*TE*, 82–99).

5. Lundgren-Gothlin, *Sex and Existence*, 231. In *Simone de Beauvoir, Philosophy and Feminism*, Nancy Bauer also sees a Sartrean influence on the concepts of freedom and transcendence in *Pyrrhus and Cinéas*. She writes: "The idea that all human beings are forced by the fact of their unimpeachable metaphysical liberty to [do one thing or another], the idea that Beauvoir has been at pains to elaborate and defend for almost all of *Pyrrhus et Cinéas*, is pure Sartre" (145). Sonia Kruks also characterizes transcendence in *Pyrrhus and Cinéas* in Sartrean terms: "Transcendence," she writes, "is the upsurge of the for-itself in the world, but it becomes concrete, it particularizes itself in the specific projects of individuals" ("Beauvoir: The Weight of Situation," 51).

6. Bauer's main point concerning *Pyrrhus and Cinéas* is that this early work reflects a Hegelian influence in its treatment of the self; Kruks argues that although *Pyrrhus and Cinéas* employs Sartrean notions of freedom and transcendence, Beauvoir develops a more reasonable account of situation and oppression than Sartre develops (Bauer, *Simone de Beauvoir*, 137–58; Kruks, "Beauvoir: The Weight of Situation," 47–55).

7. See especially the section of *Pyrrhus and Cinéas* titled "The Instant," 95–100.

8. Pascal, *Pensées*, 37.

9. Lundgren-Gothlin, *Sex and Existence*, 230.

10. Eva Lundgren-Gothlin has argued that Beauvoir's concepts of transcendence and immanence in *The Second Sex* are influenced more by Hegel and Marx than by Sartre. She argues that a Hegelian influence on the concepts of transcendence and immanence is particularly clear in Beauvoir's anthropological description of the historical development of human society, in which the pure repetition of life in its generality is transcended for the singularity of existence in the public realm. Notably, Beauvoir reported in a 1985 interview with Lundgren-Gothlin that she read Hegel's *Phenomenology of Spirit* and Kojève's *Introduction to the Reading of Hegel* during the war years, although she herself did not attend the seminars on Hegel given by Alexandre Kojève in

the 1930s, which related the works of Hegel and Marx to phenomenology and existentialism. See Lundgren-Gothlin, *Sex and Existence,* chaps. 4 and 7, esp. pp. 57–59.

11. Both Sartrean characterizations of transcendence occur on page lix of *The Second Sex.* In one passage, Beauvoir links transcendence and immanence with Sartre's *en-soi:* "Every time transcendence falls back into immanence, stagnation, there is a degradation of existence into the '*en-soi*'—the brutish life of subjection to given conditions—and of liberty into constraint and contingence" (*SS,* lix).

12. See especially *The Second Sex,* xxvii, 65–69, 186–87, 226, 313–14, 451–52, 470–74, 477–80, 505, 551, 634, and 675.

13. I am using the 1952 [1993 reprint] Knopf edition of *The Second Sex.*

14. Consider especially 78–83 of *The Ethics of Ambiguity.*

15. Siegfried, "Gender Specific Values," 426.

16. Lloyd, *The Man of Reason* (University of Minnesota Press, 1993), esp. 100–101. Lloyd argues that transcendence is necessarily a transcendence of what is feminine, so that the transcendence requires excluding and surpassing of feminine immanence. The transcendence/immanence dichotomy is itself masculinist, she argues, insofar as "it is only from a male perspective that the feminine can be seen as what must be transcended" (101).

17. In one relevant usage of "immanence" in *Being and Nothingness,* Sartre says that he does not wish to refer to being-in-itself as immanence (*BN,* lxv).

18. In *The Other Within: Ethics, Politics and the Body in Simone de Beauvoir,* Fredrika Scarth unearths a crucial distinction in *The Second Sex* between enforced maternity and *maternité libre;* she also demonstrates that, for Beauvoir, having a child can be a valid engagement with the world. See also Margaret Simons, *Beauvoir and* The Second Sex, 73–91, and Linda Zerilli, "A Process without a Subject," 111–35. Like Scarth, Zerilli reinterprets Beauvoir's discussions of the maternal body, whereas Simons demonstrates that Beauvoir's characterization of motherhood is considerably less negative in later portions of *The Second Sex.*

19. See my article "The Sisyphean Torture of Housework," 121–43.

20. See Kristana Arp, *The Bonds of Freedom,* and Sonia Kruks, "Beauvoir: The Weight of Situation." Kruks argues that Beauvoir better appreciates the situated nature of freedom and that she preceded Sartre in working toward an existentialist social philosophy. Notably, however, Karen Green argues against these claims in "Sartre and de Beauvoir on Freedom and Oppression."

21. Thomas Anderson has argued that although Sartre argues for unimpeachable human freedom in *Being and Nothingness,* in *The Notebooks for an Ethics* he sketches a more nuanced account of human freedom, emphasizing the limitations imposed upon freedom by embodiment or historical circumstance (Anderson, *Sartre's Two Ethics,* chaps. 2–5).

22. Kristana Arp has written most extensively on Beauvoir's distinction of an ethical freedom apart from Sartrean ontological freedom (*Bonds of Freedom,* 64ff.). In contrast with my interpretation of ethical freedom and transcendence, Arp associates transcendence with subjectivity and ethical freedom with actions that oppose oppressive practices. Thus, she does not see ethical freedom as realized in transcendent activity. Furthermore, because Arp sees transcendence as associated primarily with the upsurge of consciousness, and immanence as associated with materiality, she considers it prob-

lematical and even nonsensical that Beauvoir characterizes the oppressed as reduced to immanence (138–40). In my interpretation, in contrast, it makes sense to speak of the oppressed as reduced to immanence, for immanence refers primarily to the labor necessary to perpetuate life. For Beauvoir, oppression divides the world into two clans: one segment of humanity achieves transcendence through constructive or creative endeavors, while another segment becomes relegated to the mere maintenance of life (*EA*, 80–82).

23. Arp, "Conceptions of Freedom," 28.

14 Freedom F/Or the Other

Gail Weiss

> It is not true that the recognition of the freedom of others limits my own
> freedom: to be free is not to have the power to do anything you like; it is to be
> able to surpass the given toward an open future; the existence of others as a
> freedom defines my situation and is even the condition of my own freedom.
> —Simone de Beauvoir, *The Ethics of Ambiguity*

> My fundamental project toward the other—whatever may be the attitude I
> assume—is twofold: first there is the problem of protecting myself against the
> danger which is incurred by my being-outside-in-the-Other's-freedom, and
> second there is the problem of utilizing the other in order finally to totalize the
> detotalized totality which I am, so as to close the open circle, and finally to be
> my own foundation.
> —Jean-Paul Sartre, *Being and Nothingness*

In the passages above, both Beauvoir and Sartre indissolubly link freedom to
the Other. It is clear, for both philosophers, that freedom is always lived, that is,
embodied and expressed, within an intersubjective context. And yet Beauvoir
and Sartre offer very different views of this fundamental connection between
freedom and human beings' relationships with one another. For Beauvoir, there
is no freedom for the self without freedom for the Other; indeed, she asserts that
the freedom of others is a necessary condition for an individual's own freedom.
For Sartre, the Other's freedom offers an illusory promise of self-closure: by
confirming my objective existence in the Other's world, the Other totalizes me,
but this totalization confers a fixed essence upon a being that has no essence,
and therefore it is a falsification. I must, he maintains, "protect myself" against
the dangers posed by the Other's objectification of me, dangers that arise as a
result of my "being-outside-in-the-Other's-freedom," in order not to surrender
to the bad faith of denying my freedom and/or my responsibility for the situation I share with the Other.

Setting their respective claims about freedom and the Other side by side reveals that Beauvoir and Sartre have different ontological concerns that in turn have important existential, ethical, and political consequences. I will begin by offering a critical examination of how Sartre's depiction of the Other as a possible threat to my freedom contrasts with Beauvoir's emphasis on the obligations that the Other imposes on any individual who seeks to realize her freedom. While both thinkers articulate a primary dependency relationship between myself and the Other, I will argue that Sartre ends up with a disjunctive tension between freedom and the Other insofar as affirming one's own freedom seems almost necessarily to involve a subordination of the freedom of the Other, whereas for Beauvoir, my own freedom can only be realized if I simultaneously affirm the freedom of the Other.[1] Ultimately, I will claim that Beauvoir offers us more resources for securing individual and collective freedom than Sartre does, and she enables us to make better sense of the ways in which one's own freedom can be seriously undermined by the actions of other human beings.

The Ethics of Ambiguity was published five years after *Being and Nothingness,* and Beauvoir's own comments on freedom and the Other in the former text constitute a direct response to Sartre as well as to his critics.[2] In what follows, I will argue that Beauvoir's positive understanding of how one individual can "bring the seeds of liberation" to another offers a much-needed corrective to the dominant Sartrean model in which the alterity of the Other is, first and foremost, perceived to be a threat to one's own freedom.

Addressing what it means for a person to be free, Beauvoir states quite emphatically both that the Other should not be understood as limiting my freedom and that being free doesn't mean that one is always able to do what one wants. While I take the first claim to be an implicit criticism of Sartre's own one-sided focus on the constraining role played by the Other in the exercise of one's freedom, the second claim seems to be aimed more at a very prevalent misreading of *Being and Nothingness* by several 1940s proponents as well as detractors, insofar as these latter interpreted Sartre's work, and existentialism more generally, as giving unlimited license to the individual to dictate the terms of her relationships with others and with her situation.

Why is this a misreading of the Sartrean position, one might ask? After all, Sartre claims that even though the situation may be perceived as presenting insuperable obstacles to my freedom, nonetheless, "there is no constraint here since my freedom eats into my possibles and since correlatively the potentialities of the world indicate and offer only themselves" (*BN,* 348).[3] Depicted as an experience of pure transcendence (both self-transcendence, since through freedom one escapes a fixed essence, and a transcendence of the givens of the situation), individual freedom, which is no less and no more than consciousness of freedom, has no internal constraints of its own for Sartre. While I may appear to be externally constrained by my situation, it is still up to me to determine my possibilities (and therefore the meaning and value of those possibilities) within any given situation. "For," Sartre observes in his 1969 interview with the *New Left Review,*

> I believe that a man can always make something out of what is made of him. This is the limit I would today accord to freedom: the small movement which makes of a totally conditioned social being someone who does not render back completely what his conditioning has given him.[4]

While I may choose to modify my possibilities in the face of the facticity of the situation and the challenges it poses to my free projects, I might also persist in a futile course of action, my intentions thwarted by my situation—both options, for Sartre, are equally an exercise of my freedom even though the former course will be more practically efficacious than the latter.

The central claim he is making is that freedom cannot be limited by the facticity of one's situation since the two are ontologically distinct experiences that human beings live simultaneously. To be free, on his account, is to experience oneself as able to transcend the givens of one's situation even if this is only done through imagining the possibility of one's situation being otherwise. This is why he believes that even the prisoner confined to a cell is as free as someone who has never been incarcerated.

Sartre posits an absolute Cartesian divide between these two essential features of the for-itself, freedom and facticity, maintaining that the former cannot be limited or affected directly by the latter because they are essentially different phenomena: freedom is grounded in no-thing, or nothingness, whereas my facticity is grounded upon the materiality of my world.[5] If human freedom cannot be constrained by facticity, however, the situation becomes more complicated when we consider the relationship *between* freedoms as it plays out in our daily interactions with others. Can our own freedom be compromised by the freedom of others? What, exactly, is the relation between my own freedom and the freedom of the Other for Sartre? To address these questions requires that we closely examine the relation Sartre posits between being-for-itself and being-for-others.

Hell Is Other People

Garcin's infamous utterance, "Hell is—other people!" at the end of Sartre's play *No Exit* frequently functions as a shorthand for the latter's entire conception of being-for-others (*Ex*, 45).[6] Indeed, the power of the line continues to reverberate more than sixty years after it was first penned by Sartre and uttered on stage. The simplicity of this statement is directly at odds with its enormous ontological implications, and the powerful economy of expression Sartre uses is highly seductive, whether it is intended to sum up *in toto* or just to reveal a crucial dimension of our being-for-others.

Who hasn't experienced the truth of Garcin's outburst on more than one occasion in her life? Whether intentional or unintentional, physical or psychical, being tortured by others is not only a common experience but, it would seem, an inevitable one, especially as depicted by Sartre. For in *No Exit*, the chief way in which Garcin is tortured by Estelle and Inez is that he cannot compel them to view him according to his own dishonest self-image. Nor, for that matter, can Estelle compel Inez and Garcin to love her in a way that will confirm her own narcissistic desires. Sartre depicts Inez alone, as more torturing than tortured. Indeed, Inez fairly quickly confesses to Garcin and Estelle that while she was still alive, she tortured her lover, Florence, by repeatedly reminding her of the death of her husband. In Inez's words, the story was "a dead men's tale. With three corpses to it. He to start with; then she and I" (*Ex*, 25).

Although Garcin and Estelle are tortured by one another and by Inez, this does not mean that they are not themselves torturers, for both of them are responsible for creating enormous misery in the lives of others. Garcin daily abuses the wife who loves him, and Estelle murders her newborn child, an act that leads the baby's father to commit suicide. Although these are admittedly extreme examples, for Sartre, sharing a situation with other human beings clearly means not only that they can torture me but that I have the ability to torture them. "There's no need for red-hot pokers," as Garcin observes, when I am able to torture the Other merely by a look or an utterance that judges him in his freedom and finds him wanting (*Ex*, 45).

It should not be surprising that Sartre so often depicts the look of the Other in such strong, negative terms in *Being and Nothingness*. The look, he tells us, creates an "internal hemorrhage" in my world, making me feel as if my entire existence is being sucked down a drain-hole that has been unplugged by the Other. Subjected to the look, my world "bleeds" toward the Other (*BN*, 350). Although the look is manifested through the eyes, Sartre insists that the former cannot be reduced to the latter. This is because the look, on his account, is a direct expression of my freedom, whereas the eyes themselves are part of my facticity. The eyes are the vehicle for the look, but the two are distinct for Sartre, each constituting an irreducible dimension of human existence.

While the eyes, according to Sartre, are merely the material "support" for the look, and other objects can express the look as readily as the eyes, the freedom of the Other expressed through the look possesses the same transcendent quality as my own freedom. This is why the look of the Other "makes me be beyond my being in this world and puts me in the midst of the world which is at once *this world* and beyond this world" (*BN*, 350). It is important to unpack this latter claim in some depth, however, in order to see exactly what this encounter with the freedom of the Other offers me and not only what it takes from me.

Being Within and Beyond the World

As Sartre depicts it in *Being and Nothingness,* my encounter with the freedom of the Other, as it unfolds through the look (though it undoubtedly is manifested in many other ways as well), is primarily a threatening, extremely unsettling experience. The Other threatens to rob me of my world, challenging my freedom at its very core, leaving me like a beggar at the mercy of the Other's totalizing judgment. As a supplicant, totally dependent upon the Other who alone has the power to confer objectivity on my existence, I seek from the Other, not food, but something far more elusive, namely, his recognition and respect. Given Sartre's own philosophical influences, it should not be surprising if the Hegelian master-slave dialectic comes to mind here, a relationship of dependency if there ever was one, but one with a surprising twist, since in Hegel's analysis, the master needs the slave more than the slave has ever needed the master.

For Sartre, the look of the Other has the power to transport me, at one stroke, beyond the comfort and security of the world as I have known it, to a world that is nonetheless, to re-invoke Sartre's language, "at once *this world* and beyond this world." It is this world because the look of the Other appears within this world that I share with the Other, and yet it also takes me beyond this world because I am transported beyond the world *as I know it* and placed in the midst of a world *known by the Other.* Thinking about this process in terms of freedom, in particular, one might say that the Other threatens my freedom precisely because the Other is free to regard me as she pleases; I cannot bend the Other's freedom to my will in any way.[7] Above all, Sartre emphasizes the radical divide between my own consciousness and the consciousness of the Other. While I am a being-for-others as well as a being-for-itself, being a being-for-others means that I am an object of the Other's conscious awareness. My freedom is recognized by the Other but cannot be directly affected by the Other unless I choose to let the Other limit my freedom, in which case the choice is still mine and not the Other's; and in either case, my freedom is grounded in nothingness, so it cannot, technically speaking, be limited by anything at all.

In *Being and Nothingness*, Sartre offers us a predominantly antagonistic model of interpersonal relationships in which the Other and I both fight to recover our freedom and transcendence from the Other's attempts to render us mere objects in their world. Inevitably, Sartre implies, exercising my own freedom will conflict with the Other's exercise of her freedom. And this is precisely because, as I have noted, we continue to share the same world, whose resources are not infinite but are themselves limited and so cannot be equally enjoyed by all. To the extent that my projects compete with others' projects and that not all of the projects can be fulfilled simultaneously, one or more of us will be robbed of the opportunity to bring our project to completion. While this may lead to frustration and irritation toward the Other, Sartre emphasizes that it is our choice to persist in pursuing a project that we may not be able to fulfill (whether because it conflicts with the Other's project or because the project was not well conceived or well executed and therefore not capable of being realized to begin with) or to redirect ourselves toward other projects that are more capable of being achieved.

Thus, the Other continually threatens my freedom because her freedom has the same absolute, totalizing quality as my own and is exercised in one and the same world. Yet the Other can never truly threaten my freedom because my freedom is not something either I or the Other choose to have in the first place, so it can't be taken away by the Other nor can I relinquish it of my own accord. Just like the project of bad faith, then, the threat that the Other poses to my freedom can never be fully enacted. Just as I am incapable of successfully lying to myself, on Sartre's account, so too am I incapable of having my freedom taken away from me by the Other.

Ultimately, for Sartre, the important issue is not whether the Other *can* actually take my freedom from me but rather a matter of recognizing that the freedom of the Other generates a profound existential insecurity regarding my totalizing grasp on the world of my concern. For, as he reiterates throughout his phenomenological descriptions of the profoundly unsettling experience of recognizing one's being-for-others in *Being and Nothingness,* each being-for-itself has exclusive access to her own consciousness of the world. Each of us experiences the world, that is, through our consciousness of it, and no matter how close we are to others, we cannot share this experience directly with them. One's unique perspective on the world of one's concern is totalizing, moreover, insofar as it encompasses any possible or actual object of one's awareness. It persists in and through the experience of being-for-others even if we feel as if the Other has the power to rob us of our sovereign grasp of the world through her own totalizing gaze. The Other threatens us with the power of reducing us to an object in her world, and yet we disarm the Other of her threat by reaffirming our subjectivity through our own consciousness of, and response to, the Other who threatens us. Even to succumb to the will of the Other is, on Sartre's account, an expression of one's free subjectivity. Indeed, only death can render us finally and fully an object for the Other.

The Promise of Freedom

Although Beauvoir, like Sartre, views the ontological freedom of the for-itself as something absolute that cannot be given to one or taken away from one by another, she makes a crucial distinction between this basic ontological freedom, which human beings are born with, and what she calls willed, or genuine freedom, which one must actively choose to possess.[8] Moreover, and most importantly for this discussion, she claims that this willed freedom is not equally possible for all human beings because, unlike ontological freedom, it can be directly affected and even eviscerated by one's actual experiences, that is, the facticity of one's life. Whereas, as we have seen, Sartre's absolute Cartesian division between the materiality of the in-itself, or non-conscious being on the one hand, and the nonmaterial transcendence of consciousness on the other hand, renders the latter incapable of being directly diminished or enhanced by the former, Beauvoir provides a way of understanding how and why the actual empirical conditions of one's life can truly affect one's ability to exercise one's freedom for better as well as for worse.

One consequence of her distinction between the basic ontological freedom possessed by every for-itself and the ethical freedom that human beings must will to possess (and even then never manage to possess fully, since it is an existential task for a lifetime rather than an action completed once and for all), though it is not fully developed in *The Ethics of Ambiguity,* is that the genuine realization of one person's freedom requires the *confirmation* of my freedom by others and vice versa. For it is not enough merely to work to liberate another person or persons from the shackles of an oppressive experience, since this can be done even for others whom one still may view as inferior to oneself; rather, one must work to secure the freedom of others so that they, in turn, are free to pursue their own lives on *their own terms.* And this requires that one affirm the oppressed individual's own freedom to make her own choices, that is, confirm her own subjectivity even as she must in turn confirm one's own. I am calling this process of mutual recognition the "promise" of freedom, since, like any promise, it requires two parties who bind themselves to one another in a shared commitment to uphold their trust in one another. The promise is bound by no more and no less than the freedom of the parties who bring it into existence. It is also a promise in the anticipatory sense insofar as it points us toward what Derrida refers to as a freedom to come. He depicts this as-yet-unrealized freedom toward which the ethical subject is directed as

> what arises unforeseeably, what both calls upon and overwhelms my responsibility (my responsibility *before* my freedom—which it nonetheless seems to presuppose, my responsibility in heteronomy, my freedom without autonomy.

For Derrida, this freedom is an event, an

> *arrivance* that would surprise me absolutely and to whom or for whom, to which or for which I could not, and may no longer, *not respond*—in a way that is as responsible as possible: what happens, what arrives and comes down upon me, that to which I am exposed, beyond all mastery. Heteronomy, then—the other is my law.[9]

Though it is beyond the scope of this chapter to address Derrida's own rich conceptions of freedom and responsibility as they are articulated in these passages and elsewhere in his work, I do think he is capturing at least two essential insights that are present in Beauvoir's discussion of freedom and responsibility more than fifty years earlier in *The Ethics of Ambiguity*: first, that ethical freedom is grounded in an experience of heteronomy, not autonomy (that is, in Sartrean and Beauvoirian language, an experience of being-for-others and not just being-for-itself); and secondly, that the Other demands my response, not just at some places and times, but always and unconditionally. Beauvoir stresses that whether and how I respond to this call of/to the Other is ultimately up to me and me alone, but both she and Derrida would agree that I am fundamentally bound by/to the Other, whether or not I acknowledge that this is so.

Ultimately, I would argue, this Beauvoirian "promise of freedom," leads to a more nuanced and satisfying account of how human beings experience their being-for-others than the account of being-for-others offered by Sartre in *Being and Nothingness* and other early works such as *No Exit*, even while it intensifies the demands of freedom because it requires that I must work actively to affirm the Other's freedom in order to realize my own. Perhaps the best way of explaining the positive role others can and must play in enabling us to experience ethical freedom, on Beauvoir's account, is by turning to her discussion of how others can rob us of the possibility of pursuing this promise of freedom altogether.

Broken Promises

In *The Ethics of Ambiguity* and *The Second Sex*, as well as in her journal, *America Day by Day*, Beauvoir suggests that severe oppression can render it impossible for an individual to will her freedom, that is, to choose to exercise self-consciously the ontological freedom she already possesses. In cases where one is repeatedly forced into subservience to another person, she implies, an individual may lack the existential resources necessary to assert her freedom positively and efficaciously as a person who exists for-herself and not just for-the-other.[10] What are these existential resources? Beauvoir does not discuss them in any detail, yet she implies that they can provide one with the power that comes from realizing that an alternative (i.e., non-oppressed) existence is not only possible but a goal one should be striving for in one's thoughts and actions in response to one's oppressive situation. If ethical freedom consists in willing "to be a disclosure of being," willing to remain open to new possibilities that may offer themselves for becoming other than what one is or has been, then these possibilities must themselves be capable of being imagined as potentially realizable within one's own existence or they will not be possibilities at all but merely figments of one's imagination.

If there are extreme material and/or psychical constraints placed upon one's existence for an extended period of time, Beauvoir maintains, one may fail to see them as contingent aspects of one's existence but rather see them as givens that totally define who one is and what one can be. Rather than experiencing oneself as a totalizing consciousness, such a person experiences herself as totalized by her situation. Whereas Sartre would be forced to characterize this individual as being in bad faith for failing to recognize that she nonetheless possesses the ontological freedom that all for-itselves do, in fact, possess, Beauvoir suggests that the experience of severe oppression can render one incapable of attaining *consciousness* of one's freedom and that one therefore cannot be blamed for failing to will one's freedom from the limits imposed on one by the Other or by one's situation. In such circumstances, she argues, it becomes the responsibility, not of the oppressed individual, but of other human beings to expand her horizons in emancipatory ways so that a new future becomes possible for her, even if at first this appears only as a distant possibility. In Beauvoir's words:

There are cases where the slave does not know his servitude and where it is necessary to bring the seed of his liberation to him from the outside: his submission is not enough to justify the tyranny which is imposed upon him. The slave is submissive when one has succeeded in mystifying him in such a way that his situation does not seem to him to be imposed by men, but to be immediately given by nature, by the gods, by the powers against whom revolt has no meaning; thus, he does not accept his condition through a resignation of his freedom since he cannot even dream of any other. (*EA*, 85)

This passage is striking not only because of the passionate eloquence of Beauvoir's prose but also because of how subtly, yet decisively, she is parting company with a Sartrean understanding of freedom as an inviolable experience of transcendence that can never actually be diminished by the actions of others. Let us examine her words closely here in order to see both how others can rob an individual (or group) of the ability to experience "genuine" freedom and why, in such circumstances, those human beings who are able to will their freedom have a moral obligation to introduce this possibility to the oppressed individual(s) in such a manner that she (or they) can seize upon it concretely and thereby participate as an active agent in her (their) own emancipation.

Both Beauvoir and Sartre reject determinism in any form, especially concerning those aspects of experience historically deemed to be "natural." As Beauvoir explains in the first chapter of *The Second Sex*, the "data of biology" are viewed as prime exemplars of the natural, and they are often cited as establishing the limits of human beings' bodily capacities and desires. The problem, however, is that human beings have all too often exceeded these allegedly God-given (or nature-given) attributes, desiring bodies they are not supposed to desire, exhibiting capacities that do not correspond to the "natural" bodies they supposedly possess. Whether this is a matter of transgressing boundaries ascribed to one's sex, to one's race, or even to one's entire species, the data of biology, and therefore our concomitant understanding of the natural, have been undermined by the "polymorphous perversity," to use Foucault's language, of the diverse bodies they are intended to describe.[11]

While it is possible to deconstruct the notion of the "natural" by pointing out how this very notion has been historically constructed and applied to particular aspects of human as well as nonhuman existence in order to suggest that these latter cannot, or at least should not, be altered or changed, and even though one can show, as many feminist, critical race, and disability theorists have, how this invocation of determinism has traditionally operated to privilege some bodies and some bodily experiences over others, nonetheless this doesn't mean that people still can't experience their situations (or at least key aspects of their situations) as natural and inevitable and therefore as incapable of being changed. In Beauvoir's example above, for instance, the slave does not "know" his servitude because it is not experienced as the servitude of one free subjectivity to another; rather, the slave's situation appears to be "immediately given," that is, natural and unalterable. Such a person is mystified, she claims, because the thoroughgoing nature of his oppression makes him incapable of realizing that he has the power to radically transform his situation by living it on his own terms, even as he is forced to continue serving the Other.

By carving out this exception of the severely oppressed person who cannot be blamed for failing to will her freedom to live otherwise than according to the dictates of the Other, Beauvoir is acknowledging that: (1) freedom remains an empty word unless it is concretely realizable; (2) not everyone is capable of realizing their freedom; and (3) this is not always due to their own bad faith, but rather can be due to the power of the facticity of the situation itself to diminish one's experience of transcendence as a free human being. And, as Beauvoir amply demonstrates in *The Second Sex,* this has been a common experience for women throughout history although, she is always quick to point out, women have also played an active role in perpetuating their allegedly natural subordination to men.

For Beauvoir, it is not so much a matter of whether or not one views one's situation as natural that determines whether one is blameless or blameworthy for accepting that one occupies a subordinate status in comparison to the other (regardless of whether the source of one's "inferior" position is due to one's gender, class, race, religion, age, or bodily abilities), but whether one possesses what I have been calling the "existential resources" to question the notion of the natural with which one has been socialized. If one has these resources but refuses to use them, one is in bad faith; if one has been deprived of these resources due to severe oppression, one is not. Thus, we are led back to the question of what, exactly, these existential resources consist in and why those who have them are, on Beauvoir's account, under an ethical obligation to provide them for others, not only to open up the promise of freedom to the Other, but in so doing, to establish this promise for themselves as well.

The Existential Resources of Freedom

Though Beauvoir never explicitly states that she is breaking with a Sartrean conception of being-for-itself and being-for-others as two separable (albeit jointly experienced) dimensions of human existence, it is clear that her own account of how one's own freedom can only be actively affirmed to the extent that one also affirms (by working toward) the freedom of others undermines any strict ontological division between being-for-itself and being-for-others. By claiming that being-for-others is not an ontological structure of the for-itself, Sartre sets up a hostile dynamic between myself and the Other whereby each of us seeks our own freedom despite the Other, whose autonomous consciousness constantly threatens the hegemony of my own interpretations of the world we share with one another. While Beauvoir certainly recognizes that conflict is an indispensable feature of social existence, she also maintains that it is not the only, much less the paradigmatic model for describing the possibilities that flow from human relationships.

As Kristana Arp observes, the "bonds of freedom," for Beauvoir, entail that my freedom can only be meaningful insofar as I exercise it not only on my own behalf but also on behalf of the Other. By bonding myself to the Other, I pledge my freedom to her freedom, indissolubly linking our respective fates in an intersubjective existence that we create together. Realizing my own freedom, then, can never consist of freeing myself from the burden of helping to secure the freedom of the Other; instead, I must work with and for the Other to provide the concrete resources necessary for us both to pursue the promise of freedom.

Though Sartre also views human beings as responsible for improving the lives of others as well as ourselves, I am arguing that he doesn't give us a positive account of the kinds of resources we can actually provide to the Other to help her will her freedom, nor does he acknowledge that the Other can deprive us of these resources altogether through their domination. Instead, the Other always seems to pose a threat to my freedom, and I recover my freedom (which, as we have seen, the Other can never really rob me of in the first place) by reestablishing the absolute dichotomy between my own subjective experience of the world and that of the Other.

Debra Bergoffen reveals Beauvoir's distinctive contribution to existential ethics through the concept of "erotic generosity." Beauvoir, Bergoffen emphasizes, does not view willing to be a disclosure of the world as a burden we are forced to take up as a condition of ethical freedom, but rather as a source of joy that binds us indissolubly to others, allowing us to embrace their alterity as well as the otherness of the world as a whole:

> If we align the thought of the joy of disclosure with the idea of the erotic
> as disclosing the emotional warmth of the world, we find that the erotic

event captures the otherness of being as it makes us at home in the world. As fleshed intentionalities we pursue the disclosure of otherness because we find it joyful. We find the disclosure of otherness joyful because it is part of an emotionally warm/welcoming world.[12]

Passionately affirming the connections between one's own existence and the existence of others is the only means, for Beauvoir, of realizing one's own freedom; in this way, freedom for myself is always freedom for the Other: "Passion is converted to genuine freedom only if one destines his existence to other existences through the being—whether thing or man—at which he aims, without hoping to entrap it in the destiny of the in-itself." "Thus," she adds, "we see that no existence can be validly fulfilled if it is limited to itself. It appeals to the existence of others."[13]

The promise of freedom, as Beauvoir depicts it, is never a singular achievement but an ongoing collective task whose joys and sorrows we can and must take up together. It is always, as Derrida notes, yet to come, and yet, as Beauvoir observes, providing those who are oppressed with the basic existential resources necessary to pursue this promise is our only hope for securing its future.

Notes

1. I am invoking the notion of a dependency relation as it has been defined by feminist care ethicists such as Eva Kittay in *Love's Labor*.

2. The publication of Merleau-Ponty's *Phenomenology of Perception* in 1945, sandwiched between Sartre's and Beauvoir's texts with its own concluding chapter on "Freedom," marks a crucial intervention in this conversation and had a profound influence on Beauvoir's view of the intersubjective dimensions of freedom, though I am unable to do justice to Merleau-Ponty's distinctive understanding of the relationship between freedom and the Other here. I would not in any way want to imply, however, that only these three authors were engaged in this conversation. Hegel is certainly an important historical interlocutor for all three, as is Husserl; within the horizon of World War II within which Beauvoir, Sartre, and Merleau-Ponty were all writing, the question of how to realize one's own freedom in a world that is shared with (quite often in the form of domination by) others was paramount for virtually any twentieth-century intellectual who was concerned with social and political issues.

3. I am using the 1992 Washington Square Press edition.

4. Sartre, "Itinerary of a Thought," 7. I am grateful to Christine Daigle for recommending this passage to illustrate the persistence of individual freedom for Sartre in the face of social conditioning.

5. It is important to note that facticity is not co-extensive with materiality, since the facticity of my situation, for Sartre, extends to nonmaterial aspects of the situation as well. The facticity of a human being includes her body, her past (including her past

choices and the tradition or culture into which she was born), and both her intimate and non-intimate relationships with others; though each of these is grounded in the materiality of a given situation, they also cannot be understood in purely material terms.

6. I am using the 1976 Vintage edition.

7. Of course this does not mean that I am incapable of exercising power over the Other. One may force the Other to do one's bidding if the Other occupies a position of economic or physical subservience; however, the point is that even if the Other is compelled to satisfy my desires, I cannot compel the Other to freely perform a task for me, nor can I compel the Other to love or respect me if she hasn't made these choices or experienced these feelings of her own accord.

8. I am using "possess" in a figurative sense here, for of course freedom, whether we are talking about the basic freedom of the Sartrean for-itself or Beauvoir's sense of willed freedom, can never be a possession in the first place.

9. Derrida, *For What Tomorrow,* 52.

10. Beauvoir does not discuss cases of extreme material hardship where this is not perpetrated by another person for the latter's own benefit. Her examples of severe oppression are always a function of one person being objectified and dominated by another. Nonetheless, I would argue that her account of severe oppression can and should be extended to situations where the cause of the oppression is not another person or persons but a person's (or group's) being deprived of the basic resources necessary to fulfill the basic requirements of human existence even when this deprivation is not directly attributable to the actions of other human beings (e.g., political-historical conflicts). Natural disasters, for instance, can create experiences of severe oppression. Even if one wants to argue that these are never entirely natural because human beings have decisively intervened in nature and affected its processes, the point is that there is no one person in these situations who is the cause of the other's oppression or who actively seeks to oppress the person who suffers from such disasters.

11. Foucault, *History of Sexuality,* 47.

12. Bergoffen, *Philosophy of Simone de Beauvoir,* 190.

13. Ibid., 67.

Bibliography

Anderson, Thomas. *The Foundation and Structure of Sartrean Ethics.* Lawrence: Regents Press of Kansas, 1979.

———. *Sartre's Two Ethics: From Authenticity to Integral Humanity.* Chicago: Open Court, 1993.

Andrew, Barbara. "Beauvoir's Place in Philosophical Thought." In *The Cambridge Companion to Simone de Beauvoir,* ed. Claudia Card. Cambridge: Cambridge University Press, 2003.

Arendt, Hannah. "Philosophy and Politics." *Social Research* 57, no. 1 (Spring 1990): 73–103.

Arp, Kristana. "Beauvoir's Concept of Bodily Alienation." In *Feminist Interpretations of Simone de Beauvoir,* ed. Margaret A. Simons, 161–77. University Park: Pennsylvania State University Press, 1995.

———. *The Bonds of Freedom: Simone de Beauvoir's Existentialist Ethics.* Chicago: Open Court, 2001.

———. "Conceptions of Freedom in Beauvoir's *The Ethics of Ambiguity.*" *International Studies in Philosophy* 31, no. 2 (1999): 25–34.

Bachelard, Gaston. *La Psychanalyse du feu.* Paris: Gallimard, 1937. Trans. A. C. Ross, *The Psychoanalysis of Fire.* Boston: Beacon Press, 1968.

———. *L'Eau et les rêves: Essai sur l'imagination de la matière.* Paris: José Corti, 1942.

Bair, Deirdre. *Simone de Beauvoir: A Biography.* New York: Summit Books, 1990.

———. *Simone de Beauvoir.* London: Jonathan Cape, 1990.

Barnes, Hazel. *The Literature of Possibility: A Study in Humanistic Existentialism.* London: Tavistock, 1961 [1959].

———. "Sartre and Sexism." *Philosophy and Literature* 14, no. 2 (1990): 340–47.

———. "Sartre's *War Diaries*: Prelude and Postscript." In *Sartre's Life, Times and Vision du Monde,* ed. William McBride. New York: Garland Press, 1997.

Bataille, Georges. *Death and Sensuality: A Study of Eroticism and the Taboo.* New York: Arno Press, 1977. Trans. by Leslie Ann Boldt as *Inner Experience.* Albany: State University of New York Press, 1988.

Baudelaire, Charles. *The Flowers of Evil.* Trans. Anne-Marie de Grazia.

http://www.grazian-archive.com/quiddity/Baudelaire.htm, [1855]
1988. Original *Les fleurs du mal.*

Bauer, Nancy. *Simone de Beauvoir, Philosophy and Feminism.* New York: Columbia
University Press, 2001.

Beauvoir, Simone de. *L'Invitée.* Paris: Gallimard, 1943.

———. *Pyrrhus et Cinéas.* Paris: Gallimard, 1944.

———. *Le sang des autres.* Paris: Gallimard, [1945] 1996. Trans. by Yvonne Moyse
and Roger Senhouse as *The Blood of Others.* Harmondsworth: Penguin,
1964.

———. "La phénoménologie de la perception de Maurice Merleau-Ponty." In *Les
Temps modernes* 1, no. 2 (1945). Trans. as "A review of *The Phenomenology
of Perception* by Maurice Merleau-Ponty." In *Simone de Beauvoir: Philosophical Writings,* ed. Margaret A. Simons, with Marybeth Timmermann
and Mary Beth Mader. Urbana and Chicago: University of Illinois Press,
2004.

———. "Littérature et métaphysique." In *Les Temps modernes* I (6–9): 1153–63.
Paris, 1946.

———. *Pour une morale de l'ambiguïté.* Paris: Gallimard, 1947, 1994.

———. "Idéalisme moral et réalisme politique." ["Moral Idealism and Political
Realism"]. In *L'Existentialisme et la sagesse des nations,* 55–101. Paris: Editions Nagel, 1948. [Originally published in *Les Temps modernes,* November
1945.]

———. *The Ethics of Ambiguity.* Trans. Bernard Frechtman. New York: Citadel
Press, 1948 (repr. 1975, 1976, 1991, 1994).

———. *Le Deuxième sexe I: les faits et les mythes.* Paris: Gallimard, [1949] 1993.
Trans. by H. M. Parshley, *The Second Sex.* Harmondsworth: Penguin, 1987.

———. *Le Deuxième sexe II: l'expérience vécue.* Paris: Gallimard, [1949] 1991.
Trans. by H. M. Parshley as *The Second Sex.* Harmondsworth: Penguin,
1987.

———. *America Day by Day.* Trans. Patrick Dudley. London: Duckworth, 1952.

———. *The Second Sex.* Trans. H. M. Parshley. New York: Knopf, 1953.

———. *She Came to Stay.* New York: World Publishing Co., 1954.

———. "Merleau-Ponty et le pseudo-sartrisme." In *Les Temps modernes* 114–15
(1955): 2072–2122. Reprinted in *Privilèges.* Paris: Gallimard, collection
Les essais LXXVI, 1955, 203–72. Trans. by V. Zaytzeff and F. Morrison as
"Merleau-Ponty and Pseudo-Sartreanism." *International Studies in Philosophy* 21, no. 3 (1989): 3–48.

———. *Faut-il brûler Sade?* Paris: Gallimard, 1955.

———. *La Force de l'âge.* Paris: Gallimard, 1960.

———. *The Prime of Life.* Trans. Peter Green. Cleveland: World Publishing, 1962.

———. *Memoirs of a Dutiful Daughter.* Harmondsworth: Penguin, 1963.

———. *La Force des choses.* Paris: Gallimard, 1963.

——. *Une Mort très douce.* Paris: Gallimard, 1964. Trans. by Patrick O'Brian as
    A Very Easy Death. New York: Putnam, 1966.
——. *The Second Sex.* Trans. and ed. H. M. Parshley. New York: Alfred A. Knopf,
    1964, 1971.
——. *Force of Circumstance.* Trans. Richard Howard. London: Readers Union,
    1966.
——. *The Mandarins.* Trans. Leonard L. Friedman. London: Fontana Books,
    1972. *Les mandarins,* vol. 1. Paris: Gallimard, 2001.
——. *La Cérémonie des adieux,* suivi de *Entretiens avec Jean-Paul Sartre.* Paris:
    Gallimard, 1974, 1981. (Cited as *Entretiens.*)
——. *The Second Sex.* New York: Vintage Books, 1974.
——. *Tout compte fait.* Paris: Gallimard, 1978. Trans. by Patrick O'Brian as *All
    Said and Done.* New York: Paragon House, 1993.
——. "Interférences. Entretien de Michel Sicard avec Simone de Beauvoir et
    Jean-Paul Sartre." *Obliques* 18–19 (1979): 325–29.
——. *Pour une Morale de L'ambiguïté.* Paris: Gallimard, 1979.
——. "Interview de Simone de Beauvoir par J.-F. Rolland." *L'Humanité
    Dimanche,* 19 December 1954. In *Les écrits de Simone de Beauvoir,* ed.
    Claude Francis and Fernande Gontier, 358–62. Paris: Gallimard, 1979.
——. "Mon expérience d'écrivain." Lecture given in Japan, 11 October 1966. In
    Les écrits de Simone de Beauvoir, ed. Claude Francis and Fernande Gontier,
    439–457. Paris: Gallimard 1979.
——. *When Things of the Spirit Come First: Five Early Tales.* Trans. Patrick
    O'Brian. New York: Pantheon Books, 1982.
——. *Lettres au Castor et à quelques autres, II.* Paris: Gallimard, 1983.
——. *Lettres à Sartre.* Paris: Gallimard, 1983.
——. *Adieux: A Farewell to Sartre.* Trans. Patrick O'Brian. New York: Pantheon
    Books, 1984.
——. *The Second Sex.* Trans. H. M. Parshley. New York: Vintage Books, 1989.
——. *Journal de Guerre.* Paris: Gallimard, 1990.
——. *Lettres à Sartre.* Paris: Gallimard, 1990.
——. *The Prime of Life.* Trans. Peter Green. New York: Paragon House, 1992.
——. *Force of Circumstance,* Vol. 1. Trans. Richard Howard. New York: Paragon
    House, 1992.
——. *Letters to Sartre.* Trans. and ed. Quintin Hoare. New York: Arcade Pub-
    lishing, 1993.
——. *All Said and Done.* Trans. Patrick O'Brian. New York: Paragon House, 1993.
——. *The Second Sex.* Trans. and ed. H. M. Parshley. New York: Knopf, 1952
    [1993 reprint].
——. "Merleau-Ponty and Pseudo-Sartreanism." In *The Debate Between Sartre
    and Merleau-Ponty,* ed. Jon Stewart. Northwestern University Press, 1998.
——. *Pyrrhus and Cinéas.* In *Simone de Beauvoir: Philosophical Writings,* ed.

Margaret Simons with Marybeth Timmermann and Mary Beth Mader. Urbana: University of Illinois Press, 2004.

——. *Simone de Beauvoir: Philosophical Writings*. Ed. Margaret A. Simons with Marybeth Timmermann and Mary Beth Mader. Urbana: University of Illinois Press, 2004.

——. *Simone de Beauvoir: Diary of a Philosophy Student, Volume 1, 1926–27*. Ed. Barbara Klaw, Sylvie Le Bon de Beauvoir, and Margaret A. Simons with Marybeth Timmermann. Urbana and Chicago: University of Illinois Press, 2006.

——. *Anne, ou quand prime le spirituel*. Paris: Gallimard, Folio, 2006.

——. *Who Shall Die?* Trans. Patrick O'Brien. New York: Pantheon Books.

Becker, Ernest. *The Denial of Death*. New York: Free Press, 1973.

Bell, Linda. Review of Anderson's *Foundation and Structure of Sartrean Ethics* in *Man and World* 14 (1981): 223–34.

——. *Sartre's Ethics of Authenticity*. Tuscaloosa: University of Alabama Press, 1989.

Bennington, Geoffrey. *Jacques Derrida*. Chicago and London: University of Chicago Press, 1993.

Bergoffen, Debra. "The Look as Bad Faith." In *Philosophy Today* 36 (Fall 1992): 221–27.

——. "Out from Under: Beauvoir's Philosophy of the Erotic." In *Feminist Interpretations of Simone de Beauvoir*, ed. Margaret A. Simons. University Park: Pennsylvania State University Press, 1995.

——. *The Philosophy of Simone de Beauvoir: Gendered Phenomenologies, Erotic Generosities*. Albany: State University of New York Press, 1997.

——. "Simone de Beauvoir and Jean-Paul Sartre: Woman, Man and the Desire to be God." In *Constellations* 9, no. 3 (2002): 409–18.

——. "Marriage, Autonomy, and the Feminine Protest." In *The Philosophy of Simone de Beauvoir, Critical Essays*, ed. Margaret A. Simons. Bloomington: Indiana University Press, 2006.

——. "Bad Faith and *The Second Sex*." Presented at the annual conference of the United Kingdom Society for Sartrean Studies (UKSSS), London, October 2006.

Bernstein, Richard. *Praxis and Action*. Philadelphia: University of Pennsylvania Press, 1971.

Boulé, Jean-Pierre. *Sartre Médiatique: La Place de l'Interview dans son Oeuvre*. Fleury-sur-Orne: Minard, 1993.

——. *Sartre, Self-Formation and Masculinities*. New York, Oxford: Berghahn Books, 2005.

Brosman, Catherine S. *Simone de Beauvoir Revisited*. Boston: Twayne Publishers, 1991.

Burstow, Bonnie. "How Sexist Is Sartre?" *Philosophy and Literature* 16, no. 1 (1992): 32–48.

Butler, Judith. *Bodies That Matter: On the Discursive Limits of "Sex."* New York and London: Routledge, 1993.

———. *Gender Trouble: Feminism and the Subversion of Identity.* New York: Routledge, 1990.

Chaperon, Sylvie. "1949–1999: Cinquante ans de lecture et de débats français." In *Cinquantenaire du Deuxième sexe,* ed. Christine Delphy and Sylvie Chaperon. Paris: Éditions Syllepse, 2002.

Cixous, Hélène. "Extreme Fidelity." In *Hélène Cixous Reader,* ed. Susan Sellers. New York: Routledge, 1994.

Cohen-Solal, Annie. *Sartre: 1905–1980.* Paris: Gallimard, 1985.

Collins, Margery L., and Christine Pierce. "Holes and Slime: Sexism in Sartre's Psychoanalysis." In *Women and Philosophy: Toward a Theory of Liberation,* ed. Carol C. Gould and Marx W. Wartofsky. New York: Capricorn Books, 1976.

Contat, Michel. *Pourquoi et comment Sartre a écrit "Les Mots."* Paris: P.U.F., "Perspectives critiques," 1996.

———. "Introduction: une autobiographie politique?" In *Pourquoi et comment Sartre a écrit "Les Mots."* Paris: P.U.F., "Perspectives critiques," 1996.

Contat, Michel, and Michel Rybalka. *Les Écrits de Sartre.* Paris: Gallimard, 1970.

Crimp, Douglas. "Getting the Warhol We Deserve." In *Social Text* 59 (1999): 49–66.

Daigle, Christine. "The Ambiguous Ethics of Beauvoir." In *Existentialist Thinkers and Ethics,* ed. Christine Daigle, 120–41. Montreal and Kingston: McGill/Queen's University Press, 2006.

Derrida, Jacques. *Marges de la philosophie.* Paris: Minuit, 1972. Trans. Alan Bass as *Margins of Philosophy.* Hemel Hempstead: Harvester Wheatsheaf, 1982.

———. "From Restricted to General Economy." In *Writing and Difference,* 251–77. London: Routledge, 1978.

———. "Women in a Beehive: A Seminar with Jacques Derrida." In *Men in Feminism,* ed. Alice Jardine and Paul Smith. New York: Methuen, 1987.

———. *Acts of Literature.* Ed. Derek Attridge. London and New York: Routledge, 1992.

Derrida, Jacques, and Elisabeth Roudinesco. *For What Tomorrow . . . A Dialogue.* Trans. Jeff Fort. Stanford, Calif.: Stanford University Press, 2004.

Detmer, David. *Freedom as a Value: A Critique of the Ethical Theory of Jean-Paul Sartre.* La Salle, Ill.: Open Court, 1986.

Deutscher, Max. *Genre and Void: Looking Back at Sartre and Beauvoir.* Hampshire, England, and Burlington, Vt.: Ashgate, 2003.

Deutscher, Penelope. "Reconstructive 'Delirium'—of Beauvoir, Merleau-Ponty, and 'Pseudo-Sartreanism.'" Presented at NASS 2006, Fordham University, N.Y., October 28, 2006.

Diprose, Rosalyn. *The Bodies of Women*. London and New York: Routledge, 1994.

———. "Generosity: Between Love and Desire." *Hypatia* 13, no. 1 (Winter 1998): 1–20.

———. *Corporeal Generosity: On Giving with Nietzsche, Merleau-Ponty and Levinas*. Albany: SUNY Press, 2001.

Douglas, Mary. *Purity and Danger: An Analysis of the Concepts of Pollution and Taboo*. New York: Praeger, 1966.

Drummond, John. "Respect as a Moral Emotion: A Phenomenological Approach." In *Husserl Studies* 22, no. 1 (2006): 1–27.

Edwards, Paul. *Encyclopedia of Philosophy*. New York and London: Collier Macmillan, 1967.

Elias, Norbert. *Die Gesellschaft der Individuen*. Suhrkamp: Verlag, 1987.

Evans, Debbie. "Beauvoir's *L'Invitée*: The Necessity of Writing Against the Contingent." *Simone de Beauvoir Studies* 21 (2004–2005).

Foucault, Michel. *The History of Sexuality: An Introduction*, Vol. 1. Trans. Robert Hurley. New York: Vintage Books, 1990.

———. *Préface à la transgression, Critique*. In Suzanne Guerlach's *Literary Polemics: Bataille, Sartre, Valery, Breton*. Stanford, Calif.: Stanford University Press, 1997.

Fretz, Leo. "Individuality in Sartre's Philosophy." In *The Cambridge Companion to Sartre*, ed. Christina Howells, 67–102. Cambridge: Cambridge University Press, 1992.

Fuchs, Jo-Ann. "Female Eroticism in *The Second Sex*." *Feminist Studies* 6, no. 2 (1980).

Fullbrook, Edward. "An Introduction to 'Two Unpublished Chapters of *She Came to Stay*.'" In *Simone de Beauvoir: Philosophical Writings*, ed. Margaret A. Simons, with Marybeth Timmermann and Mary Beth Mader. Urbana: University of Illinois Press, 2005.

———. "*She Came to Stay* and *Being and Nothingness*." In *The Philosophy of Simone de Beauvoir: Critical Essays*, ed. Margaret A. Simons, 42–64. Bloomington: Indiana University Press, 2006.

Fullbrook, Edward, and Kate Fullbrook. *Simone de Beauvoir and Jean-Paul Sartre: The Remaking of a Twentieth-Century Legend*. London: Harvester, 1993. New York: Basic Books, 1994.

———. "The Absence of Beauvoir." In *Feminist Interpretations of Jean-Paul Sartre*, ed. Julien S. Murphy, 45–63. University Park: Pennsylvania State University Press, 1999.

———. "Sartre's Secret Key." In *Rereading the Canon: Feminist Interpretations of Simone de Beauvoir*, ed. Margaret A. Simons, 97–112. University Park: Pennsylvania State University Press, 1994.

———. "Whose Ethics: Sartre's or Beauvoir's?" *Simone de Beauvoir Studies* 12 (1995): 84–90.

———. "Leveling the Field/Tampering with the Icons: On 'Refining and Remaking the Legend of Beauvoir.'" *Simone de Beauvoir Studies* 13 (1996): 13–24.

———. "Beauvoir's Literary-Philosophical Method." *Simone de Beauvoir Studies* 14 (1997): 29–38.

———. "Simone de Beauvoir." In *A Companion to Continental Philosophy*, ed. Simon Critchley, 269–280. Oxford: Blackwell, 1998.

———. *Beauvoir: A Critical Introduction*, Cambridge, UK: Polity Press, 1998; and Cambridge, Mass.: Blackwell, 1998.

———. "Beauvoir and Plato: The Clinic and the Cave." In *The Existential Phenomenology of Simone de Beauvoir*, ed. Lester Embree, 53–66. Amsterdam: Kluwer, 2001.

———. "*Le deuxième sexe* à l'épreuve du genre littéraire." In *Cinquantenaire du Deuxième Sexe*, ed. Christine Delphy et al., 97–104. Paris: Syllepse, 2002.

———. "Simone de Beauvoir." In *Companion to Modern French Thought*. Routledge, 2005.

———. *Sex and Philosophy: Rethinking de Beauvoir and Sartre*. London: Continuum, 2008.

Fullbrook, Edward, and Margaret A. Simons. "Simone de Beauvoir and Jean-Paul Sartre." In *Gendering Western Philosophy: Pairs of Men and Women Philosophers from the 4th century B.C.E. to the Present*. Prentice-Hall, forthcoming.

Gatens, Moira. *Feminism and Philosophy: Perspectives on Difference and Equality*. Cambridge: Polity Press, 1993.

Golomb, Jacob. *In Search of Authenticity from Kierkegaard to Camus*. London: Routledge, 1995.

Green, Karen. "Sartre and de Beauvoir on Freedom and Oppression." In *Feminist Interpretations of Jean-Paul Sartre*, ed. J. Murphy. University Park: Pennsylvania State University Press, 1999.

Grosz, Elizabeth. *Volatile Bodies: Toward a Corporeal Feminism*. Bloomington: Indiana University Press, 1994.

Guerlach, Suzanne. *Literary Polemics: Bataille, Sartre, Valery, Breton*. Stanford, Calif.: Stanford University Press, 1997.

Guignon, Charles, and Derk Pereboom, eds. *Existentialism: Basic Writings*. Indianapolis: Hackett, 1995.

Hegel, G. W. F. *The Phenomenology of Mind*. Trans. J. B. Baillie. New York: Harper and Row, 1967.

———. *The Phenomenology of Spirit*. Trans. A. V. Miller. Oxford: Oxford University Press, 1977.

Heidegger, Martin. *Sein und Zeit*. Tübingen: Neomarius Verlag, 1962. Trans. John Macquarrie and Edward Robinson as *Being and Time*. New York: Harper and Row, 1962.

———. *Being and Time.* Oxford: Blackwell, 1995.

Heinämaa, Sara. "Women—Nature, Product, Style? Rethinking the Foundations of Feminist Philosophy of Science." In *Feminism, Science, and the Philosophy of Science,* ed. Lynn Hankison Nelson and Jack Nelson, 289–308. Dordrecht: Kluwer, 1996.

———. "'What Is a Woman?' Butler and Beauvoir on the Foundations of Sexual Difference." In *Hypatia* 12, no. 1 (1997): 20–39.

———. *Toward a Phenomenology of Sexual Difference: Husserl, Merleau-Ponty, Beauvoir.* Lanham, Md.: Rowman & Littlefield, 2003.

———. "Introduction [to 'A Review of *The Phenomenology of Perception* by Maurice Merleau-Ponty']." In *Simone de Beauvoir: Philosophical Writings,* ed. Margaret A. Simons, with Marybeth Timmermann and Mary Beth Mader. Urbana and Chicago: University of Illinois Press, 2004.

———. "'Through Desire and Love': Simone de Beauvoir on the Possibilities of Sexual Desire." In *Sex, Breath and Force: Sexual Difference in a Post-Feminist Era,* ed. Ellen Mortensen. Lanham, Md.: Lexington Books, 2006.

Hengehold, Laura. "Beauvoir's Parrhesiastic Contracts: Frank-speaking and the Philosophical-political Couple." In *The Philosophy of Simone de Beauvoir: Critical Essays,* ed. Margaret A. Simons, 178–200. Bloomington: Indiana University Press, 2006.

Howells, Christina. *Derrida, Deconstruction from Phenomenology to Ethics.* Cambridge: Polity Press, 1998.

Husserl, Edmund. *Philosophie als strenge Wissenschaft.* Frankfurt: Vittorio Klostermann, 1911. English: "Philosophy as Rigorous Science." In *Phenomenology and the Crisis of Philosophy,* trans. Quentin Lauer. New York: Harper Torchbooks, 1965.

———. *Ideen zu einer reinen Phänomenologie und phänomenologischen Philosophie, Erstes Buch: Allgemeine Einführung in die reine Phänomenologie.* Ed. Walter Biemel. Haag: Martinus Nijhoff, 1913. English: *Ideas: General Introduction to Pure Phenomenology.* Trans. W.R. Boyce Gibson. New York, London: Collier, 1962.

———. *Ideen zu einer reinen Phänomenologie und phänomenologischen Philosophie, Zweites Buch: Phänomenologische Untersuchungen zum Konstitution.* Ed. Marly Bimel. Haag: Martinus Nijhoff, 1952. English: *Ideas Pertaining to a Pure Phenomenology and to a Phenomenological Philosophy, Second Book: Studies in the Phenomenological Constitution.* Trans. Richard Rojcewicz and André Schuwer. Dordrecht, Boston, London: Kluwer Academic Publishers, 1993.

———. *Die Krisis der europäischen Wissenschaften und die transzendentale Phänomenologie: Eine Einleitung in die phänomenologische Philosophie.* Ed. Walter Biemel. Haag: Martinus Nijhoff, 1954. English: *The Crisis of*

European Sciences and Transcendental Phenomenology: An Introduction to Phenomenological Philosophy. Trans. David Carr. Evanston, Ill.: Northwestern University, 1988.

———. Zur Phänomenologie der Intersubjektivität, Texte aus dem Nachlass, Dritter Teil, 1929–35. Ed. Iso Kern. Haag: Martinus Nijhoff, 1973.

Hyppolite, Jean. Genèse et structure de la 'Phénoménologie de l'esprit' de Hegel. Paris: Aubier Montaigne, 1946.

Idt, Geneviève. Le Mur de Jean-Paul Sartre, techniques et contexte d'une provocation. Paris: Larousse université, 1972.

———. "Simone de Beauvoir's Adieux: A Funeral Rite and a Literary Challenge." In Sartre Alive, ed. Ronald Aronson and Adrian van den Hoven, 366–69. Detroit: Wayne State University Press, 1991.

Irigaray, Luce. Ce sexe qui n'en est pas un. Paris: Minuit, 1977. English: This Sex Which Is Not One. Trans. Catherine Porter with Carolyn Burke. Ithaca, N.Y.: Cornell University Press, 1985.

———. Éthique de la différence sexuelle. Paris: Minuit, 1984. English: An Ethics of Sexual Difference. Trans. Carolyn Burke and Gillian C. Gill. Ithaca, N.Y.: Cornell University Press, 1993.

Kail, Michel. "Jean-Paul Sartre." In Revue Philosophique de la France et de l'Étranger. Paris, N°3, 120ème année, 339–54.

———. Simone de Beauvoir philosophe. Paris: P.U.F., 2006.

———. "Le masculin et le féminin. Sartre et Beauvoir, regards croisés." Sens Public. Revue électronique internationale. www.sens-public.org/article.php3?id_article=427 (accessed August 26, 2007).

———. "La conscience n'est pas sujet: Pour un matérialisme authentique." Revue philosophique de la France et de l'étranger 121, no. 3 (1996): 339–54.

Käll, Lisa. "Encountering Self and Other: Intersubjectivity in Sartre and Merleau-Ponty." Masters thesis, Hoger Instituut voor Wijsbegeerte, Katholieke Universiteit Leuven, 2000.

———. "Beneath Subject and Object: The Expressive Body in Light of the Sartrean Gaze." Presented at the Society for Phenomenology and Existentialist Philosophy (SPEP), Loyola University Chicago, October 10–12, 2002.

———. "The expressive body in light of the Sartrean gaze." In Nordic Society for Phenomenology. University of Helsinki, Finland, April 25–27.

———. "Expressive Selfhood." Ph.D. diss., University of Copenhagen, 2007.

Kant, Immanuel. Grounding for the Metaphysics of Morals. Trans. James W. Ellington. Indianapolis: Hackett, 1993.

Kierkegaard, Søren. Sickness unto Death. Trans. Alastair Hannay. Harmondsworth: Penguin, 1989.

Kittay, Eva. Love's Labor: Essays on Women, Equality, and Dependency. New York: Routledge, 1999.

Klaw, Barbara. "Sexuality in Beauvoir's *Les Mandarins*." In *Feminist Interpretations of Simone de Beauvoir*, ed. Margaret A. Simons. University Park: Pennsylvania State University Press, 1995.

Kojève, Alexandre. *Introduction à la lecture de Hegel*. Paris: Gallimard, 1947. English: *Introduction to the Reading of Hegel: Lectures on the Phenomenology of Spirit*. Trans. James H. Nichols. Assembled by Raymond Queneau, ed. Alan Bloom. London and New York: Basic Books, 1969.

Kristeva, Julia. *Pouvoirs de l'horreur*, Paris: Seuil, 1980. English: *Powers of Horror*. Trans. Leon S. Roudiez. New York: Columbia, 1982.

———. *Colette*. Trans. Jane Marie Todd. New York: Columbia University Press, 2004. Original: *Le génie féminin III: Colette*, Paris: Fayard, 2002.

Kruks, Sonia. *Situation and Human Existence: Freedom, Subjectivity and Society*. New York: Routledge, 1990.

———. "Simone de Beauvoir: Teaching Sartre about Freedom." In *Sartre Alive*, ed. Ronald Aronson and Adrian van den Hoven. Detroit: Wayne State University Press, 1991.

———. "Simone de Beauvoir: Teaching Sartre about Freedom." In *Feminist Interpretations of Simone de Beauvoir*, ed. Margaret A. Simons. University Park: Pennsylvania State University Press, 1995.

———. "Beauvoir: The Weight of Situation." In *Simone de Beauvoir: A Critical Reader*, ed. Elizabeth Fallaize. New York: Routledge, 1998.

———. *Retrieving Experience: Subjectivity and Recognition in Feminist Politics*. Ithaca, N.Y.: Cornell University Press, 2001.

Lacan, Jacques. *Le Séminaire de Jacques Lacan, Livre XX: Encore*, 1972–1973. Ed. Jacques-Alain Miller. Paris: Editions du Seuil, 1975. Trans. by Bruce Fink as *The Seminar of Jacques Lacan, Book XX: Encore*, 1972–1973. New York: W.W. Norton, 1998.

———. *Écrits, A Selection*. Trans. Bruce Fink. London: W.W. Norton, 2002.

Lacoin, Elisabeth. *Correspondance et carnets d'Elisabeth Lacoin, 1914–1929*. Paris: Seuil, 1991.

Lacoste, Guillermine de. "Sartre's Itinerary from Self-Presence to Abandon." In *Philosophy Today* 42, no. 2 (Fall 1998): 284–89.

———. "Le Trouble chez Beauvoir (re)marqué par Bergoffen." Presented at the Société Américaine de Philosophie de Langue Française meeting at the APA convention, Washington, D.C., 1998.

———. "The Transformation of the Notion of Transparency on which Beauvoir's and Sartre's Pact Was Based." In *Simone de Beauvoir Studies*, Vol. 15, 1998–1999.

Langer, Monika. "Sartre and Merleau-Ponty: A Reappraisal." In *The Debate between Sartre and Merleau-Ponty*, ed. Jon Stewart, 93–117. Evanston, Ill: Northwestern University Press, 1998.

———. "Beauvoir and Merleau-Ponty on Ambiguity." In *The Cambridge Compan-*

ion to *Simone de Beauvoir*, ed. Claudia Card. Cambridge: Cambridge University Press, 2003.

Lecarme, Jacques. "Sartre palimpseste." In *Pourquoi et comment Sartre a écrit Les Mots*. Paris: P.U.F., "Perspectives critiques," 1996.

Lecarme-Tabone, Eliane. "Le couple Beauvoir-Sartre face à la critique féministe." In *Les Temps modernes*, June–July 2002, no. 619, 19–42.

———. *Mémoires d'une jeune fille rangée de Simone de Beauvoir*. Paris: Gallimard, "Folio," 2000.

Le Dœuff, Michèle. *Hipparchia's Choice: An Essay Concerning Women, Philosophy, etc.* Trans. Trista Selous. Oxford, Cambridge: Blackwell, 1991. New York: Columbia University Press, 2007. [Original: *L'étude et le rouet*, 1989.]

Léon, Céline. "Can the Second Sex be One?" In Simone de Beauvoir Ten Years Later, *Simone de Beauvoir Studies* 13 (1996): 25–44.

Linsenbard, Gail. "Beauvoir, Ontology, and Women's Human Rights." In *Hypatia* 14, no. 4 (1999): 145–62.

Lloyd, Genevieve. *The Man of Reason: "Male" and "Female" in Western Philosophy*. London: Methuen, 1984. Minneapolis: University of Minnesota Press, 1993.

Louette, Jean-François. "La dialectique dans 'L'enfance d'un chef.'" In *Études Sartriennes* IV (1990): 125–51.

———. *Silences de Sartre*. Toulouse: Presses Universitaires du Mirail, 1995.

Lundgren-Gothlin, Eva. "Gender and Ethics in the Philosophy of Simone de Beauvoir." In *Nora: Nordic Journal of Women's Studies* 1, no. 3 (1992): 3–13.

———. *Sex and Existence: Simone de Beauvoir's The Second Sex*. Trans. Linda Schenck. Hanover, NH: Wesleyan University Press, 1996.

———. "Reading Simone de Beauvoir with Martin Heidegger." In *The Cambridge Companion to Simone de Beauvoir*, ed. Claudia Card. Cambridge: Cambridge University Press, 2003.

MacIntyre, Alasdair. *After Virtue: A Study in Moral Philosophy*. Notre Dame, Ind.: University of Notre Dame Press, 1981.

Mahon, Joseph. *Existentialism, Feminism, and Simone de Beauvoir*. New York: St. Martin's Press, 1997.

Marso, Lori Jo, and Patricia Moynagh, eds. *Simone de Beauvoir's Political Thinking*. Urbana and Chicago: University of Illinois Press, 2006.

Mauss, Marcel. *Essai sur le don: Forme archaïque de l'échange*. Trans. Ian Cunnison, *The Gift: Forms and Functions of Exchange in Archaic Societies*. New York: Norton, 1967.

McBride, William. "Merleau-Ponty and Sartre." In *Merleau-Ponty's Later Works and Their Practical Implications: The Dehiscence of Responsibility*, ed. D. Davis. Amherst, Mass.: Humanity Books, 2001.

———. "Sartre's *War Diaries*: Prelude and Postscript." In *Sartre's Life, Times and Vision du Monde*, ed. William McBride. New York: Garland Press, 1997.

———. "Sartre e Beauvoir all'asse del ventesimo secolo." In *La fenomenologia et l'oltre-fenomenologia: Prendendo spunto dal pensiero francese,* ed. G. In-vitto. Trans. P. Invitto. Milan: Mimesis Edizioni, 2006.

McGill, V. J. "Sartre's Doctrine of Freedom." *Revue internationale de philosophie,* no. 8, April 1949.

Merleau-Ponty, Maurice. *Phénoménologie de la perception,* Paris: Gallimard, [1945] 1993.

———. "Le doute de Cézanne." In *Sens et non-sens,* Paris: Gallimard, [1945] 1995. English: "Cézanne's doubt." In *Sense and Non-Sense.* Trans. Hubert L. Dreyfus and Patricia Allen Dreyfus. Evanston, Ill.: Northwestern University Press, 1964.

———. "Sartre and Ultra-Bolshevism." In *The Debate between Sartre and Merleau-Ponty,* ed. Jon Stewart, 355–447. Evanston, Ill.: Northwestern University Press, 1998.

———. *Les Aventures de la dialectique.* Paris: Gallimard, 1955.

———. *Phenomenology of Perception.* Trans. Colin Smith. London: Routledge and Kegan Paul, 1962.

———. "Metaphysics and the Novel." In *Sense and Non-Sense.* Trans. Hubert L. Dreyfus and Patricia Allen Dreyfus, 26–40. Evanston, IL: Northwestern University Press, 1964. French: "Le Roman et la métaphysique." *Cahiers du Sud,* no. 270, March 1945.

———. "Le philosophe et son ombre." In *Éloge de la philosophie et autres essais.* Paris: Gallimard, 1960.

Moi, Toril. *Feminist Theory and Simone de Beauvoir.* Cambridge: Blackwell, 1990.

———. *Simone de Beauvoir: The Making of an Intellectual Woman.* New York: Blackwell, 1994.

———. *What Is a Woman? And Other Essays.* Oxford: Oxford University Press, 1999.

———. "While We Wait: Notes on the English Translation of *The Second Sex.*" In *The Legacy of Simone de Beauvoir,* ed. Emily R. Grosholz. Oxford: Oxford University Press, 2004.

Monteil, Claudine. *Les amants de la liberté.* Paris: J'ai Lu, 2002.

Morris, Phyllis Sutton. *Sartre's Concept of a Person.* Amherst: University of Massachusetts Press, 1976.

———. "Sartre and Objectification: A Feminist Perspective." In *Feminist Interpretations of Jean-Paul Sartre,* ed. Julien S. Murphy. University Park: Pennsylvania State University Press, 1999.

Mui, Constance. "Sartre and Marcel on Embodiment: Reevaluating Traditional and Gynocentric Feminisms." In *Feminist Interpretations of Jean-Paul Sartre,* ed. Julien S. Murphy, 105–22. University Park: Pennsylvania State University Press, 1999.

Nietzsche, Friedrich. *Gay Science*. Trans. Walter Kaufmann. New York: Random House, 1974.

Noddings, Nel. *Caring: A Feminine Approach to Ethics and Moral Education*. Berkeley: University of California Press, 1986.

Pacaly, Josette. *Sartre au miroir*. Paris: Klincksieck, 1980.

Pascal, Blaise. *Pensées*. Trans. A. J. Krailsheimer. London: Penguin, [1966] 1995.

Pierce, Christine. "Philosophy." *Signs* 1, no. 2 (1975): 487–503.

Pilardi, Jo-Ann. "Female Eroticism in the Works of Simone de Beauvoir." In *The Thinking Muse: Feminism and Modern French Philosophy*, ed. Jeffner Allen and Iris Marion Young, 18–34. Bloomington: Indiana University Press, 1989.

Rowley, Hazel. *Tête-à-tête: The Tumultuous Lives and Loves of Simone de Beauvoir and Jean-Paul Sartre*. New York: HarperCollins, 2005.

Rybalka, Michel. "Les Chemins de la liberté. Notice." In *Oeuvres Romanesques*. Paris: Gallimard, La Pléiade, 1981.

Sallenave, Danièle. "Avant-propos." ["Preface" to *Anne, ou quand prime le spirituel*.] Paris: Gallimard, Folio, 2006.

Sartre, Jean-Paul. *La Nausée*. Paris: Gallimard, 1938.

———. *L'Être et le néant: Essai d'ontologie phénoménologique*. Paris: Gallimard, [1943] 1998.

———. *Baudelaire*. Trans. Martin Turnell. New York: A New Directions Paperbook, [1947] 1967.

———. *Baudelaire*. Paris: Gallimard, 1947.

———. *Qu'est-ce la littérature?* In *Situations II*. Paris: Gallimard, 1948.

———. *Baudelaire*. Trans. Martin Turnell. Norfolk, Conn.: New Directions, 1950.

———. *No Exit and Three Other Plays*. Trans. Stuart Gilbert. New York: Vintage Books, 1955.

———. *Being and Nothingness*. Trans. Hazel E. Barnes. New York: Washington Square Press, 1956.

———. *Being and Nothingness*. New York: Philosophical Library, 1956.

———. *Transcendence of the Ego*. Trans. F. Williams and R. Kirkpatrick. New York: Noonday Press, 1957.

———. "Dos Passos and '1919.'" In *Literary Essays*. New York: Philosophical Library, 1957.

———. *Critique de la raison dialectique*, vol. 1. Paris: Gallimard, 1960.

———. *Saint Genet, Actor and Martyr*. New York: G. Braziller, 1963.

———. *Les Mots*. Paris: Gallimard, 1964.

———. "Merleau-Ponty." In *Situations*, vol. 4. Paris: Gallimard, 1964. For the posthumously published version, see "Merleau-Ponty." *Revue internationale de philosophie* 152–53 (1985): 3–29.

———. *Nausea*. Trans. Lloyd Alexander. New York: New Directions, 1964.

———. *Nausea*. Trans. Robert Baldwick. Harmondsworth: Penguin, 1965.

——. *L'Être et le néant.* Paris: Gallimard, 1971.

——. "What's Jean-Paul Sartre Thinking Lately?" Interview with P. Bénichou, in *Esquire* 78, no. 6 (December 1972).

——. "The Childhood of a Leader." In *The Wall.* Trans. Lloyd Alexander. New York: New Directions Publishing Corp., 1975.

——. "No Exit." In *No Exit and Three Other Plays.* Trans. S. Gilbert. New York: Vintage International, 1976.

——. *Critique of Dialectical Reason.* Trans. Alan Sheridan-Smith. Ed. Jonathan Rée. London: NLB, 1976.

——. "Sartre et les femmes." Interview avec Catherine Chaine. *Le Nouvel Observateur,* 31 janv. 1977.

——. Interview avec Jean Le Bitoux et Gilles Barbedette. *Libération,* printemps 1980. Special issue on Sartre.

——. *Oeuvres romanesques.* Paris: Gallimard, 1981.

——. *Lettres au Castor: et à quelques autres, 1940–1963.* Paris: Gallimard, 1983.

——. *Cahiers pour une morale.* Paris: Gallimard, 1983.

——. *Les Carnets de la drôle de guerre.* Paris: Gallimard, 1983.

——. *War Diaries.* Trans. Quintin Hoare. London: Verso Editions, 1984.

——. *The War Diaries: November 1939–March 1940.* Trans. Quintin Hoare. New York: Pantheon Books, 1985.

——. *The Transcendence of the Ego: An Existentialist Theory of Consciousness.* Trans. F. Williams and R. Kirkpatrick. New York: Hill and Wang, 1989.

——. *Being and Nothingness.* Trans. Hazel E. Barnes. New York: Washington Square Press, 1992.

——. *Notebooks for an Ethics.* Trans. David Pellauer. Chicago: University of Chicago Press, 1992.

——. *Quiet Moments in a War: The Letters of Jean-Paul Sartre to Simone de Beauvoir 1940–1963.* Trans. Lee Fahnestock and Norman MacAfee, ed. Simone de Beauvoir. New York: Charles Scribner's Sons, 1993.

——. "Interview à propos de *L'Idiot de la famille*," avec Michel Contat et Michel Rybalka. *Le Monde,* 14 mai 1971. Trans. by Paul Auster and Lydia Davis as "On the Idiot of the Family." In *Life/Situations, Essays Written and Spoken by Jean-Paul Sartre.* New York: Pantheon Books, 1997.

——. *Huis Clos.* In *Théâtre complet.* Paris: Gallimard, 2005.

——. "Itinerary of a Thought." In *Conversations with Jean-Paul Sartre,* ed. Perry Anderson, Ronald Fraser, Quintin Hoare, and Simone de Beauvoir. London: Seagull Books, 2006.

——. *Conversations with Jean-Paul Sartre.* Ed. Perry Anderson, Ronald Fraser, Quintin Hoare, and Simone de Beauvoir. Oxford: Seagull Books, 2006.

——. "Existentialism Is a Humanism." In *Existentialism: Basic Writings,* ed. Charles Guignon and Derk Pereboom. Indianapolis: Hackett, 1995.

Scarth, Fredrika. *The Other Within: Ethics, Politics and the Body in Simone de Beauvoir.* New York: Rowman and Littlefield, 2004.

Schlipp, Paul. *The Philosophy of Jean-Paul Sartre.* La Salle, Ill.: Open Court, 1981.

Schwarzer, Alice. *Simone de Beauvoir Today: Conversation 1972–1982.* London: Chatto and Windus, 1984.

Siegfried, Charlene Haddock. "Gender Specific Values." In *The Philosophical Forum* XV (Summer 1984): 425–42.

Simons, Margaret. "Sartre and Beauvoir: The Question of Influence." In *Eros* 8, no. 1 (June 1981): 25-42.

———. "The Silencing of Simone de Beauvoir: Guess What's Missing from *The Second Sex.*" In *Women's Studies International Forum* 6 (1983): 231–38. Reprinted in *Beauvoir and* The Second Sex: *Feminism, Race, and the Origins of Existentialism.* Lanham, Md.: Rowman & Littlefield, 1999.

———. "Beauvoir and Sartre: The Philosophical Relationship." In *Simone de Beauvoir, Witness to a Century.* New Haven, Conn.: Yale University, Yale French Studies, 1986.

———, ed. *Feminist Interpretations of Simone de Beauvoir.* University Park: Pennsylvania State University Press, 1995.

———. "An Appeal to Reopen the Question of Influence." In *Philosophy Today,* 42 (suppl.) (1998): 17–24.

———. *Beauvoir and* The Second Sex: *Feminism, Race and the Origins of Existentialism.* New York: Rowman & Littlefield, 1999.

———. "Beauvoir's Early Philosophy." In *Beauvoir and* The Second Sex: *Feminism, Race, and the Origins of Existentialism.* Lanham, Md.: Rowman & Littlefield, 1999.

———. "Beauvoir Interview (1979)" In *Beauvoir and* The Second Sex: *Feminism, Race, and the Origins of Existentialism.* Lanham, Md.: Rowman and Littlefield, 1999.

———. "Sexism and the Philosophical Canon: On Reading Beauvoir's *The Second Sex.*" Reprinted as chapter 8 in *Beauvoir and* The Second Sex: *Feminism, Race and the Origins of Existentialism,* 101–114. Lanham, Md.: Rowman and Littlefield, 1999.

———. "Beauvoir's Philosophical Independence in a Dialogue with Sartre." *Journal of Speculative Philosophy* 14, no. 2 (2000): 87–103.

———. "L'indépendance de la pensée philosophique de Simone de Beauvoir." In *Les Temps modernes,* 57ème année, Juin–Juillet 2002, no. 619, "Présences de Simone de Beauvoir," 43–52.

Simont, Juliette. *Jean-Paul Sartre, un demi-siècle de liberté.* Paris, Brussels: De Boeck, 1998.

Sokolowski, Robert. *The Formation of Husserl's Concept of Constitution.* The Hague: Martinus Nijhoff, 1964.

Stack, George. *Sartre's Philosophy of Social Existence.* Saint Louis: Open Court, 1977.

Stewart, Jon. *The Debate Between Sartre and Merleau-Ponty.* Evanston, Ill.: Northwestern University Press, 1998.

Stone, Robert. "Freedom as a Universal Notion in Sartre's Ethical Theory." *Revue internationale de philosophie,* nos. 152–53 (1985): 137–48.

Tidd, Ursula. *Simone de Beauvoir, Gender and Testimony.* Cambridge: Cambridge University Press, 1999.

Todd, Olivier. *Un Fils rebelle.* Paris: Grasset, 1981.

van den Hoven, Adrian. "*Nausea:* Plunging below the Surface." In *Sartre Alive,* ed. Ronald Aronson and Adrian van den Hoven, 227–39. Detroit: Wayne State University Press, 1991.

———. "Censures et autocensure dans *La Nausée* de Jean-Paul Sartre et les déboires de la contingence." In *Censure et autocensure et art d'écrire,* sous la direction de Jacques Domenach, 270–80. Nice: Editions Complexe, 2005.

Veatch, Henry. *For an Ontology of Morals.* Evanston, Ill.: Northwestern University Press, 1971.

Veltman, Andrea. "The Sisyphean Torture of Housework." In *Hypatia* 19, no. 3 (Summer 2004): 121–43.

Vintges, Karen. "*The Second Sex* and Philosophy." In *Feminist Interpretations of Simone de Beauvoir,* ed. Margaret A. Simons. University Park: Pennsylvania State University Press, 1995.

———. *Philosophy as Passion: The Thinking of Simone de Beauvoir.* Bloomington: Indiana University Press, 1996.

Waldenfels, Bernhard. "Leibliche Erfahrung zwischen Selbsheit und Andersheit." In *Vernunft—Entwicklung—Leben,* eds. Ulrich Bröckling, Stefan Kaufmann, and Axel Paul. Munich: W. Fink, 2004.

Ward, Julie K. "Beauvoir's Two Senses of 'Body' in *The Second Sex.*" In *Feminist Interpretations of Simone de Beauvoir,* ed. Margaret A. Simons, 223–42. University Park: Pennsylvania State University Press, 1995.

Warnock, Mary. *The Philosophy of Sartre.* London: Hutchinson University Press, 1965.

Wehr, Demaris. *Jung and Feminism, Liberating Archetypes.* Boston: Beacon Press, 1989.

Zahavi, Dan. *Husserl's Phenomenology.* Stanford, Calif.: Stanford University Press, 2003.

Zaytzeff, Veronique, trans. *The Debate between Sartre and Merleau-Ponty.* Evanston, Ill.: Northwestern University Press, 1998.

Zerilli, Linda. "A Process without a Subject: Simone de Beauvoir and Julia Kristeva on Maternity." *Signs* 18, no. 1 (1992): 111–35.

Contributors

Debra Bergoffen is Professor of Philosophy and is affiliated with the Women's Studies and Cultural Studies faculties at George Mason University. She is author of *The Philosophy of Simone de Beauvoir: Gendered Phenomenologies, Erotic Generosities* and editor of several anthologies. She has authored numerous articles on Simone de Beauvoir, Luce Irigaray, Friedrich Nietzsche, and Jean-Paul Sartre. She is currently working on a book on genocidal rape and human rights titled *Between Rape and Justice: Toward a Politics of the Vulnerable Body.*

Christine Daigle is Associate Professor of Philosophy and Director of the Centre for Women's Studies at Brock University (St. Catharines, Ontario). She is President of the North American Sartre Society. She is author of *Le nihilisme est-il un humanisme? Étude sur Nietzsche et Sartre* and editor of *Existentialist Thinkers and Ethics,* for which she also contributed the chapter "The Ambiguous Ethics of Simone de Beauvoir."

Matthew C. Eshleman is Assistant Professor at the University of North Carolina, Wilmington. His work on Sartre appears in *Philosophy Today, Sartre Studies International,* and *History of Philosophy Quarterly.* He recently received a Cahill Grant to work on Foucault and Hellenistic philosophy.

Debbie Evans is an independent scholar whose research interests focus on the writings of Sartre, Beauvoir, Heidegger, Hegel, and Derrida. Her work has appeared in *Sartre Studies International* and *Simone de Beauvoir Studies.* She is currently working on a book on Sartre and Beauvoir entitled *Public Images, Private Lives.*

Edward Fullbrook is a research fellow at the School of Economics at the University of the West of England (Bristol). In addition to his work in economics, he has authored or co-authored more than twenty essays and three books on Sartre and Beauvoir, including *Sex and Philosophy: Rethinking de Beauvoir and Sartre.*

Jacob Golomb is the Ahad Ha'am Professor of Philosophy at the Hebrew University of Jerusalem and acts as the philosophical editor of the Hebrew University Magnes Press. His books include *Nietzsche's Enticing Psychology of Power; Introduction to Philosophies of Existence; In Search of Authenticity: From Kierkegaard to Camus;* and *Nietzsche in Zion.*

Kevin W. Gray is a doctoral candidate at Laval University and adjunct instructor of philosophy at Marist College. He works principally in twentieth-century Marxism, existentialism, and critical theory. His work has appeared in *Simone de Beauvoir Studies* and *Radical Philosophy Review.* He has contributed the chapter "Sartre et la révolution hongroise?" to the volume *Sartre, l'intellectuel et la politique.*

Sara Heinämaa is senior lecturer of theoretical philosophy at the University of Helsinki (Finland). She has contributed work on Beauvoir to *Hypatia* and the *Cambridge Companion to Beauvoir.* She is author of *Toward a Phenomenology of Sexual Difference* and co-editor of *Consciousness: From Perception to Reflection.*

Michel Kail is Professeur agrégé of Philosophy at the Lycée Sophie-Germain (Paris) and has been, from 1986 to 2007, a member of the editorial board of Sartre and Beauvoir's own political and literary magazine, *Les Temps modernes.* He is author of *Simone de Beauvoir philosophe* and co-author, with Françoise Bagot, of *Jean-Paul Sartre: Les Mains sales.* He edits the journal *L'Homme et la Société, revue internationale de recherches et de synthèses en sciences sociales.*

Sonia Kruks is Danforth Professor of Politics at Oberlin College. She has published numerous works on twentieth-century political thought and contemporary feminist political theory, including *Retrieving Experience: Subjectivity and Recognition in Feminist Politics* and *Situation and Human Existence: Freedom, Subjectivity and Society.* She has published work on Beauvoir in *Hypatia* and *Feminist Studies.*

Guillermine de Lacoste is an independent scholar and researcher. She has taught philosophy at Newton College of the Sacred Heart and Tufts University. Her work has appeared in *Philosophy Today, Sartre Studies International,* and *Simone de Beauvoir Studies.* She has contributed chapters to several books, including *Feminist Interpretations of Jean-Paul Sartre.* She is currently working on a book manuscript, *Existentialism's Enigmas Deciphered by Psychoanalysis: Sartre and Kierkegaard.*

Eliane Lecarme-Tabone is maître de conférences honoraire of the Université de Lille-III (France). She is author, with Jacques Lecarme, of *L'Autobiographie,* where her particular focus was the use of autobiography by women. She has published several studies on the works of Simone de Beauvoir. Her most recent writings include *Mémoires d'une jeune fille rangée de Simone de Beauvoir* and *Le Deuxième sexe de Simone de Beauvoir*.

William L. McBride is the Arthur G. Hansen Distinguished Professor of Philosophy at Purdue University. He is the author of *Sartre's Political Theory*. He has contributed work on Beauvoir to the book *The Contradictions of Freedom: Philosophical Essays on Simone de Beauvoir's 'The Mandarins'* and he has contributed work on Sartre to numerous journals and books. He is the co-founder and first President of the North American Sartre Society and the Secretary General of the International Federation of Philosophical Societies.

Adrian van den Hoven is Emeritus Professor of French Language and Literature at the University of Windsor (Ontario). He is translator of Sartre's *Truth and Existence* and *Hope Now: The Sartre-Benny Lévy Interviews of 1980*. He has co-edited the collection of essays *Sartre Today: A Centenary Celebration*. He is Past President of the North American Sartre Society and founding editor of *Sartre Studies International*.

Andrea Veltman is Assistant Professor of Philosophy at James Madison University. Her work on Beauvoir has been published in *Hypatia*. Her essay "Transcendence and Immanence in the Ethics of Simone de Beauvoir" appears in *The Philosophy of Simone de Beauvoir: Critical Essays* (Indiana University Press, 2006). In addition to publishing on Simone de Beauvoir, she has also edited *Social and Political Philosophy: Classic and Contemporary Readings* and *Oppression and Moral Agency,* Special Issue of *Hypatia* (Winter 2009).

Gail Weiss is Professor of Philosophy and Director of the Human Sciences Program at The George Washington University. She has published several essays and book chapters on Beauvoir and contributed the chapter "Challenging Choices: An Ethic of Oppression" to *The Philosophy of Simone de Beauvoir: Critical Essays* (Indiana University Press, 2006). She is currently completing a monograph entitled *Beauvoir's Ambiguities: Philosophy, Literature, Feminism*.

Index

existentialism, 2–3, 6–8, 10n1, 11n11, 48n27, 56, 83, 98, 141n28, 148–149, 155, 159n6, 213, 239nn10,20, 242; existentialist ethics, 10n1, 31, 34, 44, 76–77, 83, 89n49, 149–150, 152, 223, 232–233, 237, 252; existentialist philosophy, 4, 6, 93, 125, 157; French existentialism, 65, 83, 117, 222; Sartrean existentialism, 118, 230

facticity, 5, 17–19, 21–23, 26–29, 32–35, 77, 162, 164, 191, 225, 230–231, 237, 243–244, 247, 251, 253n5
feminism, 10, 15–16, 26–27, 29, 38–39, 43, 47n22, 48nn27,31, 49, 53, 58–61, 63n17, 66, 90, 94, 103, 114n53, 117, 129–130, 133–134, 136–138, 141nn9,18, 143, 163, 194, 196, 230–232, 239n16, 250, 253n1
flesh, 27–28, 36–39, 42–43, 50, 59, 61, 64n39, 73, 88n40, 91, 137–138, 140n6, 142n33, 214–215, 253. *See also* embodiment
la force des choses, 161, 176, 179n32
free indirect discourse, 204–206, 208–213
freedom, 3, 5, 8, 14, 17–26, 32, 42–43, 48n27, 50, 53–55, 60, 63n17, 72–82, 84n11, 85n20, 86nn26,35, 87nn36,37,38, 88nn39,40,41,42, 89nn44,47, 107–108, 117, 131–135, 144, 146, 150–157, 163–168, 172, 176, 177n11, 178n12, 179n32, 181, 198, 205, 217, 222–237, 238n4, 239n21, 241–253, 253nn2,4, 254n8; absolute freedom, 5, 8, 18, 31, 33–34, 44, 66–72, 78, 84n10, 176, 224, 237; ethical freedom, 24, 76, 223, 232–234, 237, 239n22, 248–249, 252; freedom and intersubjectivity, 65–66, 80–82, 89n47; freedom of consciousness, 46n20, 47n20, 97–102, 155, 224–225; freedom of/for Others, 5, 12n13, 24–28, 33, 55, 62n17, 67–72, 80–81, 88nn39,42,43, 99, 108–109, 152, 156, 223–224, 232–234, 237, 238n2, 241–249, 251–253, 253n2, 254n7; ontological freedom, 77–78, 85n14, 86n27, 164, 176, 178n12, 223, 232–233, 239n22, 247, 249; situated freedom, 5, 31, 33–34, 44, 45n4, 66–69, 70, 84n14, 126, 155–156, 162–170, 176, 177n7, 179nn31,32, 222–223, 229, 232, 237, 238nn1,6, 239n20, 241–243, 249–251, 254n10. *See also liberté*

generosity, 8, 42, 44, 56–57, 88n43, 108, 121, 165, 178n13, 186, 198, 231, 252
God, 71–72, 78–80, 82–83, 206–207, 212, 215, 217, 250

Hegel(ian), 13, 20, 82, 86n33, 90–110, 111nn5,8,14, 112nn19,30,31, 114nn39,41,48,51, 140n6, 155, 199, 222–223, 225–226, 228, 231, 238nn6,10, 239n10, 245, 253n2; *The Phenomenology of Spirit*, 90, 93–95, 98–100, 102–104, 106–108, 110, 112nn19,31, 238n10
Heidegger(ian), 7, 57, 73, 108, 110, 114n55, 194, 199–200; *Being and Time*, 114n55; *Dasein*, 114n55, 141n16, 226; *Mitsein* (Being-with), 108, 110, 114n55, 115n56, 191, 199, 224
history, 1, 5, 13–14, 17, 21–22, 26, 32, 42–43, 48n25, 60, 66, 74, 77, 91, 103–104, 106–107, 110, 117–118, 122–123, 135, 147, 153–154, 166, 169, 173, 194, 198, 200, 202n10, 207, 225, 230, 237, 238nn10,21, 250–251, 253n2, 254n10
Husserl(ian), 6, 79, 97, 99, 106, 108, 112n30, 113n33, 130–132, 140n7, 141nn8,9, 193–194, 200, 201n5, 234, 253n2; affectivity, 130–131; countersense, 79, 83

I, 94, 98, 106, 112n31, 113n33, 144. *See also* ego
immanence, 40, 42, 53, 107, 119, 149, 159n8, 198, 223, 226–232, 238n10, 239nn11,16,17,22, 240n22. *See also* transcendence
intentional, 16–18, 23, 28–29, 102, 132, 144–145, 147, 153, 224–227, 244, 253
intersubjective, 14, 31, 34, 65–66, 71–73, 80–82, 88n43, 89nn44,47, 103, 108, 110, 114n55, 119–120, 158, 191, 241, 252, 253n2. *See also* freedom, freedom and intersubjectivity

jouissance, 51, 62n5, 95, 101
judgment, 9, 109, 161, 163–169, 171–172, 176, 232

Kant(ian), 12n13, 74–75, 79, 81, 86n33, 88n43, 89n46, 149, 163–166, 189, 194, 232; categorical imperative, 81, 86n33, 166
Kierkegaard, Søren, 3, 6, 136–137, 199

lack, 4, 14, 24, 38, 51, 60, 62n5, 63n22, 66, 88n40, 96–98, 135, 165, 174, 195, 235, 249
Les Temps modernes, 9, 12nn16,17,18, 61, 117, 196
liberté, 164–165, 169, 176, 177n11, 178n12, 223, 233. *See also* freedom
limit(ation), 24, 36, 42, 68–69, 90–91, 94–95, 102, 104, 136, 145, 148, 154, 164, 166,

199–200, 206, 225, 239n21, 241–243, 246, 249–250
logos, 92, 111n5
look, 8, 17, 20–21, 25–27, 29, 32, 35, 45n12, 101–102, 109–110, 114n46, 147, 225, 244–245; gaze, 20, 68, 101, 109, 115n59, 207, 247

Marx(ism), 15, 77, 149, 155, 166, 189, 198, 231, 238n10
master-slave dialectic, 13, 90–95, 98–108, 110, 112n19, 114nn39,41,46,51, 245. *See also* slave
mauvaise foi, 75. *See also* bad faith
Merleau-Ponty, Maurice, 7, 9, 12n16, 15–17, 19–21, 27, 30–34, 40, 47nn22,24, 69, 70–71, 73, 85n23, 117, 119, 123, 131–132, 140nn6,7, 141n15, 162, 167–168, 177nn7,9, 178n20, 189–193, 196, 201nn3,5, 202n10, 216, 253n2; "Les Aventures de la dialectique," 189; *Phenomenology of Perception,* 32, 47n24, 70, 178n20, 253n2; "Sartre and Ultra-Bolshevism," 31
metaphysic(al), 89n46, 90–91, 95, 98, 101, 105–106, 108, 110, 111nn3,14, 125, 160, 163, 189, 225, 227–228, 230–231, 238n5
mind, 34, 41, 70, 91, 98, 113n33, 114n46, 191, 195, 199, 229

negate, 18, 27, 77, 94, 97, 102, 105, 109, 147, 151, 155, 229
Nietzsche, Friedrich, 3, 6, 49, 50, 82, 83, 141n9, 192, 199; *The Gay Science,* 49
nihilism, 6, 167, 178n22
normative, 66, 73, 75, 77–83, 87n35, 88n43, 89n44, 163, 168, 228, 231–233
nothingness, 38, 140n6, 224, 232, 243, 246

object, 13–14, 23, 36, 40, 42–43, 45n13, 57, 68, 81, 85n20, 94, 96–97, 101, 104, 106, 108, 113n33, 114n39, 129–133, 141n8, 145, 147, 150–152, 156, 171, 178n13, 183, 190, 193, 197, 219–220, 224, 230, 232, 234–235, 246–247; Me-as-object, 35, 85n18, 100; object of perception, 20, 102, 130, 132
objective, objectivity, 44, 51–52, 61, 74–75, 78, 82–83, 88n41, 89, 102, 128–129, 135, 137, 139, 139n2, 147–148, 150–153, 155, 157, 166, 171, 191, 224, 241, 245
ontology, 37, 39, 73, 76–77, 105, 125, 138–139, 139n2, 140nn2,6, 155, 159, 159n4, 178n12,

190, 192, 194, 198–199, 223, 226, 228, 231, 242–244, 252; ontological meanings, 128–130, 132, 135–137. *See also* freedom, ontological freedom; phenomenology, phenomenological ontology
oppression, 13, 15–16, 21, 24–25, 42, 49, 67, 69–70, 72, 86n27, 87n35, 90, 103–108, 110, 116, 149, 157, 161, 165–167, 170, 178n21, 205, 223, 228, 238n6, 239n22, 240n22, 247, 249–251, 254n10
the Other, 3, 13–14, 21, 35–37, 42–44, 45nn12,13, 49–54, 57–60, 62, 73, 85n19, 89nn44,46, 93–95, 100–106, 110, 111n14, 112n18, 113n34, 114nn39,49, 125, 143, 145–148, 150, 152–153, 158, 165, 194, 197, 224; existence of Others, 24, 73, 85n19, 99, 102, 147–148, 150, 241, 253; problem of the Other, 5, 113n37, 156–157. *See also* freedom, freedom of/for Others

Parshley, Howard, 11n9, 50, 124, 196
passive(ly), 13–14, 17, 38, 46n16, 49, 51–53, 55, 59, 92, 130, 133, 151, 179n31, 184, 224, 226–228, 234
patriarchy, 14–15, 17, 23, 26, 28–29, 42, 54, 61, 90, 105, 117, 123
perception, 15, 20–21, 27, 29, 89n44, 101–102, 118, 130–132, 134, 141n16, 189, 194, 235
perspective, 2, 25–26, 94, 110, 113n33, 149, 176, 192, 198, 239n16, 246
phenomenology, 7, 10n1, 15–17, 22, 27, 29, 45, 76, 92, 97, 99, 106, 119, 130–132, 139n2, 140nn6,7, 144, 147, 163, 168, 190, 224, 239n10, 246; gendered phenomenology, 40, 44, 46n14; phenomenological ontology, 31–32, 35, 128. *See also* existential, existential phenomenology
political, 1–2, 5, 10, 15–29, 32, 66, 129, 158–159, 161–166, 168–170, 172, 174–176, 178n22, 182, 193–194, 196, 204, 211, 222, 234, 236, 242, 253n2, 254n10
praxis, 145, 147–148
project, 16, 27, 31, 33–36, 38–39, 42, 44, 46n20, 49, 63n25, 67, 72–73, 79–83, 85n20, 92, 97, 99, 109, 130, 135, 144, 146, 148–149, 153, 155, 157–158, 160, 162, 164–165, 175, 177n10, 178n16, 179n31, 210, 215–216, 223–227, 230, 233–237, 238n5, 241, 243, 246
psychoanalysis, 18, 30, 61, 132, 134–135, 138, 139n2, 140nn2,6, 141n24, 186; psychoanaly-

sis of things, 128, 130, 137, 139. *See also* existential, existential psychoanalysis

psychological, 19, 54, 58, 68, 191, 202n10, 204, 207

puissance, 164, 178n12

reality, 18, 21–22, 24, 80, 87n35, 94, 105, 130, 138, 148, 155, 166–167, 176, 191, 205–207, 210, 212, 216–217, 220; human reality, 34, 76–77, 86n27, 128, 224

reciprocity, 14, 25, 28–29, 44, 49–51, 53–57, 59–60, 62, 62n5, 99, 104, 108–110, 115n57, 144, 148, 157, 165, 233

responsibility, 14, 18–20, 24, 26, 153, 161, 164, 166, 168–170, 176, 177n6, 241, 248–249

Roquentin, 53, 60, 101, 206, 216, 218, 220

Rybalka, Michel, 58, 98, 185

Sartre's works: *Baudelaire,* 114n46, 141n25; *Being and Nothingness,* 4–6, 8–9, 12n13, 18–19, 31–35, 40, 44–45, 53, 55, 67–70, 72–73, 75–76, 83n2, 84n11, 85nn17,19, 90, 93, 95–106, 108, 110, 111n15, 112n31, 113n32, 117–123, 128–129, 131–132, 134, 138, 141n28, 143–152, 156, 159n4, 161–162, 164–165, 167, 178nn13,20,22, 191, 193–195, 197, 199–200, 222, 224–225, 232–233, 239nn17,21, 241–242, 244–246, 248; "The Childhood of a Leader," 101, 181, 184–186; *Critique of Dialectical Reason,* 8, 10, 83n2, 110, 143–149, 157, 190–191, 193, 200; "Erostrate," 181; "Existentialism Is a Humanism," 74–75, 78, 223; *Huis Clos,* 113n37; *Idiot of the Family,* 141n24, 179n28, 193; *The Imagination,* 4, 9; "Intimacy," 186; *La Nausée,* 203, 206, 216, 220; "La République du silence," 191; *Le Mur,* 203–204, 206; *Le Soleil de minuit,* 180–181; "L'Enfance d'un chef," 184, 204, 216; "Les Communistes et la paix," 189; *Les Mots,* 58–59, 193, 199; *Les Mouches,* 11n12; *L'Être et le néant,* 50, 85n17, 196; *L'Existentialisme est un humanisme,* 5, 223; *L'Idiot de la famille,* 58–59; *Littérature et métaphysique,* 91–92; *Nausea,* 4, 9, 53, 101, 125, 186; *No Exit,* 111, 113n37, 243, 244; *Notebooks for an Ethics,* 4, 9, 44, 54–57, 61, 64n35, 85n16, 110, 165, 178n13, 199, 239n21; "Réponse à Claude Lefort," 189; "The Roads to Freedom," 193; *Saint Genet,* 110, 141n24; *A Sketch for a Theory of Emotions,* 9; *Transcendence of the*

Ego, 4, 9, 97, 99, 113n33, 144, 238n4; "The Wall," 184; *The Wall,* 180–181, 185; *War Diaries,* 2–3, 96–97, 101, 122; "What is Literature?" 110; *The Words,* 181–182

Simons, Margaret, 3, 6, 8, 60, 93, 96, 118, 124, 200, 222

situation, 3–5, 20, 32, 35, 40, 45n8, 82, 87n35, 91, 102, 107, 111n15, 130, 151, 153–154, 161, 169, 171–175, 178n16, 214, 216, 225, 234, 244, 253n5; situated body, 36, 42, 45n4, 47nn22,24; situation of women, 13–16, 19, 25–26, 34, 104, 116, 126, 157, 162, 177n5, 231. *See also* freedom, situated freedom

Skepticism, 95, 103

slave, 5, 13, 23, 25, 43, 54, 67, 69–70, 82, 84n11, 86n26, 90, 94–95, 100–107, 110, 112n19, 114n52, 178n12, 232–235, 245, 250–251. *See also* master-slave dialectic

slime, 38–39, 44, 46nn17,18, 52–53, 62n11, 129–130, 132–139, 141nn20,21, 194; and holes, 38–39, 106, 135, 140n6, 194

social, 5–6, 17–19, 21, 23, 27, 40, 43, 47n25, 53, 60, 63n22, 67–69, 80–81, 85n20, 86n35, 108, 119, 125, 129, 140n6, 146–148, 155, 158–159, 159n4, 165, 168, 173, 177n5, 191–192, 195, 204–208, 234, 236–237, 239n20, 243, 252, 253nn2,4

solipsist(ic), 68, 85nn19,21, 100, 102

spirit(ual)(ism), 22, 28, 66, 73, 98, 106, 133, 137, 151, 154, 181, 183–185, 192, 197, 216–217

subjectivity, 13, 15, 19–20, 23–24, 26–27, 36, 48n29, 51–52, 54–55, 80, 88n41, 97, 128, 132, 139, 147–148, 151–153, 155–156, 191, 224–225, 227, 230, 232, 234, 237, 239n22, 247, 251–252; subjective values, 74–75, 78, 87n35

subject, 13–14, 19–20, 22–23, 31, 38, 42, 49, 52, 63n17, 79, 82, 101–102, 104, 106, 108, 126, 134–136, 140n6, 141nn8,16, 144, 148–150, 152, 155, 158, 179nn28,31, 190, 192, 248; body-subject, 40, 47n24; free subject, 54, 230; philosophy of subject, 143, 145–146; subject-object, 16, 21, 73, 110, 120, 145, 147, 156

transcendence, 25, 28, 49, 83, 85n15, 86n27, 91–92, 99, 101–102, 114n41, 119, 129, 140n6, 147, 150, 157–158, 159n8, 165, 198, 222, 238n10, 239nn11,16, 240n22, 244; transcendence and consciousness, 34, 36, 38–40, 42, 97, 114n44, 130, 145, 149, 224–228, 233–234,

Printed and bound by CPI Group (UK) Ltd, Croydon, CR0 4YY

13/04/2025

14656543-0005